...ly indus-
...nsformed
...and poor
...theoreti-
...nological
...he essays
...e dynam-
...w public
...nal level,
...th levels.
...IEs with
...for poli-
...tion to a
...licy field.

...urrently,
...nt of the
...aught at
...Science
...demy of
...estigious
...of more
...ncluding
ic Devel-
...d British
...ean gov-
...nd sub-

...d Public
...has also
...and he
...n and on
...the President's Council of Economic Advisers in Washington, D.C. Professor
Nelson is best known for his work on long-run economic change, including, with
Sidney Winter, the development of a formal evolutionary theory of economic
change. His major recent books include *The Sources of Economic Growth* (1996),
Technonationalism and Technoglobalism: Conflict and Cooperation (with Sylvia
Ostry, 1995), *National Innovation Systems: A Comparative Analysis* (1993), and
Sources of Industrial Leadership: Studies of Seven Industries (with David C.
Mowery, 1999).

Advance Praise for *Technology, Learning, and Innovation*

TECHNOLOGY, LEARNING, AND INNOVATION

Experiences of Newly Industrializing Economies

Edited by

LINSU KIM

Korea University

RICHARD R. NELSON

Columbia University

CAMBRIDGE
UNIVERSITY PRESS

PUBLISHED BY THE PRESS SYNDICATE OF THE UNIVERSITY OF CAMBRIDGE
The Pitt Building, Trumpington Street, Cambridge, United Kingdom

CAMBRIDGE UNIVERSITY PRESS
The Edinburgh Building, Cambridge CB2 2RU, UK   http://www.cup.cam.ac.uk
40 West 20th Street, New York, NY 10011-4211, USA   http://www.cup.org
10 Stamford Road, Oakleigh, Melbourne 3166, Australia
Ruiz de Alarcón 13, 28014 Madrid, Spain

© Linsu Kim and Richard Nelson   2000

First published 2000

Printed in the United States of America

Typeface Times Roman 11/12.5 pt.   *System* QuarkXPress [BTS]

A catalog record for this book is available from the British Library.

Library of Congress Cataloging in Publication data
Kim, Linsu.
Technology, learning and innovation : experiences of newly industrializing
economies / Linsu Kim, Richard R. Nelson.
p.   cm.
Includes bibliographical references and index.
ISBN 0-521-77003-3 – ISBN 0-521-77987-1 (pbk.)
1. Technology and state – Developing countries.   2. Technological innovations –
Developing countries.   I. Nelson, Richard R.   II. Title.
T49.5 .K54   2000
338.9'27'091724 – dc21
99-040248
CIP

ISBN   0 521 77003 3   hardback
ISBN   0 521 77987 1   paperback

Contents

Contributors

Mark Dodgson, *Australian National University*

Geert Duysters, *Technological University, Eindhoven, the Netherlands*

Martin Fransman, *Edinburgh University*

John Hagedoorn, *MERIT, the Netherlands*

Michael Hobday, *University of Sussex, England*

Jorge Katz, *ECLAC, Santiago, Chile*

Linsu Kim, *Korea University*

Sanjaya Lall, *Oxford University*

KongRae Lee, *Science and Technology Policy Institute (STEPI), Seoul, Korea*

Won-Young Lee, *Office of the President, the Republic of Korea*

Bengt-Åke Lundvall, *Aalborg University, Denmark*

Richard R. Nelson, *Columbia University*

Howard Pack, *Wharton School, University of Pennsylvania*

David J. Teece, *University of California, Berkeley*

Morris Teubal, *Hebrew University, Jerusalem, Israel*

Preface

Technological advance has been the key driving force in industrialized countries, accounting for the lion's share of productivity growth. Recently, several newly industrializing economies (NIEs) such as Korea, Taiwan, Singapore, and Hong Kong have transformed themselves from technologically backward and poor to relatively modern and affluent economies. Despite a recent economic crisis, each of these countries now has a significant collection of industrial firms producing technologically complex products and competing effectively against firms based in industrially advanced countries. Industrial development is, indeed, a process of acquiring technological capabilities and translating them into product and process innovations in the course of continuous technological change. How did these countries do it?

Some economists argue that what lies behind rapid development in these countries is simply very high investment rates in physical and human capital that enabled movements along a production function. In contrast, other economists recognize the importance of these types of high investment rates but have placed risk-taking entrepreneurship, effective learning, and innovation as central in their analyses.

Ten essays and four commentaries in this volume take the latter view and analyze the process of technological progress at both the macro and micro levels. They discuss how firms, particularly those in electronics and automobiles, have dynamically accumulated technological capabilities at the micro level, how public policies have shaped the process of technological progress at the national level, and what problems some of these countries face today at both levels. In addition, the volume provides a comparative picture of East Asian NIEs and their Latin American counterparts. The discussion also offers useful lessons for policies in other developing countries.

This volume is a compendium of papers presented in Seoul in May 1997 at the International Conference on the Innovation and Competitiveness in Newly Industrializing Countries held in commemoration of the tenth anniversary of the Science and Technology Policy Institute (STEPI). The organizers of the conference were extremely fortunate in being able to invite a group of leading scholars in the field to participate in and present original papers for the conference. We believe that the conference was successful in providing new insights into the understanding of the process of technological learning and innovation in NIEs.

Many individuals contributed significantly to make the conference productive and stimulating. The participants would like to extend their gratitude to the members of STEPI, particularly Dr. Dal-Hwan Lee, Dr. Sung-Chul Chung, Dr. Joonghae Suh, Dr. Young-Rak Choi, and Dr. Taeyoung Shin, who successfully organized the conference. They also extend their gratitude to discussants for their constructive comments.

CHAPTER 1

Introduction

Linsu Kim
Richard R. Nelson

TECHNOLOGY AND INDUSTRIALIZATION IN NEWLY INDUSTRIALIZING ECONOMIES

From the beginnings of the modern discipline, economists writing about economic growth have recognized technological advance as its key driving force (Smith, 776; Marx, 1867; Schumpeter, 1911). In the 1950s and 1960s many studies tried to measure the contribution of technological change to economic growth in countries operating at the frontiers of technology (Solow, 1957; Denison, 1962). The conclusion was that technological advance accounted for the lion's share of growth in worker productivity. Since that time, a vast empirical and theoretical literature has grown up on technological progress in the advanced industrial nations.

More recently, a number of economists have turned their attention to the mechanisms of technological advance in the development of economies that, initially at least, have been far behind the frontiers. The acquisition and progressive mastering of technologies that are new to them, if not to the world, obviously has been a central aspect of the newly industrializing economies (NIEs) that have grown so rapidly over the past thirty years (Pack and Westphal, 1986; Kim, 1997).

Since the early 1960s, countries such as Korea, Taiwan, Singapore, and Hong Kong have transformed themselves from technologically backward and poor to relatively modern and affluent economies. Each now has a significant collection of industrial firms producing technologically complex products and competing effectively against firms based in industrially advanced countries. While Korea recently has been undergoing an economic crisis, due in large part to financial mismanagement, no one denies the strong technological capabilities that Korea has built up.

1

The key question is, how did the NIEs do it? And what are the lessons for policies in other developing countries?

Some economists argue that what lies behind rapid development in these countries is simply very high investment rates that enabled movements along a production function (Young, 1993; Kim and Lau, 1994; Krugman, 1994). They insist that the greater portion of increased output can be explained by increases in physical and human capital, which brought along modern technology as a more or less automatic by-product. Nelson and Pack (1999) call these arguments "accumulation theories." In contrast, other economists have placed learning about and learning to master new technologies as central in their analysis and focused on what was involved in this achievement. To be sure, acquiring and assimilating the technologies of advanced countries required high rates of investment in physical and human capital. But in addition, this demanded risk-taking entrepreneurship, effective learning, and innovation (Pack and Westphal, 1986; Amsden, 1989; Kim, 1997). Nelson and Pack (1999) call these arguments "assimilation theories."

Regardless of one's theoretical explanation of what has happened, the evidence that new capabilities have been acquired is dramatic. For instance, Korea's export increased from a mere $40 million in 1960 to $125 billion in 1995, with virtually all the increase represented by products that Korea did not know how to produce at the start of the era. In the mid-1960s, Korea began exporting textiles, apparel, toys, wigs, plywood, and other labor-intensive mature products. Ten years later, ships, steel, consumer electronics, and construction services from Korea challenged established suppliers from the industrially advanced countries. By the mid-1980s, computers, semiconductor memory chips, videocassette recorders, electronic switching systems, automobiles, industrial plants, and other technology-intensive products were added to Korea's list of major export items. Korea is now working on such next-generation products as multimedia electronics, high-density television, personal communication systems, and a new type of nuclear breeder. Vogel (1991) concludes that no nation has tried harder than Korea and come so far so quickly – from handicrafts to heavy industry, from poverty to prosperity, from inexperienced imitators to modern planners, managers, and engineers.

The authors of the chapters in this volume are all "assimilation theorists" concerning the phenomena in question. They regard as very misleading the proposition that the remarkable expansion of capabilities of these economies came about more or less automatically as a result of these nations' high rates of investment in physical and human capital. They believe that learning, entrepreneurship, and innovation that have occurred in these economies are extremely important in their own right, and that understanding "how they did it" is the key to perception of the policies needed to effect such transformations.

An important element of the viewpoint shared by the authors is an analysis of how the successful NIEs moved from imitation in the 1960s to innovation by the 1990s. We sketch out key elements of that common view below.

FROM IMITATION TO INNOVATION

The rapid industrialization going on in NIEs in the 1960s and 1970s stemmed largely from imitation – reverse engineering of existing foreign technologies. When relatively simple products are involved, as they were then, reverse engineering does not require specialized investment in research and development (R&D). Only a low level of learning occurs since the firm cannot and is not required to generate new knowledge. Nevertheless, even simple reverse engineering rarely occurs in a vacuum. Reverse engineering involved activities that sensed the potential needs in the market, activities that located knowledge or products that would meet the market needs, and activities that would infuse these two elements into a new project. Reverse engineering also involved purposive search for relevant information, effective interactions among technical members within a project team and with marketing and production departments within the firm, effective interactions with other organizations such as suppliers, customers, and – for more complex products and technologies – local R&D institutes and universities. Such activity required the willingness to take risks and to learn from experience. Considerable trial and error and try-again learning generally was involved in achieving a satisfactory result.

Imitation does not necessarily mean illegal counterfeits or clones of foreign goods; it can also be legal, involving neither patent infringement nor pirating proprietary know-how. Mansfield (1984) shows that 60 percent of patented innovations were imitated legally within four years of their introduction. Imitation ranges from illegal duplicates of popular products to truly innovative new products that are merely inspired by a pioneering brand. Schnaar (1994) categorizes several distinct imitations: counterfeits or product pirates, knockoffs or clones, design copies, creative adaptations, technological leapfrogging, and adaptation to another industry.

Counterfeits and knockoffs are duplicative imitations, but one is illegal and the other is legal. Counterfeits are copies that sell under the same premium brand name as the original, often (but not always) of low quality, robbing the innovator of due profits. In contrast, knockoffs or clones are in most cases legal products on their own right, copying closely the pioneering products in the absence or expiration of patents, copyrights, and trademarks but selling with their own brand names at far lower prices. Clones often surpass the original in quality.

Duplicative imitation conveys no sustainable competitive advantage to the imitator in a technological sense, but it sustains competitive edge in price if the imitator's wage cost is significantly lower than the originator's. For this reason, duplicative imitation, if legal, is an astute strategy in the early industrialization of low-waged, catching-up countries, as the technology involved is generally mature and readily available and duplicative imitation of mature technology is relatively easy to undertake.

Duplicative imitation alone, however, is insufficient if a NIE is to achieve further industrialization. Both creative imitation and innovation are required not only to catch up in existing industries but also to challenge advanced countries in new industries. Design copies, creative adaptations, technological leapfrogging, and adaptation to another industry are creative imitations. Design copies mimic the style or design of the market leader but carry their own brand name and unique engineering specifications. Creative adaptations are innovative in the sense that they are inspired by existing products but differ from them. Technological leapfrogging can occur to a late entrant's advantage when the latecomer gains access to newer technology and uses it with a more accurate understanding of the growing market than was possessed by the original innovator. Adaptation to another industry illustrates the application of innovations in one industry for use in another. Creative imitations aim at generating imitative products but with new performance features. They involve not only such activities as benchmarking but also notable learning through substantial investment in R&D activities to create imitative products, the performance of which may be significantly better or production cost considerably lower than the original. Bolton (1993) argues that Japanese strategy represents these features.

Innovation is defined as a pioneering activity, rooted primarily in a firm's internal competencies, to develop and introduce a new product to the market for the first time. The distinction between innovation and creative imitation is, however, blurred. Most innovations do not involve breakthrough inventions but are deeply rooted in existing ideas. On the other hand, as Nelson and Winter (1982) note, imitators working with an extremely sparse set of clues might claim the "innovator" title, since most of the problem is really solved independently.

Many skills and activities required in reverse engineering have easily been transformed into activities called R&D, as some NIEs approached the technological frontier. Skills and activities required in these processes are in fact the same as in the innovation process in R&D.

Several industries in these countries, such as semiconductors, electronics, and biotechnology, are stretching their R&D activities to transform themselves into effective creative imitators as well as innovators. The innovation drive of newly industrializing economies in selective industries in the 1990s is marked by intensified in-house R&D activities and participation in global alliances and reflects their aspiration to become members of the industrially advanced community. In other words, technology and innovation become watchwords in these countries for strengthening competitiveness in the preparation for the twenty-first century. This volume presents articles contributed by leading scholars in the field to discuss innovation and competitiveness in NIEs, particularly those in East Asia.

ORGANIZATION OF THE VOLUME

This volume has four parts, with two to four chapters in each. Each part is concluded by a short commentary on the chapters therein.

Part I provides a broad prospective in two chapters. In Chapter 2, using the experience of the Asian and other industrializing countries, Sanjaya Lall discusses how industrial technological capabilities differ at the national level and the role that policy plays in these differences. He not only offers ten important features of enterprise-level technology capability development but also illustrates how national technological capability can be built on the basis of microlevel capabilities. In Chapter 3, Howard Pack notes that only a small group of Asian countries have succeeded in industrialization even though many developing countries pursued similar strategies. He discusses this success as the outcome of several interrelated features. They include the successful countries' openness to and their ability and willingness to learn from foreign knowledge, their response to competitive pressure from the export market to increase their productivity, and the high productivity of foreign technology as its dissemination and successful use was enhanced by an educated domestic labor force. In conclusion, he notes that although the considerable turmoil experienced currently by some of the NIEs is likely to be a temporary problem, their longer-term difficulty lies in continuing to expand the modern sectors efficiently. At the end, Lundvall provides a short commentary on the two chapters, in which he also introduces his own thoughts on the topics.

Part II examines in four chapters the ways firms learn at the microeconomic level. In Chapter 4, David Teece presents a model of dynamic capability of a firm. He argues that firms are the domains in which economic development really takes place, and that the competence and capabilities of a firm rest fundamentally on organizational processes, market positions, and paths. He also concludes that competence can provide competitive advantage and generate profits only if it is based on a collection of routines, skills, and complementary assets that are difficult to imitate. The chapter provides implications for firms in newly industrializing economies. In Chapter 5, Mike Hobday compares similarities and differences in technological learning in electronics between the OEM (original equipment manufacture) system prevalent in East Asia and the system led by transnational corporations (TNCs) in Southeast Asia. He concludes that despite structural problems, both approaches contributed significantly to industrial innovation and national economic growth. He also discusses future prospects and challenges for newly industrializing economies.

In Chapter 6, KongRae Lee analyzes how a passenger car producer in Korea as a user accumulated technological capabilities and became a major player in the industry. He examines in detail how the car producer accumulated reverse engineering capabilities through learning by operating the imported capital goods and imitating them, how it assimilated them through learning by designing, and how it became an independent designer through creative learning. He also discusses similar evidence in other industries. In Chapter 7, Geert Duysters and John Hagedoorn discuss different forms of international strategic technology alliances and why strategic alliances shift from traditional equity agreements to more flexible nonequity agreements. They also present empirical data on international strategic technology alliances within the Triad (namely Japan, the United States, and fifteen member countries in Europe), and between the Triad and NIEs. They conclude that Korean firms mostly account for the Triad-NIEs alliances, and that they are clustered in such high-technology industries as electronics, micro-information technologies, and bioengineering. Then Part II concludes with a commentary by Martin Fransman, who also provides his own thoughts on the topics.

Part III analyzes public policies for innovation in Asian NIEs. In Chapter 8, Mark Dodgson examines the relative strengths and weaknesses of science and technology in East Asian NIEs and analyzes the policies being pursued to assist the development of science, technology, and innovation. Despite broad differences in industrial structures, government-business relationships, and legal and financial systems among the emerging Asian nations, he concludes that infrastructure-building policies, such as creating network-oriented intermediary institutions, have a distinct impact on the development of technology diffusion and creation capabilities. In contrast, Won-Young Lee discusses in Chapter 9 the evolution of science and technology policy in Korea's industrial development in the past three decades. He postulates that technological development in Korea has undergone three stages: imitation, internalization, and generation. He then discusses the distinctive characteristics and efficacy of policies at each stage. He also examines the interaction between industrial policy and science and technology policy. Then, Morris Teubal provides a commentary on the two chapters with his own thoughts.

Part IV concludes the volume with two chapters. In Chapter 10, Jorge Katz presents the Latin American experience of technological learning during the import substitution period and the effect of recent structural change on manufacturing. He concludes that economic growth in Latin American countries was by no means as impressive as it had been in the East Asian nations. But an increasing degree of technological sophistication as an outcome of the learning dynamics resulted in a rapid expansion of labor productivity and of manufacturing exports in Argentina, Brazil, and Mexico in the 1970s. Such progress could not, however, be sustained under the macro-economic and trade policies put in place during the 1980s. Rather, there has been a rise of relatively low-technology labor-intensive industries in the 1980s and 1990s and a large shift of industrial specialization toward raw material processing. In Chapter 11, Linsu Kim discusses how Korea's national innovation system, which functioned relatively effectively in the past, has become problematic in recent years. He diagnoses Korea's problem in such areas as government bureaucracy, industrial structure, quality in education, R&D infrastructure, financial institutions, corporate management, and deteriorating sociocultural factors. That is, the greatest strengths in Korea's national innovation system in the past have become its most serious liabilities in recent years. He also provides a prescription for its reengineering. Finally, Howard Pack provides a commentary on the two chapters with his own thoughts on the topics.

REFERENCES

Amsden, Alice, H. 1989. *Asia's Next Giant: South Korea and Late Industrialization.* New York: Oxford University Press.

Bolton, Michele K. 1993. "Imitation versus Innovation." *Organization Dynamics,* Winter, 30–45.

Denison, Edward F. 1962. *The Sources of Economic Growth in the United States and the Alternatives before Us.* New York: Committee for Economic Development.

Kim, J. I., and L. J., Lau. 1994. "The Sources of Economic Growth in the East Asian Newly Industrialized Countries." *Journal of Japanese and International Economics,* (18), 235–271.

Kim, Linsu. 1997. *Imitation to Innovation: The Dynamics of Korea's Technological Learning.* Boston: Harvard Business School Press.

Krugman, Paul. 1994. "The Myth of Asia's Miracle." *Foreign Affairs*, December, 62–78.

Mansfield, Edwin. 1984. "R&D and Innovation." In Zvi Griliches (ed.), *R&D, Patents, and Productivity.* Chicago: University of Chicago Press, 142–143.

Marx, Karl. 1867. *Capital.* New York: Modern Library, 1934; first published in 1867.

Nelson, Richard R., and Howard Pack. 1999. "The Asian Miracle and Modern Growth Theory." *The Economic Journal*, 109, 416–436.

Nelson, Richard R., and Sidney G. Winter. 1982. *The Evolutionary Theory of Economic Change.* Cambridge, MA: Belknap Press.

Pack, Howard, and Larry E. Westphal. 1986. "Industrial Strategy and Technological Change: Theory versus Reality." *Journal of Development Economics*, 22, 87–128.

Schnaar, Steven P. 1994. *Managing Imitation Strategy: How Later Entrants Seize Markets from Pioneers.* New York: Free Press.

Schumpeter, Joseph. 1911. *The Theory of Economic Development.* Cambridge, MA: Harvard University Press, 1968; first published in 1911.

Smith, Adam. 1776. *The Wealth of Nations.* New York: Modern Library, 1937; first published in 1776.

Solow, R. M. 1957. "Technical Change and the Aggregate Production Function." *Review of Economics and Statistics*, 39, 312–320.

Vogel, Ezra F. 1991. *The Four Little Dragons: The Spread of Industrialization in East Asia.* Cambridge, MA: Harvard University Press.

Young, Alwyn. 1993. "The Tyranny of Numbers: Confronting the Statistical Realities of the East Asian Growth Experience." *Quarterly Journal of Economics*, 110, 641–680.

PART I

A Broad Prospective on Innovation in Newly Industrializing Economies

Technological Change and Industrialization In the Asian Newly Industrializing Economies: Achievements and Challenges

Sanjaya Lall

INTRODUCTION

The process of technological change in developing countries is one of acquiring and improving on technological capabilities rather than of innovating at frontiers of knowledge. This process essentially consists of learning to use and improve on technologies that already exist in advanced industrial economies. This is not a trivial or costless task, and industrial success depends on how well the process is managed: since all countries have access to the same international array of technical knowledge and equipment, a critical determinant of industrial performance is different rates of technological learning by different countries. This chapter uses the experience of the Asian newly industrializing economies (NIEs) (the "Tigers") and other industrializing countries to illustrate how industrial technological capabilities differ at the national level and the role that policy plays in these differences.

In the process, it revisits the debate on industrial policy, arguing that an evolutionary perspective gives better insights into market failures in technology and information than conventional approaches that tend to gloss over crucial technological phenomena. Despite a growing acceptance of a market friendly role for the government, industrial policy (in the sense of selectivity in government interventions) is considered unhealthy in current development thinking. The reasons for this hostility are more political than economic. A consideration of the technology devel-

I am grateful to the participants at the STEPI conference for comments and to Professor Nelson for subsequent suggestions on an earlier draft.

13

opment process at the microlevel provides a strong and valid economic case for industrial policy, and the East Asian case provides the empirical backing. The ramifications of both are spelled out here, and implications drawn for Asian countries that have failed to become Tigers.

National technological capability is the complex of skills, experience, and effort that enables a country's enterprises to efficiently buy, use, adapt, improve, and create technologies. While the individual enterprise remains the fundamental unit of technological activity, national capability is more than a sum of individual firm capabilities. It comprises the nonmarket system of interfirm networking and linkages, ways of doing business, and the web of supporting institutions. These affect significantly how firms interact with each other and the efficacy with which they exchange the information needed to coordinate their activities and to benefit from collective learning. This systemic aspect is something that conventional neoclassical theory does not deal with satisfactorily: the perfect competition paradigm shies away from dealing with widespread and diffuse externalities and fuzzy learning phenomena.[1] As such, it is not well suited to analyzing or explaining how technological activity occurs in the real world. Evolutionary perspectives are much better able to do this, and if supplemented with considerations of market efficiency and failure, they can provide very useful insights into how and why some countries manage technological development and change better than others. This is what this chapter tries to do, building upon, but also deviating, from the national innovation systems approaches that have also been used by evolutionary analysts to look at technology in a national setting.

How may one measure or compare national capabilities? Conventional economics, given its analytical underpinnings, tends not to treat the issue as a real one (thus the tendency by some theorists to dismiss wholly the concern with national competitiveness[2]), and so cannot provide the tools needed. However, it is possible to use indirect, but intuitively plausible, indicators of such capability, drawing on different aspects and outcomes of techno-

---

[1] See Richardson (1996), based on his pioneering work in the 1960s. Also see Stiglitz (1996) for a succinct review of the relevance of recent information theory for industrial policy in developing countries.

[2] See, for instance, Krugman (1996).

logical activity. But why *national* capabilities? Is it not misleading to think of national capabilities when technological learning is part of, and strongly conditioned by, activity in other countries? Not necessarily. While international flows of technology are clearly critical to national technological effort, not all countries are able to tap available knowledge equally. Taking into account differences in economic management, there remain differences in the *national* bases of (nontransferable) assets that determine each country's competence in effectively using technologies. The national boundary defines a common set of incentives and factor markets, attitudes, and business systems within which firms learn. It makes analytical sense to think of national capabilities as long as these learning systems differ. With the accelerating pace of technological change and trade and investment flows, national learning abilities are becoming more rather than less important. This is particularly true of developing countries, where intercountry differences tend to be larger.

TECHNOLOGICAL EFFORT IN DEVELOPING COUNTRIES

Nature of Enterprise Technological Learning

Developing countries obtain industrial technologies mainly from the industrialized world, and their main technological problem, at least initially, is to master, adapt, and improve on the imported knowledge and equipment. A large body of research suggests that this is not a straightforward task.[3] The hardware is available equally to all countries, but the disembodied elements of technology cannot be bought or transferred like physical products. Technical knowledge is difficult to locate, price, and evaluate, and its transfer cannot be wholly embodied in equipment or instructions, patents, designs, or blueprints. Unlike the sale of a good, where the transaction is complete when physical delivery has taken place, the successful transfer of technology can be a prolonged process, involving local learning to complete the transaction. The embodied elements can be used at best practice levels only if they

---

[3] See, among others, Bell and Pavitt (1993), Dahlman, Ross-Larson, and Westphal (1987), Enos (1992), Evenson and Westphal (1995), Katz (1987), Lall (1992), Pack (1992), Pack and Westphal (1986), Teitel (1993) and Teubal (1996).

are complemented by a number of tacit elements that have to be developed locally (Nelson, 1990).

The need for local learning exists in all cases, even when the seller of the technology provides advice and assistance, though the extent and costs of learning can vary greatly according to the technology, firm, and country context. Technological learning calls for conscious, purposive, and incremental efforts – to collect new information, try things out, create new skills and operational routines, and strike new external relationships.[4] This process must be located at the production facility and embodied in the institutional and organizational setting of the manufacturing enterprise. It is strikingly different from textbook depictions of how technology is transferred and used in developing countries.[5]

Let us summarize ten important features of enterprise-level technology capability development.

First, learning is a real and significant process. It is vital to industrial development and is primarily conscious and purposive rather than automatic and passive. This aspect of capability development is ignored in conventional economics, which assumes that all firms have equal and full knowledge of all available technologies (on a given production function) and can use the selected technology efficiently and instantaneously (knowledge about the existence of a technology is assumed to include knowledge about its "tacit" elements). At most, it accepts automatic learning by doing, arising from production and involving little or no risk or conscious effort. In the capability approach, by contrast, such passive learning is a relatively small part of the process. Thus, firms using a given technology for similar periods need not be equally proficient. Each would be at the point given by the intensity and efficacy of its deliberate capability-building efforts.

Second, firms do not have full information on technical alternatives and function with imperfect, variable, and rather hazy knowledge of technologies they are using. As a result, there is no

---

[4] The theoretical antecedents of this are the evolutionary theories of change developed by Nelson and Winter (1982). For extensions and related approaches see Dosi (1988), Dosi et al. (1988), Metcalfe (1995), and Stiglitz (1987, 1996).

[5] The dynamics of firm capability building is a large and complex subject that cannot be addressed here, but another paper in this volume (Teece, 1997) deals with it in greater detail.

uniform, predictable learning curve for a given technology. Each firm may have a different learning experience, depending on its initial situation and subsequent efforts. Each faces an element of risk, uncertainty, and additional cost in learning. Differences between learning given technologies are expected to be larger between firms in different countries and at differing levels of development.

Third, firms may not know how to build up the necessary capabilities – learning itself often has to be learned (Stiglitz, 1987). In a developing country, knowledge of traditional, stable, and simple technologies may not be a good base on which to learn how to master modern technologies. Thus, enterprises may not be able to predict if, when, how, and at what cost they would learn enough to become fully competitive, even when the technology is well known and mature elsewhere. This adds to the uncertainty and risk inherent in the learning process. For a latecomer to a technology, the fact that others have already undergone the learning process is thus a both a benefit and a cost – a benefit in that they can borrow from the others' experience, to the extent that this is accessible, and a cost in that they will necessarily be relatively inefficient during the learning process, and so have to bear a loss if they have to compete on completely open markets. The extent of the cost and risk depends on how new the technology is relative to the entrant's base of knowledge, how developed the supporting factor markets are, how deep it wants its learning to go, and how fast the technology itself is changing.

Fourth, firms cope with these uncertain conditions not by maximizing a well-defined objective function but by developing organizational and managerial *satisficing* routines, which they adapt over time as they collect new information, learn from experience, and imitate other firms (Nelson and Winter, 1982). Thus, learning tends to be path dependent and cumulative. Firms "move along particular trajectories in which past learning contributes to particular directions of technical change, and in which the experience derived from those paths of change reinforces the existing stocks of knowledge and expertise" (Bell and Pavitt, 1993, p. 168). Once embarked on, technological trajectories are difficult to change suddenly, at the national as well as the firm level, and patterns of specialization tend to persist over long periods. The stock of past capabilities and routines provides the base on which firms develop the capabilities to cope with new technologies: change is certainly possible, but it is conditioned by the past.

Fifth, the learning process is highly technology specific, since technologies differ greatly in their learning requirements. For instance, some technologies tend to be more embodied in equipment while others have greater tacit elements. Process technologies (like chemicals or paper), for instance, are more embodied than engineering technologies (machinery, automobiles, or electronics), and demand different – often less – effort. Different technologies involve different learning costs, risks, and duration, and they differ in their linkages. In this sense, it is possible to think of easy and difficult technologies (e.g., garment assembly is "easier" than textile manufacture, which is "easier" than making textile machinery, and so on). Capabilities built up in one manufacturing activity may not be easily transferable to another, and policies to promote learning in one may not be very useful in another. Similarly, different technologies can involve different breadth of skills and knowledge, with some needing a relatively narrow range of specialization and others a very wide range.

Sixth, different technologies can also have different degrees of dependence on interaction with outside sources of knowledge or information, such as other firms, consultants, capital goods suppliers, or technology institutions. It is important to bear in mind these differences in technology-specific features, which determine learning costs, risks, duration, and linkages, in considering how capabilities can be promoted by policy. A set of policies that conduces to the development of one set of capabilities may not be suited to another because of the completely different requirements.

Seventh, capability building involves effort at all levels – shop floor, process and product engineering, quality management, maintenance, procurement, inventory control, outbound logistics, and relations with other firms and institutions. Innovation, in the conventional sense of formal research and development (R&D) activity leading to new products or processes, is at one end of the spectrum of technological activity; it does not exhaust it. Note that what appear at first sight to be routine and easy technical functions, like quality management or maintenance, can be very difficult to master in a developing country. Most learning in developing countries arises in these and similarly mundane technical activities. However, formal R&D does become increasingly important in more complex technologies, where even efficient absorption requires distinct search and experimentation.

Eighth, technological development can take place within a given learning process to different depths. The attainment of a minimum level of operational capability (know-how) is essential to all industrial activity. While difficult to acquire, depending on the technology and initial stock of capabilities, this may not lead automatically to the development of deeper capabilities, the ability to understand the principles of the technology (know-why). The deeper the levels of technological capabilities aimed at, generally the higher the cost, risk, and duration involved. It is possible for an enterprise to become and stay a good user of imported technologies, with efficient process engineering, quality control, and maintenance routines, without developing the ability to decode the processes to the extent needed to significantly adapt, improve, or reproduce them, or to create new products or processes. This may not be optimal for a company's long-term capability development, since it remains dependent on other firms for all major improvements to its technologies.

While there are exceptions, depending on the costs involved, the development of know-why is an important part of overall learning (Nelson, 1993). It allows enterprises to select more efficiently the new technologies they need, lower the costs of buying these technologies, adapt and improve on them more effectively, add more value by using their own knowledge in production, and develop autonomous innovative capabilities. The lack of deeper capabilities may, on the other hand, restrict a firm's ability to move up the technology scale, in terms of even using higher levels of know-how in their given activity, diversifying into other activities, or coping with unexpected demands of technological change. Note that know-why development is needed not only for innovating at the frontier: even good "follower" strategies, where firms efficiently imitate and adapt technologies developed by others, requires good know-why capabilities.

Ninth, technological learning in a firm does not take place in isolation; the process is rife with externalities and interlinkages (see Greenwald and Stiglitz, 1986; Richardson, 1996; and Stiglitz, 1996, 1997). The most important direct interactions are those with suppliers of inputs or capital goods, competitors, customers, consultants, technology suppliers, and so on. Technological linkages also occur with firms in unrelated industries, technology institutes, extension services and universities, industry associations, and training institutions. Many such linkages are not mediated by markets but take place informally. Not all are deliberate or cooperative; some learning involves imitating and stealing knowledge. Where information and skill flows cohere around a set of related activities, clusters of industries emerge, with collective learning occurring in the group as a whole. The tapping of these cluster effects can be a very effective means of accelerating technological competence.

Finally, technological interactions take place both within a country and with other countries. Imported technology provides the most important initial input into technological learning in developing countries. Since technologies change constantly, moreover, access to foreign sources of innovation remains vital to continued technological progress. Technology import is not, however, a substitute for indigenous capability development; the efficacy with which imported technologies are used depends on local efforts. Domestic technological effort and technology import are largely complementary. However, not all modes of technology import are equally conducive to indigenous learning. Much depends on how the technology is packaged with complementary factors, whether it is available from other sources, how fast it is changing, how developed local capabilities are, and the policies adopted to stimulate transfer and deepening.

The main distinction here is between internalized (within a multinational company) and externalized (licensing or other arm's length transactions) modes of technology transfer. In general, internalized modes are very efficient for transferring know-how, but less so for transferring know-why. Externalized modes are more effective for generating local know-why, but may be more expensive in the short term for accessing know-how, and they do not allow access to those new technologies that are not for sale. However, these generalizations need qualification: even for accessible technologies, externalized modes can be wasteful if used in a protected setting to achieve technological self-reliance (as earlier in India; see Lall, 1987), rather than, as in Japan or Korea, to supplement strong design and development efforts.

Internalized modes can boost local know-why if induced to do so by appropriate policy interventions (as in Singapore), or when there is already a substantial base of local research capabilities (as in highly industrialized countries) (Cantwell, 1989).

In many technologies, it is increasingly unrealistic to think of alternatives to internalized modes of access, as costs of innovation grow and the deployment of technologies has to be at scales that require global production and distribution networks. Nevertheless, it remains important, or becomes even more important, for developing countries to deepen their technological base in this globalizing world. Where international competitiveness becomes the prime consideration in attracting new, high value-added foreign direct investment, countries must offer production sites that have not just low wages but world-class technical and management skills. To upgrade these, and to attract new, higher value-added activities, they must provide a growing base of advanced manufacturing and design skills and flexible and specialized supplier and support networks. Furthermore, to capture some of the externalities generated by technologically advanced multinational corporations (MNCs), they must have domestic firms with the ability to learn from them.

National Technological Capabilities

National technological capability is, as noted, more than the sum of capabilities of individual firms in a country. It is an innovation system, which includes the externalities and synergy generated by the learning process, ways of doing business, and the knowledge and skills residing in related institutions. The term *innovation system* has been widely used in the recent technology literature to analyze the complex of factors that affect national technological activity (Lundvall, 1992; Nelson, 1993). The system being considered here is very similar, but the capability approach differs from the Lundvall/Nelson one in that it places more emphasis on the incentive regime, particularly trade policies, and, as explained later in this chapter, introduces market failure considerations to mediate between firm- and country-level capabilities. The role of policies is considered in terms of their effectiveness in overcoming these market failures that affect firm-level technological activity. This provides a more coherent and systematic structure to the analysis of national systems.

The development of national capability shares many features of learning at the enterprise level. Countries undergo costly, uncertain, prolonged, and unpredictable learning, even when the technologies concerned are well known abroad. Entry into different technologies involves different learning processes, and the simple act of production does not ensure that efficient learning has occurred. National learning is path dependent and cumulative, and patterns of specialization are difficult to change quickly; the national base of capabilities and learning determines how well countries are able to cope with new technologies. Growing national technological maturity involves the industrial sector's ability to move from easy to complex technologies, and within given sets of technologies, from know-how to know-why. At each stage, there may be costs, risks, delays, and externalities; these are likely to rise at higher levels of technology and capability development.

What determines how well countries develop technological capabilities? In a simple neoclassical world, countries optimize, under free market conditions, by choosing from a known array the techniques appropriate to their relative factor prices and costlessly use these as best practice. In an evolutionary world with complex learning processes and externalities, the ability to select and deploy technologies efficiently cannot be taken for granted in this way. Many requirements of learning may involve serious market failure, and it cannot be assumed that over time countries will move automatically and efficiently into more difficult technologies – or into taking on more complex tasks within given technologies – simply in response to rising wage/interest ratios. Technological upgrading and deepening require enterprises to invest in more advanced – and so more costly, uncertain, and prolonged – learning processes. In the presence of externalities and deficient factor markets, such investments may not take place in free markets. They may require policies to overcome market failures – to tackle learning costs, promote externalities and linkages, coordinate factor market improvements with technological needs, and develop institutions.

In standard theory, interventions are justified only by the presence of market failures.[6] The role of government in overcoming certain market failures is now widely accepted in the development literature. However, there is a debate over whether interventions should be purely functional (aimed at remedying generic market failures, without favoring particular activities or sets of activities over others) or should include selective elements.[7] Examples of functional interventions are the fostering of primary or secondary schooling, the provision of basic infrastructure, or the stimulation of general export orientation. Selective interventions involve influencing the allocation of resources between activities, and industrial policy requires directing resources at particular manufacturing activities rather than others by trade restrictions, credit allocation/subsidization, discrimination on technology or foreign investment inflows, and so on. The neoclassical approach has shifted from denying that any market failures exist to arguing that only failures that call for functional interventions should be remedied by policy. Failures that call for selectivity are either not

---

[6] Though it is convenient to use the *market failure* terminology to discuss the role of government interventions, it may not be the most appropriate framework for analyzing policy in developing countries, especially where technological change is concerned. *Market failure* in neoclassical theory is a deviation from a market clearing equilibrium under conditions of perfect competition, and the remedy is to return to (a theoretically achievable) static optimum. This may not be possible, or even desirable, in markets that characterize modern industry. Some argue that perfect competition is undesirable as a theoretical construct under conditions of increasing returns and uncertain and unpredictable technological change (Richardson, 1996). Information economics suggests that whenever information is imperfect, externalities diffuse, and markets incomplete (including all future markets for risk), invariably the case with technical change, free markets cannot in principle meet the strict requirements of optimality in resource allocation (Stiglitz, 1996). It is misleading to think of market failure as something that can, or should, be remedied in order that the economy can be brought back to a desired (static) optimum (Lipsey, 1994). In developing countries, where technological learning is essential to industrial development, externalities are rife, and markets highly imperfect – indeed, when new markets, agents or endowments are being created – it is difficult to describe policy as "remedying market failure in the neoclassical sense. Where economies of scale exist in intermediate products, leading to multiple equilibria (Rodrik, 1996), government policy should aim to move from low to high productivity/technology paths. Again, this is not really dealing with market failure since equilibrium could in theory be reached in any of the multiple possibilities. However, this chapter cannot deal with such fundamental issues. We continue to use the market failure terminology for purposes of exposition but remind the reader that the term includes strategic interventions that have little to do with achieving static resource optimization.

[7] See, for instance, World Bank (1993) for the espousal of functional interventions, and Amsden (1989, 1994), Pack and Westphal (1986), Lall (1992, 1994, 1996), and Wade (1990, 1994), on the need for selectivity.

important or, if they are, their economic cost is always less than the cost of inherent government failure. This moderate neoclassical approach is not theoretically justifiable, nor does it reflect accurately the experience of interventions in technology development in many newly industrializing countries (Lall, 1996).

The theoretical deficiencies can be traced to the simplifying assumptions on technology that underlie the neoclassical analysis. A more realistic framework, reflecting the features of technological learning described above, yields a different set of policy prescriptions. A simple framework for looking at the determinants of technology development (Lall, 1992) classifies the determinants under *incentives*, *factor markets* and *institutions*, and derives the role of policy by identifying the market failures that may arise in technological learning for each. Note that this ignores the firm-specific processes of capability building, which can differ greatly (Teece, 1997, and the case study of Samsung in Choi, 1997). It focuses instead on the common elements of learning by firms in a common national environment – it asks why, given firm level differences, some countries produce a larger number of dynamic and competitive firms than others. It assumes, in other words, that the common set of markets, rules, and institutions that make up a national economic unit has a significant effect on the behavior and capabilities of the firms within that unit.

Incentives

The main incentives affecting investment in technological capabilities arise from the macroeconomic environment, trade policy, domestic industrial policies, and domestic demand. The importance of good *macro management* is now universally accepted and will not be discussed further here. The role of *trade policies* is more complex. Participation in trade enables a country to realize its existing comparative advantage and take advantage of scale economies in capital-intensive activities. Facing world competition is an effective stimulus to building technological capabilities, and close contact with export markets is an excellent, and partly free, source of technological information. The dangers of intervening in trade through prolonged and haphazard protection are also well known. Classic import-substitution, with haphazard and open-ended protection for all activities with no regard to efficiency, clearly breeds inefficiency and technological sloth. Export-orientation has been conclusively shown to be a better strategy.

It does not follow, however, that completely free trade is optimal. Free markets cannot, by definition, give the right signals for resource allocation in the presence of market failures. Apart from the textbook cases of market failure from externalities, public goods, and monopolistic markets, the failures that affect technology development arise from the nature of the learning process: its uncertain and unpredictable duration, its variability by technology, the problem of financing learning costs in imperfect markets, increasing returns, and the presence of widespread link-ages (which can also vary by activity).[8] Thus, free markets can lead to underinvestment in difficult technologies with high learning costs, exceptional risks, long learning periods, and widespread externalities. These market failures arise both from the problem of encouraging entry by firms into difficult and scale-intensive technologies and taking on more complex technological tasks, and of coordinating economic decisions by agents where there are collective learning phenomena to capture valuable externalities. It follows that efficient interventions to restore efficient resource allocation must vary by activity according to its technology and linkages. Uniform support across activities in the presence of these technology-specific differences makes as little sense as noninter-vention – there can be good economic reasons for selectivity in government interventions.

Trade interventions can take the form of subsidies or protec-tion; economists prefer the former on theoretical grounds, but governments prefer the latter on practical (revenue) ones. Theory dictates that all such interventions should be carefully geared to remedying or taking advantage of market failures and should be removed once the failures have been overcome (though the diffuse externalities inherent in technological development may never entirely disappear). They should not be of the haphazard, open-ended, and nonselective sort typical in import-substituting regimes. In the nature of the phenomenon, all such interventions are difficult to design; they require enormous information, are prone to rent-seeking behavior, and can remove the incentive for

---

[8] For theoretical expositions, see Rodrik (1996), Stiglitz (1994, 1996), and Lall (1996).

the very learning they seek to promote. This is difficult, but not impossible, since what is being sought is not one unique static optimum but a range, where the precise outcomes are not as important as the ability to stimulate a process of widespread and dynamic learning. Effective trade interventions of selective types were in fact mounted in several East Asian economies, under certain conditions.[9] Note also that the information needs of follower countries are not as difficult as those of frontier countries, where picking winners at the frontiers of technology is much more risky and difficult.

As far as *domestic industrial policies* are concerned, the removal of artificial barriers to competition provides the best stimulus to technological development. Thus, there is a critical role for antitrust policies, elimination of artificial barriers to entry, and protection of intellectual property rights. In fact, vibrant domestic competition is one of the best ways of offsetting some of the distortions that may be created by restricting import competition. However, the ideal is not necessarily the small, anonymous firm of textbook-perfect competition models. Given the scale economies inherent in many industrial activities, not just in production but also in technology development (in the more advanced stages where formal R&D becomes significant), export marketing (especially where a firm launches its own outlets and brand names rather than remaining a supplier to foreign buyers or a provider of original equipment manufacture products[10]), and investing overseas, it may be desirable to allow, even promote, large size or spread that can allow firms to undertake the necessary investment and risk. This is what some governments did to allow their industries to enter difficult technologies and develop advanced export and foreign investment capabilities, while pro-

[9] These conditions are strong leadership commitment to competitiveness, flexibility in policy making, skilled and insulated bureaucracy, supporting interventions in factor markets, close interaction with industry, and exposure to export competition (while retaining a protected domestic market to cushion learning) to discipline both firms and the government. The World Bank (1993) documents some of these in the East Asian case, even though it comes out against selective trade interventions. Also see Stiglitz (1994, 1996), and for a critique of the Bank analysis, Lall (1994).

[10] OEM refers to *original equipment manufacture*, where a developing country firm makes a product to designs and specifications provided by a foreign firm, which sells the product under its own name. Most of the high-end technological and marketing activity remains with the foreign firm, with its concomitant value added and learning. For an analysis of OEM as a means to export growth in East Asia, see Hobday (1995).

moting fierce domestic competition between the large firms and groups. Again, there was selectivity involved.

Domestic demand can play an important role in influencing national capabilities, for two reasons. First, the quality of local demand (the sophistication of buyers, development of marketing channels, intensity of competition) affects the development of product, quality management, and marketing skills (Porter, 1990). Second, the size of the domestic market influences the kinds of activities that can be undertaken, given that some kinds of technological learning require interacting with local markets; the greater costs involved in exporting mean that learning on export markets is not feasible unless there are multinational companies involved or the domestic resource cost advantage is very large.[11] Thus, large countries can foster capabilities in more scale-intensive activities than smaller economies; since the effective size of the domestic market depends not only on total incomes but also its distribution, greater equity, with a broader base of demand, can be more conducive to the development of such capabilities. Here policies have to be functional rather than selective.

Factor Markets

The most important factor markets in technology development are skills (especially technical skills), finance for technological activity, and access to information, domestic and foreign.[12] The importance of skills and the role of government in promoting education and training is so widely acknowledged that it does not need extensive discussion; what should be noted is that policies to promote human capital for technology development may need to be fairly selective at higher levels. At the start of the industrialization process, the provision of literate labor may suffice. As technologies in use become more demanding, the education system has to provide more specific technical, engineering, and scientific skills. One of the most distinctive features of new technologies is their need for a broad range of technical skills as well as different kinds of skills that involve team work and multitasking (Capelli and Rogovsky, 1994). To the extent that the education and train-

---

[11] The threshold effects of market size during development are investigated by Murphy et al. (1989).
[12] Physical infrastructure is vital, but this is obvious and need not be separately discussed here.

ing systems fail to anticipate and provide for these needs, there is a need for selective interventions by the government.

Capital market failures in developing countries, arising from missing or asymmetric information and adverse selection, can lead to underfinancing of risky or long gestating technological investments. Most capital market interventions take the form of directed/subsidized credit to selected clusters, industries, or firms – all highly selective policies. Many such policies have not been effective in promoting technological dynamism, but, as with trade policies, some Tigers have been able to use them to promote industrial and technological development by carefully integrating them with other incentive and factor market interventions and imposing requirements on beneficiaries in terms of competitive performance in export markets (Stiglitz, 1996; Stiglitz and Uy, 1996).

In information markets, access to foreign technology is vital to technology development, but the mode of access affects technological deepening. A passive reliance on foreign technologies, without interventions to ensure local effort to absorb and deepen them, may be suboptimal. Interventions can take different forms: with internalized technology transfer, they can seek to guide foreign direct investment (FDI) into more complex activities, induce existing foreign investments to upgrade the technological content of their activities, and/or promote the diffusion of technology and skills from foreign affiliates to local firms. Such selective interventions may coexist with noninterventionist policies in trade (e.g., Singapore). With externalized forms, policies can stimulate greater absorption and deepening in local firms, by exposure to international markets, R&D incentives, and support and entry into more complex technologies (e.g., Korea).

Several factor market interventions have to be selective rather than functional, for three reasons. First, several factor market needs are specific to particular activities; if they lack the information or coordination to meet these needs, interventions must be applied to remedy these specific deficiencies. For instance, the skill needs of new electronics technologies may not be fully foreseen by education markets, or the financial needs of emerging new technologies may not be addressed by capital markets. Second, the government's resources for supporting factor markets are limited, and to allocate among competing uses entails selectivity at a high level of priority setting (say, between education and other uses).

Third, where the government is already targeting particular sectors for promotion in product markets, factor markets have to be geared to those objectives.

Institutions

Institutions here takes the narrow sense to refer to bodies that support industrial technology, such as education and training, standards, metrology, technical extension, R&D, long-term credit, technology and export information, and so on. These institutions may be government run, started by the government but run autonomously, or started and managed by industry associations or private interests. Many are set up on nonmarket terms, at least initially, in response to perceived gaps in the market provision of inputs into technology development. The literature on technology (see, for instance, the country studies in Nelson, 1993) stresses the significance of such institutions for supporting enterprise efforts to develop their knowledge and capabilities. The catalytic role of government in launching many institutions is acknowledged, as is the fact that such interventions are often highly selective and geared to the objectives of industrial policy.

The outcome in terms of the development of national technological capabilities depends on the complex interaction of these variables on firm-level learning processes. However, not all market failures call for government intervention. Markets may improve, private agents may remedy failures by nonmarket means, and the cost of intervention may outweigh its benefits. The risk of government failure needs particular emphasis, particularly when selectivity (with its attendant effects on resource allocation and rent seeking) is involved. The history of development is littered with well-intentioned but inefficient interventions. Most interventions have not been well designed or truly selective (i.e., aimed at market failures in a few activities at a time), or implemented with flexibility or discipline. Thus, import substitution gave unlimited, unselective, and open-ended protection to all industrial activities and did not offset its disincentives to technological development. It was often overlaid with noneconomic objectives such as nationalism, socialism, or self-reliance. Governments often failed to integrate their interventions in product and factor markets; thus, activities promoted by protection were not provided with the necessary technical skills or institutional support.

This being said, however, it remains the case in theory that where market failures exist, or where multiple equilibria are possible, the outcome can be improved by appropriate policies. The fact that policies have often been badly designed and implemented in the past is not a case against intervention as such (Shapiro and Taylor, 1990). A general case against industrial policy can only be established if it is argued that interventions cannot be better designed and implemented. This is difficult to establish on an a priori basis, though some economists do assert this without further justification or evidence (and ignoring the evidence of East Asia).[13] Apart from those with this ideological bent, however, most analysts would agree that this is an empirical, context and time-specific, matter. Moreover, since government capabilities are themselves acquired, policy analysis must include a central component of improving intervention capabilities themselves. The correct answer on the role of government has to be contingent and cannot be not universal.

INDICATORS AND DETERMINANTS OF TECHNOLOGICAL COMPETENCE

Industrial success depends on how each country learns and organizes itself to use constantly changing industrial technologies on its technological competence. Every country uses technology in some form or another, but it is possible to stay static at the bottom of the technology chain, providing basic inputs like extracting natural resources or deploying unskilled labor in simple manufacturing. However, a shallow base of capabilities, specializing in the operation of a limited number of simple activities with few spillovers, can lead to growth in a liberalized world economy only as long as these activities remain competitive – or the resource base is very large. Growth will slow down as these advantages erode and are not added to, as new entrants provide low-skilled labor at lower cost, or technological progress makes such simple competencies unnecessary. Sustained growth requires a steady

---

[13] However, Krugman argues that, despite the theoretical case for interventions, a "Realist" (which presumably he considers himself and all those who agree with him) "does not share the interventionist propensities of the Strategist, because he regards acting on the theoretical possibilities for activism to be virtually certain to do more harm than good" (1996, p. 23).

move up the ladder of technology, the building up of the system for collective learning. In a world of rapid technological change, moreover, what is critical is the depth and flexibility of the system – the ability to deal with technical change as a process.

This section looks at proxies for systemic technological capabilities across Asian economies. There cannot be an unambiguous comparative measure of this, and the usual measures have deficiencies. Growth rates of gross domestic product (GDP) or industrial value added do capture technological capabilities, but they also reflect many other factors. The relative structure of manufacturing may indicate industrial depth but does not take technical efficiency or differences in local technological effort into account. Research and development and education data capture inputs into technological effort, but not technological output or structural trends. Total factor productivity (TFP) estimates, the common neoclassical measure of technological activity, face serious methodological and interpretation problems. However, this does not mean that we cannot say anything: a mixture of different indicators, if used carefully, can furnish plausible indicators, as long as their defects are borne in mind.

Export Performance and Structure

Of the various measures of technological performance, data on manufactured exports are perhaps the most usable. They are relatively easy to calculate, indicate prima facie international efficiency, and show structural trends. However, they may not be good indicators of competence in large economies that have large nonexporting sectors, or where incentives discriminate in favor of domestic markets. Export data do not also distinguish between different levels of technology used in a given product group (between simple and complex processes). Nor do they distinguish between exports by foreign and domestic firms, which may be important when these reflect different technological inputs and competence. However, some deficiencies may be offset by looking at trade regimes, local technological content of exports and the role of FDI in trade.

We start with aggregate figures, with the focus on ten Asian countries – the Four Tigers (Hong Kong, Singapore, Korea, and Taiwan), the three "new Tigers" (Indonesia, Malaysia, and

Table 2.1. *Exports from selected Asian countries (1994)*

Country	Merchandise exports			Manufactured exports
	Value ($ million)	Growth rate (1980–90)	Growth rate (1990–94)	Value ($ million)
Hong Kong (a)	28,739	11.5	−0.3	27,302
Singapore (a)	57,963	12.1	10.9	56,224
Korea	96,000	13.7	7.4	89,280
Taiwan	92,847	11.6	5.9	86,348
Indonesia	40,054	5.3	21.3	21,229
Malaysia	58,756	11.5	17.8	41,129
Thailand	45,262	14.3	21.6	33,041
China	121,047	11.4	14.3	98,048
India	21,553	6.3	7.0	16,165
Pakistan	6,636	9.5	8.8	5,641

Notes: (a) Excluding re-exports.
Sources: World Bank, *World Development Report*, 1996; Asian Development Bank, *Key Indicators of Developing Asian and Pacific Countires*, 1994; *Hong Kong External Trade*, February 1996; *Singapore Trade Statistics*, 1996.

Thailand), and three large countries with considerable import-substitution pasts (India, China, and Pakistan). Table 2.1 shows that in 1994 the largest exporters, both of merchandise and manufactures, were China, Korea, Taiwan, Malaysia, and Singapore.[14] The fastest rates of growth in 1990–94 were for Thailand, Indonesia, Malaysia, China, and Singapore. Hong Kong was the only country in the group that had declining exports (re-exports excluded), a dramatic deterioration on its earlier performance. Of the larger Tigers, Korea showed a stronger long-term performance than Taiwan. China outperformed the other large economies, and by 1994 emerged as the largest single exporter of manufactures in the group – and in the whole developing world. The general export performance, higher than in other developing regions, suggests considerable technological dynamism. However, these data reveal little about the nature of technological activity, in particular, the levels or kinds of technologies being deployed or of the nature of local capabilities.

[14] Note that the data for Singapore and Hong Kong exclude re-exports, which account for 40 percent of total merchandise exports for the former and 81 percent for the latter.

Let us look, therefore, at the technological composition of manufactured exports. There are numerous ways to categorize this. A frequently used one, high and low technology, is highly aggregated and conceals interesting differences in export performance, especially between developing countries that are largely exporting simple products. A breakdown by technological characteristics is more useful (Table 2.2); the industries in each category are shown in the chapter appendix, Table 2A.1.

There are inevitable overlaps between the categories (e.g., resource-based industries can be very capital intensive), and the groups are broad (for instance, many electronics exports are labor intensive); but if carefully used, the classification is helpful. Labor-intensive products tend to be at the low end of the technological spectrum, with low requirements of technical skills. Products in the scale-intensive group use complex, capital-intensive technologies, but are generally not at the cutting edge of technology (this also applies to many resource-based exports). Within the scale-intensive group, there is a distinction between process (e.g., chemicals) and engineering industries (e.g., automobiles); the latter tend to have more difficult learning requirements, be very linkage intensive, and involve a larger variety of skills. Differentiated manufactures are more sophisticated engineering products involving advanced design, research, and manufacturing skills, while science-based products use leading edge technologies. In broad terms, we call the last three categories *technologically advanced*, and the last two *high-tech* products. Resource-based products are not considered further here because their competitive edge is too specific to merit generalization.

Table 2.3 shows the technological breakdown of manufactured exports by the ten countries since 1980.[15] The highest concentration on labor-intensive exports (primarily textiles and garments) is currently in Pakistan (94%), followed at some distance by China (58%), Hong Kong (54%), India (50%), Indonesia (49%), and Thailand (38%). There is some correlation between labor intensity of exports and factor costs, but it is far from perfect. The lowest wages are probably in China and Indonesia, while Hong Kong is a high-wage economy. The export structure also reflects the

---

[15] Data for the Tigers go up to 1994, the others to 1992. The calculations are at the two-digit Standard International Trade Classification (SITC) level. I am grateful to Simon Dradri for his help with the data.

Table 2.2. *Technological basis of competitive advantage*

Activity Group	Major Competitive Factor	Examples	Growth Rates (a)		Distribution of World Manufactured Trade	
			1980–90	1990–95	1980	1995
Resource-intensive	Access to natural resources	Aluminum, food processing, oil refining	7.4	6.6	18.8	15.1
Labor-intensive	Cost of unskilled, semi-skilled labor	Garments, footwear, toys	9.5	7.7	17.4	17.9
Scale-intensive	Length of production runs	Steel, autos, paper, chemicals	7.8	7.0	27.8	23.7
Differentiated	Products tailored to varied demands	Advanced machinery, TVs, power generating equipment	8.4	8.6	24.3	23.4
Science-based	Rapid application of science to technology	Electronics, biotechnology, pharmaceuticals	12.6	13.3	11.4	19.9

Note: (a) Total world manufactured trade grew at 8.8% per annum during 1980–90 and at 8.5% during 1990–95.
Source: Classification from OECD (1987); trade data from World Bank trade database.

Table 2.3. *Distribution of manufactured exports by technological categories (%)*

	China		Korea		Taiwan		Singapore		Hong Kong	
	1985	1992	1980	1994	1980	1994	1980	1994	1980	1994
Resource-based	4.3	6.3	7.3	3.8	9.4	6.8	6.5	3.3	2.0	3.7
Labor-intensive	66.6	58.4	49.5	27.8	53.9	32.7	16.9	8.5	65.8	54.3
Scale-intensive	17.6	11.2	25.8	27.2	9.4	13.9	20.9	10.5	1.2	4.2
Differentiated	5.3	17.2	14.7	35.6	23.7	30.9	50.3	46.3	16.7	21.4
Science-based	0	1.1	2.7	5.6	3.6	15.8	5.4	31.4	14.3	16.4

	Indonesia		Malaysia		Thailand		India		Pakistan	
	1980	1992	1980	1992	1980	1992	1980	1992	1980	1992
Resource-based	14.7	29.5	11.0	5.4	53.9	20.1	26.5	28.7	15.5	4.5
Labor-intensive	28.9	48.7	18.4	17.4	28.4	38.3	55.4	49.6	84.5	93.8
Scale-intensive	20.2	7.6	4.9	5.3	4.3	5.6	11.2	17.1	0.0	0.0
Differentiated	19.0	7.6	60.1	29.6	13.4	15.7	4.1	1.2	0.0	0.0
Science-based	0	0.9	3.8	42.3	0.0	20.3	2.8	3.4	0.0	1.7

Notes: Figures for Singapore and Hong Kong are for total manufactured exports (including re-exports). No data for China are available for 1980, so the starting year is 1985.
Source: Calculated from UN trade data.

underlying industrial and technological structure, which in turn is determined by the industrial policies pursued (Lall, 1996).

With industrial development there is a general tendency for the share of labor-intensive products to decline. But again there are exceptions: in Indonesia and Pakistan the shares have risen over time. As for more technology-based products, the figures below show the shares of technologically advanced (Figure 2.1) and high-tech (Figure 2.2) products for these countries. These suggest the following:

- The most technologically advanced exporters are Singapore, followed by Malaysia, Taiwan, and Korea. Hong Kong has the lowest technological content of exports of the Tigers. Pakistan is the least advanced; Indonesia is the next lowest, with India and China slightly ahead.
- In the narrower category of high-tech products, the leader is Malaysia, followed by Singapore, Taiwan, and Korea. The weakest is Pakistan, followed by India, Indonesia, and China.
- The technology intensity of manufactured exports has been growing for all countries except Indonesia, where the rapid

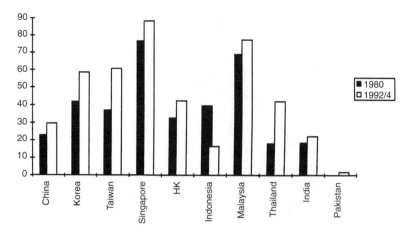

Figure 2.1. Shares of technologically advanced products (%).

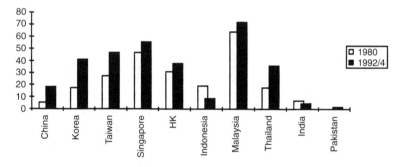

Figure 2.2. Shares of high-tech products (%).

growth of labor- and resource-intensive exports has swamped other exports (though this growth has also been rapid, if from a small base) (Lall and Rao, 1995).

Accepting the problems of aggregation and simplification inherent in these calculations, the results accord with general knowledge about technological capability in these countries. However, some qualifications have to be made to these indicators if they are to indicate the domestic technological base more accurately. In particular, we have to account for the level of technology involved in the export activity, and the role of MNCs in export and technological activity.

Level of Technology

The local technological content of similar exports can vary between countries, according to the level and extent of local inputs of components, equipment, and technical knowledge. For instance, a high-technology export in one country may come from locally assembled imported components, with few local inputs, physical or technological; in another, it may be based on substantial local equipment, components, design, development, and engineering. These clearly show different capabilities to deal with technological change. Asian countries differ greatly in this respect. Malaysia's high-tech exports are driven primarily by electronics and electrical assembly activity in export enclaves. While the activity has upgraded in process technology and product range, there are still few domestic linkages and very low local technological input (Lall et al., 1994). Capabilities have certainly developed, but they are mainly in operating imported technologies. Singapore is also driven by MNC-based operations, but the processes and products are at a higher level of sophistication, use more advanced skills, and involve more local technological activity. However, there are still relatively low levels of design and development activity, which is done overseas by the MNCs involved.

By contrast, high-tech exports from Korea and Taiwan have significant local linkages (both equipment and components) and far more local technological input up to basic design stages. Korea is ahead of Taiwan, with a more diverse and heavier industrial structure and far greater R&D effort. Of the Tigers, Hong Kong has the lowest technological input, having remained specialized in light consumer goods (though within this there has been considerable upgrading); in addition, even its high-technology exports are simpler than in the other Tigers, consisting largely of electronic items like games and watches. Thailand is also basically at the assembly stage in technologically advanced products, but its rate of growth in such activities is phenomenal, and in more traditional activities there is a lot of local depth. China's high-tech exports have a mixture of assembled and manufactured items, the former largely off-loaded from the Tigers. India has a deep and backward

Table 2.4. *Inward foreign direct investment (FDI)*

Country	Annual FDI Inflows ($ million)							FDI as % GDI (a)	
	1984–89	1990	1991	1992	1993	1994	1995	1984–89	1990–94
H Kong	1,422	1,728	538	1,918	1,667	2,000	2,100	12.2	6.7
Singapore	2,239	5,575	4,879	2,351	5,016	5,588	5,302	28.3	28.4
Korea	592	788	1,180	727	588	809	1,500	1.4	0.7
Taiwan	691	1,330	1,271	879	917	1,375	1,470	3.3	3.0
Indonesia	406	1,093	1,482	1,774	2,004	2,109	4,500	1.6	3.5
Malaysia	798	2,333	3,998	5,183	5,006	4,348	5,800	8.8	22.4
Thailand	676	2,444	2,014	2,116	1,726	640	2,300	4.4	4.3
China	2,282	3,487	4,366	11,156	27,515	33,787	37,500	1.8	11.6
India	133	162	141	151	273	620	1,750	0.2	0.5
Pakistan	136	244	257	335	354	422	639	2.0	3.6

Note: (a) GDI stands for gross domestic investment. The figures are simple annual averages.
Source: UNCTAD, *World Investment Report 1996*, Geneva.

integrated production structure, but one that past policies have burdened with high costs and technological lags.

Role of MNCs

A strong foreign presence has mixed implications for the local technological activity in export activity. In industrially advanced countries, MNC export activity can have significant inputs of indigenous content and design, and interact with and contribute to the local know-why base. In low-wage, less industrialized countries, MNC exports are driven mainly by cheap labor, and have low levels of local technological content. Between these two, a number of combinations of MNC presence and technological activity are possible. Asian countries show the whole range. Note that even in cases of MNC-driven assembly activity, there may be considerable creation of local technological capabilities – but the learning tends to be concentrated in operational capabilities rather than know-why.

FDI has played very different roles in these countries. In terms of the share of FDI in gross domestic investment, Singapore is the most FDI-intensive economy in the region (and probably in the world), followed by Malaysia (Table 2.4). Then comes China, with a startling growth in the share of FDI in investment in the 1990s, the bulk coming from overseas Chinese enterprises. At the other end of the spectrum, India and Korea have traditionally had very low levels of reliance on foreign investment. It is interesting to note the differences between the Tigers in FDI policies: Korea and Taiwan, particularly the former, emphasized externalized technology transfer, while Singapore strongly targeted internalized modes and Hong Kong had a laissez faire attitude (Lall, 1995a). The first two had selective policies on entry, restricting FDI where domestic capabilities were adequate (or were being protected). Once allowed in, investors were induced to diffuse technologies locally. Singapore also used selectivity strongly to attract investors into targeted activities and, later, to upgrade their technological content. Only Hong Kong left FDI and technology transfer entirely to market forces.

In terms of export contribution, MNCs account for around 25 percent of manufactured exports from Hong Kong, 70 percent from Malaysia, 90 percent from Singapore, and 17 percent from Taiwan (Ramstetter, 1994). The figure for Korea is probably significantly lower than for Taiwan, given Korea's much lower reliance on inward FDI and predominant role of its *chaebol* (large private conglomerates) in export activity. Thailand and Indonesia depend heavily on MNCs in many export activities, but large parts of the industrial sector are in local hands. Chinese labor-intensive exports largely originate from investors from the other NIEs, mainly Hong Kong and Taiwan, but a number of local firms are also becoming active exporters in a range of products. MNCs are not significant exporters from India and Pakistan.

Export activity may not be a good indicator of technological strength in large inward-oriented countries. China and India probably possess technological capabilities far in advance of that suggested by their export structures, though many may not currently be at best practice international levels (on India, see Lall, 1987). In the other countries, where trade plays a larger role in manufacturing, the patterns shown earlier may not be unrepresentative of the underlying technological structure.

Taken on the whole, the evidence suggests that the most advanced technological capabilities are in Korea and Taiwan. Singapore is strong in a narrow range of high-tech activities, where some deeper capabilities are developing; because of its heavy dependence on MNCs, however, it is weak in design and development. Hong Kong has good operational capabilities in light industry but little technological depth. The new Tigers have relatively shallow industrial structures, with Thailand the most advanced and Indonesia the least. Of the large economies, China and India have fairly developed capabilities but with significant inefficiencies and lags. Pakistan lags overall.

Role of Governments

Governments intervened both selectively and functionally in promoting technology development in the NIEs. The patterns of intervention varied enormously, from wholesale planning and import substitution to selective measures to guide and develop markets and minimal selectivity.[16] The import-substituting economies intervened massively, but without discrimination: they supported, without any limit on time or cost, any manufacturing activity set up within them. They imposed no offsetting requirements of export growth or international competitiveness. And they often constrained domestic competition. The results of these haphazard, unselective interventions was large areas of inefficiency and technological sloth (on India see Lall, 1987). Of the Tigers, Hong Kong and Singapore did not use trade interventions, though Singapore influenced resource allocation by targeting and guiding foreign investment. Korea and Taiwan intervened significantly in trade, using the whole range of quantitative restrictions, tariffs, procurement, and other administrative measures to promote selected industries. They offset these interventions by strong export incentives and targeting, and coordinated investments across firms, activities, and industries as well as across product and factor markets, where they subsidized and allocated credit, targeted human capital formation, and encouraged technological activity. As noted, they also restricted FDI inflows to deepen their indigenous technological capabilities. The new Tigers had a mixture of policies.

The dynamism of comparative advantage as discussed reflects the nature of interventions. The countries that managed to build up the most advanced base of capabilities were those that intervened most heavily and efficiently – *efficiently* in this context means being selective, offsetting the effects of intervention by export orientation, and coordinating related activities and factor

---

[16] See, of the vast literature, Amsden (various), Wade (1990), World Bank (1993), Pack (1997), Pack and Westphal (1986), Westphal (1990), Stiglitz (1996), Rodrik (1995), and Lall (1996).

markets. Simple and impressionistic as this evaluation is, it gives us a base to differentiate between the technological bases in these economies. The following subsections look at some of the inputs into the capability development base.

The Human Capital Base

The human capital base is represented here by educational enrollments, though it is far from a perfect measure. Education is not equal to capabilities, but it provides the base on which learning takes place; without further technology-specific experience and search, formal qualifications do not yield know-how or know-why. Thus, formal education is only one way to create skills; on-the-job learning, training, and experimentation are often more important. Nevertheless, since formal education is generally a necessary condition for industrial skill acquisition, enrollment data *can* serve as a reasonable proxy in the absence of other comparative human capital formation data. Even this measure suffers from differences in definition, quality, and relevance between countries, but there is little we can do to correct for this.

Table 2.5 shows general enrollments at three levels as well as tertiary students abroad and the adult literacy rate. While most countries claim to have universal primary enrollment, there is still considerable illiteracy in Pakistan, India, and to a lesser extent, China, Indonesia, and Malaysia. Secondary enrollment rates are very high in the Tigers, with Korea and Taiwan at developed country rates. Hong Kong and Singapore are slightly behind, followed by Malaysia, China, and India.[17]

The quality of schooling is also apparently higher in the Tigers than in South or Southeast Asia: dropout rates are lower, and there is a stronger emphasis on numeracy, which is particularly relevant for emerging information-based technologies. The Tigers tend to surpass even the developed Western countries in mathematics (OTA, 1990; UK Cabinet Office, 1996). In the latest and most comprehensive international test for mathematics and science (Third International Math and Science Study), which covered a half-million thirteen-year-old children in forty-one

---

[17] Pack (1997) has a stimulating analysis of the evolution of the education systems, and some of their differences, in the Tiger economies.

Table 2.5. *Educational enrollments and literacy rates*
Most recent available (percent of age group)

Country	Primary	Secondary	Tertiary	Percent tertiary abroad (a)	Adult literacy rate
Hong Kong	102	75	21	32	91
Singapore	107	78	19 (b)	25	90
Korea	101	93	48	2	97
Taiwan	100	88	38	NA	NA
Indonesia	114	43	10	2	83
Malaysia	93	59	7	38	82
Thailand	98	37	19	1	94
China	109	52	6	3	79
India	105	45	6	1	50
Pakistan	65	17	3	9	36

Note: (a) 1987–88 (b) Figure for 1995, referring to % or persons aged 18 who are university graduates. In addition to these, Singapore also has 27% that are polytechnic graduates.
Sources: World Bank, *World Development Indicators 1997*; UNESCO, *Statistical Yearbook*, various; UNDP, *Human Development Report 1995*; Government of Taiwan, *Taiwan Statistical Data Book*, 1994; data from Singapore Economic Development Board Website.

countries, the top four places were secured by Singapore, Korea, Japan, and Hong Kong in mathematics; in science, Singapore was top, Japan third, and Korea fourth (the second place was held by the Czech Republic), with Hong Kong coming twenty-fourth ("World Education League," 1997). The bottom two places were held by Colombia and South Africa in both. The only other participating country from our Asian sample was Thailand, which came twentieth in mathematics and twenty-first in science.

In tertiary-level enrollments, Korea and Taiwan are at developed country levels; then come Hong Kong and Thailand (around 20%). There are four countries with tertiary enrollments of 5% to 10%: India, Indonesia, Malaysia, and Singapore, Well behind the others come Pakistan (3%) and China (2%). There are high proportions of tertiary students going overseas in Hong Kong, Singapore, and Malaysia. The larger Tigers have in place attractive incentives for nationals studying or working overseas to return, and in both Korea and Taiwan these nationals have provided an important input into the countries' capability development. Singapore places more emphasis than other countries on nonuniversity technical education.[18] Its system of employee training is reputed to be one of the world's finest, and enterprises are given strong incentives and subsidies to use it (Lall, 1996, chap. 3). To compensate for specialized skill shortages, the Singapore government allows very liberal use of high-level expatriate manpower.

The observed pattern generally corresponds to the distribution of technological capabilities traced above. The correspondence is not exact: the stock of educated manpower is not reflected fully by current enrollment levels. China stands out by virtue of its very low tertiary enrollments combined with a booming export sector – clearly, exporters find sufficient skilled manpower for the relatively low levels of technology that they use.

Enrollment at the tertiary level in technical subjects, more relevant for our purposes, is shown in Table 6.2. This table includes some advanced industrial countries for comparison, and shows not just wide differences between the Asian countries but also that Asian countries, like Korea and Taiwan, are now ahead of many technological leaders in the Organization for Economic Cooperation and Development (OECD) in technical skill creation.

Take enrollments in all technical subjects, which may be a good indicator of the general technical base in a country. The norm in European countries (Table 2.6 shows only the technological leaders, and this may not apply to others) is around 1%, while for the United States it is 1.47%. The norms for Korea and Taiwan are 1.66% and 1.45%, respectively, higher than Europe or Japan; Korea is ahead of the United States, and Taiwan is about the same. There is a large range among the other Asian countries: the lowest figure (below 0.1%) is for Pakistan, with India, China, Indonesia, and Malaysia slightly better (under 0.2%). These are all countries with relatively simple exports, with the exception of Malaysia, which basically engages in a low-technology operation in a high-tech industry. China and India have large absolute numbers, with

---

[18] The figure for Singapore is higher if polytechnic enrollments are included. According to data provided by the Coat Review Committee in 1996, polytechnic enrollment was nearly double that of universities in Singapore. However, these data are expressed as percentages of primary one cohorts rather than as the relevant age group, so we cannot compare them directly with the other countries.

Table 2.6. *Tertiary-Level students in technical fields (numbers and percent)*

Country	Year	Natural science		Math & computer		Engineering		All technical subjects (a)		Science + math & computers + engineering		Ratio of engineers to scientists
		Nos.	% population	Nos.	% population	Nos.	% population	Nos.	% population	% total tertiary	% population	
Hong Kong	1992	5,503	0.095	6,661	0.115	14,788	0.256	35,068	0.607	30.3	0.47	2.69
Singapore	1994	1,281	0.046	1,420	0.051	13,029	0.465	16,767	0.599	20.4	0.56	10.17
Korea	1993	75,778	0.172	145,948	0.331	367,846	0.834	730,346	1.655	31.2	1.34	4.85
Taiwan	1993	16,823	0.080	32,757	0.157	179,094	0.857	303,964	1.454	42.3	1.09	10.65
Indonesia	1992	22,394	0.012	13,117	0.007	205,086	0.109	315,325	0.167	13.4	0.13	9.16
Malaysia	1990	8,775	0.049	4,557	0.025	12,693	0.071	32,222	0.180	21.4	0.15	1.45
Thailand	1992	77,098	0.135	1,292	0.002	105,149	0.185	249,952	0.439	15.9	0.32	1.36
China	1993	95,492	0.008	174,862	0.015	1,156,735	0.098	1,831,966	0.155	31.7	0.12	12.11
India	1990	869,119	0.102	—	—	216,837	0.025	1,236,414	0.146	27.9	0.146	0.25
Pakistan	1991	29,433	0.025	—	—	41,244	0.035	75,168	0.065	34.0	0.065	2.55
Memo item: Some OECD countries												
Japan	1991	59,030	0.048	20,891	0.017	488,699	0.394	730,637	0.590	19.6	0.46	8.28
France	1991	266,299	0.467	N/A	N/A	123,514	0.217	614,159	1.078	21.2	0.68	0.46
Germany	1993	310,435	0.384	N/A	N/A	389,182	0.481	805,801	0.997	37.3	0.87	1.25
Netherlands	1992	16,707	0.110	8,742	0.058	N/A	N/A	137,510	0.905	N/A	0.17	N/A
UK	1992	105,983	0.183	76,430	0.132	219,078	0.378	596,404	1.029	26.3	0.69	2.07
USA	1990	496,415	0.199	525,067	0.210	801,126	0.320	3,676,985	1.471	13.3	0.73	1.63

Notes: (a) All technical subjects include the three categories earlier plus medical, architecture, trade and crafts, and transport and communications.
OECD = Organization for Economic Cooperation and Development.
Sources: UNESCO. *Statistical Yearbook 1995*; Government of Taiwan, *Taiwan Statistical Yearbook, 1994*; data from Ministry of Education, Singapore.

Table 2.7. *Research and development (R&D) expenditures*

Country	Year	As % of GDP Total	As % of GDP By industry	R&D per capita ($)
Hong Kong	1995	0.1	N/A	19.8
Singapore	1992	1.0	0.6	153.6
Korea	1995	2.7	2.0	271.1
Taiwan	1993	1.7	0.8	179.6
Malaysia	1992	0.4	0.17	11.2
Thailand	1991	0.2	0.04	3.1
Indonesia	1993	0.2	0.04	1.5
China	1992	0.5	N/A	2.4
India	1992	1.0	0.22	3.1
Pakistan	1987	0.9	0.0	2.6
Memo item: Some OECD countries				
Japan	1995	3.0	1.9	1225.6
France	1994	2.4	1.5	544.8
Germany	1991	2.3	1.5	674.8
UK	1994	2.2	1.4	383.6
USA	1995	2.4	1.7	655.2

Note: OECD = Organization for Economic Cooperation and Development.
Sources: UNESCO, *Statistical Yearbooks*; STEPI (1997); Taiwan Government (1994).

may not feed into the capabilities of local firms. Hong Kong, in line with its specialization in low-technology activities, lacks a significant R&D base. There are pockets of technological development in large economies like China and India, some of it quite advanced (space and defense technology in China or chemicals and pharmaceuticals in India), but much of the industrial sector does not invest in significant R&D. Of the new Tigers, only Malaysia has some R&D capability, but this is largely confined to the product engineering units of a few large MNCs (the bulk is in twenty-five electronics firms; World Bank, 1996). Pakistani industry conducts practically no formal R&D.

Table 2.8 shows R&D manpower per million population. Korea has the highest number in developing Asia, followed by Taiwan, Singapore, and China (which apparently has 1.3 million scientists and engineers in R&D, higher in absolute numbers than the United States, which has fewer than 1 million). Malaysia follows some distance behind; Indonesia, India, and Thailand come next with roughly equal numbers of R&D scientists and engineers. Pakistan again lags well behind the other countries. The leading Asian economies are still a long way from technological leaders like Japan, but Korea and Taiwan now have more R&D scientists and engineers per head than pre-unification Germany and are not too far behind France.

Total Factor Productivity Growth

A number of exercises have been done recently on total factor productivity (TFP) growth in East Asia.[20] These have given rise to debate on whether growth in the East Asian economies was driven more by high rates of factor accumulation (which they clearly had) or by TFP increases. This growth accounting does not, at first sight, seem to concern the present discussion of technological capabilities. However, in the neoclassical growth accounting approach, the TFP residual measures economywide technical progress (i.e., after the contribution of the primary factors, physical and human capital and labor, have been taken into account). The TFP findings have three implications for our discussion:

- If TFP growth is low in the Tigers, there has been little technical progress and, by implication, little technological effort. This implies that low technological capabilities are no barrier to using new technologies successfully, contrary to the arguments of this paper.
- The relative rates of TFP growth among the Asian economies may be a good indicator of their technological capabilities and give a different ranking of capabilities from the export, educational, and technological data used here.
- If simple accumulation is the real explanation of growth in East Asia, then all governments have to do is to ensure the

[20] For early results see Pack (1988), and for a recent exposition, Barro and Sala-I-Martin (1995). The World Bank (1993) *Miracle* study argued that conventional factors (capital and skill accumulation and labor) explained the bulk (60–90%) of East Asian growth, but that TFP growth was higher than in developed countries and other regions. Young (1994a and b), using different data, reduced the role of TFP growth and strengthened that of physical investment, concluding that high rates of saving were the main engine of Asian growth. Young's data were used by Krugman (1994) to argue that the Asian "miracle" was a myth, its economic challenge exaggerated, and the much-vaunted role of Asian governments fallacious.

Table 2.8. *Scientists, engineers and technicians in research and development (R&D)*

Country	Year	R&D S&E per million population	R&D technicians per million population
Hong Kong	1990	N/A	N/A
Singapore	1987	1284	583
Korea	1992	1976	347
Taiwan	1991	1673	573
Indonesia	1988	181	N/A
Malaysia	1988	326	69
Thailand	1991	174	51
China	1992	1129	428
India	1990	151	114
Pakistan	1990	56	80
Memo Item: Some OECD countries			
Japan	1992	5677	869
France	1991	2267	2972
Germany (a)	1989	1634	867
Netherlands	1991	2656	1777
USA	1988	3780	

Note: (a) Former Federal Republic only.
S&E = Scientists and engineers
Sources: UNESCO, *Statistical Yearbook 1995*; *Taiwan Province of China Statistical Data Book*, 1994.

right macroeconomic conditions for high rates of saving and foreign investment inflows and mount functional interventions to ensure that human capital formation takes place. There is no role for technology policy, nor for selective interventions in trade and industry.

The data provided by Young (1994a) suggest that TFP growth rates over 1960–93 in East Asia were moderate: Hong Kong achieved the highest (2.2%), followed by Taiwan (1.8%), Korea (1.2%), and Singapore (−0.4%). These figures are similar to those achieved by the OECD countries or Latin America. The ranking of countries differs from the one derived here. Does this mean, then, that there was little technological effort in Asia, using technologies depended solely on factor accumulation, the rankings yielded by our more structural indices are wrong, and there is no need to consider policies apart from the market friendly ones espoused by neoclassical economists?

Not necessarily. The TFP approach suffers difficulties that qualify its results significantly.[21] At the less significant level, there are well-known data and methodological problems. The measurement of the basic factors, in particular physical capital, is fraught with problems. Total factor productivity estimates capture a range of influences other than technology, such as capacity utilization, increasing returns to scale, and imperfect competition (Hall, 1990). This is why different estimates come up with widely varying results. In contrast to the Young results, for instance, the World Bank (1993) finds that the East Asian Tigers had relatively high rates of TFP growth. Moreover, the estimates cover entire economies rather than just the manufacturing sector, which is our present concern.

The real problem with the approach arises, however, at a more fundamental level. TFP estimation is based on an identity, and cannot, as such, distinguish the validity of different underlying causal relationships.[22] However, its underlying theory makes certain critical assumptions of the standard neoclassical type, involving perfect markets, no technological learning, equal access to information, and so on. These assumptions constrain the estimations and determine the nature of the results – with different assumptions, the estimations could yield quite different results from the same data. The existing calculations per se cannot determine which set of assumptions is more valid. This can be decided only on the basis of theory and empirical analysis.

Cappelen and Fagerberg (1995) put this as follows:

For the Young-Krugman interpretation to be credible, it is not enough to argue that the predictions of the theory seem to fit the evidence, when this evidence may equally well be consistent with other theoretical perspectives. Rather, what should be done is to show that the assumptions of the theory (on which the interpretation is based) suit the East Asian experience. Thus, one has to ask questions of the type: Did perfect competition prevail (i.e., no large firms with market power, no economies of scale and so on)? Was new technology equally available to all firms,

[21] See Cappelen and Fagerberg (1995), Kwon (1994), Nelson and Pack (1996), Rodrik (1994, 1995) and, in more general terms, Stiglitz (1996).

[22] This point is made forcefully by Nelson and Pack (1996). This is why the same data yield different conclusions and rankings of countries according to TFP growth if assumptions regarding, say, economies of scale, are changed, as Kwon (1994) does with a reworking of the World Bank data.

domestically as well as abroad, independently of factor accumulation (and other efforts)? As long as these (deeper) questions are ignored, studies of the type presented by Young should be regarded as descriptions, reflecting among other things the underlying assumptions, rather than tests . . . exercises of this type are not well suited for making judgments on causality. (p. 185)

As far as technological capability is concerned, the assumptions on technology make TFP exercises particularly ill-suited to assessing technological competence and effort; learning, technological lags, and market failures are simply ruled out by the model. It is taken as a premise that factor accumulation occurs along a given and known production function along which firms move smoothly, without any additional risk, effort, or cost and in a world without externalities or market failures (Nelson and Pack, 1996). There is therefore no interaction between accumulation (moving into more capital and skill intensive technologies) and technological effort: technical change comes only from a shift of the function. In real life, as shown by numerous detailed studies, this distinction between moves along and of the production function is untenable. The process of simple accumulation (if efficiently carried out) requires enormous technological effort, which must vary according to the nature and complexity of the technologies used, the extent of linkages with other activities, the risk and duration of the learning process, and the degree of depth to which local capabilities are developed.

In the standard TFP model, where all capital accumulation is assumed to occur without technological effort, the residual cannot show such effort. In a realistic world, such as the one we have been considering, it is not clear what the residual *does* capture. Clearly, when some countries are moving into very complex and demanding technologies with considerable indigenous absorptive effort, TFP exercises do not serve as reliable guides to technological capabilities, and we have to return to other indicators of technological effort.

This also has implications for government policy. In the TFP model, the government appears only as the facilitator for the main engine of growth: factor accumulation. It has, on neoclassical assumptions, no role in influencing resource allocation between activities. Once the assumptions of accumulation without learning and perfect markets are dropped, however, there immediately appears a strong potential role for the government in overcoming

the failures that affect technological development. These interventions often *have* to be selective.

In sum, the TFP approach does not further our analysis, and
its results do not negate our ranking of capabilities. Nor does the
supposed debunking of the Asian "miracle" add anything to the
understanding of the role of governments, since much of this role
is simply assumed away.

Summing Up

Given the risks inherent in assessing something as amorphous as
"national technological capability," the measures given here are
admittedly rough and impressionistic. Nevertheless, they are quite
useful. Policy makers and analysts do think in terms of technological strengths and weaknesses, leads and lags, and "national
innovation systems" (see Nelson, 1993, and Lundvall, 1992). If
the earlier argument about learning and capabilities has any
validity, making an assessment of future technological prospects
is worthwhile.

Of the ten emerging Asian economies considered here, Korea
stands out as the clear technological leader on almost every criterion. Its industrial sector has considerable depth and integration,
with competitive capabilities over a very wide range of activities
(including practically all heavy producer goods industries) that
have been developed largely without reliance on direct foreign
investment, largely on the basis of indigenous learning, skills, and
R&D effort. Its leading firms are multinationals in their own right
in many frontier activities, challenging established multinationals
on their home ground, and competing in industries where it was
thought that developing country firms could not play an independent role. Korea is followed by Taiwan, which has a narrower
industrial base and a preponderance of small and medium-size
enterprises (SMEs). This gives it more flexibility but less depth in
technology generation; as the industrial sector approaches technological frontiers, this may prove a disadvantage. It may account
for the fact that Taiwanese manufacturing output and manufactured exports have been growing consistently slower than Korea's
over the past decade or more (see the chapter appendix, Table
2A.2). Nevertheless, some of its leading firms are world leaders in
their technologies; its superlative network of technology support

institutions gives the smaller enterprises the backup they need to keep pace with technological change.

Of the smaller Tigers, with narrower spheres of competence, Singapore is distinctly ahead of Hong Kong in technological terms. Despite its smaller size and higher wages, which may be expected to lead to faster deindustrialization, Singapore continues to register among the highest rates of industrial and export growth in the region, while Hong Kong is suffering a rapid contraction of its manufacturing sector (Appendix, Table 2A.2) and falling exports. The industrial structures of the two countries have diverged greatly, with Singapore transforming itself into a center for high-tech electronics and chemical production (with concomitant technological capabilities) and Hong Kong remaining in light consumer goods with low technological content. The Hong Kong economy has continued to grow by moving into services largely directed at the mainland, but its rate of growth is lower than that of Singapore, which has also increased its service sector considerably without running down industry. However, Singapore's edge lies in providing an efficient and high-skill base for MNC activity rather than in its own technological capabilities. These capabilities are growing, partly as MNCs are induced to set up research facilities there in certain selected areas, but they are not comparable to those in the larger Tigers.

In terms of emerging technologies, Korea and Taiwan seem the best placed in the foreseeable future. Korea has an edge over Taiwan in the most R&D-intensive activities, where it seems set to emerge as a technological leader. Taiwan has smaller niches of innovativeness, in which it is likely to remain an advanced production center. Singapore will also participate fully and at the high value-added end, but not in the creation of new technologies. It is making efforts to induce MNCs to relocate R&D activities to Singapore, but this is likely to succeed in only a few cases. Hong Kong, if it were not being absorbed by the mainland, would be set for reversion to an entrepot for China, with little technological base beyond design and marketing of low-technology consumer goods.

None of the new Tigers has a significant technological base.[23]

---

[23] On Malaysia see Lall et al. (1994), Lall (1995b) and World Bank (1996), and on Indonesia see Lall and Rao (1995).

Their high dependence on FDI for technology upgrading and diversification has served them extremely well in the past, but they are conscious of the constraints of this strategy. They are making efforts to upgrade from essentially low-level assembly to more value-added manufacturing with deeper local roots, and to develop their "know-why" bases by trying to raise local content, encouraging technological activity, building technology institutions, and/or entering higher-technology activities with state-owned enterprises (the last in Malaysia and Indonesia). The results so far are mixed. There are a few successes, but these are insufficient to influence the technological base as a whole and they are not developing a tradition of autonomous R&D in the private sector. They suffer from shortages of technical manpower that will prevent them from following an aggressive FDI-targeting strategy like Singapore (the new rules of international investment would in any case limit such efforts).

On present trends, the new Tigers seem set to remain efficient implementers of new technology, as producers at low to medium levels of technological sophistication. Domestic firms will dominate in the simpler technologies, and MNCs in high-tech ones. This may allow them to sustain high rates of growth as in the past; on the other hand, with a strong competitive threat from lower-cost economies or those with larger technological bases, they may lose momentum as these competitors offer similar incentives to foreign investors and improve their infrastructures. As the initial advantages of the Tigers erode, their continued growth will depend on the success of their efforts to move up the technological ladder.

Of the larger economies, China and India have deep and diverse industrial sectors that suffer serious technological and organizational lags. They have the domestic market size, experience, and proven research skills to move to high levels of production and innovation in new technologies, but to achieve this on a wide basis would require further massive reforms to the incentive systems and a reduction in the past role of the government in the economy. In the longer term, it would also call for large investments in high-level technical manpower and physical infrastructure – of special importance to these economies. Pakistan combines the weaknesses of several countries in the group, with a weak industrial structure, low attraction to FDI, a small human capital base, and minuscule levels of local technological activity. Unless all these are improved, it seems poorly placed to participate in the new technological paradigm, even as an implementer of know-how.

The foregoing arguments suggest that maximizing the national benefit from new technologies requires considerable domestic capabilities. These capabilities have to go beyond those of an efficient low-end user of advanced technologies (know-how) to those needed for more complex production with those technologies, and finally to having some autonomous innovative capability (know-why). A few countries in emerging Asia have already established the necessary base and will share fully in the rewards of the new technologies as users and innovators. Others have developed operational capabilities and will benefit as efficient producers as long as they can retain a competitive edge; in the longer term they will have to deepen their technological capabilities. Others have the potential to develop deep capabilities but will have to undergo massive reforms. Still others have neither an efficient production base for new technologies nor the immediate prospect of deepening their technology base.

There are important lessons to be drawn from the technological successes of the three leading Tigers. Each adopted strong policies to boost its technological development, but they were guided by very different strategies: Korea, with a strongly national based and targeted drive into heavy, high-tech industry; Taiwan, with an SME-dominated structure guided by the government into skill and technology intensive activities, with inputs from selectively used FDI and a superlative extension and technology support system; and Singapore, with its targeted use of FDI to upgrade industry into an advanced and specialized center for production, fully integrated into the global system of leading MNCs. Each had very active interventions, with a mixture of functional and selective elements. All demonstrate that selectivity can shape the industrial and technological structure in beneficial ways, and governments do not fail in improving upon imperfect markets.

Let us briefly consider the policy lessons under each main determinant of technology development, focusing on technology policies specifically.

Incentives

Each of the three technological leaders in emerging Asia acted upon the incentive regime in the context of a strongly export-oriented regime. This openness and close contact with the world market was crucial to the success of their strategies. Korea had the strongest ambitions to develop a diverse, deep, and advanced industrial structure and had to mount the most comprehensive set of interventions to achieve this in a relatively compressed period.[24] These interventions included quantitative and tariff restrictions on imports, strong export subsidies and targeting, subsidized and guided credit, and the promotion of giant conglomerates. These interventions shaped the nature of industrial development at a very detailed – often product and technology – level. There was also the technological effort needed to compete in world markets, with export orientation providing the discipline on firms and bureaucrats. Entire sets of heavy industries were promoted together to exploit linkages and externalities, with changes being made as events unfolded and some activities proved unviable.

Taiwan did not have the political economy to mount such detailed interventions, but it did use trade policies to guide the technological upgrading of the economy very successfully. Public enterprises were used to enter areas where the private sector was reluctant. However, it could not achieve the industrial depth attained by Korea. Singapore used FDI targeting and incentives within a free trade context to upgrade industry from its simple initial stages to capital- , skill- , and then technology-intensive activities, targeting particular industries and then mounting concerted campaigns to realize their entry and growth. As with Taiwan, public enterprises were used to spearhead particularly difficult activities.

The market failures addressed by these policies were noted earlier; unpredictable, risky, and variable costs of learning, externalities, capital market deficiencies, and coordination problems, which lead in free markets to underinvestment in demanding and linkage-intensive technologies and to shallow learning. In addition there was a strong element of creating new markets, leading the

---

[24] As Pack (1997) notes, the need for intervention was less at the start of the industrialization process, when relatively simple, labor-intensive techniques were being learned and the country's comparative advantage in these products drove its export engine.

industrial sector in new directions, that are difficult to describe as remedying market failure in the strict sense of restoring a static competitive equilibrium: the interventions were determined by strategic objectives rather than achieving efficient market clearing with existing factor endowments.

The nature and extent of interventions depended on these objectives, concerning the nature of the new technologies to be mastered and the depth of local capability desired within those. Korea, with the strongest ambitions, had to mount the most pervasive and detailed interventions. Singapore, on the other hand, content to stay in the MNC framework at the production end of selected advanced technologies, could combine free trade with incentives to foreign investors and the provision of skills. Its technology strategy entailed lower levels of local learning than in Korea, even within similar technologies, so the protection was less. The contrast between Singapore and Hong Kong, both practicing free trade, should also be noted: the latter had no targeting or deliberate upgrading of FDI; therefore it experienced little deepening of the industrial sector and subsequent "hollowing out" at wages lower than in Singapore.

The lessons for countries that wish to deepen the industrial structure depend on their present situation and strategies. For those that have strong indigenous industrial groups, a degree of promotion of entry into complex technologies would seem to be desirable, if this is done in a strongly export-oriented setting, factor markets are adequate, and their bureaucrats have the information, skills, honesty, and independence to mount selective policies. In countries that have highly protected industrial sectors already engaged in heavy industry, but brought up under the irrational and pervasive umbrella of strong import-substitution, there is a need for considerable liberalization before any selectivity is considered. For those that wish to rely on FDI, a strategy of guidance for entry and upgrading is needed, again if combined with the skills and infrastructure needed to attract MNCs, and the bureaucratic information, skills, and efficiency required.

Factor Markets and Institutions

Each of the successful Tigers also intervened, often selectively, in factor markets to ensure that these cohered to the targeting pursued elsewhere. In *human capital* markets, they intervened pervasively to boost enrollments and focus them on technical fields. The specific subjects were often in line with technologies chosen for encouragement. Industrial training was encouraged by subsidies to or levies on firms, with considerable investment in government training institutions. Efforts were made to gear training to emerging technological needs, often by getting industry involved in the management of training and education institutions. The data given earlier are sufficient testimony to the efficacy of these interventions and to their relative weakness in the non-Tiger economies.

In *technology development*, interventions differed by national objectives on building up domestic capabilities. The Tigers with the strongest R&D ambitions undertook a range of targeted interventions to promote technological activity. These ranged from infant industry promotion and the support of large firms to credit subsidization, technology targeting, FDI restrictions, the development of research institutions and extension services, and the financing of links between industry and universities. The most powerful impetus came, however, from the strong export orientation of the regime, which forced firms to invest in formal R&D to absorb new technologies to best practice levels, enter new areas, and lower the costs of importing technology. A great deal of technological effort in the early years was based on copying foreign technologies, and the countries adopted a fairly relaxed attitude toward intellectual property protection. As the industrial sectors matured and drew nearer to technological frontiers, local R&D needed greater protection; in addition, pressures for stronger intellectual property regimes grew internationally. Today, the Tigers have become, or are becoming, quite strict on patent, copyright, and brand name laws, though lapses still occur.

In Korea, the desire to have a local base capable of autonomously absorbing and then creating technologies led to a heavy emphasis on externalized modes of technology import. The surge in Korean technological activity was the result of policies to enter heavy industry and promote the *chaebol* (which account for the bulk of R&D expenditures; see Kim, 1997) while forcing them, by several other incentives and subsidies, to enter export markets, import technology at arm's length, and support

R&D.[25] The government targeted strategic technologies for promotion, often by getting private industry to collaborate with public research institutes in projects paid for by the government. The financing of technology expenditures was also fostered by a large number of subsidized credit and venture capital schemes (Korea has the largest indigenous venture capital industry of developing countries in Asia).

In Taiwan much effort went into setting up research institutions that could import technologies and diffuse them to its SMEs; in some cases, the government itself set up joint ventures with foreign companies to import very advanced technology (as with Philips for semiconductor manufacture). FDI was induced by local content rules and other incentives to diffuse technology to local suppliers and competitors. There was very active technology targeting.[26] Private R&D was encouraged by a variety of incentives: provision of funds for venture capital; financing for enterprises that developed strategic industrial products (of which 151 were

[25] The Designated R&D Program has, since 1982, supported private firms undertaking research in core strategic technology projects in industry approved by the Ministry of Science and Technology. It funded up to 50 percent of R&D costs of large firms and up to 80 percent for SMEs. Between 1982 and 1993, this program funded 2,412 projects, which employed around 25,000 researchers at a total cost of around $2 billion, of which the government contributed 58 percent, resulting in 1,384 patent applications, 675 commercialized products and $33 million of direct exports of know-how. Its indirect contribution in terms of training researchers and enhancing enterprise research capabilities was much larger. The value of grants under the program in 1994 was $186 million, of which 42 percent was directed at high technology products like new specialty chemicals. The Industrial Technology Development Program was started in 1987 to subsidize up to two-thirds of the R&D costs of joint projects of national interest (National Research Projects) between private firms and research institutes. Between 1987 and 1993 this program sponsored 1,426 projects at the cost of $1.1 billion, of which the subsidy element from the government was 41 percent. In 1994, the program gave grants of $180 million (with 31 percent going to high-technology products), a significant increase from $69 million in 1990. The Highly Advanced National (HAN) Project was launched in 1992 to support the development of high-technology products in which Korea could become competitive with advanced industrial countries in a decade or two (Product Technology Development Project), and the development of essential "core" technologies in which Korea wanted to have an independent innovative base (Fundamental Technology Development Project). So far, eleven HAN projects have been selected, and during 1992–94 the government provided $350 million of subsidies for them. In this brief period, the program resulted in 1,634 patent applications and 298 registrations (Lall, 1996).

[26] A Science and Technology (S&T) Program was started in 1979, targeting energy, production automation, information science, and materials science technologies for development. In 1982, biotechnology, electro-optics, hepatitis control, and food technology were added to this list. In 1986, the current S&T Development Plan (1986–95) was launched, continuing the targeting of strategic areas of technology, setting a target for 1995 of 2 percent of GDP for total R&D.

selected in 1982 and 214 in 1987); encouragement of product development by private firms by providing matching interest-free loans and up to 25 percent of grants for approved projects;[27] full tax deductibility for R&D expenses, with accelerated depreciation for research equipment; special incentives for enterprises based in the Hsinchu Science Park (with government financial institutions able to invest up to 49 percent of the capital); and requiring larger firms (turnovers exceeding new Taiwan [NT] $300 million) to invest 0.5 percent to 1.5 percent of sales, depending on the activity, in R&D. The government also launched large-scale research consortia, funded jointly with industry, to develop critical industrial products such as 16M DRAM and 4M SRAM chips.

Singapore, despite its dependence for basic technology on MNCs, has several programs to strengthen local technology (Lall, 1996). In 1962 it launched a fund to help SMEs modernize their equipment. In the mid-1970s several other schemes for financial assistance were added, of which the most significant was the Small Industries Finance Scheme to encourage technological upgrading. The 1985 venture capital fund was set up to help SMEs acquire capital through low-interest loans and equity. In 1987, a U.S. $519 million scheme was launched to cover eight programs to help SMEs, including product development assistance, technical assistance to import foreign consultancy, venture capital to help technology startups, robot leasing, training, and technology tie-ups with foreign companies.[28] Over 1976–88, total financial assistance by the Singapore government to SMEs amounted to U.S. $1.5

---

[27] By the end of 1992, the government had granted new Taiwan (NT) $2 billion in matching interest-free loans and NT $1 billion in research grants, mostly to the information and communications industries. The provision of grants was limited to products involving high technology, while loans were available, on approval, to most industries.

[28] In addition, the Singapore Institute of Standards and Industrial Research (SISIR) disseminated technology to SMEs, and helped their exports by providing information on foreign technical requirements and how to meet them. The National Productivity Board provided management advice and consultancy to SMEs. The Technology Development Center helped local firms to identify their technology requirements and purchase technologies; it also designed technology upgrading strategies. Since its foundation in 1989, the TDC provided over 130 firms with various forms of technical assistance. It also administered the Small Industry Technical Assistance and Product Development Assistance Schemes (SITAS) to help firms develop their design and development capabilities. It gave grants of over $1 million for 29 SITAS in the past five years, mainly to local enterprises. Its earnings have risen to a level where its cost-recoverable activities are self-financing.

billion. In 1991 the Singapore government launched a technology plan with an R&D target of 2 percent of GDP by 1995; in the early 1990s, the figure was around 1 percent. It selected a number of sectors for technology development,[29] and established a U.S. $2 billion fund for R&D. It launched public R&D facilities, as in biotechnology, to catalyze research in selected activities, getting world-class researchers to come to Singapore and then persuading private firms to participate in the research.

Technology support is also an active area of policy in the new Tigers, but it has a long way to go before it can match the depth and reach of the older Tigers.[30] India is in the midst of a thoroughgoing reform of its public R&D system, trying to make it more relevant to the needs of industry; the initial results are quite encouraging. Similar efforts are underway in China and Pakistan, but this author is unable to comment on them.

In general, government technology institutions have not been very effective in stimulating industrial technology development in most countries, but the experience of the Tigers and some advanced industrial countries suggests that they can be.[31] The scarcity of resources and skills for such institutions means that they should be carefully targeted at activities that will be most relevant and useful for preparing industry to cope with new technologies. The institutions should have significant private sector inputs into their management and operations, and their incentive structures should be such that staff spend much of their effort in applied technological work rather than in pure science.

FDI will have to play a more prominent role than in the past as an agent of technology transfer and technological activity. The kinds of selectivity used by Korea and Taiwan may not be feasible in the near future, and it is likely that most countries will offer similar sets of incentives and "level playing fields" to all investors. This does not mean that FDI can be left passively to market forces. On the contrary, there may be market failures in attracting MNCs,

---

[29] These activities are information technology, microelectronics, electronic systems, advanced manufacturing technology, materials technology, energy and water resources, environment, biotechnology, food and agro-technology, and medical sciences.

[30] On Malaysia, see World Bank (1996), and on Indonesia, Lall and Rao (1995).

[31] However, Pack (1997) argues persuasively that even the Tigers' public technology institutions did not contribute very greatly to in-firm technological development.

allocating their investments and upgrading their technologies over time. A pro-active strategy of targeting FDI and inducing it into more complex activities has proved to be extremely effective, and some such strategies may remain feasible in the future. Of course, no amount of targeting can work if local factor markets are not appropriate for high value-added activities by MNCs; this requires large investments in education and training, suppliers, infrastructure, and support institutions.

As far as *capital markets* are concerned, selective interventions were plentiful in the larger Tigers. Theory suggests that these were necessary, and the evidence shows that they were effective (Stiglitz and Uy, 1996). There are certainly dangers inherent in allocating capital and subsidizing it to particular users, and the experience of capital market interventions elsewhere has not been happy. However, the Tigers' experience suggests that financial targeting should not be ruled out altogether, if it is part of a carefully formulated industrial strategy and is flexibly and competently administered. Otherwise it can lead to waste, rent seeking, and technical inefficiency.

There is no single optimum path to technological development. A number of different strategies are possible, depending on each country's objectives and political economies. There are necessarily some common elements, such as the creation of human capital, efficient technology support systems, access to new technologies, and close contacts with world markets. However, many other critical elements of strategy can differ, and these determine the resulting industrial structures and technological bases. We must note, however, that many of the interventionist strategies noted in this chapter are not feasible in the emerging international rules of the game of trade, investment, and political relations. The growing convergence of policies enforced by these rules has many beneficial effects but also significant potential costs. And its underlying philosophy is driven more by faith than rationality and evidence.

REFERENCES

Amsden, A. 1989. *Asia's Next Giant: South Korea and Late Industrialization.* New York: Oxford University Press.
Amsden, A. 1994. "Why Isn't the Whole World Experimenting with the

East Asian Model to Develop? Review of *The East Asian Miracle.*" *World Development*, 22(4), 627–634.

Barro, R. J., and Sala-I-Martin. 1995. *Economic Growth.* New York: McGraw-Hill.

Bell, M., and K. Pavitt. 1993. "Technological Accumulation and Industrial Growth: Contrasts between Developed and Developing Countries." *Industrial and Corporate Change*, 2(2), 157–210.

Cantwell, J. 1989. *Technological Innovation and the Multinational Corporation.* Oxford: Blackwell.

Cappelen, A., and J. Fagerberg. 1995. "East Asian Growth: A Critical Assessment." *Forum for Development Studies*, 2, 175–195.

Capelli, P., and N. Rogovsky. 1994. "New Work Systems and Skill Requirements." *International Labor Review*, 133(2), 205–220.

Choi, Y. 1997. "Techno-Management Capability: The Samsung Semiconductor Case." Draft paper, Science and Technology Policy Institute, Seoul.

Dahlman, C. J., B. Ross-Larson, and L. E. Westphal. 1987. "Managing Technological Development: Lessons from Newly Industrializing Countries." *World Development* 15(6), 759–775.

Dosi, G. 1988. "Sources, Procedures, and Microeconomic Effects of Innovation." *Journal of Economic Literature*, 36(4), 1120–1171.

Dosi, G., C. Freeman, R. R. Nelson, G. Silverberg, and L. Soete (eds.). 1988. *Technical Change and Economic Theory.* London: Pinter.

Enos, J. 1992. *The Creation of Technological Capabilities in Developing Countries.* London: Pinter.

Evenson, R. E., and L. E. Westphal. 1995. "Technological Change and Technology Strategy." In J. Behrman and T. N. Srinivasan (eds.), *Handbook of Development Economics*, Vol. IIIb. Amsterdam: North Holland, 2209–2299.

Freeman, C. 1995. "The 'National System of Innovation' in Historical Perspective." *Cambridge Journal of Economics*, 19(1), 5–24.

Freeman, C., and C. Perez. 1988. "Structural Crises of Adjustment, Business Cycles and Investment Behavior." In G. Dosi et al. (eds.), *Technical Change and Economic Theory.* London: Pinter, 38–66.

Greenwald, B., and J. E. Stiglitz. 1986. "Externalities in Economies with Imperfect Information and Incomplete Markets." *Quarterly Journal of Economics*, 101, 229–264.

Hall, R. E. 1990. "Invariance Properties of Solow's Productivity Residual." In P. A. Diamond (ed.), *Growth, Productivity, Unemployment.* Cambridge, MA: MIT Press, 71–112.

Hobday, M. G. 1995. *Innovation in East Asia: The Challenge to Japan.* Cheltenham: Elgar.

Katz, J. M. (ed.). 1987. *Technology Generation in Latin American Manufacturing Industries.* London: Macmillan.

Kim, L. 1997. *From Imitation to Innovation: Dynamics of Korea's Tech-*

nological Learning. Cambridge, MA: Harvard Business School Press.

Krugman, P. R. 1994. "The Myth of Asia's Miracle." *Foreign Affairs*, 73, November–December, 62–78.

Krugman, P. R. 1996. "Making Sense of the Competitiveness Debate." *Oxford Review of Economic Policy*, 12(3), 17–25.

Kwon, J. 1994. "The East Asian Challenge to Neoclassical Orthodoxy." *World Development*, 22(4), 635–644.

Lall, S. 1987. *Learning to Industrialize: The Acquisition of Technological Capabilities in India.* London: Macmillan.

Lall, S. 1992. "Technological Capabilities and Industrialization." *World Development*, 20(2), 165–186.

Lall, S. 1994. " 'The East Asian Miracle' Study: Does the Bell Toll for Industrial Strategy?" *World Development*, 22(4), 645–654.

Lall, S. 1995a. "Industrial Strategy and Policies on Foreign Direct Investment in East Asia." *Transnational Corporations*, 4(3), 1–26.

Lall, S. 1995b. "Malaysia: Industrial Success and the Role of Government." *Journal of International Development*, 7(5), 759–774.

Lall, S. 1996. *Learning from the Asian Tigers: Studies in Technology and Industrial Policy.* London: Macmillan.

Lall, S. et al. 1994. *Malaysia's Export Performance and Its Sustainability.* Study prepared for the Asian Development Bank, Manila.

Lall, S., and K. Rao. 1995. *Indonesia: Sustaining Manufactured Export Growth.* Study prepared for the Asian Development Bank, Manila.

Lipsey, R. G. 1994. "Markets, Technological Change and Economic Growth." *Pakistan Development Review*, 33(4), 327–352.

Lundvall, B.-A. 1992. *National Systems of Innovation: Towards a Theory of Innovation and Interactive Learning.* London: Pinter.

Metcalfe, J. S. 1995. "Technology Systems and Technology Policy in an Evolutionary Framework." *Cambridge Journal of Economics*, 19(1), 25–46.

Murphy, K. M., A. Schliefer, and R. Vishny. 1989. "Income Distribution, Market Size and Industrialization." *Quarterly Journal of Economics*, 104, 537–564.

Nelson, R. R. 1990. "On Technological Capabilities and Their Acquisition." In R. E. Evenson and G. Ranis (eds.), *Science and Technology: Lessons for Development Policy.* Boulder, CO: Westview Press, 71–80.

Nelson, R. R. (ed.). 1993. *National Innovation Systems: A Comparative Analysis.* Oxford: Oxford University Press.

Nelson, R. R., and H. Pack. 1996. "Firm Competencies, Technological Catch-up, and the Asian Miracle." Columbia University and University of Pennsylvania, draft paper for sixth conference of the International Joseph A. Schumpeter Society.

Nelson, R. R., and S. J. Winter. 1982. *An Evolutionary Theory of Economic Change*. Cambridge, MA: Belknap Press.

OECD. 1987. *Structural Adjustment and Economic Performance*. Paris: Organization for Economic Cooperation and Development.

OTA. 1990. *Making Things Better: Competing in Manufacturing*. Washington, DC: Office of Technology Assessment, U.S. Senate.

Pack, H. 1988. "Industrialization and Trade." In H. B. Chenery and T. N. Srinivasan (eds.), *Handbook of Development Economics*, Vol. I. Amsterdam: North-Holland, 333–379.

Pack, H. 1992. "Learning and Productivity Change in Developing Countries." In G. K. Helleiner (ed.), *Trade Policy, Industrialization and Development*. Oxford: Clarendon Press, 21–45.

Pack, H. 1997. "Research and Development in the Industrial Development Process." In this volume.

Pack, H., and L. E. Westphal. 1986. "Industrial Strategy and Technological Change: Theory versus Reality." *Journal of Development Economics*, 22(1), 87–128.

Porter, M. 1990. *The Competitive Advantage of Nations*. New York: Basic Books.

Ramstetter, E. 1994. "Employment-Related Characteristics of Foreign Multinationals in Selected Asian Economies." Background paper for UNCTAD, *World Investment Report 1994*, Geneva.

Richardson, G. B. 1996. "Competition, Innovation and Increasing Returns." Aalborg: Danish Research Unit for Industrial Dynamics, DRUID Working Papers, No. 96–10.

Rodrik, D. 1994. "King Kong Meets Godzilla: The World Bank and *The East Asian Miracle*." In A. Fishlow et al., *Miracle or Design: Lessons from the East Asian Experience*. Washington, DC: Overseas Development Council, 13–54.

Rodrik, D. 1995. "Asian Growth: Miracle or Myth." *Foreign Affairs*, 74(2), 175–176.

Rodrik, D. 1996. "Coordination Failures and Government Policy: A Model with Applications to East Asia and Eastern Europe." *Journal of International Economics*, 40(1/2), 1–22.

Shapiro, H., and L. Taylor. 1990. "The State and Industrial Strategy." *World Development*, 18(6), 861–878.

Stiglitz, J. E. 1987. "Learning to Learn, Localized Learning and Technological Progress." In P. Dasgupta and P. Stoneman (eds.), *Economic Policy and Technological Development*. Cambridge: Cambridge University Press, 125–55.

Stiglitz, J. E. 1989. "Markets, Market Failures and Development." *American Economic Review Papers and Proceedings*, 79(2), 197–202.

Stiglitz, J. E. 1994. *Whither Socialism?* Cambridge, MA: MIT Press.

Stiglitz, J. E. 1996. "Some Lessons from the East Asian Miracle." *The World Bank Research Observer*, 11(2), 151–177.

Stiglitz, J. E. 1997. "Market Failures, Public Goods, and Externalities." In E. Malinvaud (ed.), *Development Strategy and the Market Economy*. Oxford: Oxford University Press.

Stiglitz, J. E., and M. Uy. 1996. "Financial Markets, Public Policy and the East Asian Miracle." *The World Bank Research Observer*, 11(2), 249–276.

Teece, D. 1997. "Firm Capabilities and Economic Development: Implications for the Newly Industrializing Economies." In this volume.

Teitel, S. 1993. *Industrial and Technological Development*. Washington, DC: Inter-American Bank–Johns Hopkins University Press.

Teubal, M. 1996. "R&D and Technology Policy in NICs as Learning Processes." *World Development*, 24(3), 449–460.

UK Cabinet Office. 1996. *Competitiveness: Creating the Enterprise Centre of Europe*. London: Her Majesty's Stationery Office.

UNIDO. 1995. *Industry Global Report 1995*. Vienna: United Nations Industrial Development Organization.

Wade, R. 1990. *Governing the Market: Economic Theory and the Role of Government in East Asian Industrialization*. Princeton, NJ: Princeton University Press.

Wade, R. 1994. "Selective Industrial Policies in East Asia: Is *The East Asian Miracle* Right?" In A. Fishlow, C. Gwin, S. Haggard, D. Rodrik, and R. Wade, *Miracle or Design? Lessons from the East Asian Experience*. Washington, DC: Overseas Development Council, 55–80.

Westphal, L. E. 1990. "Industrial Policy in an Export-Propelled Economy: Lessons from South Korea's Experience." *Journal of Economic Perspectives*, 4(3), 41–59.

World Bank. 1993. *The East Asian Miracle: Economic Growth and Public Policy*. New York: Oxford University Press.

World Bank. 1996. *Made in Malaysia: Technology Development for Vision 2020*. Study prepared for the Ministry of Science, Technology and the Environment, Government of Malaysia.

"World Education League: Who's Top?" (1997, March 29). *The Economist* (London), 25–27.

Young, A. 1994a. "The Tyranny of Numbers: Confronting the Statistical Realities of the East Asian Growth Experience." New York: National Bureau of Economic Research, Working Paper No. 4680.

Young, A. 1994b. "Lessons from the East Asian NICs: A Contrarian View." *European Economics Review Papers and Proceedings*, 38.

APPENDIX

Table 2A.1. *Industries classified by technology*

Resource-intensive	Labor-intensive	Scale-intensive	Differentiated	Science-based
Food, beverages, tobacco	Textile, wearing apparel, and footwear	Paper, paper products, printing, publishing (excluding pulp, paper and paperboard)	Engines and turbines Agricultural machinery and equipment	Other chemical products and pharmaceuticals
Leather, excluding footwear and wearing apparel Wood and cork products (excluding furniture)	Furniture and fixtures, (excluding primarily metal) Metal scrap, fabricated metal products (excluding machinery and equipment	Industrial chemicals Rubber products	Metal and woodworking machinery Special industrial machinery	Office, computing, and accounting machinery
Pulp, paper and paperboard	Other manufacturing industries	Iron and steel	Machinery and equipment (excluding electric not elsewhere classified)	Aircraft
Petroleum refineries. Misc. products of petroleum and coal Other non-metallic mineral products		Pottery, china, earthenware, glass and glass products Plastic products (not classified elsewhere)	Electrical machinery, apparatus, appliances, and supplies Watches and clocks	Professional, scientific, measuring, and controlling equipment
Non-ferrous metal basic industries		Transport equipment, excluding aircraft	Photographic and optical goods	Biotechnology

Source: OECD, *Structural Adjustment and Economic Performance*, Paris, 1987.

67

SANJAYA LALL

Table 2A.2. *Rates of manufacturing growth in Tigers (% per annum)*

	1980–85	1985–90	1990–93
Hong Kong	3.0	2.9	−1.1
Singapore	1.3	10.3	4.4
Korea	9.3	10.3	4.6
Taiwan	6.5	5.8	3.4

Sources: Calculated from UNIDO, *Industry Global Report 1995*.

CHAPTER 3

Research and Development in the Industrial Development Process

Howard Pack

INITIAL VIEWS

In arriving at a synthesis of current knowledge about the role of research and development (R&D) in the development process, several lessons can be derived from considering the view that was dominant in the decades immediately after World War II. There was a widespread belief that a technology shelf or backlog existed that could be relatively easily exploited to benefit the less-developed countries (LDCs) (Gerschenkron, 1962). Overlooked was the reality that some of this technology, particularly technology that was skill- or capital-intensive, was inappropriate for the majority of developing countries which had many workers and limited amounts of capital. Some of the technology transferred was inappropriate in two dimensions: it was too complex to be operated efficiently, thus leading to low output growth; and it economized on unskilled labor, the plentiful factor in most countries.

Simultaneously, a much different view evolved that the LDCs needed to develop their own science and technology base. Partly, this represented an attempt to assuage the wounds of colonialism and perceptions of technological inferiority. Partly, local technological development was perceived as a parallel effort to import-substituting industrialization (ISI), which became the regnant policy regime in the 1950s and continued through the 1980s. Proponents of local science and R&D were suspicious

Support from the University of Pennsylvania Research Foundation is gratefully acknowledged. Helpful comments were received from participants at the 10th Anniversary International Conference of the Science and Technology Policy Institute, Seoul, Korea, May 26–29, 1997.

about the benefits of international technology transfer.[1] Elaborate
codes were developed to regulate direct foreign investment and
technology licensing either to limit the influence of foreign firms
or reduce "excess" payments for licenses (Mytelka, 1978). Foreign
technology, like foreign products, was viewed with suspicion. Technology transfer did not represent an opportunity but another
mode of potential exploitation.

These suspicions led to efforts to increase technological education as well as the establishment of research institutions. In some
countries such as Argentina the level of university science education was quite good, but this had little impact on the industrialization process, the science institutions being largely divorced
from the needs of industry. Given the budget constraint of governments, high-level science education often came at the expense
of elementary education, which was more relevant to initial industrialization. Latin American and African nations often spent
roughly the same percentage of gross domestic product (GDP) on
education as many of the Asian newly industrializing economies
(NIEs) but a far higher percentage on university education (World
Bank, 1993). In many nations there was a lack of incentive for
industrial firms to improve their productivity, hence a limited
induced demand for the R&D institutions to respond to the needs
of industry.

Through the 1970s, discussions of science and technology policy
and the role of human resources in industrialization often
proceeded without much reference to the actual or prospective
experience of developing countries. Whereas the analysis of agricultural technology, especially the Green Revolution, generated
an enormous empirical literature replete with statistical analysis
of diffusion patterns and rates of return on local adaptive
research, there was no systematic collection of firm level data
on research, human capital, and industrialization (Evenson and
Westphal, 1995). However, the explosive growth of a small group
of Asian countries – Hong Kong, Korea, Singapore, and Taiwan
(for expository convenience lumped together as the NIEs) – has
generated a corpus of detailed empirical case studies of tech-

---

[1] Such views characterized much of the dependency literature. See, for example, Dos
Santos, 1970, and Kumar, 1985.

nology strategies that have been employed (Dahlman and Sananikone, 1990; Hobday, 1995; Kim, 1997).

For the last thirty years a small group of Asian nations has been conspicuously successful. Yet many of the policies they pursued and many characteristics of their economies were not much different from those followed in other less-successful countries. They often selectively protected individual sectors as did many poorly performing import-substituting countries (World Bank, 1993). Their primary education levels were high but initially lower than those prevailing in countries such as Argentina. University education at the beginning of their rapid ascent was not widespread. Their investment levels were not particularly unusual in the period that saw the beginning of rapid growth. Yet despite these unpromising elements, these nations succeeded in generating rapid and generally efficient industrial growth. Once rapid growth was initiated, education levels, investment, and technical investments grew, but these can be viewed as largely an endogenous response to growing income per capita. And clearly, once investments increased as a share of GDP, further improvements occurred in a mutually reinforcing cycle.

Nevertheless, it was not factor accumulation alone that guaranteed successful growth. Otherwise many East European countries would have succeeded rather than imploded. Moreover, even relatively poor nations such as India have had fairly high rates of investment in physical capital and selected areas of human capital and have not succeeded. The NIEs were somehow able to transmute whatever investments they made into sustained growth in productivity, which gave them a bonus from factor accumulation that was not reaped by other LDCs. We thus concentrate here on the ability of the NIEs to move toward international best practice that accounts for their productive utilization of labor and investment. This success was the outcome of several interrelated features including (1) their openness to foreign knowledge and their ability and willingness to tap international technology markets; (2) the pressures brought to bear on firms to increase their productivity to continue to increase exports rather than to use the knowledge obtained to extract rents from the domestic economy, thus creating a demand for foreign technology; and (3) the high productivity of foreign technology as its dissemination and successful use were enhanced by an educated domestic labor force (Nelson and Pack, 1999).

In each of these dimensions, the NIEs we study differed in major respects from other nations with some similarities in initial conditions or policies. I first review briefly some of the relevant history, then provide more detail.

Export Growth and Openness to Knowledge

A major distinguishing feature of the NIEs has been their rapid growth in industrial exports (Pack, 1997). While they followed standard ISI policies for varying lengths of time, even continuing selective protection after switching to more open policies, a variety of means were adopted simultaneously to ensure rapid growth in exports. Export growth became the standard by which all policies were judged, including those that provided initial protection for infant industries. The emphasis on exports was a manifestation of the view that the world economy presented an opportunity rather than a threat.

The perceived benefits from exporting were paralleled by the assumption that foreign knowledge presented an enormous potential asset whose selective utilization could greatly improve domestic productivity. This path was first explored in the postwar period by Japan, which took advantage of knowledge embodied in Western, usually U.S., equipment and also extensively utilized technology licensing to enter new areas of production (Ozawa, 1974; Nagaoka, 1989). The openness to foreign knowledge was a major distinguishing characteristic in Japan, and later in the other NIEs, compared to ISI economies with superficial similarities.[2] The transferred technology was then used with increasing effectiveness by the recipient firms (Kim, 1997; Hobday, 1995).

---

[2] Japan's interest in foreign technology and its ability to adapt it to local conditions and improve it goes back to the late nineteenth century. Indian firms, even under British rule, were less successful at these activities in the same period in the cotton textile industry. The basis of postwar policies were set more than a half century earlier. On the Japanese and Indian experiences in textiles, see Otsuka, Ranis, and Saxonhouse, 1988.

In countries as diverse as Argentina and India, there was a deep suspicion of the benefits of foreign knowledge. In Argentina and other Latin American countries, dependency theory had permeated the views of many intellectuals and policy makers (Packenham, 1992). All contact with technology from the "core" was assumed to be impoverishing, whether in the form of equipment or disembodied knowledge provided by licensing agreements. Thus, utilization of foreign technology, whether imported foreign equipment or knowledge brought by multinationals or licensing agreements, was interpreted as inimical to sustained national development. Self-sufficiency in technology generation as well as in the production of goods was believed to be a key to successful industrial development. In India, some of the hostility to foreign technology reflected the Gandhian legacy extolling the virtues of simple, labor-intensive technologies. Another strand of thought, represented in India by Mahalanobis, stressed the need to develop the domestic machinery sector, then perceived to be the source of the alleged economic success of the Soviet Union.

While the countries of East Asia undertook a variety of efforts to foster the inflow of international knowledge, the ISI countries often hindered the inflow of knowledge in a manner analogous to their attempts to limit imports of goods. In India, direct foreign investment (DFI) and foreign licensing agreements were closely monitored and generally discouraged. In the Latin American countries, licensing agreements were subject to intense scrutiny lest local firms pay "excessive" charges (Chudnovsky, 1981). The opportunity cost of domestic generation of imported technologies was never compared to royalties for such technologies. While a few ISI countries, primarily in Latin America, were open to direct foreign investment, there was little attention either to generating exports through them (as there was in Singapore) or to directing these investments to new high-technology sectors where they might generate externalities as local firms observed their behavior and local employees left to form their own firms or work for domestic companies. The latter form of technology transfer was particularly important in Taiwan in sectors such as electronics (Schive, 1990).[3] In most inward-looking countries, multinational

---

[3] For a detailed discussion of other technological benefits derived by Taiwan from DFI, see Ranis and Schive, 1985.

corporations (MNCs) were mainly viewed as a source of additional investment and employment for firms whose output was, like their domestic counterparts, directed to the protected internal market.

In the Asian countries, one or two modes of technology transfer were usually limited by government policy. Korea, for example, actively discouraged direct foreign investment following the earlier example of Japan. Taiwan was somewhat less restrictive, viewing DFI as a means of entry into new technological areas. Singapore encouraged massive inflows but as the economy developed was open to DFI only in increasingly advanced production areas. Nevertheless, other channels appropriate to the stage of development were always open. Thus, Korea never seriously restricted technology licensing by limiting royalty rates or insisting on no restrictive clauses, such as prohibiting exports to third countries (World Bank, 1979). In contrast, the Latin American countries that were members of the Andean Pact engaged in a microscopic inspection of each technology contract, despite the near impossibility of preventing firms from attempting to live up to the agreements (Mytelka, 1978).

International Technology Markets

There are varying degrees of imperfection in the markets for knowledge. For example, a number of empirical studies find that licensing payments exceed, by a considerable magnitude, the marginal cost of the dissemination of existing knowledge (Contractor, 1980). It may nevertheless be wise for a country to make such payments given the opportunity cost of domestic generation of the technology. More important, some technologies, especially in new research-intensive sectors such as chemicals, machinery, and electronics appear not to be traded at all: there are missing markets. Countries desiring to have their firms enter these areas, when it is justified by changing factor proportions, have resorted to a large number of modes including joint ventures, strategic alliances, inducing the return of nationals who have been educated and worked abroad, and so on.

Domestic Capability

Knowledge imported from the rest of the world has had a magnified impact in the NIEs because of the high-quality labor force and the technological learning that has been a characteristic of many of the local firms. The interaction of knowledge from abroad and domestic capacity was critical. Evidence from other countries shows some with very high education levels (or pockets of high capacity as in India) and many research institutes. Nevertheless, they have not realized rapid growth in industrial productivity. The difference is evident in several features of the Asian NIEs: their rapid acquisition of external technological knowledge; their substantial capacity to utilize the knowledge transferred and to improve it; and the competitiveness of the markets in which products were sold.

It has been convincingly argued that a primary effect of education is to facilitate the ability to deal with rapid change (Nelson and Phelps, 1966; Schultz, 1975). If technology is changing slowly, the payoff to education will be low. If a centuries-old agricultural technology is employed, the benefit to a farmer of having become literate and numerate may be small. Empirically derived rules of thumb developed from generations of experience may yield productivity close to the maximum feasible level. If, however, high-yield variety seeds are employed and optimal planting dates as well as the dosage and date of application of fertilizer and water are much more sensitive to weather conditions, the farmer's ability to perform the requisite calculations becomes critical to obtaining the maximum yield from the new technology. The productivity of education in industry will be even higher, as in many instances there can be no approximate rules of thumb for entirely new processes and products. In the absence of rapid technological change, most production will have been routinized, and education that equips people to deal with change will have a limited marginal benefit. Thus, even in sub-Saharan Africa, which is generally thought to suffer from a shortage of skilled labor, the presence of educated managers has little payoff in improved productivity in the face of a very low inflow of new technology (Pack and Paxson, 1999).

Although the highly educated labor force within a country

may generate some purely indigenous innovations, they are likely to be less productive than if they are able to utilize their talents on a proven body of knowledge that is being introduced into the country for the first time. Local R&D inevitably has failures whereas gaining a mastery of technologies that are *known* to work in other countries has few dead ends.

None of this implies that no domestic effort at small innovations is desirable. If nothing else, such effort improves a nation's ability to more effectively master internationally available technology. Effort to generate domestic technology should thus occur simultaneously with the effort to master international technology. Indeed, it is necessary to do so as international competitors constantly improve their own productivity. But it would be incorrect to conclude that countries should spend large funds in original R&D rather than engage in the small efforts to improve imported processes and products. For example, it has been argued that imported technology reduces the quantity and quality of local effort, discouraging local capabilities which in the long run would have greater social marginal productivity.[4] Concern about such substitution effects has been voiced in Latin America and India and is remarkably similar to arguments favoring import-substituting industrialization. Several arguments militate against this view.

First, in the now advanced countries, during their periods of initial rapid growth the available evidence suggests that total factor productivity rarely grew at more than 2 percent per year. Nor is this growth rate currently exceeded in the OECD countries that are at the technology frontier, even though they benefit from considerable technology transfer among themselves. This evidence implies that even substantial investment in high levels of domestic education and research infrastructure are unlikely to lead to rates of total factor productivity (TFP) growth[5] based solely on local effort that would allow a country to close its gap relative to the world frontier. Most LDCs need to achieve growth in per capita income in excess of 5 percent per year to begin to close the absolute gap,

---

[4] For an econometric evaluation of this argument in India, see Basant and Fikkert, 1994.

[5] TFP growth is used as a shorthand for the effectiveness of the use of inputs. For a discussion of the requirements for its usefulness, see Nelson and Pack, 1999.

and the surest road to this is to borrow and improve available international technology.[6]

Obviously countries that can accumulate physical and human capital more rapidly than the OECD countries may move toward the latter's per capita income levels with a smaller contribution from TFP growth. The outstanding example of this is Singapore, which achieved high rates of growth of accumulable factors while moving along an international best practice production function supplied by direct foreign investors.

Available estimates of TFP levels in developing countries relative to the OECD indicate differences of 60 percent or 70 percent. Closing gaps of such magnitude is more certain and offers larger quantitative benefits than the intrinsically uncertain new R&D.

Second, the productivity growth of LDCs that have emphasized domestic education and R&D but have not taken full advantage of the possibilities offered by international technology transfers has been approximately zero.[7] In countries such as Argentina and India, this may partly reflect the simultaneous pursuit of ISI. Yet analyses of ISI, which emphasize the static loss in efficiency, offer no compelling explanation of the failure of productivity to grow. While the absence of competitive pressure to reduce costs is often used to explain low TFP growth, firms that could improve productivity would realize greater profits from such effort. A complementary explanation is that ISI regimes, as noted earlier, are usually either accompanied by a hostility toward the inflow of knowledge or lack the ability to extract technical information in very imperfect markets, an imperfection that an international orientation, such as that derived from exporting, helps to overcome.

---

[6] More precisely, if an LDC (L) is to close the absolute gap in per capita income (Y/P) relative to the United States (U), the growth rates of Y/P, namely, $(Y/P)^*_L$ and $(Y/P)^*_U$ must satisfy the following:

$$(Y/P)_L^* - (Y/P)_U^* > \log Y_U - \ln Y_L$$

If the LDC has $500 per capita income, and the U.S. $20,000, to close the absolute gap, $(Y/P)^*_L - (Y/P)^*_U$ must exceed 3.7 percent per year. Thus with $(Y/L)_U^*$ of 1.5 percent per year, reduction of the absolute productivity gap requires $(Y/L)_L^*$ of 5.2 percent, a rate achieved only in the Asian NIEs. Even if the LDC begins with a per capita income of $3,000, closing the absolute gap requires $(Y/L)_L^*$ of 3.4 percent per year, a figure achieved by only a few developing countries over a sustained period.

[7] For a review of the evidence through the mid-1980s, see Pack, 1988. Evidence for more recent years for a number of countries is provided by the various authors in Helleiner, 1994.

Finally, we note that technology inflows that are not comple-mented by domestic absorptive ability will have little if any impact on a country's productivity. Imagine that Bolivia, Chad, or Nepal were the beneficiaries of a new foreign aid facility that allowed them to obtain, free, any technology licenses they desired. Most observers would agree that, by itself, such knowledge could not generate a sustained growth in productivity on the part of purely local firms in these countries that are characterized by low levels of human capital and organization ability. To think of this in more contemporary terms, a free package of a powerful computer, a spreadsheet program and manuals, the five best books providing expositions, templates, and video tutorials will not allow those below a high threshhold of literacy and numeracy to successfully construct and manipulate spreadsheets.

Market Forces

The preceding sections argue that the interaction of knowledge from abroad and high domestic abilities were the critical feature allowing the NIEs to achieve their high productivity growth rates. But the resulting productivity growth might have been lower, even with this favorable constellation of factors, had firms not faced incentives to utilize their lower costs to achieve still greater export growth or efficient import substitution. Firms in Korea were compelled, by export targets, to improve productivity to increase their exports (Pack and Westphal, 1986). Taiwanese firms had strong incentives to export as a result of a chronically underval-ued exchange rate.

Competitive forces are important not mainly for improved static allocation, though that is consequential, but for ensuring that the technology transferred and local efforts to improve it are not misdirected. In some cases foreign technology has been used simply to achieve lower costs than competitors within a protected local market, after which firms have rested on their laurels. In other cases, considerable domestic effort has been expended by firms that had little chance of long-run competitiveness but which were currently protected (Katz, 1987). Eventually, with the correct technology and competitiveness policies, LDCs will approach world best practice. The harder task then begins of trying to push ahead the technology frontier itself rather than borrowing. But by that time the country is developed and is reasonably well prepared for this new effort, some of which has inevitably already been taking place simultaneously with technology borrowing.

A CLOSER EXAMINATION OF THE ASIAN EXPERIENCE
AND ITS IMPLICATIONS FOR SCIENCE, TECHNOLOGY,
AND HUMAN RESOURCES

Early Industrial Development

The Gang of Four (Hong Kong, Korea, Singapore, Taiwan) all began with brief interludes of import substitution but then switched to export orientation, the earliest exports largely consisting of labor-intensive manufactured products.[8] In these products, the relevant technology is largely embodied in imported equipment, and the requisite additional noncodified production knowledge is easily acquired from consultants or former employees of developed country firms. A literate and numerate labor force is the important requisite at this stage of production, the need for highly trained engineers and scientists being relatively limited. Thus, countries trying to emulate the growth pattern of the NIEs would, at an early stage, need to emphasize high-quality, widely available primary education. Simultaneously there needs to be a slow accumulation of higher capacities to allow an eventual transition to more complex growth. This would militate in favor of encouraging promising students to obtain high school and university education; the latter might well be outside the country, given the expense of high-quality university education and the government budget constraints.

Even at this early stage of development of the labor-intensive industries, there is a compelling need for increasing competitive pressures if industry is to progress. This can be seen most readily from the experience of the Indian textile industry, which has accumulated enormous industrial experience over a century of production. Three regional textile research institutes – ATIRA, BITRA, and SITRA – have been established in three regions to serve the sector and are supported by the firms in each institute's

---

[8] The shift from import substitution to export orientation should not be overstated. Certainly Korea and Taiwan continued to offer quite high levels of protection to firms in selected industries through the 1980s. See, for example, World Bank, 1993.

area. Given their source of funding, research is inevitably oriented
to actual production problems encountered by the constituent
firms. The published documents of these organizations demonstrate that they are the technical peers of textile research
institutes in the OECD countries.[9] Yet the rate of growth of productivity in the Indian textile industry during much of the post-
independence period has been very low (Ahluwalia, 1985)
whereas that in the NIEs has been quite high despite the absence
of comparable research institutions.

The primary reason for the low productivity growth is the
absence of competitive incentives for the Indian textile firms to
adopt the hardware and software that have been developed, the
latter including knowledge about such mundane but critical
production knowledge as how to reduce the number of broken
yarns during spinning. Until the reforms of 1991, individual firms
faced legal restrictions on their ability to expand their share of the
domestic market. Simultaneously, the foreign trade regime discouraged exports. Thus, even with superb researchers and excellent institutional structure, there was no payoff to either education
or R&D in the Indian textile sector. In contrast, textile companies
in Hong Kong, Korea, and Taiwan experienced rapid rates of productivity growth. While they employed competent, locally trained
engineers, there were no formal institutions comparable to the
three Indian ones. The firms relied on knowledge conveyed by
machinery manufacturers, foreign consultants, and importantly, on
suggestions by foreign purchasers of their products (Rhee, Ross-
Larson, and Pursell, 1984). The purchasers, having discovered a
reliable source of low-cost, high-quality products, were anxious
to enhance the quality of local production. Thus, the very act of
exporting became a source of improved technical knowledge sub-
stituting for expensive domestic research institutes. Moreover, the
NIE firms faced a very large world market that could be pene-
trated if they could improve cost and quality and if trade policy
encouraged exporting.

Thus, in the early stages of industrialization, a concentration
on relatively simple, relatively labor-intensive products dictated
by static comparative advantage may have beneficial growth

---

[9] See, for example, Ahmedabad Textile Industry's Research Association, 1973, and South
    India Industry's Textile Research Association, 1974.

effects. Machinery for production is available from a large number of manufacturers and the software can be obtained from manufacturers, consultants, and trade periodicals. There is relatively little proprietary knowledge in the simpler sectors. If this route is to be followed, widespread primary education and a competitive environment are required. Most of the critical technical resources from equipment to production engineering advice can be obtained freely or at low cost in the international market. Those nations that place disproportionate parts of their education budgets in higher education and which regulate expatriate visas and outlays for equipment are not likely to be successful in this early industrial phase. Conversely, provision of primary education, allowing the inflow of foreign knowledge, and establishing a competitive atmosphere are likely to stimulate early industrial development. A more elaborate industrial strategy replete with formal R&D and high-level education produced by the local school system is redundant.

More Complex Industrial Development

Countries that succeed in the initial stages of development, concentrating on relatively labor-intensive products, will eventually encounter changed circumstances calling for new stances. Wage rates will start to rise and it will become necessary to switch into less labor-intensive areas of production. Japan and the other NIEs have already gone through such a "graduation" and countries such as Indonesia, Malaysia, and Thailand in Asia, and perhaps a few of the Latin American countries, are currently in such a transition.

The appropriate strategies, again based on the NIE experience, appear to be openness to foreign technology, the encouragement of local R&D within firms rather than in government-sponsored institutions, and an upgrading of education. The openness of the Asian NIEs with respect to licensing can be seen in Table 3.1, which shows the ratio of licensing payments to value added in manufacturing for three Asian and three Latin American countries. For most periods, the Asian countries exhibited significantly higher ratios. And Table 3.2 indicates the increasing size of local R&D, much of it at the firm level, accompanied by a growing number of patents issued to domestic innovators in Taiwan in recent years. Although a similar pattern of R&D exists for Korea,

Table 3.1. *Ratio of licensing payments to manufacturing value added*

Years	Korea	Hong Kong	Singapore	Argentina	Brazil	Chile
1966–70	na	na	na	0.22	0.36	0.07
1971–75	0.29	na	na	0.09	0.11	0.03
1976–80	0.23	0.13	0.76	0.08	0.06	0.04
1981–85	0.24	0.16	1.05	0.11	0.04	0.02
1986–90	0.44	0.17	1.61	2.87	0.02	0.00

Source: C. Dahlman, H. Pack, and L. Westphal, *Industrialization in Developing Countries*, forthcoming.

Table 3.2. *Research and development and patenting activity in Taiwan*

Year	R&D/GDP	Total Patents	Taiwanese Nationals' Patents	Foreign Patents
1981	0.95[a]	6,265	2,897	3,368
1986	0.98	10,526	5,800	4,726
1991	1.65[b]	27,281	13,555	13,726

Notes: a, 1984; b, 1990.
Source: Taiwan Statistical Data Book, 1992, Tables 6.7, 6.8.

Hong Kong firms undertook much less research and yet continued to thrive as they obtained considerable knowledge at low cost in relatively low-technology sectors.

With the need for firms to identify new processes and new product areas in which they can compete, there will be a greater demand for workers whose education allows them to scan world markets and to deal with rapid change. At this stage, a growing level of high school and perhaps junior college graduates become a factor facilitating the necessary change in production. Some university graduates are important, particularly those trained in science and engineering, as ability to tap international knowledge becomes greater insofar as much of the knowledge has a different scientific base than that characterizing the earlier stage of development. In particular, such sectors as clothing, leather goods, textiles, toys, and wood products employ a technology that would be recognizable to a nineteenth-century manufacturer. In contrast, many of the newer products have a biological, chemical, or

Table 3.3. *The role of returning nationals in Taiwan*

Period	Returning Students/ Students Abroad	Returning to Industry/ Total Returning Students
1952–61	0.08	na
1962–85	0.04	0.16
1986–89	0.34	0.30

Source: Calculated from *Taiwan Statistical Data Book*, 1990, Tables 14.12, 14.13.

electronic basis that depends on modern science, and much of the relevant knowledge is proprietary. There is thus a need for greater local, highly educated manpower to identify, evaluate, and improve foreign technology. Such a group requires a fairly long time to develop.

Thus, even during the period of labor-intensive, lower-technology development, a growing group of high school gradu-ates, and eventually university graduates, needs to be developed. The problem is that until the transition to a more technology-intensive phase of development occurs, a premature expansion in the number of educated will lead to disappointment and perhaps discourage enrollment. Without technology-intensive industry, there is often little demand for the skills of these graduates. Despite the technocratic optimism in the 1960s by researchers developing optimizing education planning models designed to address such issues (Tinbergen and Bos, 1964), there is no easy solution to the time phasing of improved education.

Korea and Taiwan had early large increases in science and tech-nology enrollment – indeed in all university education – but it was not necessarily demand driven. While such anticipatory accumu-lation of skills had an important benefit when industrial upgrad-ing began, it is not a path that can be urged on other countries as part of an industrial strategy. Indeed, both countries suffered from a considerable "brain drain" until their higher technology indus-tries began to expand. Thus, as Table 3.3 shows, Taiwan had a relatively small return of its foreign-educated students until indus-trial growth had shifted to more modern sectors. The experience of Singapore is also germane in this respect. It had considerably lower levels of education than the other Asian Tigers but was able to substitute foreign skills – the staff of multinationals – for unavailable domestic skills. If expatriates can ease the path to the next stage of industrialization, they offer a substitute for the early and potentially politically explosive growth of under-employed university graduates.

It is worth emphasizing that the skills that are relevant are science and technology training rather than law or liberal arts. Argentina in 1960 had one of the highest average levels of education of any country, but its industry suffered from a relative shortage of technicians, compounded by adverse incentives. Indeed, a large supply of lawyers may encourage the type of coun-terproductive surveillance of foreign technology inflows charac-teristic of the Andean Pact nations. Conversely, the establishment of science and technology institutes, even those devoted to facili-tating industrialization, may not be necessary or as productive as it initially appears to outsiders. For example, the Korean Institute of Science and Technology (KIST) and the Industrial Technology Research Institute (ITRI) in Taiwan have been widely viewed as critical to the rapid growth of newer, higher-technology industries. Yet firm-level studies of the development of competitiveness in these industries in both Korea and Taiwan rarely find that these institutions were critical to the success of firms (Hobday, 1995; Kim, 1997). Rather, the ability of firms to obtain knowledge from abroad, through licenses, equipment purchases, strategic alliances, and returning nationals, is a recurrent theme for firms in newer industries. Moreover, this knowledge was improved upon by engi-neers on the firms' own staffs (Kim, 1997). While KIST and ITRI played an important role in a few technological areas, the critical element was the initiative of entrepreneurial firms and their own internal R&D that improved on foreign technology. Publicly sup-ported research consortia, whether SEMATECH in the United States or the fifth-generation computer project in Japan, do not have a compelling record of economic success. A few examples from Japan in large-scale integrated circuits are offset, even in that country, by any number of failed efforts.

Thus, for the second stage of development, the relevant human resource strategy is to build up the local education base or facili-tate the substitution of foreign skills during a transition period. Japan, Korea, and Taiwan followed the first path; Singapore the second. Necessary complements are a willingness to facilitate

foreign technology transfer whether to local firms or by investment by MNCs. As in the early stage of industrialization, human
resource development is a critical part of a package. The weight
of the components of a successful package can vary from the
high DFI–relatively low education route of Singapore to the low
DFI–high education path of Japan and Korea. There is no single
optimum.

Occasionally the Singapore route has been criticized, with
claims that there is insufficient transfer of technical knowledge to
local employees and firms. The import of this argument is elusive.
In Taiwan, employees of MNCs have regularly left them and
begun their own competitive firms in identical or related products.
If this has not occurred in Singapore, it is unrelated to MNCs
per se but requires answers as to why such mobility is lacking.
Attitudes toward risk taking, regulation, and the development
of financial markets are more plausible candidates than the ability
of firms to prevent local workers from obtaining relevant knowledge. The prevalence of small firms in Taiwan and the high private
saving rate, with savings often invested directly in small
enterprises, was important. Even in the United States, with well-
specified employment contracts and an effective judicial process,
it has been impossible for firms to prevent employees from utilizing their knowledge in spinoff firms. On the other hand, such spin-
offs are apparently rare not only in Singapore but also in Japan,
supporting the view that it is not the unwillingness to share technology with workers but the general economic environment that
limits the seepage of knowledge from established MNCs to startup
firms.

R&D POLICIES THAT HAVE NOT WORKED

In early postwar discussions of appropriate policies for science
and technology, suggestions were often made that developing
nations establish research institutes that were freestanding or
were affiliated with universities. There was often a mixture of
motives, including a positive view of the potential contribution
of such institutions and a desire to reduce brain drain by having
a research center attractive to scientists and engineers who had
been trained abroad. There is, however, no systematic evidence
that any of these centers has made a significant contribution to

sustained industrial development. As noted earlier, even the most widely admired of such institutes, KIST and ITRI, which were established with the mandate to aid industrial development, do not have documented success. Indeed, a number of recent studies about the acquisition of technological abilities in Korea and Taiwan cite the role of foreign technology transfers and internal firm-level efforts as much more important than that of the publicly supported research institutes (Hobday, 1995; Kim, 1997).

The argument for publicly supported research institutes is that they will perform basic research whose results are likely to be nonappropriable and therefore would not be undertaken by private sponsors. While this constitutes a valid argument for public support, most knowledge relevant for industrial success in LDCs is not frontier knowledge but a transfer of existing knowledge from more industrialized countries. In Korea, and especially at ITRI in Taiwan, there was an attempt in the electronics sector to develop expertise in some areas of production that could then form the basis for the development of local industry. Intensive firm-level studies suggest, however, that even such well-designed and thought out programs were not very important for the development of the local electronics sector (Hobday, 1995; Kim, 1997). Rather, this sector, certainly in Taiwan, relied on licensing of technology, returning Taiwanese nationals who had been educated and had worked in the United States, and the knowledge obtained by nationals who had worked in multinationals within Taiwan. All this was improved on, often quite imaginatively, by graduates of the local engineering programs (often junior colleges), who constituted the research staff of the electronics firms. Only rarely do firms indicate a major contribution from ITRI.

The limited role of public research institutes is not surprising. In sectors in which there is a rapidly evolving technology frontier and knowledge is proprietary, the public sector is likely to learn the proprietary knowledge in OECD firms with a significant lag. But it was hardly useful to learn to produce a 256 K chip when the world standard changed to one or four megabytes. In older sectors with more slowly evolving technologies, public institutions would seem a fifth wheel given that much of the information is not proprietary and can be identified and purchased by individual firms. It is arguable that the large fixed costs involved in the search for information lead to high average costs but low marginal cost for information acquisition and thus justify public search and dissemination in traditional sectors; however, there are no documented cases of such institutions succeeding in the postwar period. In Meiji, Japan, the manufacturers' association in textiles did perform these and other functions (including machinery design), but this effort seems to have been a phenomenon more likely to succeed in an earlier period of technology diffusion (Otsuka, Ranis, and Saxonhouse, 1988).

At the present time, it would appear that government-supported efforts to identify technology are not likely to be needed in the nontechnology-intensive sectors. If one firm succeeds in this enterprise, it will serve as a beacon to other firms in industry, encouraging them to emulate its effort. In these sectors, given the ease of access to technology, one can expect quick imitation once the new methods have proved profitable in the LDC. While a combination of high fixed-search costs and capital market imperfections might preclude either a leading firm from succeeding or followers from imitating it, the success of small-scale firms in Hong Kong and Taiwan in traditional sectors suggest this is not an insuperable barrier. The obstacles to obtaining technology lie in other limitations, and public technology institutes are, at best, a very indirect and costly method of redressing them.

There is no intent to imply that firm-level R&D efforts are always socially desirable. There is considerable evidence, especially in Latin America, that some firms have undertaken imaginative R&D to augment their production when they are unable to obtain additional foreign equipment (Katz et al., 1987) due to foreign exchange shortages imposed by poor macroeconomic management. Others have tried to improve the usefulness of locally available inputs when tariffs or quantitative restrictions have limited their access to foreign intermediates. Even when these efforts have been "successful," much of the case study material suggests that the rate of return on such effort has been quite low relative to what would have occurred with additional investment in foreign equipment. Moreover, much of the effort was undertaken in sectors that did not have a long-term comparative advantage. Thus, even where technically successful, the R&D effort almost surely had low rates of return, though few studies have calculated such returns rather than simply documenting the technological effort.

NEW GENERATIONS OF PROBLEMS IN THE NIES

There has been a large amount of statistical research on the determinants of convergence in per capita income between initially poor and advanced economies, but such studies cannot address many of the interesting questions facing the countries that have already reduced the income gap relative to the OECD countries. A principal question is this: Can the gap be narrowed even more?

Consider nations such as Korea and Taiwan that have achieved 40 percent of the per capita income of the United States compared with less than 10 percent in 1960. The typical statistical study that attempts to explain this convergence correctly identifies the rapid growth rate of capital stock and educated labor as important components of such performance. What is often overlooked is that such accumulation would have run into severely diminishing returns had it not been for the improvement in technological knowledge, which insured that the newly available factors were used efficiently. Many countries with high rates of factor accumulation have not enjoyed such spectacular growth, reflecting their inability to master new technologies (Nelson and Pack, 1999). Even if the NIEs maintain their very high investment/GDP ratios, the rate of growth of the capital stock will decline, given that the capital-labor ratios are much higher than they were at the beginning of the process. Unless there is continuing rapid growth in technological capabilities, some significant slowing in the rate of growth is likely. Can the onset of diminshing returns be delayed by entering areas in which the firms can obtain rents from sales of their products abroad?

In the more labor-intensive product areas in which the NIEs are already active, there are still possibilities for upgrading and reducing costs to maintain or increase export shares in the world market and to maintain the existing share of the domestic market. While productivity has grown significantly, they are still considerably below OECD levels (Pilat, 1994). In these sectors, it will, however, become increasingly difficult to match the costs of new competitors such as China, the Philippines, and Vietnam, given the very low wage levels of these countries. Hence, a decreasing percentage of investment will be allocated to traditional products and greater percentages to new product areas that are more skill- and capital-intensive and utilize newer technologies.

In new product areas, there will be intense competition both among the NIEs and vis-à-vis the OECD countries. In principle, the introduction of new innovative goods or services could generate sufficiently high returns to keep aggregate growth rates high. But it is precisely in high-tech areas that it is very difficult to achieve a self-sustaining niche in world markets. The competition over the next decade will be of a different type from that faced by policy makers in the 1965–90 period. Replication of earlier efforts by governments to guide sectoral development toward high-income elasticity, more technology-intensive products are likely to prove fruitless. There are few high-income elasticity markets with static unchanging demands for standardized commodities such as steel and television sets. Rather, many of the markets with high-income elasticity change with extraordinary rapidity, and their evolution, even over six months, is often unpredictable. Hence, as firms enter product areas in which specifications change rapidly, there will be a premium on avoiding product areas in which product cycles are exceptionally short.

Government targeting of individual sectors is unlikely to prove effective. Huge firms like IBM and Intel continually generate new products that reflect enormous cumulative research experience. Even firms as large as Samsung and Daewoo are unlikely to match the continuing rapid introduction of new products by such large U.S. firms.[10] More emphasis will have to be placed on smaller, innovative enterprises.

Can one envision efforts in which the major firms in the NIEs will be successful in the increasingly competitive international market? Some companies, such as Acer, Daewoo, and Samsung, are already at the research frontier and engaging in large R&D expenditures to obtain commercially useful knowledge. Exchanges of information with companies of comparable size in other OECD countries through strategic alliances is already occurring and will become more widespread. But neither internal research within the current industrial structure nor the sharing of knowledge with OECD competitors is likely to confer a unique benefit that will allow the generation of rents. Long-term success will require an entrepreneurial culture that produces Korean and

---

[10] As an example, within a week Intel and IBM announced new, radically more powerful microprocessors and methods of producing them, leaving both American and Japanese competitors likely to fall behind these firms. See "New Intel Chip," 1997.

Taiwanese counterparts to Microsoft, Dell, and Oracle, to name only three of the high-technology companies in the United States that began as very small enterprises within the last fifteen years.

There has been a considerable debate about differing development strategies in Korea and Taiwan. Korea's has been built mainly by fostering large-scale firms through a skewing of tax and credit market policies. Taiwan, with more neutral policies, has developed a more vigorous small- and medium-enterprise sector. If large-scale R&D is the answer to competing in the world market, Korean firms clearly enjoy a better position. However, if nimbleness in shifting among rapidly changing product specifications is important, given the accelerating pace of technological innovation, Taiwanese firms appear to have an advantage.[11] Future success does not necessarily consist of one or the other but of a mixture of large- and small-firm efforts.

Focusing more narrowly on Korea, more size neutral policies are clearly in order. The government emphasis for three decades on the *chaebol* (conglomerate) as a major instrument of industrialization has almost certainly run into rapidly diminshing returns, as shown by bankruptcies in 1996 and 1997. A change toward more neutral tax and credit policies should encourage the emergence of smaller, perhaps more innovative firms. But this shift will not necessarily occur automatically or rapidly. In Korea, as in Japan, several generations have been conditioned to a view that big is better in terms of both income and job security. An entrepreneurial culture that encourages recent graduates to start their own firms is not yet in sight, even if public policies are more supportive.

Assuming that more neutral policies are adopted, how can the Korean economy improve its short- to medium-term prospects and find new products and/or processes that will improve its export outlook? Korean firms have demonstrated excellence in both manufacturing and marketing (MM). Casual empiricism suggests they have been less successful at generating new innovations with commercial possibilities. If this characterization is correct, a mode for acquiring capacities complementary to the existing ones will be important as more neutral incentives gradually lead to the development of smaller, perhaps more innovative firms.

[11] There has, however, been no quantitative investigation at a detailed industrial classification of export success by firm size.

One route immediately suggests itself – namely, the search for underexploited pools of potentially marketable knowledge in nations where these are not complemented by local MM skills. Countries such as Israel and Russia satisfy this criterion. In both there is a considerable pool of scientists and engineers having knowledge with commercial potential. Neither of these countries possesses the MM skills of Korea. While Korean firms have attempted technology alliances and purchases in Western Europe and the United States, domestic competitors in those nations are likely to have pored over the opportunities presented by smaller firms and university-based researchers. There are probably fewer underinvestigated technology opportunities than exist in Israel and Russia, and perhaps in some former East Bloc countries.

CONCLUSIONS

In the years after World War II, economists and social scientists who were proponents of modernization believed that the task of industrial development would be relatively simple given the extensive shelf of technology that could be exploited. A half century later it is apparent that efficient industrial growth is the exception rather than the norm. A relatively small set of countries have experienced a sustained rapid growth in industrial value added at international prices. Their success has been due to their ability to tap the existing backlog of technology and to efficiently absorb it. Most of this success was attributable to firm-level efforts, abetted by a well-educated labor force. Little, if anything, was due to government-sponsored technology institutions. The framework within which this unprecedented success was achieved was consistent competitive pressure even when domestic markets were protected (Pack and Westphal, 1986).

Although many of the NIEs are currently undergoing considerable turmoil due to some macroeconomic mismanagement and insufficient regulation of their financial systems, it is likely that these are temporary problems that will be solved. The longer-term difficulty lies in continuing to expand the modern sectors efficiently. Young (1995) argued that Korean and Taiwanese growth, along with that of Singapore, has been fueled largely by factor accumulation. Undoubtedly, factor accumulation has contributed to aggregate growth, but it is also remarkable that these economies, even by Young's calculation, have exhibited positive total factor productivity growth, unlike many LDCs that have absorbed less labor and capital. Nelson and Pack (1999) offer an explanation of this success in terms of successful absorption of foreign technology.

After the current macroeconomic and financial crises pass, the difficult task of the NIEs will be to find new niches within world markets. Some of these will undoubtedly be in services, some in new industrial products. The formulas that were followed in the past of intensive government guidance are unlikely to be of much use. New, more flexible economic and social organizations will have to develop if further convergence of the NIEs toward the GNP per capita levels of the OECD countries is to be achieved.

REFERENCES

Ahluwalia, Isher Judge. 1985. *Industrial Growth in India.* Delhi: Oxford University Press.

Ahmedabad Textile Industry's Research Association. 1973. *Standards for Costs of Yarn Spinning.* Ahmedabad: Ahmedabad Textile Industry Research Associates.

Amsden, Alice. 1989. *Asia's Next Giant: South Korea and Late Industrialization.* New York: Oxford University Press.

Basant, Rakesh, and Briak Fikkert. 1996. "The Effects of R & D, Foreign Technology Purchase, and Domestic and International Spillovers on Productivity in Indian Firms." *Review of Economics and Statistics,* 78, 187–199.

Chudnovsky, Daniel. 1981. "Regulating Technology Imports in Some Developing Countries." *Trade and Development* 3, Winter.

Contractor, Farok J. 1980. "The Profitability of Technology Licensing by U.S. Multinationals." *Journal of International Business Studies,* Fall.

Dahlman, Carl J., and Ousa Sananikone. 1990. "Technology Strategy in the Economy of Taiwan: Exploiting Foreign Linkages and Investing in Local Capacity." Washington, DC: World Bank, Industry and Energy Department.

Dos Santos, T. 1970. "The Structure of Dependence." *American Economic Review, Papers and Proceedings,* pp. 231–236.

Evenson, Robert, and Larry E. Westphal. 1995. "Technological Change and Technology Strategy." In Jere Behrman and T. N. Srinivasan, (eds.), *Handbook of Development Economics,* Vol. 3A. Amsterdam: Elsevier Science, 2209–2299.

Gerschenkron, Alexander. 1962. *Economic Development in Historical Perspective.* Cambridge, MA: Harvard University Press.

Helleiner, G. K. 1994. *Trade Policy and Industrialization in Turbulent Times*. London: Routledge.

Hobday, Mike. 1995. *Innovation in East Asia: The Challenge to Japan*. London: Edward Elgar.

Katz, Jorge, et al. 1987. *Technology Generation in Latin American Manufacturing Industries*. London: Macmillan.

Kim, Linsu. 1997. *From Imitation to Innovation: Dynamics of Korea's Technological Learning*. Boston: Harvard Business School Press.

Kumar, Nagesh. 1985. "Cost of Technology Imports: The Indian Experience." *Economic and Political Weekly*, 20 (35), M103–M114.

Mytelka, L. K. 1978. "Licensing and Technology Dependence in the Andean Group." *World Development*, April, 28–42.

Nagaoka, Sadao. 1989. "Overview of Japanese Industrial Technology Development." Industry Series Paper 6. Washington, DC: World Bank, Industry and Energy Department.

Nelson, Richard R., and E. Phelps. 1966. "Investment in Humans, Technological Diffusion, and Economic Growth." *American Economic Review*, 56, May, 69–75.

Nelson, Richard R., and Howard Pack. 1999. "The Asian Growth Miracle and Modern Growth Theory." *The Economic Journal*, 109, 416–436.

"New Intel Chip Holds Twice as Much Data." (1997, September 18). *Washington Post*, p. E1.

Otsuka, K., G. Ranis, and G. Saxonhouse. 1988. *Comparative Technology Choice: The Indian and Japanese Cotton Textile Industries*. London: Macmillan.

Ozawa, Terutomo. 1974. *Japan's Technological Challenge to the West, 1950–74: Motivation and Accomplishment*. Cambridge, MA: MIT Press.

Pack, Howard. 1988. "Industrialization and Trade." In H. B. Chenery and T. N. Srinivasan (eds.), *Handbook of Development Economics*. Amsterdam: North-Holland, 333–380.

Pack, Howard, and Larry E. Westphal. 1986. "Industrial Strategy and Technological Change: Theory vs. Reality." *Journal of Development Economics*, 22, 87–128.

Pack, Howard. 1997. "The Role of Exports in Asian Economic Development and Lessons for Latin America." In Nancy Birdsall and Fred Jaspersen (eds.), *Pathways to Growth*. Baltimore: Johns Hopkins University Press.

Pack, Howard, and Christina Paxson. 2000. "Is African Manufacturing Skill Constrained?" In E. Szirmai (ed.), *The Industual Experience of Tanzania*. London: Macmillan, 1–18.

Packenham, Robert. 1992. *The Dependency Movement*. Cambridge, MA: Harvard University Press.

Pilat, Dirk. 1994. *The Economics of Rapid Growth: The Experience of Japan and Korea*. Brookfield, VT: Elgar.

Ranis, Gustav, and Chi Schive. 1985. "Direct Foreign Investment in Taiwan's Development." In Walter Galenson (ed.), *Foreign Trade and Investment: Economic Development in the Newly Industrializing Asian Countries*. Madison: University of Wisconsin Press, 80–96.

Rhee, Yung, Bruce Ross-Larson, and Gary Pursell. 1984. *Korea's Competitive Edge: Managing Entry into World Markets*. Baltimore: Johns Hopkins University Press.

Schive, Chi. 1990. *The Foreign Factor: The Multinational Corporations' Contribution to the Economic Modernization of the Republic of China*. Stanford, CA: Hoover Institution Press.

Schultz, Theodore W. 1975. "The Value of the Ability to Deal with Disequilibria." *Journal of Economic Literature*, 13, September, 827–846.

South India Textile Research Association. 1974. *Modernization in Spinning*. Coimbatore: South India Textile Research Association.

Tinbergen, Jan, and H. C. Bos. 1964. "A Planning Model for the Education Requirements of Economic Development." In OECD, *The Residual Factor in Economic Growth*. Paris: OECD, 147–169.

World Bank. 1979. *Korea: Development of the Machinery Industries*. Washington, DC: World Bank, Industrial Development and Finance Department.

World Bank. 1993. *The East Asian Economic Miracle*. Washington, DC: World Bank.

Young, Alwyn. 1995. "The Tyranny of Numbers: Confronting the Statistical Realities of the East Asian Growth Experience." *Quarterly Journal of Economics*, 110, 641–680.

Commentary

Bengt-Åke Lundvall

The chapters in Part I are by two of the world's most experienced experts on development strategies in developing countries and basically they address the same set of issues: How to explain the relative success of the Asian Tigers in terms of economic growth? What lessons can be learned for developing countries and other countries? Specifically, the authors try to sort out the role of public policies and the role of openness to the external world. In what follows, I point to areas of consent and areas of disagreement between the two authors as well as raise a few questions that their analyses leave unanswered. First, I will sum up the main argument of each author.

SANJAYA LALL ON THE NEED FOR SECTOR-SPECIFIC GOVERNMENT POLICY

The chapter by Sanjaya Lall gives a broad perspective on the role of technology in economic growth. He specifies several fundamental characteristics of technological learning (uncertainty, cumulativeness, embeddedness, externalities, etc.) that make it difficult to capture this process by standard economic models assuming rational, maximizing agents with a unique equilibrium state as the point of reference. He develops a model of a national innovation system giving strong emphasis to the incentives regime and public policies. He specifies the main elements of the system as being, respectively, incentives, factor markets, and institutions (defined as organizations that constitute the public knowledge infrastructure). A major part of the chapter is the presentation of indicators of technological competence for a number of Asian countries showing that Korea, Taiwan, and Singapore exhibit the strongest technological capacities on almost all measures.

95

On the basis of this analysis, Lall discusses the role of government with reference to the experience of the most successful Asian economies. His general conclusion is that there is a role for governments, not only in promoting the general framework conditions, but also in targeting and supporting specific sectors with a great growth potential.

HOWARD PACK ON THE IMPORTANCE OF FOREIGN TECHNOLOGY

Howard Pack also takes the history of the Asian Tiger economies as the basis for considering what is an adequate technology policy in a developing country. He distinguishes three different phases that are more or less demanding with respect to technological competence and specifies the policy needs at each stage. At an early stage, primary education, export orientation, and openness to foreign technology are crucial for success. Later, there will be a need for more sophisticated technologies, engineering skills, and research and development. Finally, the third stage will be even more demanding in terms of innovative capabilities, including the creation of new enterprise.

Pack strongly emphasizes the openness to foreign technology and to competition and entrepreneurship. He states that governments have a role in promoting education and training whereas attempts to establish a public technological infrastructure are regarded as not useful. He also warns against overly ambitious attempts to create an indigenous science base.

CONSENSUS POINTS – EXPORT PROMOTION AND HUMAN CAPITAL

On a number of points the two authors are in complete agreement; others reflect differences in emphasis. On a few their analyses point in different directions. The most fundamental point of consensus relates to the role of technology in economic development. They both argue that the capability to develop, absorb, and efficiently utilize technology has been crucial for the outstanding growth in the Tiger economies. Both refer to the growth accounting exercises by Young showing that the growth in total factor productivity (sometimes labeled the rate of technical progress in the vocabulary of standard economics) has not been outstanding in these economies compared to, for instance, the OECD (Organization for Economic Cooperation and Development) economies. But they give convincing and complementary arguments for why one should not accept an interpretation giving technological competence a secondary role in economic development.

They also agree on the importance of two factors behind the progress of the Tiger economies: export orientation and investment in human capital. One point of almost universal agreement in the development debate supported by the two authors is that import-substitution strategies give the wrong incentives for building technology competence while export promotion gives the right ones.

Comparing the experience of Latin America and Asia, respectively, it is difficult to avoid such a conclusion. Even so, there might be a need for clarifying and specifying the dynamics involved. As pointed out by Pack, there is no simple theoretical link from import-substitution strategies to weak *dynamic* performance in a standard economic model of micro-economic behavior (the link would be to static misallocation, which would be of minor importance for the rate of economic growth). On this background, Pack argues that the crucial variable is not import substitution as such, but, as part of the import-substitution philosophy, a general negative attitude to foreign technological opportunities among firms and politicians. Another part of the explanation could be that the weakening of competition has a negative impact on the effort to engage in learning.

Another issue relates to how far governments should go in supporting export and what means they should use. If competition pressure affects efforts to learn positively, it is not obvious that a "chronically undervalued currency" should promote dynamic efficiency (as argued by Pack in the case of Taiwan). What are the specific mechanisms that translate growing sales abroad into technological learning? One general mechanism might be that the degree of x-efficiency as well as the effort to promote innovation reflects not only the intensity of competition but also the positioning of firms in international production networks. (By getting involved in a close cooperation with foreign firms that are demanding in terms of quality and flexibility, domestic firms may enhance their competitiveness.) This kind of reasoning would, however, imply a theory of micro-economic behavior of the kind indicated in the first part of the Lall chapter (standard economic assumptions of representative or best practice firms in terms of management competence would have to be fundamentally revised). It would also extend the policy agenda to include attempts to facilitate the transition to organizational and management better practices. Finally, it would point to a need to give more emphasis to training in management and to research in organization theory as contrasted to technical skills and natural science, so strongly privileged in the development literature.

The other point of agreement is that the investment of human resources has been crucial for building technological competence and international competitiveness. This covers investments in primary as well as secondary education. Both chapters illustrate the enormous investments in these areas in Korea and Taiwan as well as the dramatic results in terms of training new generations of engineers and scientists. There are certainly differences in emphasis here, since Pack warns against overinvestment in the more advanced stages of training, but the general thrust is the same.

When considering the future of the Tiger economies, it might be of interest to go behind these numbers and look at qualitative dimensions. There have been international comparisons indicating good capacities in mathematics and other disciplines for Korean and Taiwanese students. But there are other dimensions that might become more decisive for economic performance in the future. In a context of rapid change, the kind of training given to workers may be of great importance for the capability to adapt and innovate (this is not in contradiction with the general assumption that training promotes the capability to master change; see Pack).

How far does the education and training system reproduce authoritarian relationships in terms of generation and gender gaps in the different Asian economies? This might prove to be a serious problem in a rapidly changing economy where it is crucial to obtain broad participation and to distribute widely individual responsibility. Also the need for individual creativity may be increasing in the new phase of development. And, finally, this gives a further argument for why, currently, the crucial bottlenecks of the Tiger economies may be in social science and management competencies rather than in natural science and technology.

THE MAJOR DISAGREEMENT – THE DEGREES OF OPENNESS AND STATE INTERVENTION

While both authors favor openness to foreign technology and export orientation strategies, they differ in their assessment of what national governments can and should do. Lall argues that selective and sector-specific intervention is needed and that the crucial step is to go from know-how to know-why, implying that the national agents hereby establish their own indigenous capabilities to innovate.[1] This will not take place if the initiative is left to private initiative and multinational firms. National governments need to intervene to direct investments – domestic as well as foreign – educated labor, and finance toward sectors with a strong growth potential. Also, they should build technological infrastructure in these areas. Some forms of protectionism may be called for – for instance, by giving sector-selective permits to foreign investors – to realize such strategies.

Pack argues strongly for the positive potential of market processes and for the strategic importance of openness and access to foreign technology. A suitably trained labor force, extreme openness to foreign technology, and export orientation should in principle be enough to create the necessary dynamics. He argues that there are practically no examples of successful government intervention. Even what has been quoted in the literature as positive examples establishing technological institutes in Korea (KIST) and Taiwan (ITRI) seem to be of marginal impact when firms are asked about the role of these institutes in the development of new technologies.

To give a fair judgment between these two views, there is a need both for detailed historical analysis and for an assessment of how

---

[1] The implicit idea in Lall's analysis that "know-how" always represents a lower and more primitive level of knowledge than "know-why" may be misleading. Often it is easier to get access to know-why knowledge in a codified form than to get access to the necessary know-how that can be learned only by doing, using, or interacting. Here, we prefer the idea of a spiral movement going back and forth between codified/know-why and tacit/know-how knowledge proposed by Nonaka (1991). For an alternative view on the concepts of know-how and know-why, see Lundvall and Johnson (1994).

the present situation differs from the past. Here I will give some observations that might be of relevance for the debate. First, I find it somewhat peculiar that both authors, and especially Howard Pack, tend to emphasize technology as process technology rather than as "product technology." What seems to characterize both Japan and the Asian Tiger economies – as compared with other less successful developing economies – is that they have moved massively into new product areas where it was far from obvious that they had an original comparative advantage. Lall, like many other sources, indicates that governments did play a major role in this connection. Is it not that role that has to be analyzed rather than the absorption of process technology?[2]

Second, regarding the role of technological institutes, I believe that Howard Pack makes a strong point when he argues that these normally will not be at the forefront of technology and that it would be a mistake to regard them as technological vanguards of the economy. But I am much less convinced that they have no role to play in diffusing technology to the average and laggard firms. Especially in innovation systems, dominated by small firms such as the Taiwanese, there may be a major role for speeding up diffusion through such organizations. This function may be much more important than their direct contribution to the development of brand-new technologies.

ABOUT THE FUTURE

To agree on the past may, as we have seen, be quite difficult. It is still more difficult to agree on the development strategies of the future. Even if it could be demonstrated that a specific policy strategy had been successful in the past, we could not conclude that it ought to be applied in the current context. Major changes in the last decade have created a new context for national systems of innovation. This also raises the possibility that systems that were

---

[2] Specifically, it would be interesting to know more about what role "reverse engineering" has played in the development strategies of the Asian Tiger economies. This mode of integrating new technology from abroad has apparently proved its effectiveness in the case of Japan (Freeman, 1987). It may be that this way of accessing foreign technology is especially useful in moving into new and promising product areas since multinational firms may be especially reluctant to give away product technology insights in areas where market growth is expected to be substantial.

highly successful a decade ago may run into serious trouble today, and vice versa.

Some of the major changes have to do with a speeding up of the rate of change and with a movement toward a more intangible economy where certain knowledge-intensive business services begin to play a strategic role for the overall industrial dynamics. Growing complexity and accelerating change impose a need for rapid learning in terms of forgetting some old and building new competencies. In order to cope with new challenges in terms of new technological opportunities, new competitors, and new market developments, it is no longer sufficient to have a stable and deep stock of knowledge. In this new kind of learning economy, it is the capability to access and create new knowledge that determines the success of individuals, firms, and countries.

A fundamental question is how far the different Asian economies are prepared to cope with this new context. At the end of his chapter, Howard Pack points to the problems related to the highly concentrated Korean economy and its extreme reliance on the small number of *chaebols*, and he also indicates the growing importance of services for successful export strategies. I share these concerns, but I also believe that the implications of the new context are much wider and more fundamental. Actually, the core debate about what national governments should or should not do might need a recasting in light of these changes.

Obviously there is some kind of role for government policy in the learning economy. It is generally accepted that the market cannot by itself channel the right amount of resources to the creation of knowledge and that there are difficult tradeoffs relating to the diffusion of knowledge and the establishment of intellectual property rights, respectively. It is also obvious that the capability to learn is unevenly distributed in many different dimensions (among individuals, firms, regions, sectors, technologies, etc.) and that this capability can be affected by public policy. At the same time, there is a lot of evidence that direct public intervention in specific learning processes may be detrimental for efficiency. Therefore, the key role of government must be to shape the economic structures and institutions that promote learning in areas where there is much to learn and where the returns to learning are high. A key role is to break up structures and institutions that block learning or lead to "lock-ins" and to create new ones that help to establish new learning trajectories.

REFERENCES

Freeman, C. 1987. *Technology and Economic Performance: Lessons from Japan*. London: Pinter.

Lundvall, B.-A., and Johnson, B. 1994. "The Learning Economy." *Journal of Industrial Studies*, 1(2), 23–42.

Nonaka, I. 1991. "The Knowledge Creating Company." *Harvard Business Review*, November–December, 2, 96–104.

PART II

How Firms Learn

CHAPTER 4

Firm Capabilities and Economic Development: Implications for Newly Industrializing Economies

David J. Teece

INTRODUCTION

The increase in the stock of useful knowledge and the extension of its application are the essence of modern economic growth. This much is understood. There is also recognition that the augmentation of the stock of useful knowledge as well as the extension of its application takes place primarily by business firms, admittedly pursuant to institutional structures and rules laid down by government.

Despite the centrality of the business firm to economic growth and economic development, development economics has given relatively short shrift to the firm as the agent of economic development. While firms are by no means neglected, the weight of the literature focuses on the role of macro-economic variables and the public sector in the development process. Capital availability, exchange rates, savings, and taxation issues are all well recognized and comprehensively studied, although their impact is still uncertain. The poor state of the development economics literature is possibly due to the relative neglect of the study of firms and the institutions that support firms.

In this chapter, recent work on the theory of the firm is discussed. In particular, recent work on competences and capabilities is discussed to see whether the enabling factors and the forces that assist economic development can be better illustrated. Over the last decade-and-a-half, a considerable amount of research and writing has been going on, principally at business schools, articulating a "dynamic capabilities" theory of firm performance and strategy.[1] To date, this body of writing has developed based on insights from the recent history of innovative firms in advanced industrial countries. While the institutional context is often rather different from what exists in newly industrialized countries, many of the basic processes of learning and advancement taking place inside the firm are applicable in other contexts as well. Indeed, a firm that is a new entrant into a market in the United States or other advanced industrial country experiences challenges not unlike those of the newcomer located in a newly industrialized country. While the local talent and the local knowledge base may be different, the processes of catching up and organizing for continuous innovation have important similarities. Thus, the purpose of this chapter is to describe certain concepts which some have found to be important to understanding the growth and development of firms in the developed countries, suggesting that the fundamental processes may in fact be more general, as some scholars believe to be the case (see, for instance Kim, 1993; Dodgson and Kim, 1997).

COMPETENCES AND CAPABILITIES

There are many dimensions of the business firm that must be understood if one is to develop distinctive competences/capabilities in business firms. In this chapter, I identify several classes of factors that will help determine a firm's strength. I am especially interested in developmental activities at the level of the firm. There is always a *static* aspect to firm performance, such as how to minimize cost for a given output level. But in the developmental context, *dynamic* issues are more important. The fundamental question then becomes, How does one profitably grow the business?

Such developmental activity has two major dimensions: (1) how to leverage existing assets into new and/or related business, and (2) how to learn, and how to combine and recombine assets to establish new businesses and address new markets. The challenge is to make sense of the rapidly changing context of global business and to find new ways of doing things. This typically involves

---

[1] This chapter draws in part on Teece, Pisano, and Shuen, 1997, "Dynamic Capabilities and Strategic Management," *Strategic Management Journal*, 18(7).

new business models and transformational activity inside the firm as well as with customers, suppliers, and competitors. Thus, where possible I try to distinguish between static and dynamic elements. I also endeavor to assess the particular role of business processes, market positions, and expansion paths in shaping economic development at the level of the firm.

Processes

Organizational processes have four roles: coordination/integration (a static concept); routinization; learning (a dynamic concept); and reconfiguration (also a dynamic concept). I discuss each in turn.

Coordination/Integration

While the price system supposedly coordinates the economy, managers effectuate cooperation/coordination/integration activity inside the firm (Barnard, 1938). How efficiently and effectively internal coordination or integration is achieved is very important (Aoki, 1990).[2] The same is true for external coordination.[3] Increasingly, competitive advantage requires the integration of external activities and technologies. The growing literature on strategic alliances, the virtual corporation, buyer-supplier relations, and technology collaboration evidences the importance of external integration and sourcing. External coordination is rather different from internal coordination, however, as one cannot appeal to hierarchy to effectuate action.

Routinization

Organizational performance is effectuated in large measure through standard ways of performing organizational tasks. Such

---

[2] Indeed, Ronald Coase, author of the pathbreaking 1937 article "The Nature of the Firm," which focused on the costs of organizational coordination inside that firm as compared to across the market, half a century later has identified as critical the understanding of "why the cost of organizing particular activities differs among firms" (Coase, 1988, p. 47). I argue that a firm's distinctive ability needs to be understood as a reflection of distinctive organizational or coordinative capabilities. This form of integration (i.e., inside business units) is different from the integration between business units; they could be viable on a stand-alone basis (external integration). For a useful taxonomy, see Iansiti and Clark (1994).

[3] Shuen (1994) examines the gains and hazards of the technology make-vs.-buy decision and supplier co-development.

procedures can be thought of as "routines." There is some field-based empirical research that provides support for the notion that the nature of business processes and routines inside the firm provide the source of differences in firms' competence in various domains. For example, Garvin's (1988) study of eighteen room air-conditioning plants reveals that quality performance was not related to either capital investment or the degree of automation of the facilities. Instead, quality performance was driven by special organizational routines. These include routines for gathering and processing information, for linking customer experiences with engineering design choices, and for coordinating factors and component suppliers.[4] The work of Clark and Fujimoto (1991) on project development in the automobile industry also illustrates the role played by coordinative routines. Their study reveals a significant degree of variation in how different firms coordinate the various activities required to bring a new model from concept to market. These differences in coordinative routines and capabilities seem to have a significant impact on such performance variables as development costs, development lead times, and quality.

Furthermore, Clark and Fujimoto tend to find significant firm-level differences in coordination routines, and these differences seemed to have persisted for a long time. This finding suggests that routines related to coordination are firm specific in nature. While these findings have been derived from firms in advanced countries, there is no reason to suppose that they are not applicable to firms in developing countries as well.

Also, the notion that competence/capability is embedded in distinct ways of coordinating and combining helps to explain how and why seemingly minor technological changes can have devastating impacts on incumbent firms' abilities to compete in a market. Henderson and Clark (1990), for example, have shown that incumbents in the photolithographic equipment industry were sequentially devastated by seemingly minor innovations. However, while seemingly minor, the innovations in question had major impacts on how systems had to be configured. Difficulties were experienced because systems-level or "architectural" innovations often require new routines to integrate and coordinate engineering tasks. These findings and others suggest that produc-

---

[4] Garvin (1994) provides a typology of organizational processes.

tive systems display high interdependency, and that it may not be possible to change one level without changing others. This appears to be true with respect to the "lean production" model (Womack and Roos, 1991) which has now transformed the manufacturing organization in the automobile industry.[5] Lean production requires distinctive shop floor practices and processes as well as distinctive higher-order managerial processes. Put differently, organizational processes often display high levels of coherence, and when they do, replication may be difficult because it requires systematic changes throughout the organization and also among interorganizational linkages, which might be very hard to effectuate. Thus, partial imitation or replication of a successful model may yield zero benefits.[6]

---

[5] Fujimoto (1994, pp. 18–20) describes key elements as they existed in the Japanese auto industry as follows: "The typical volume production system of effective Japanese auto makers of the 1980s (e.g., Toyota) consists of various intertwined elements that might lead to competitive advantages. Just-in-Time (JIT), Jidoka (automatic defect detection and machine stop), Total Quality Control (TQC), and continuous improvement (Kaizen) are often pointed out as its core subsystems. The elements of such a system include inventory reduction mechanisms by Kanban system; levelization of production volume and product mix (heijunka); reduction of muda (non-value adding activities), mura (uneven pace of production), and muri (excessive workload); production plans based on dealers' order volume (genyo seisan); reduction of die set-up time and lot size in stamping operation; mixed model assembly; piece-by-piece transfer of parts between machines (ikko-nagashi); flexible task assignment for volume changes and productivity improvement (shojinka); multitask job assignment along the process flow (takotei-mochi); U-shape machine layout that facilitates flexible and multiple task assignment; on-the-spot inspection by direct workers (tsukurikomi); fool-proof prevention of defects (poka-yoke); real-time feedback of production troubles (andon); assembly line stop cord; emphasis on cleanliness, order, and discipline on the shop floor (5-S); frequent revision of standard operating procedures by supervisors; quality control circles; standardized tools for quality improvement (e.g., 7 tools for QC; QC story); worker improvement in preventive maintenance (Total Productive Maintenance); low-cost automation for semi-automation with just-enough functions); reduction of process steps for saving of tools and dies, and so on. The human resource management factors that back up these elements include stable employment of core workers (with temporary workers in the periphery); long-term training of multiskilled (multitask) workers; wage system based in part on skill accumulation; internal promotion to shop floor supervisors; cooperative relationships with labor unions; inclusion of production supervisors in union members; generally egalitarian policies for corporate welfare, communication, and worker motivation. Parts procurement policies are also pointed out often as a source of the competitive advantage; relatively high ratio of parts outsourcing; multilayer hierarchy of supplier; long-term relations with suppliers; relatively small number of technologically capable suppliers at the first tier; subassembly functions of the first-tier parts makers; detail-engineering capability of the first-tier makers (design-in, back box parts); competition based on long-term capability of design and improvements rather than bidding; pressures for continuous reduction of parts price; elimination of incoming parts inspection; plan inspection and technical assistance by auto makers, and so on."

[6] For a theoretical argument along these lines, see Milgrom and Roberts (1990).

The notion that there is a certain rationality or coherence to processes and systems is not quite the same concept as corporate culture. Corporate culture refers to the values and beliefs that employees hold; culture can be a de facto governance system, as it mediates the behavior of individuals and economizes on more formal administrative methods. Rationality or coherence notions are more akin to the Nelson and Winter (1982) notion of organizational routines. However, the routines concept is a little too amorphous to properly capture the congruence among processes and between processes and incentives.

Consider a professional service organization like an accounting firm. If it is to have relatively high-powered incentives that reward individual performance, then it must build organizational processes that channel individual behavior; if it has weak or low-powered incentives, it must find symbolic ways to recognize the high performers, and it must use alternative methods to build effort and enthusiasm. What one may think of as styles of organization in fact contain necessary, not discretionary, elements to achieve performance.

Recognizing the congruences and complementarities among processes, and between processes and incentives, is critical to the understanding of organizational capabilities. In particular, they can help us explain why architectural and radical innovations are so often introduced into an industry by new entrants. The incumbents develop distinctive organizational processes that cannot support the new technology, despite certain overt similarities between the old and the new. The frequent failure of incumbents to introduce new technologies can thus be seen as a consequence of the mismatch that so often exists between the organizational processes needed to support the conventional product/service and the requirements of the new. Radical organizational reengineering will usually be required to support the new product, which may well do better embedded in a separate subsidiary where a new set of coherent organization processes can be fashioned.[7]

Learning

Learning is perhaps even more important than routinization. The two concepts are obviously linked. Learning is a process by which

---

[7] See Abernathy and Clark (1985).

repetition and experimentation enable tasks to be performed better and quicker and new production opportunities to be identified.[8] In the context of the firm, if not more generally, learning has several key characteristics. First, learning involves organizational as well as individual skills.[9] While individual skills are relevant, their value depends on their employment in particular organizational settings. Learning processes are intrinsically social and collective and occur not only through the imitation and emulation of individuals, as with teacher-student or master-apprentice, but also because of joint contributions to the understanding of complex problems.[10] Learning requires common codes of communication and coordinated search procedures. Second, the organizational knowledge generated by such activity resides in new patterns of activity, in "routines," or a new logic of organization. As indicated earlier, routines are patterns of interactions that represent successful solutions to particular problems. These patterns of interaction are resident in group behavior, though certain subroutines may be resident in individual behavior. Collaborations and partnerships can be vehicles for new organizational learning, helping firms to recognize dysfunctional routines and preventing strategic blind spots.

Reconfiguration and Transformation
In rapidly changing environments, there is obviously value in the ability to sense the need to reconfigure the firm's asset structure, and to accomplish the necessary internal and external transformation (Amit and Schoemaker, 1992; Langlois, 1994). This requires constant surveillance of markets and technologies, the willingness to adopt best practice, and the ability to see things differently and act accordingly. The capacity to see things differently, then reconfigure and transform, is itself a learned organizational skill. The more frequently practiced, the easier it is accomplished.

Change is costly and so firms must develop processes to minimize low payoff change. The ability to calibrate the requirements for change and to effectuate the necessary adjustments would appear to depend on the ability to scan the environment, to eval-

---

[8] For a useful review and contribution, see Levitt and March (1988).
[9] See Mahoney (1995).
[10] There is a large literature on learning, although only a small fraction of it deals with organizational learning. Relevant contributors include Levitt and March (1988), Levinthal and March (1981) and Nelson and Winter (1982).

uate markets and competitors, and to quickly accomplish reconfiguration and transformation ahead of competition. Firms that have honed these capabilities are sometimes referred to as high-flex firms.

Positions

The competitive posture of a firm is determined not only by its learning processes, the excellence of its operations, but also by the coherence of its internal and external processes and incentives, its asset and market positions, and the regulatory and policy environment in which it is embedded. By assets, I mean its difficult-to-trade knowledge assets and assets complementary to them, as well as its reputational and intangible assets. These help determine its market share and profitability at any time.

Technological Assets

While there is an emerging market for know-how (Teece, 1981), much technology does not enter it. This is either because the firm is unwilling to sell it[11] or because of difficulties in transacting in the market for know-how (Teece, 1980). A firm's technological assets may or may not be protected by the standard instruments of intellectual property law. Either way, the ownership, protection, and utilization of technological assets are clearly key differentiators among firms. The same applies to complementary assets.

Complementary Assets

Technological innovations require the use of certain related assets to produce and deliver new products and services. Prior commercialization activities require and enable firms to build such complementarities (Teece, 1986). Such capabilities and assets, while necessary for the firm's established activities, may have other uses as well. Such assets typically lie downstream. New products and processes either can enhance or destroy the value of such assets (Tushman, Newman, and Romanelli, 1986). Thus the development of computers enhanced the value of IBM's direct sales force in office products, while disk brakes rendered useless much of the auto industry's investment in drum brakes.

[11] Managers often evoke the "crown jewels" metaphor. That is, if the technology is released, the kingdom will be lost.

Financial Assets
In the short run, a firm's cash position and degree of leverage may have strategic implications. While there is nothing more fungible than cash, it cannot always be raised from external markets without the dissemination of considerable information to potential investors. Accordingly, what a firm can do in short order is often a function of its balance sheet. In the longer run, that ought not be so, as cash flow and the ability to raise capital will be more determinative.

Locational Assets
The legal, regulatory, and policy environment matters too. Uniqueness in certain businesses can stem from the institutional or "home base" environment. This may not be fully "tradable" or accessible to outsiders, since governments routinely favor domestic enterprise. More important, however, is whether the government makes credible commitments. Absent an environment for confident contracting, investment incentives will be inadequate.

Paths

Path Dependencies
The notion of path dependencies recognizes that "history matters." Bygones are rarely bygones, despite the predictions of rational actor theory. Thus a firm's previous investments and its repertoire of routines (its history) constrain its future behavior.[12] This follows because learning tends to be local. That is, opportunities for learning will lie in the neighborhood of what is already familiar, and thus will be transaction and production specific (Teece, 1988). This is because learning is often a process of trial, feedback, and evaluation. If too much is changing at once, the ability of firms to learn by conducting meaningful natural quasi-experiments is attenuated. Put differently, if many aspects of a firm's learning environment change simultaneously, the ability to ascertain cause-effect relationship is confounded because cognitive structures will not be formed, and rates of learning will diminish as a result.

---

[12] For further development, see Teece, Bercovitz, and de Figueiredo (1997).

The importance of path dependencies is amplified where conditions of increasing returns to adoption exist. This is a demand-side phenomenon, and it tends to make technologies and products embodying those technologies more attractive the more they are adopted. Attractiveness flows from the greater adoption of the product among users, which in turn enables them to become more developed and hence more useful. Increasing returns to adoption has many sources, including network externalities (Katz and Shapiro, 1985), the presence of complementary assets (Teece, 1986) and supporting infrastructure, learning by using, and scale economies in production and distribution. Competition between and among technologies is shaped by increasing returns. Early leads won by good luck or special circumstances can become amplified by increasing returns. This is not to suggest that first movers necessarily win. Because increasing returns have multiple sources, the prior positioning of firms can affect their capacity to exploit increasing returns. Thus, in Mitchell's (1989) study of medical diagnostic imaging, firms already controlling the relevant complementary assets could in theory start last and finish first.

In the presence of increasing returns, firms can compete passively, or they may compete strategically through technology-sponsoring activities.[13] The first type of competition is not unlike biological competition among species, although it can be sharpened by managerial activities that enhance the performance of products and processes. The reality is that companies with the best products will not always win, as chance events may cause "lock-in" on inferior technologies (Arthur, 1988) and may generate switching costs for consumers. However, while switching costs may favor the incumbent, in regimes of rapid technological change, switching costs can become quickly swamped by switching benefits. Put differently, new products employing different standards often appear suddenly in market environments experiencing rapid technological change.

---

[13] Because of huge uncertainties, it may be extremely difficult to determine viable strategies early on. Since the rules of the game and the identity of the players will be revealed only after the market has begun to evolve, the payoff is likely to lie with building and maintaining organizational capabilities that support flexibility. For example, Microsoft's recent about-face and vigorous pursuit of Internet business once the Netscape phenomenon became apparent is impressive, not so much because it perceived the need to change strategy, but because of its organizational capacity to effectuate a strategic shift.

Technological Opportunities

The concept of path dependencies is given forward meaning through the consideration of an industry's technological opportunities. It is well recognized that how far and how fast a particular area of industrial activity can proceed is in part due to the technological opportunities that lie before it. Such opportunities are usually a lagged function of the amount of forment and diversity in basic science, and the rapidity with which new scientific breakthroughs are being made.

However, technological opportunities may not be completely exogenous to industry. This is not only because some firms have the capacity to engage in or at least support fundamental research, but also because technological opportunities are often fed by innovative activity itself. Moreover, the recognition of such opportunities is affected by the organizational structures that link the institutions engaging in fundamental research (primarily the universities) to the business enterprise. Hence, the existence of technological opportunities can be quite firm specific.

Important for our purposes is the rate and direction in which relevant scientific frontiers are being advanced. Firms engaging in research and development (R&D) may find the path dead ahead closed off, though breakthroughs in related areas may be sufficiently close to be attractive. Likewise, if the path dead ahead is extremely attractive, there may be no incentive for firms to shift the allocation of resources away from traditional pursuits. The depth and width of technological opportunities in the neighborhood of a firm's prior research activities thus are likely to impact a firm's options with respect to both the amount and level of R&D activity that it can justify. In addition, a firm's past experience conditions the alternatives management is able to perceive. Thus, not only do firms in the same industry face "menus" with different costs associated with particular technological choices, but they also are looking at menus containing different choices.[14]

Assessment

The assessment of a firm's competitive advantage and strategic capability is presented here as a function of the firm's processes,

---

[14] This is a critical element in Nelson and Winter's (1982) view of firms and technical change.

positions, and paths.[15] What a firm can do and where it can go are thus heavily constrained by the topography of its processes, positions, and paths. I submit that if one can identify a firm's processes, positions, and paths and understand their interrelationships, one can at least predict the performance of the firm under various assumptions about changes in the external environment. One can also evaluate the richness of the menu of new opportunities from which the firm may select, and its likely performance in a changing environment.

The parameters I have identified for determining performance are quite different from those in the standard textbook theory of the firm, and in the competitive forces and strategic conflict approaches to the firm and to strategy.[16] Moreover, the agency theoretic view of the firm as a nexus of contracts would put no weight on processes, positions, and paths. While agency approaches to the firm may acknowledge that opportunism and shirking may limit what a firm can do, they do not recognize the opportunities and constraints imposed by processes, positions, and paths. Moreover, the firm is much more than the sum of its parts (or a team tied together by contracts).[17] Indeed, to some extent individuals can be moved in and out of organizations and, so long as the internal processes and structures remain in place, performance will not necessarily be impaired. A shift in the environment is a far more serious threat to the firm than is the loss of key individuals, as individuals can be replaced more readily than organizations can be transformed. Furthermore, the dynamic capabilities view of the firm would suggest that the behavior and performance of a particular firm may be quite hard to replicate, even if its coherence and rationality are observable. This matter and related issues involving replication and imitation are taken up in the section that follows.

---

[15] I also recognize that the processes, positions, and paths of customers also matter. See the earlier discussion on increasing returns, including customer learning and network externalities.

[16] In both, the firm is still largely a black box. Certainly, little or no attention is given to processes, positions, and paths.

[17] See Alchian and Demsetz (1972).

Replicability and Imitability of Organizational Processes and Positions

Thus far, I have argued that the competences and capabilities (and hence competitive advantage) of a firm rest fundamentally on processes, positions, and paths. However, competences can provide competitive advantage and generate superior profits only if they are based on a collection of routines, skills, and complementary assets that are difficult to imitate.[18] A particular set of routines can lose their value if they support a competence that no longer matters in the marketplace, or if they can be readily replicated or emulated by competitors. Imitation occurs when firms discover and simply copy another firm's organizational routines and procedures. Emulation occurs when firms discover alternative ways of achieving the same functionality. There is ample evidence that a given type of competence (e.g., quality) can be supported by different routines and combinations of skills. For example, the Garvin (1988) and Clark and Fujimoto (1991) studies both indicate that there is no one "formula" for achieving either high quality or high product development performance.

Replication
Replication involves transferring or redeploying competences from one concrete economic setting to another. Since productive knowledge is embodied, this cannot be accomplished by simply transmitting information. Only in those instances where all relevant knowledge is fully codified and understood can replication be collapsed into a simple problem of information transfer. Too often, the contextual dependence of original performance is poorly appreciated, so unless firms have replicated their systems of productive knowledge on many prior occasions, the acts of replication and transfer are often impossible absent the transfer of people, though this can be minimized if investments are made to convert tacit knowledge to codified knowledge. Often, however, this is simply not possible.

In short, organizational capabilities, and the routines upon

---

[18] I call such competences distinctive. See also Dierickx and Cook (1989) for a discussion of the characteristics of assets that made them a source of rents.

which they rest, are normally rather difficult to replicate.[19] This constrains the ability of firms to grow. Even understanding what all the relevant routines are that support a particular competence may not be transparent. Indeed, Lippman and Rumelt (1992) have argued that some sources of competitive advantage are so complex that the firm itself, let alone its competitors, does not understand them.[20] As Nelson and Winter (1982) and Teece (1982) have explained, many organizational routines are quite tacit in nature. Imitation can also be hindered by the fact that few routines are "stand-alone"; coherence may demand that a change in one set of routines in one part of the firm (e.g., production) requires changes in some other part (e.g., sales).

Some routines and competences seem to be attributable to local or regional forces that shape firms' capabilities at early stages in their lives. Porter (1990), for example, shows that differences in local product markets, local factor markets, and institutions play an important role in shaping competitive capabilities. Differences also exist within populations of firms from the same country. Various studies of the automobile industry, for example, show that not all Japanese automobile companies are top performers in terms of quality, productivity, or product development (see, for example, Clark and Fujimoto, 1991). The role of firm-specific history has been highlighted as a critical factor explaining such firm-level (as opposed to regional or national-level) differences (Nelson and Winter, 1982). Replication in a different context may thus be rather difficult.

At least two types of strategic value flow from replication. One is the ability to support geographic and product line expansion. To the extent that the capabilities in question are relevant to customer needs elsewhere, replication can confer value.[21] Another is that the ability to replicate also indicates that the firm has the foundations in place for learning and improvement. Considerable

---

[19] See Szulanski's (1993) discussion of the intrafirm transfer of best practice. He quotes a senior vice president of Xerox as saying "You can see a high performance factory or office, but it just doesn't spread. I don't know why." Szulanski also discusses the role of benchmarking in facilitating the transfer of best practice.

[20] If so, it is my belief that the firm's advantage is likely to fade, as luck does run out.

[21] Needless to say, there are many examples of firms replicating their capabilities inappropriately by applying extant routines to circumstances where they may not be applicable, such as Nestle's transfer of developed-country marketing methods for infant formula to the Third World (Hartley, 1989). A key strategic need is for firms to screen capabilities for their applicability to new environments.

empirical evidence supports the notion that the understanding of processes, both in production and in management, is the key to process improvement. In short, an organization cannot improve what it does not understand. Deep process understanding is often required to accomplish codification. Indeed, if knowledge is highly tacit, it indicates that underlying structures are not well understood, which limits learning because scientific and engineering principles cannot be as systematically applied.[22] Instead, learning is confined to proceeding through trial and error, and the leverage that might otherwise come from the application of scientific theory is denied.

Imitation

Imitation is simply replication performed by a competitor. If self-replication is difficult, imitation is likely to be even harder. In competitive markets, it is the ease of imitation that determines the sustainability of competitive advantage. Easy imitation implies the rapid dissipation of the innovator's superior profits.

Factors that make replication difficult also make imitation difficult. Thus, the more tacit the firm's productive knowledge, the harder it is to replicate by the firm itself or its competitors. When the tacit component is high, imitation may well be impossible, absent the hiring away of key individuals and the transfer of key organization processes.

However, another set of barriers impedes imitation of certain capabilities in advanced industrial countries. This is the system of intellectual property rights, such as patents, trade secrets, and trademarks, and even trade dress.[23] Intellectual property protection is of increasing importance in the United States, as the courts, since 1982, have adopted a more pro-patent posture. Similar trends are evident outside the United States. Besides the patent system, several other factors cause a difference between replication costs and imitation costs. The observability of the technology or the organization is one such important factor. Whereas vistas

---

[22] Different approaches to learning are required depending on the depth of knowledge. Where knowledge is less articulated and structured, trial and error and learning-by-doing are necessary, whereas in mature environments where the underlying engineering science is better understood, organizations can undertake more deductive approaches or what Pisano (1994) refers to as "learning-before-doing."

[23] Trade dress refers to the "look and feel" of a retail establishment – for example, the distinctive marketing and presentation style of The Nature Company.

into product technology can be obtained through strategies such as reverse engineering, this is not the case for process technology, as a firm need not expose its process technology to the outside in order to benefit from it.[24] Firms without product technology, on the other hand, confront the unfortunate circumstances that they must expose what they have in order to profit from the technology. Secrets are thus more protectable if there is no need to expose them in contexts where competitors can learn about them.

One should not, however, overestimate the importance of intellectual property protection; yet it presents a formidable imitation barrier in certain particular contexts. Intellectual property protection is not uniform across products, processes, and technologies, and is best thought of as "islands" in a sea of open competition. If one is not able to place the fruits of one's investment, ingenuity, or creativity on one or more of the islands, then one indeed is at sea.

I use the term *appropriability regimes* to describe the ease of imitation. Appropriability is a function both of the ease of replication and the efficacy of intellectual property rights as a barrier to imitation. Appropriability is strong when a technology is both inherently difficult to replicate and the intellectual property system provides legal barriers to imitate. When it is inherently easy to replicate, and intellectual property protection is either unavailable or ineffectual, then appropriability is weak. Intermediate conditions also exist.

IMPLICATIONS

When firms do not have cost advantages stemming from privileged positions in "input" or "factor" markets, they must compete through innovation. The development of proprietary and difficult-to-imitate technology thus becomes increasingly important to competitive advantage.

The knowledge assets of the firms consist of high-performance business processes/routines (organizational assets) and techno-

---

[24] An interesting but important exception to this can be found in second sourcing. In the microprocessor business, until the introduction of the 386 chip, Intel and most other merchant semiproducers were encouraged by larger customers like IBM to provide second sources – that is, to license and share their proprietary process technology with competitors like AMD and NEC. The microprocessor developers did so to assure customers that they had sufficient manufacturing capability to meet demand at all times.

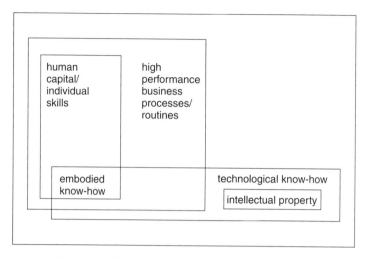

Figure 4.1. The firm's industrial knowledge assets.

logical know-how (Figure 4.1). The ability of the firm to combine and recombine, engineer and reengineer itself is critical to success. A simplified representation showing the centrality of such dynamic capabilities is contained in Figure 4.2. This shows that the firm's knowledge assets are of limited value, absent control of or access to the relevant complementary assets and complementary technologies. Hence, one must include the firm's complementary assets and its alliance structures as an integral part of the value creation capabilities of firms.[25]

The scarcity of firm-specific idiosyncratic assets and the complexity of integration and coordination processes constrains the growth of firms. Even simple replication of routines requires support from the firm's existing stocks of idiosyncratic human assets. Nor is it just managerial resources that are likely to be constraining (à la Edith Penrose); technical resources are also major constraints. Activities may be scalable in principle, but what can be accomplished in any one period is very much a function of what was in place in the prior period. The supporting infrastructure in the economy at large also matters, because this is likely to affect

---

[25] This is not to imply that all alliances add value, or that all assets inside the firm add value. For further discussion, see Chesbrough and Teece (1996).

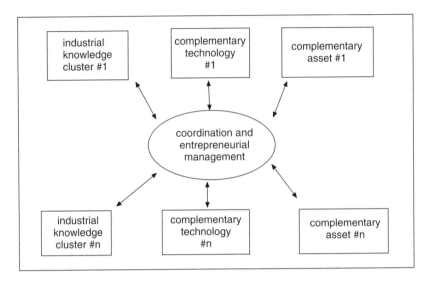

Figure 4.2. The business firm: Elements of dynamic capabilities.

the supply of appropriately educated and trained indigenous managerial and technological human resources. Indeed, the growth of firms is closely coupled to the availability in factor markets of trained personnel, indigenous or foreign.

The organization of this framework around processes, positions, and paths is hopefully instructive in some ways. The framework stresses the role of organization and management (processes) while suggesting that positioning can be undone (i.e., with original equipment manufacture, or OEM, contracts), and paths need not always disadvantage the latecomer inordinately. In laying out this framework, much has undoubtedly been overlooked. In particular, the framework is silent with respect to institutional context. However, if both product and intermediate markets are open, certain aspects of the institutional environment become a common factor and can lead to at least some similarity in firm growth and development in different country contexts. This possibility is employed in this chapter. Firm-level work on competency and capabilities in developed countries is put forward to assist the understanding of economic development in newly industrializing economies (NIEs).

RELEVANCE TO NIES

The experience of firms in NIEs, and the development process more generally, can be brought into sharper focus through the employment of the concepts outlined above. While the *positions* of firms in NIEs may not initially be advantageous, firms in NIEs can catch up by being better at *processes*, and by astutely selecting and following desirable *paths*. There are at least two structural features of advanced economies, particularly that of the United States, which facilitate catch-up by NIEs.

One is the presence of relatively open intermediate product markets. Thus firms in NIEs, although they may lack certain complementary assets needed for full scale success (i.e., distribution), can access these complementary assets through contractual relationships. In particular, the "OEM system" described by Michael Hobday (1997) and in Chapter 5 of this volume is simply a manifestation of how certain firms in NIEs have accessed complementary assets abroad and thereby shared to some degree in the benefits of innovation originating elsewhere.

The second feature is the relative openness of the international market for know-how. Firms in developed countries are willing to sell/license their know-how, often for modest fees relative to the original development costs. Coupled with (and encouraged by) the relative ease of imitation of product technology (facilitated by reverse engineering), the result is that technology developed elsewhere can in fact be readily accessed, if firms make the commitment to acquire it and establish the managerial processes to facilitate the absorption and integration of technical and industrial knowledge inside the firms.

Put differently, the disadvantages associated with poor market and asset positions can be readily overcome if there is the organizational commitment to do so, and the allocation of resources is made (relatively modest) to license-in technology. This leaves processes and paths as the differentiator. With respect to processes, many firms in advanced countries have demonstrated little in the way of special acumen in this area, enabling firms in NIEs to quickly draw even and possibly overtake them. With respect to paths, firms have some choice, but industry dynamics are likely to influence outcomes powerfully. The ability of firms in NIEs to cooperate on standards and strategies might well enable them to overcome the disadvantages of being the latecomer. In some instances, the latecomer may in fact have an advantage if new, more attractive evolutionary paths have been revealed.

Finally, the ability of firms to quickly configure and reconfigure is important to success in industries experiencing rapid change. The newcomer is less likely to be shackled by incumbency factors, such as the reluctance to cannibalize one's own products with new products. Innovation studies in developed countries reveal that the newcomers overturn the existing order with greater frequency than do other incumbents (Utterback, 1994). Looked at from the perspective of NIEs, firms located there will simply not be the incumbents in the global market. Rather, they are the challengers, bereft of the decision-making biases likely to burden firms with established market positions. Put differently, firms in NIEs have some of the same benefits as new entrants in developed countries, although their subsequent success might well lead to the same complacency.

CONCLUSION

In this chapter I have looked at basic properties of the firm with an eye toward the implications for economic development. I suggest that firms are the "engines" of economic development. Successful knowledge accumulation and the orchestration of complementary assets and technologies within a legal-political-financial and social system, enabling credible commitments and wealth accumulation, are at the heart of the process of economic development. To understand economic development, one must therefore understand the developmental processes inside firms. If firms are indeed the instruments of development, the study of economic development cannot take place separate from the study of the theory of the growth of the firm.

REFERENCES

Abernathy, W. J., and K. Clark. 1985. "Innovation: Mapping the Winds of Creative Destruction." *Research Policy*, 14, 3–22.

Alchian, A. A., and H. Demsetz. 1972. "Production, Information Costs, and Economic Organization." *American Economic Review*, 62, 777–795.

Amit, R., and P. Schoemaker. 1990. "Key Success Factors: Their Foundation and Application." University of British Columbia and University of Chicago. Working paper.

Aoki, M. 1990. "The Participatory Generation of Information Rents and the Theory of the Firm." In M. Aoki et al. (eds.), *The Firm as a Nexus of Treaties*. London: Sage.

Arthur, W. B. 1998. "Competing Technologies: An Overview." In G. Dosi et al. (eds.), *Technical Change and Economic Theory*. London: Pinter, 115–135.

Barnard, C. 1938. *The Functions of the Executive*. Cambridge, MA: Harvard University Press.

Barney, J. B., J. C. Spender, and T. Reve. 1994. *Crafoord Lectures*, Vol. 6. Bromley, U.K.: Chartwell-Bratt, and Lund, Sweden: Lund University Press.

Chesbrough, H. W., and D. J. Teece. 1996. "When Is Virtual Virtuous? Organizing for Innovation." *Harvard Business Review*, January–February, 65–73. Republished in J. S. Brown (ed.), *Seeing Things Differently: Insights on Innovation*, Cambridge, MA: Harvard Business School Press, 1997, 105–119.

Clark, K., and T. Fujimoto. 1991. *Product Development Per-formance: Strategy, Organization and Management in the World Auto Industries*. Cambridge, MA: Harvard Business School Press.

Coase, R. 1937. "The Nature of the Firm." *Economica*, 4, 386–405.

Coase, R. 1988. "Lecture on the Nature of the Firm, III." *Journal of Law, Economics and Organization*, 4, 33–47.

Dierickx, I., and K. Cook. 1989. "Asset Stock Accumulation and Sustainability of Competitive Advantage." *Management Science*, 35(12), 1504–1511.

Dodgson, M., and Y. S. Kim. 1997. "Learning to Innovate Korean Style: The Case of Samsung International." *Journal of Innovation Management*, 1(1), 53–71.

Domar, E. 1947. "Expansion and Employment." *American Economic Review*, March.

Freeman, J., and W. Boeker. 1984. "The Ecological Analysis of Business Strategy." In G. Carroll, and D. Vogel (eds.), *Strategy and Organization*. Boston, MA: Pitman, 64–77.

Fujimoto, T. 1994. "Reinterpreting the Resource-Capability View of the Firm: A Case of the Development-Production Systems of the Japanese Automakers." Faculty of Economics, University of Tokyo, draft working paper.

Garvin, D. 1988. *Managing Quality*. New York: Free Press.

Garvin, D. 1994. "The Processes of Organization and Management." Harvard Business School Working Paper #94–084.

Ghemawat, P. 1966. *Commitment: The Dynamics of Strategy*. New York: Free Press.

Harrod, R. F. 1939. "An Essay in Dynamic Theory." *Economic Journal*, March.

Hartley, R. F. 1989. *Marketing Mistakes*. New York: Wiley.

Hayes, R., and K. Clark. 1985. "Exploring the Sources of Productivity Differences at the Factory Level." In K. Clark, R. H. Hayes, and C. Lorenz (eds.), *The Uneasy Alliance: Managing the Productivity Technology Dilemma*. Boston, MA: Harvard Business School Press, 151–188.

Henderson, R. M., and K. B. Clark. 1990. "Architectural Innovation: The Reconfiguration of Existing Product Technologies and the Failure of Established Firms," *Administrative Science Quarterly*, 35, March, 9–30.

Henderson, R. M., and I. Cockburn. (eds.), "Measuring Core Competences." Massachusetts Institute of Technology working paper.

Hobday, M. 1997. *Innovation in East Asia: The Challenge to Japan*. United Kingdom: Edward Elgar.

Isansiti, M., and K. B. Clark. 1994. "Integration and Dynamic Capability: Evidence from Product Development in Automobiles and Mainframe Computers." *Industrial and Corporate Change*, 3(3), 557–605.

Kim, L. 1993. "National System of Industrial Innovation: Dynamics of Capability Building in Korea." In R. R. Nelson (ed.), *National Innovation Systems: A Comparative Analysis*. New York: Oxford University Press, Chap. 11.

Kuznets, S. 1966. *Modern Economic Growth: Rate, Structure and Spread*. New Haven, CT: Yale University Press.

Langlois, R. 1994. "Cognition and Capabilities: Opportunities Seized and Missed in the History of the Computer Industry." University of Connecticut, working paper presented at the conference on Technological Oversights and Foresights, Stern School of Business, New York University, March 11–12, 1994.

Levitt, B., and J. March. 1988. "Organizational Learning." *Annual Review of Sociology*, 14, 319–340.

Lewis, W. A. 1954. "Economic Development with Unlimited Supplies of Labor." The Manchester School, May.

Lippman, S. A., and R. P. Rumelt. 1992. "Demand Uncertainty and Investment in Industry-Specific Capital." *Industry and Corporate Change*, 1(1), 235–262.

Mahoney, J. 1995. "The Management of Resources and the Resources of Management." *Journal of Business Research*, 33(2), 91–101.

Meier, G. 1990. *International Economics*. New York: Oxford University Press.

Milgrom, P., and J. Roberts. 1990. "The Economics of Modern Manufacturing: Technology, Strategy, and Organization." *American Economic Review*, 80(3), 511–528.

Mitchell, W. 1989. "Whether and When? Probability and Timing of Incumbents' Entry into Emerging Industrial Subfields." *Administrative Science Quarterly*, 34, 208–230.

Nelson, R., and S. Winter. 1982. *An Evolutionary Theory of Economic Change*. Cambridge, MA: Harvard University Press.

North and Douglas. 1990. *Institutions, Institutional Change and Economic Performance*. New York: Cambridge University Press.

Pisano, G. 1994. "Knowledge Integration and the Locus for Learning: An Empirical Analysis of Process Development." *Strategic Management Journal*, 15, Winter Special Issue, 85–100.

Porter, M. E. 1990. *The Competitive Advantage of Nations*. New York: Free Press.

Rostow, W. W. 1956. "The Take-off into Self Sustained Growth." *Economic Journal*, March, 29–30.

Rostow, W. W. 1959. "The Stages of Economic Growth." *Economic History Review*, August, 1–17.

Shuen, A. 1994. "Technology Sourcing and Learning Strategies in the Semiconductor Industry" Unpublished Ph.D. dissertation, University of California, Berkeley.

Szulanski, G. 1993. "Intrafirm Transfer of Best Practice, Appropriate Capabilities, Organizational Barriers to Appropriation." Working paper, INSEAD.

Teece, D. J. 1980. "Economics of Scope and the Scope of an Enterprise." *Journal of Economic Behavior and Organization*, 1, 223–247.

Teece, D. J. 1981. "The Market for Know-How and the Efficient International Transfer of Technology." *The Annals of the Academy of Political and Social Science*, November 1981, 81–96.

Teece, D. J. 1982. "Towards an Economic Theory of the Multiproduct Firm." *Journal of Economic Behavior and Organization*, 3, 39–62.

Teece, D. J. 1986. "Profiting from Technological Innovation." *Research Policy*, 15(6), December, 285–305.

Teece, D. J. 1988. "Technological Change and the Nature of the Firm." In G. Dosi, et al. (eds.), *Technical Change and Economic Theory*. London: Pinter, 256–330.

Teece, D. J. 1993. "The Dynamics of Industrial Capitalism: Perspectives on Alfred Chandler's Scale and Scope (1990)." *Journal of Economic Literature*, 31, March, 199–225.

Teece, D. J., J. E. Bercovitz, and J. M. de Figueiredo. 1997. "Firm Capabilities and Managerial Decision-Making: A Theory of Innovation Biases." In R. Garud, P. Nayyar, and Z. Shapira (eds.), *Technological Innovation: Oversights and Foresights*. Cambridge: Cambridge University Press, 233–259.

Teece, D. J., G. Pisano, and A. Shuen. 1997. "Dynamic Capabilities and Strategic Management." *Strategic Management Journal*, 18(7), 509–533.

Tushman, M. L., W. H. Newman, and E. Romanelli. 1986. "Convergence and Upheaval: Managing the Unsteady Pace of Organizational Evolution." *California Management Review*, 29(1), Fall, 29–44.

Utterback, J. 1994. *Mastering the Dynamics of Innovation*. Boston, MA: Harvard Business School Press.

Williamson, O. E. 1996. *The Mechanisms of Governance*. New York: Oxford University Press.

Womack, J., D. Jones, and D. Roos. 1991. *The Machine that Changed the World*. New York: Harper-Perennial.

CHAPTER 5

East versus Southeast Asian Innovation Systems: Comparing OEM- and TNC-led Growth in Electronics

Michael Hobday

INTRODUCTION

Despite the continuing shift of world manufacturing to the newly industrializing economies (NIEs) of East and Southeast Asia (Wood, 1994; Abegglen, 1994), there is little understanding of the extent of innovation in the NIEs, or its role in the process of economic growth.[1] The countries of East Asia (e.g., South Korea and Taiwan) and Southeast Asia (e.g., Singapore, Malaysia, and Thailand) until the recent crisis were among the fastest growing economies for two decades.[2] While Taiwan and South Korea have relied on locally owned firms for their export-led industrial growth, Southeast Asia has depended largely on transnational corporations (TNCs).[3] Through the 1980s and into the 1990s, electronics has remained the largest export sector in the NIEs.

The export progress of the East Asian NIEs presents many fundamental development questions. How did local firms, with little previous experience in electronics, manage to become highly

---

[1] See the section in this chapter on perspectives on innovation for important exceptions. The chapter uses the term *innovation* mainly to refer to technological innovation. However, managerial and organizational innovations are also important. The term *NIE* refers to the fast growingeast and Southeast Asian economies (the southeast coastal region of China could also be included).

[2] For example, the Malaysian economy grew at 6.7 percent per annum over the period 1971–1990 (manufacturing at 10.3 percent). During the early 1990s, Malaysia's economic growth rose to over 8 percent per annum and manufacturing exceeded 12 percent (Lall, 1994, p. 2). Growth in 1994 and 1995 was just under 9 percent. As with each of the other NIEs, electronics exports played a major part in overall growth performance.

[3] In electronics, the contribution of TNCs to Korean and Taiwanese growth tailed off during the 1970s as local firms grew in competence. Note that Korea and South Korea are used interchangeably (as shorthand for the Republic of Korea).

successful international competitors? How did "latecomer" firms, located outside the world centers of innovation (mostly the United States and Japan), acquire the necessary technology to catch up? Likewise, the progress of Southeast Asia raises equally challenging questions. What was the role of innovation, if any, in the industrial success of the TNC exporters in Singapore, Malaysia, and Thailand? Similarly, what would induce or discourage foreign TNCs to transfer skills and technology to subsidiaries from headquarters locations?

Focusing on electronics, the aim of this chapter is to compare the paths and patterns of technological innovation in the two groups of countries and to identify the factors that underpin technological progress and export success. The chapter focuses on *how* catch-up occurred rather than the underlying investment or policy causes.[4] The method used is to compare two of the chief institutional mechanisms for electronics export: the OEM (original equipment manufacture) system prevalent in East Asia and the TNC-led growth of Southeast Asia.[5] The hope is to cast some light on the strengths and weaknesses of the various strategies for development and to assess the paths and patterns against conventional innovation wisdom.

The chapter is structured as follows. The first section briefly presents analytical perspectives on innovation and development. The next three sections describe the OEM system and how it operates in South Korea with Taiwan. Then there is a discussion on TNC-led development, focusing on Malaysia, followed by a comparison of OEM with TNC-led growth, contrasting the processes of inno-

---

[4] It is outside the scope of the chapter to attempt to assess or measure the contribution of technological change to economic growth. However, the writer assumes that technological acquisition and learning have played an important part in the catch-up growth of the NIEs at firm, sector, and national level and is therefore worthy of investigation. Although there are major disputes over the story told by the macro-economic data, there is abundant empirical evidence at the firm and product level to show that the NIEs have managed to close some of the technology gap with the advanced countries (and in some cases to overtake their competitors in the United States, Europe, and Japan). For a factor input/capital accumulation view of East Asian growth, see Young (1994, 1995) and Krugman (1994). For criticisms of the latter, see Nelson and Pack (1995), Cappelen and Fagerberg (1995), Singh (1995), Felipe (1998), and Filipe and McCombie (1998).

[5] Although TNC-led growth occurred in the early stages of South Korean growth and remains important in Taiwan the predominant mode of development has been locally owned (or latecomer) firms, especially during the 1980s and 1990s. Similarly, although local firm OEM occurs in Malaysia and Singapore, TNC activities overwhelmingly dominate in terms of industrial ownership and export sales.

vation witnessed in the NIEs with conventional "Western" innovation models. Finally, the conclusion summarizes the main findings and comments on future challenges and opportunities for the NIEs.

There is good reason for focusing on electronics (defined here to include goods, systems, subsystems, components, and electrical appliances). It is the fastest growing export industry in the NIEs and the rate of technological change has been consistently high, presenting barriers as well as opportunities for entry. As the chapter shows, despite major differences in corporate ownership, size, and strategy, each country has enjoyed a remarkable degree of success. In the future, electronics exports may well play an important role in overcoming current problems of recession and economic crisis.

PERSPECTIVES ON INNOVATION AND DEVELOPMENT

Although the strict definition of an innovation is the successful introduction of a new or improved product (or process) to the marketplace (Dorfman, 1987, p. 4; SPRU, 1972, p. 7; Kamien and Schwartz, 1982, p. 2), this approach fails to capture very important transformations that occur in firms in developing countries (and elsewhere). Many innovations occur from behind the technology frontier defined by leaders in the advanced countries. Therefore, following Nelson and Rosenberg (1993), Kim (1997), and many others (e.g., Myers and Marquis, 1969; Schmookler, 1966; and Gerstenfeld and Wortzel, 1977), this chapter defines innovation as a product or process new to the firm rather than to the world or marketplace. Many firms have grown and succeeded as a result of innovations new to the company, although not new to the world.

Innovation should be seen as a long-term *process*, rather than a once-and-for-all event. Also, nontechnological innovation, especially managerial and organizational improvements, are crucial for exploiting technology and enhancing competitiveness (Garvin, 1993; Stata, 1989; Senge, 1990; Kim, 1995). Although this chapter focuses mainly on technological innovation, it also points to important organizational innovations in the NIEs.

There is now a rich body of literature examining the processes of technological evolution at the economic, industrial, and policy levels (Nelson and Winter 1982; Kim, 1980; Kim and Dahlman,

1992; Lall, 1982, 1992; Dahlman et al., 1985; Westphal and Dahlman, 1985; Fransman and King, 1984). Several studies analyze NIE policies for industrialization, mostly focusing on single countries (e.g., Wade, 1990, for Taiwan; Amsden, 1989, for South Korea), while other work on the NIEs examines general economic conditions for successful growth (Riedel, 1988; World Bank, 1993; Hughes, 1988).[6] Until recently, the subject of firm-level innovation in the East Asian NIEs has received relatively little attention. However, there are now a few studies on how Korean and Taiwanese firms innovate (Kim, 1995, 1997; Choi, 1994; Kim and Kim, 1989; Schive, 1990; Shieh, 1992).

With respect to Southeast Asia, when the issue is raised, TNC subsidiaries tend to be criticized as "screwdriver" plants for exploiting low cost labor. However, some research on TNC subsidiaries in developed countries points to the importance of subsidiaries for enhancing competitiveness (Bartlett and Ghoshal, 1987a, 1987b). A few studies deal with the role of technology in Malaysian industrialization, focusing on interfirm linkages (Kam, 1992; Rasiah, 1994), the progress of electronics (Kassim and Salleh, 1993; O'Connor, 1993; UNDP, 1993), and foreign technology transfer (Guyton, 1994; Capannelli, 1994).

Overall, there is little knowledge of the innovation activities of TNC subsidiaries or how the rapid growth in electronics was achieved in East and Southeast Asia. Indeed, according to traditional innovation study (Utterback and Abernathy, 1975), TNC product life cycle theory (Vernon, 1966, 1975) and TNC location theory (Dunning, 1975), and theories of industrial clustering (Porter, 1990), innovation is not "supposed" to occur in the developing countries, let alone among TNC subsidiaries. Conventional wisdom holds that the advanced countries are the source of most research and development (R&D) and the technology pull of highly advanced markets (Porter, 1990).[7] The case of the NIEs is therefore a challenging one for conventional theory.

[6] Earlier studies of TNCs show the importance of international product life cycles (Vernon, 1966, 1975) and the determinants of the location of production (Dunning, 1975). However, these studies were mainly concerned with top-down corporate location decisions, rather than the actions of local subsidiaries in building innovative capacity and influencing investment location.

[7] The same sorts of arguments can be applied to locally owned Korean and Taiwanese firms, largely dislocated from the pull of advanced markets and sources of R&D.

INNOVATION IN THE OEM SYSTEM

Latecomer firms[8] from Asia faced at least two important competitive disadvantages: first, their dislocation from the major international sources of innovation and R&D; and second, their distance from advanced markets and the user-producer links essential to innovation (Von Hippel, 1988; Lundvall, 1988). A variety of institutional channels were used to overcome these barriers to entry and enable technological learning to occur including licensing, foreign direct investment (FDI), joint ventures, subcontracting, buyer activities, overseas training and education, hiring, foreign acquisitions, and joint ventures.[9]

One of the chief institutional mechanisms in electronics was the OEM system. OEM is a specific form of subcontracting that evolved out of the joint operations of TNC buyers and NIE suppliers. Under OEM, the finished product is made to the precise specification of a particular buyer (or TNC) who then markets the product under its own brand name, through its own distribution channels.

OEM takes a variety of forms and has evolved considerably since the 1960s. It was especially significant in consumer electronics, computing, peripherals, and electrical appliances (e.g., microwave ovens).[10] In Taiwan and South Korea, OEM accounted for a significant share of electronics exports during the 1970s, 1980s, and 1990s. The term OEM began to be used in the 1950s by U.S. computer makers who used East Asian suppliers to produce equipment for them. It was later adopted by U.S. TNCs in the 1960s, which used local firms to assemble and test semiconductors. Today, the term has acquired a variety of meanings (some use OEM to refer to the local supplier). To avoid confusion, in this chapter, the term OEM refers to the subcontracting system in which firms cooperate, rather than to the buyer or supplier of equipment.

---

[8] Hobday (1995) develops the idea of the latecomer firm, contrasting it with "leader" and "follower."

[9] It is beyond the scope of this chapter to compare these different channels. Dahlman and Sananikone (1990) provide an analysis for the case of Taiwan. Schive (1990) deals in depth with FDI in Taiwan.

[10] OEM is similar to other subcontracting arrangements in sectors such as bicycles and footwear (Egan and Mody, 1992).

In the past, foreign OEM partners have helped with the selection of capital equipment; the training of managers, engineers, and technicians; and advice on production, financing, and management. Successful OEM arrangements have led to close long-term technological relationships between buyers and sellers. Local learning was encouraged because the TNC depended on quality, delivery, and price of the final output.

Today, OEM overlaps substantially with "own design and manufacture" (ODM), first noted by Johnstone (1989, pp. 50–51). Under ODM the local firm carries out some or all of the product design (as well as production) tasks needed to make a good, usually according to a general design layout supplied by the TNC. In some cases the buyer cooperates with the local supplier on the design, using the skills developed by the local firm. As with basic OEM, the goods are then sold under the TNC's (or buyer's) brand name. ODM signifies the internalization of some degree of know-how in the areas of product design, product-process interfacing, manufacturing, and sometimes component design. ODM offers a mechanism for local NIE firms to capture more of the process and design value-added while still avoiding the risk of launching own-brand products. Although ODM indicates some advance in technological competence, it applies mainly to incremental or follower designs, rather than leadership product innovations based on R&D.

Table 5.1 describes the transition of the OEM system since the 1960s. Although there are no clearly defined stages, the share of basic OEM has declined as a proportion of total production. Today, many local firms produce their own brand-name goods, called "own brand manufacture" (OBM), although ODM and OEM remain important. As Table 5.1 indicates, the OEM/ODM systems have both a technological and marketing dimension, enabling firms to reach into international markets and use the system as a training school for technological learning.

OEM and ODM allowed NIE companies to export large volumes of goods, enabling economies of scale, investments in automation, and production learning. Within the system, firms developed by strenuous in-house efforts, by trial-and-error learning, and by on-the-job training. Eventually some firms mastered production and design know-how for electronics, narrowing the gap with the leaders.

Table 5.1. *Transition of NIE latecomer firms: From OEM to ODM to OBM*[a]

	Technological transition	Market transition
1960s/1970s		
OEM	Learns assembly process for standard, simple goods	Foreign TNC/buyer designs, brands, and distributes
1980s		
ODM	Local firm designs[b] and learns product innovation skills	TNC buys, brands, and distributes TNC gains PPVA[c]
1990s		
OBM	Local firm designs and conducts R&D for new products	Local firm organizes distribution, uses own brand name, and captures PPVA

[a] OEM = original equipment manufacture; ODM = own design and manufacture; OBM = own brand manufacture; note that terminology differs among users.
[b] or contributes to the design, alone or in partnership with the foreign company.
[c] post-production value-added.
Source: Hobday (1995).

However, OEM also has risks and disadvantages. It proved to be a harsh, highly competitive industrial training school for local companies. Many firms invested heavily for little or no return in the early stages, while the TNCs gained the large majority of the profits. If one firm failed to meet expectations, the buyer could always switch to another eager supplier. Even today, the local partner is often subordinated to the strategic decisions of TNC buyers, and is often dependent on the TNC for technology and components. As discussed in the section on OEM in South Korea, the system also makes it difficult for local companies to build up high-quality international brand images abroad.

OEM IN SOUTH KOREA

Industrial Development and Electronics

In South Korea, the government fostered the growth of a small number of large oligopolistic firms with sufficient resources to overcome entry barriers in electronics. These policies led to a very highly concentrated industrial structure, with three large firms dominating the industry: Samsung Electronics (later called SEC), LG, and Daewoo Electronics. Samsung began making electronics in 1969 under a joint venture with Sanyo of Japan. By 1995, SEC's sales had reached around U.S. $20 billion, with an R&D spending of about U.S. $1.2 billion.

Other fast-growing competitors include Hyundai, Anam, and Ssangyong. Except for Anam, each of these firms began as offshoots of major groups (or *chaebols*). Chaebols are the large Korean conglomerates that dominate Korean industry. As the family owners of the *chaebols* followed each other into the industry, the share of electronics in manufacturing rose from around 2.1 percent in 1970, to 6 percent in 1980, to 17.8 percent in 1988. During the 1980s, exports of electronics increased tenfold in current dollar terms. By 1991 electronics had become the largest export, accounting for some U.S. $20.2 billion, or 28 percent of total exports. By 1994 total electronics export reached around U.S. $25 billion.

Through the 1980s and into the 1990s, electronics remained the centerpiece of Korea's export-led industrialization. Product lines included color TVs and monitors, semiconductors, videocassette recorders (VCRs), camcorders, compact disc players, personal computers (PCs), and peripherals and fax machines. In 1994 semiconductors became the largest single export, amounting to an estimated U.S. $8.4 billion.[11]

Within each of the major firms, technological advance accompanied growth and diversification. Historically, progress in electronics can be divided into three broad phases. Phase 1 (late-1950s to circa 1969), which was dominated by FDI, began with the start of transistor radio production for the home market in the late 1950s. During the 1960s, U.S. and Japanese TNCs invested in cheap labor assembly activities. U.S. firms, including Motorola, Signetics, and Fairchild, began to assemble chips during the mid-1960s, followed by Japanese firms and joint Korean-Japanese ventures such as Samsung-Sanyo, Crown Radio Corporation, Toshiba, and LG-Alps Electronics (Suh, 1974, pp. 17–19).

[11] The issue of semiconductors cannot be dealt with here. Suffice it to say that DRAMs represent the most dramatic advance in Korean electronics (Choi, 1994; Mathews, 1995; Kim, 1996). South Korea has taken a world leadership position, forging ahead of many foreign TNCs in both production and design technology. In 1995 SEC sold around U.S. $20 billion in electronics of which just under 50 percent was semiconductors, a large proportion of which were DRAMs.

Phase 2 (circa 1970 to 1979) involved more local firms and joint ventures in the takeoff stage. Production increased from U.S. $45.9 million in 1968 to U.S. $3.3 billion in 1979, while exports grew from U.S. $20 million to U.S. $1.8 billion. Exports included semifinished, low-technology parts and components (mostly integrated circuits, condensers, and transistors), shipped into South Korea for final assembly by foreign firms. Also important were consumer and industrial electronics (e.g., black and white TVs, tape recorders and amplifiers, desktop calculators, and transceivers).[12] During the 1970s a substantial increase in the share of local and joint venture firms in total output occurred, although local firms were still fairly small and dispersed.

The third and current phase began during the 1980s. As the market expanded, the *chaebols* became the dominant force for production and exports. During the 1980s, the share of foreign ownership in electronics fell considerably. Japanese firms such as Matsushita, Sanyo, and NEC withdrew from joint ventures as tax advantages were canceled and firms were encouraged by the government to leave (Bloom, 1991, p. 9). The *chaebols* increased their outward investments as they invested close to customers to avoid trade restrictions. By 1994 SEC alone had twenty over- seas factories, seventeen sales subsidiaries, and twelve R&D centers (including five in Korea), and the firm's overseas produc- tion exceeded U.S. $1 billion for the first time (excluding semiconductors).

Dependence on OEM

With the growing competence of local firms in the early 1980s, the OEM system provided an alternative to joint ventures. OEM (often linked to licensing) enabled firms to export large volumes of goods under foreign brand names and distribution channels, often at the low-end, low value-added segments of the market. During the 1980s, exports were highly concentrated on a few major product lines, many of which depended on OEM. Accord- ing to Jun and Kim (1990, pp. 22–23), in the late 1980s, some 50 percent to 60 percent of color TVs and VCRs were sold under OEM brands. Important OEM brand names included Sony,

---

[12] For details, see Korea Exchange Bank (1980), pp. 172–180.

Panasonic, Mitsubishi, Zenith, Toshiba, Philips, Zenith, RCA, and Hitachi.

In PCs and peripherals the *chaebols* were also heavily reliant on OEM, although Hyundai, Samsung, Daewoo, and Trigem offered their own brands. Samsung's PC exports via OEM were as high as 95 percent in 1985. This fell to around 60 percent in 1988 and still further through the 1990s. Other firms also reduced their dependence on OEM with some degree of success.

Several surveys confirm the overall importance of OEM, although data are not usually comparable. *Electronic Business* (April 22, 1991, p. 59) put the share of OEM at 70 percent to 80 percent of total Korean electronics exports in 1990 and estimated that the largest three *chaebols* relied on OEM for 60 percent of their exports.[13] Similarly, a survey conducted in 1993 by the Korean Foreign Trade Association showed that 61 percent of all exports (including nonelectronics) to Europe were conducted on an OEM basis. At that time, very few firms had established their own sales outlets into Europe.

OEM as a Technology Training School

In many cases, Korean firms gained their first orders under OEM conditions and learned important technology and marketing skills from Japanese and U.S. partners. Transnationals and other buyers sought to ensure that production was of the highest quality at the lowest possible price. In microwave ovens, to gain its first export order from GTE, Samsung trimmed costs to a minimum, while production engineers worked long hours for seven days a week, sometimes sleeping by their machinery (Magaziner and Patinkin, 1989). In the early days, the ever-present risk of buyers switching to other OEM suppliers forced the pace of learning and intensi- fied competition.

By the late 1980s, technological activities under OEM evolved to the point of ODM, where products were designed and speci- fied, as well as manufactured, by the *chaebols* while the foreign buyer simply branded the ready-made product (Hobday, 1995). In

---

[13] It is not clear exactly how these figures were calculated, the data almost certainly exclude semiconductors.

Table 5.2. *Benefits and disadvantages of OEM/ODM in South Korea*

Benefits	Disadvantages
Scale economies	Subordination to partner
Low risk/cost entry[a]	Cycle of dependence on buyer
Access to markets	Low profit margins
Production learning	Focus on low end (of range) products
Corporate/export growth	Shallow technological roots
Joint technology development	Dependence on core components
Specialist skills in mass production	Dependence on capital goods
Ability to focus on manufacture	Little product design required[b]

[a] That is, no forward investment in marketing, distribution, or advertising.
[b] In early stages; in later stages an inability to exploit competencies fully.

some product areas, companies carried out some (or all) of the product and process tasks, according to general design layouts. Some ODM deals involved close design partnerships while others were conducted at arm's length, involving little input from the buyer. It is probable that, through the 1980s, advanced design skills and complex production technologies were internalized by most large firms, although such advances applied mostly to incremental design improvements rather than new product (leadership) designs.

The OEM system evolved as firms supplied more production and design technology, but most remained dependent on foreign firms for key components and capital goods. OEM and licensing were particularly important for products new to South Korean firms (e.g., advanced computer terminals, telecommunications exchanges, and semiconductors). As products matured and capabilities were learned, OEM became less important (e.g., in audio and TV).

Table 5.2 summarizes some of the advantages and disadvantages of the OEM/ODM system. OEM enabled substantial catch-up learning in production, providing firms with economies of scale in production in areas such as CTVs, TV picture tubes, PCs, computer monitors, printers, and VCRs. A typical learning sequence would begin with the final production stages (e.g., assembly of printed circuit boards), involving tooling and production layout. Later on, new skills would be needed for line optimization, equipment adaptation, chip layout, and design-for-manufacture. The latter required firms to learn more about product design, beginning with low-end, simple products and progressing to higher-end, more complex goods. The general advance in ODM is reflected in the proliferation of new engineering and R&D departments in Korea as well as product design teams. Within the OEM system, the rate of learning depended on in-house efforts, investments in engineering, and on-the-job training.

For their part, Japanese and U.S. firms gained from a rapid, low-cost expansion of manufacturing capacity. OEM enabled Japanese TNCs to compete by reducing production costs, particularly after the yen appreciated in the mid-1980s. Once one market leader began OEM, others quickly followed or suffered the consequences. In the case of microwave ovens, Samsung may well have enabled the U.S. firm GTE to survive under competitive pressure from Japanese suppliers (Magaziner and Patinkin, 1989).

Disadvantages included low profit margins (see discussion in the section on OME strategies) and a dependence on potential competitors for new product designs. Foreign TNCs captured most of the postmanufacturing value added and were often able to control or restrict the supply of key components, materials, new designs and capital goods, and access to new markets. Such arrangements subordinated the *chaebols* to the strategies of their senior partners and would-be competitors.[14]

OEM Strategies: Samsung (SEC) and LG

Samsung learned much about production and marketing under OEM and licensing deals. In 1981 Toshiba licensed microwave oven technology to Samsung. In 1982 Philips supplied color TV technology. Videocassette recorder technology was licensed from JVC and Sony in 1983. By the late-1980s, Samsung had acquired sufficient capabilities to begin joint developments in VCRs, camcorders, and color TVs (Koh, 1992, p. 22). One in five microwave ovens sold in the United States were made by Samsung in 1992, mostly under OEM deals with GTE.

[14] It would be wrong to overstress the disadvantages. For many firms, OEM was the best possible option leading to many new opportunities.

SEC made huge efforts to develop its own product designs and establish its own brand name overseas. It stepped up in-house R&D efforts to develop new products, assimilate advanced foreign technologies, reduce OEM dependence, and change its image from junior to equal partner in joint ventures. Under recent ventures, SEC has brought a range of assets to the table to bargain for leading-edge technologies and access to markets.[15] By the early 1990s SEC had the largest R&D center in South Korea, manufacturing operations around the world, and global leadership in semiconductor dynamic random access memory (DRAM) technology. In 1995 SEC sales reached U.S. $20.9 billion with net profits of U.S. $3.2 billion. Around one-third of total sales were accounted for by memory chips (mostly DRAMs) and roughly 80 percent to 90 percent of profits were from DRAMs.

However, despite these efforts, during the 1980s and 1990s the company continued to depend heavily on OEM. Own brand sales (excluding semiconductors) in 1989 were around 35 percent of total exports, while OEM and related sales amounted to around 65 percent of exports. Thereafter, own brand sales increased to 55 percent in 1992, to 56 percent in 1993, and to 57 percent in 1994. Put another way, the firm still depended on OEM for around 43 percent of its electronics sales (excluding semiconductors) in 1994. Although SEC had made brand progress in the United Kingdom (e.g., in fax machines), Spain (in VCRs and microwave ovens), Sweden (cordless phones), and Saudi Arabia (color TVs), in other important markets such as the United States, Germany, and Japan, own brand shares had stalled at around 2 percent to 5 percent of total sales.

Table 5.3 provides information on Samsung's profitability in electronics for the period 1992 to 1994. As can be seen, apart from semiconductors, profitability has been negative on average over the three years. Although it is not possible to identify the reasons for the poor profitability, it is likely that in consumer goods, information systems, and telecommunications, dependence on

---

[15] SEC's advance is most apparent in the semiconductor field. In 1994 Samsung agreed with NEC of Japan to swap research data on the 256 megabit DRAM, a technology well in advance of the mainstream, to share costs and risks. In 1993 it formed an eight-year alliance with Toshiba of Japan to work together on a new industry standard for flash memories, a technology invented by Toshiba.

Table 5.3. *Samsung: Profitability in electronics 1992 to 1994 (U.S. $)*

	1992	1993	1994
Consumer electronics	67	−230	39
Information systems (IS) and telecom	−32	−96	40
Semiconductors	158	960	855
Total	193	634	934

Source: Unpublished SEC company report, 1995.

low-cost, price-sensitive OEM sales was a major contributing factor.

The case of LG also indicates the continuing importance of OEM. LG is a major OEM supplier of TVs to Japanese firms such as Toshiba, Hitachi, Panasonic, and Sony. The firm has attempted to build up its own brand name in international markets. By 1994, LG's brand sales accounted for 45 percent of total revenues and the company planned to achieve 75 percent by the year 2000. In computers and peripherals LG also depended on OEM, supplying large volumes of CD-ROM drives and PCs to IBM.

In 1995, LG purchased Zenith Electronics Corporation, an American producer of TVs and consumer goods, for U.S. $351 million (following twenty-year OEM relationship). Zenith, although making losses, promised to supply LG with technology (e.g., digital TV and set-top boxes) as well as its U.S. distribution network and the Zenith brand name. The immediate effect of the takeover was an increase in LG's TV market share in the United States from 2 percent to 12 percent. Like SEC, LG has invested heavily in key components (e.g., it invested around U.S. $1.3 billion in liquid crystal display [LCD] production facilities) and formed partnerships with major companies (e.g., Philips for CDI Interactive) to acquire frontier technologies and overcome its OEM dependence.

To sum up, the cases hint at pressures on profitability within OEM and illustrate the strategic desire of Korean firms to reduce their OEM dependence. In the future, the *chaebol* hope to improve their international brand names and gain direct access to international markets.

OEM IN TAIWAN

Industrial Development in Electronics

In contrast with South Korea, OEM began in hundreds of tiny firms as well as larger family-owned groups.[16] By the early 1990s, Taiwanese firms supplied around 35 percent of the world's output of computers and peripherals. At this time there were around 700 hardware manufacturers (mostly small and medium-size enterprises [SMEs]) and about 300 software and service companies (O'Connor and Wang, 1992, pp. 53–54). The main product lines included PCs, color monitors, keyboards, mice, image scanners, and motherboards (the main circuit board used in PCs).

In the 1960s, the Taiwanese electronics industry benefited considerably from TNC investments, joint ventures, and foreign buyers. Transnational corporations helped to foster the electronics industry, as large numbers of local firms rushed in to supply them with goods and services, leading to a thriving subcontracting and OEM system.[17] Electronics accounted for around one-third of Taiwan's total FDI up until 1974 (Wade, 1990, p. 149) and for some 36 percent of total investment in 1987. Foreign direct investment led to backward linkages with local Taiwanese producers and raised the quality of exports. After the mid-1980s, the share of FDI in industrial output fell as local industry grew in stature and capability.

Compared with the structure of the electronics industry in South Korea, this industry in Taiwan is more diverse and complex. The U.S. connection also runs deeper, mostly because of close Taiwanese links with the U.S. computer industry. Taiwanese industry is made up of at least five strategic types of firms: (1) foreign TNCs and joint ventures; (2) the major local manufacturing groups; (3) high-technology startups; (4) government-sponsored ventures; and (5) traditional SMEs.

The first strategic group (TNCs and joint ventures) initiated much of the electronic industry and provided opportunities for local companies to become subcontractors, OEM suppliers,

[16] In Hong Kong, as well as Taiwan, the role of overseas Chinese in starting up SMEs in electronics was very important.

[17] See Schive (1990) for a thorough analysis of the importance of FDI to Taiwan's development.

licensees, and eventually competitors. During the 1970s and 1980s, companies such as Philips, RCA, IBM, DEC, NEC, Sanyo, Sharp, Matsushita, Epson, Hewlett-Packard, and NCR eased Taiwan's entry into the computer industry in their search for cheap labor and low-cost hardware. By the early 1990s, the world's leading computer companies were dependent on Taiwan for high resolution monitors, keyboards, printed circuit boards, graphics cards, and printers.

The second strategic group, Taiwan's major manufacturing conglomerates, also forced the technological pace of local industry. Tatung is the largest electronics producer in Taiwan ahead of Sampo, TECO, and AOC. Founded in 1919, it diversified from construction into building materials, mechanical equipment, electric fans, steel, chemicals, and telecommunications. During the 1970s, electronics became Tatung's largest operation. During the 1980s, around half of Tatung's color TVs, PCs, and hard disk drives were exported under OEM. Tatung and the others learned under OEM arrangements, advancing from simple consumer goods to computers, color display terminals, printers, video graphic adaptors, and TV monitors.

The third group, small, high-technology startups, entered with product innovation skills often gained from overseas experience in U.S. firms and universities. Many began as OEM niche market players, focusing on a narrow range of products. Of these companies ACER is the best known outside Taiwan. Other important players, mostly unheard of in the West, include First International, Mitac, Inventec, Quanta, Elite, and Twinhead. These rely heavily on OEM/ODM for sales (see Table 5.4).

The final two groups include first, the government-sponsored startups, which spun off from ERSO/ITRI or benefited from the Hsinchu Science-Based Industrial Park facilities, and second, the large numbers of traditional SMEs, which cluster around export market niches. Historically, the SMEs have been the most important source of entrepreneurial dynamism in Taiwan (Hobday, 1995).

Clustering within the OEM System

OEM in Taiwan (and Hong Kong) took place within a diversified and fast-changing industrial structure. Many small PC makers won

Table 5.4. *Taiwanese OEM/ODM^a partnerships and major computer product lines*

OEM buyer	Product	Taiwanese producer
Apple	Monitor	Tatung
	Notebook	ACER
Compaq	Monitor	ADI, Teco
	Notebook	Inventec
	PC	Mitac
Dell	Monitor	Lite-on, Royal
	Notebook	Quanta
	Motherboard	GVC, Lun Hwa, FIC
IBM	Monitor	Sampo
	Motherboard	GVC, Elite, Lung Hwa
	Notebook	ASE
Packard Bell	PC	Tatung
	Motherboard	Tatung, GVC
AST	Notebook	Quanta, Compal
DEC	Alpha PC	Elite
Gateway 2000	Monitor	Mag
	Notebook	ASE
Sharp	Notebook	Twinhead
NEC	Monitor	Tatung
	Motherboard	Elite
Hitachi	Monitor	ACER
	Notebook	Twinhead
Epson	PC	Unitron
	Notebook	ASE, Compal, Twinhead
Philips	Notebook	Kapok
Siemens Nixdorf	Monitor	Kapok
	Notebook	Quanta
Vobis	Notebook	Clevo
	Monitor	Royal

^a OEM = Original equipment manufacture.
ODM = Own design and manufacture.
Source: Market Intelligence Center, Electronic Business Asia, December 1995.

their first orders from traders in close touch with new export markets. Backward linkages were forged as new SMEs spun off from existing suppliers, often under subcontract relations with previous bosses (Shieh, 1992). Low-cost OEM proved irresistible to foreign buyers, who greatly expanded their purchasing operations in Taipei during the takeoff period of the 1980s. Many SMEs

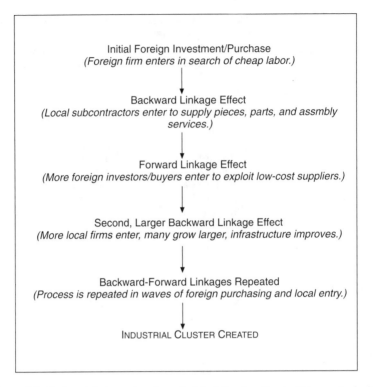

Figure 5.1. Industrial clustering from behind the frontier in Taiwan. A similar
process occurred in Hong Kong where, by the early 1990s, the backward
linkage industries employed around half the electronics industry in that
country (Fok, 1991).

failed to grow while others went bankrupt and exited the industry. Successful firms learned new skills and generated a low-cost,
highly responsive industrial infrastructure that, in turn, attracted
more foreign investment, producing a classic forward linkage
effect (Hirschman, 1958; Schive, 1990).

A self-reinforcing process of backward and forward linkages
occurred, as described in Figure 5.1. Each forward linkage encouraged more entrants, forming a further (often much larger), backward linkage effect. Successive waves of forward and backward
linkages ultimately created industrial clusters in keyboards, PCs,
consumer electronics, computer mice, fax machines, calculators,

and other product areas (Hobday, 1995). Requiring little R&D, OEM and subcontracting generated industrial clustering that needed little, if any, direct support from government. By 1989, OEM/ODM accounted for some 43 percent of Taiwanese computer hardware production, compared with 35 percent by foreign-invested companies and 22 percent for local brands. In computers alone, Taiwanese OEM/ODM sales reached around U.S. $3.5 billion in 1993, about half of Taiwan's total computer exports. The clustering effect was also stimulated by the appreciation of the Japanese yen against the new Taiwanese dollar, as production of many low-cost goods became less profitable in Japan.

During the 1990s, OEM/ODM became a prominent feature of the world computer industry involving most of the major players. Table 5.3 places several of the major U.S., European, and Japanese buyers alongside the computer product lines supplied by Taiwanese producers.

By the late 1980s, the term ODM had begun to be used widely in Taiwan. ODM provided an alternative to own brand manufacture for small firms, and signified a new stage in latecomer product innovation, going beyond the processes learned under OEM. ODM evolved out of the basic OEM system, highlighting the growing interdependence between local firms and TNCs and the learning of design skills by domestic firms. Today, many of the largest international computer suppliers depend on low-cost Taiwanese suppliers of computer hardware. The TNCs also benefit from new Taiwanese-owned operations in China.

Organizational Innovations: ODM, OBM, and OIM

During the mid-1990s another term, *original idea manufacture* (OIM) began to be used in Taiwan. Under OIM, the product idea is generated by the local firm that designs and manufactures the product, which is then sold under the brand name of the Western or Japanese TNC. Companies such as Inventec now use the term OIM to refer to themselves to reassure buyers that they have no ambitions of becoming direct, brand-name competitors (Interview, Inventec 1994). However, less publicly, many Taiwanese firms believe that unless and until they make a full transition to OBM based on in-house technology, they will remain subordinated to strategies of the TNCs and unable to compete on equal terms. The emergence of OIM is another latecomer organizational innovation in electronics.

OEM Setbacks: The Case of ACER

As the case of ACER shows, the progress of Taiwanese firms under OEM has been a long and difficult struggle, and not without significant setbacks. ACER was established as Multitech International Corporation in 1976 with just eleven engineers.[18] Sales rose from U.S. $331.0 million in 1987 to U.S. $600 million in 1988 to U.S. $3.2 billion in 1994 to around U.S. $5.7 billion in 1995. ACER's technological performance has consistently been impressive. In 1986 it launched the world's second 32-bit PC, after Compaq but ahead of IBM. In 1993 it licensed its own U.S.-patented ChipUp technology to Intel (in return for royalties), which allows a single-chip upgrade to a dual-Pentium microprocessing system. During the 1980s, ACER was among the world's largest producers of PCs, color monitors, keyboards, fax machines, and printers. It developed its own brand workstations, operating systems, and new chip designs. As a major OEM supplier to Apple, Hitachi, Canon, ITT, AT&T, and others, ACER proved its competence in processes and product design. In 1991 it diversified into semiconductors by forming a joint venture with TI to produce DRAMs within Taiwan (a U.S. $400 million facility). In 1993, up to 40 percent of ACER's output was sold under OEM/ODM. Many of ACER's original brand goods were intelligently modified and improved PC designs.

In an attempt to challenge brand leaders, ACER began to distribute its own brand products directly to customers in the United States and Europe. However, in 1992 it scaled back its OBM efforts and retreated to more traditional OEM/ODM after sustaining heavy losses (about U.S. $90 million between 1990 and 1993). Mitac and others also retreated from own brand sales, focusing instead on OEM and ODM. A chief reason for the retreat from OBM was the PC price war in 1992, which reduced the price gap between clone and brand-name suppliers, leading to large losses across the industry. Mitac, for example, lost U.S. $27.7 million in 1992. Another reason was that major U.S. firms such as Hewlett-Packard became suspicious of the brand-name strategies

---

[18] Evidence for this section is from interviews carried out in Taiwan, Johnstone (1989, pp. 51–52), and the trade press. See also Chaponniere and Fouquin (1989, p. 61).

of their suppliers, preferring not to award orders to companies with the potential of becoming head-on brand competitors. This led to the OIM strategies discussed earlier. These steps back to OEM/ODM illustrate the risks facing latecomer firms wishing to overcome their disadvantages and compete as leaders on the world stage.

To sum up, as in the case of South Korea, OEM in Taiwan enabled firms to learn both technological and marketing skills. Larger companies established marketing departments in the advanced countries and diversified their customer base. Today, a few (e.g., ACER and Tatung) have established well-known brand names abroad and organize their own distribution outlets in the advanced countries.

TNC-LED DEVELOPMENT IN MALAYSIA

Industrial Development in Electronics

Malaysia is one example of TNC-led growth in Southeast Asia. Singapore and Thailand also depend heavily on TNC-led growth. Singapore leads within the region, boasting several wafer fabrication facilities and new product design work. Throughout the 1980s and 1990s electronics has made a substantial contribution to Malaysian growth. In 1993 total exports reached around U.S. $45 billion, of which electronics accounted for roughly U.S. $20.4 billion (61 percent of manufacturing and 45 percent of Malaysia's total exports). Most other manufacturing exports were minor in comparison (e.g., textiles and clothing accounted for 6.2 percent).

The electronics industry in Malaysia began in the 1960s under that country's import-substitution policy, somewhat later than in South Korea and Taiwan. Matsushita of Japan was the first major foreign investor in 1966. Other foreign firms from Japan, the United States, and Europe entered to assemble radios, black and white TVs, electrical appliances, and simple components. In the 1970s under new export-led policies, semiconductors were produced in large volumes, providing badly needed employment and exports. The industry grew rapidly as TNCs benefited from low-cost labor as well as the ten-year, tax-free Pioneer Status. National Semiconductor, Motorola, and Intel all began assembling chips in the early-1970s.

Table 5.5. *Recent innovation examples in twelve TNCs in Malysia[a]*

Company	Total employment	Engineers/technicians % of employment	R&D[b] dept/staff	Recent innovation examples
Intel Penang	2,600	n/a	40	Reliability analysis breakthrough; development of new jigs, fixtures, machinery; new SPC[c] techniques
Motorola Penang	2,600	300[d]–11.5%	130	Cordless phone design (CT2); changes to advanced manufacturing equipment; simple application specific integrated circuit designs; new product design for manufacture
Matsushita	24,700	n/a	40	Numerous split air-conditioner design changes (e.g., voltage, style); die and mold development; design for manufacture
SEH (Shin-Etsu)	1,350	50/100–9.0%	10	Capital goods, e.g., new automated etching and slicing machines (patented); total quality management modification
Sony Electronics	8,000	500/800–16.2%	30[e]	Design specifications for Sony Discman (portable CD) development of capital goods; prototypes for new hi-fi systems
Sony Mechatronics	2,900	80/150–7.9%	n/a	Continuous improvements to processes; minor changes to locally purchased inputs
Centronix	700	30/58–12.6%	10	Telephone handset designs; new tooling specifications; design for manufacture
Inventec	3,000	130/134–8.8%	10	Calculator model designs (including LSI chip); manufacture specifications for telephone handset

Grundig	900	54/35–9.9%	38	Product designs for hi-fi and cassette recorders, design for manufacture
MEMC	640	60/60–18.8%	n/a[f]	Reengineering of production lines into cellular form, including integration of R&D into production; improvements to wafer saw and other equipment
Siemens	1,560	50/110–10.3%	8	World center for Siemens opto production and design; applied new approach to TQM[g]; development of new bonding machines with foreign suppliers
Philips/JVC	3,190	32/40[h]–2.3%	11	Design for manufacture; continuous improvements to production processes

[a] Not exhaustive (illustrative examples only); innovations are defined as commercially exploited ideas, new to the firm and/or to the country (not necessarily to the market or to the world); technological and organizational innovations are included.
[b] R&D refers to technical staff; note that R&D, and engineers and technicians are not strictly comparable across firms, as company definitions differed.
[c] SPC = statistical process control.
[d] Total engineers and technicians combined (separate details not available).
[e] Planned to expand to 70 by 1997.
[f] R&D activities integrated into production under new cellular approach to production.
[g] TQM = total quality management.
[h] This firm applied a very strict definition of "engineer" (a bachelors' degree holder) and also to "technician" (diploma holder); therefore, technical support staff are probably understated, relative to other firms in sample.
Source: Company interviews (derived from Hobday, 1996).

151

Table 5.6. *Exports of electronics from selected East and Southeast Asian NIEs*

	Population in billions (1995)	Total GDP (1994 U.S. $ billions)	Total exports (U.S. $ billions 1994, f.o.b.)	Electronics exports 1994[a] (U.S. $ billions)	Share of electronics in exports
South Korea	45.6	508	96	25	26%
Taiwan	21.5	257	93	18	20%
Malaysia	19.7	167	57	22	35%
Singapore	2.9	57	96	38	40%

[a] Electronics export data calculated from various sources: South Korea, based on data supplied by Samsung; Singapore based on official (EDB, 1992b, p. 145) data for 1991, assuming 10 percent compound average annual growth (CAAG), probably an underestimate; Malaysia based on 1993 data from MITI Malaysia (1994, pp. 34–36, p. 43, pp. 56–57), again assuming 10 percent CAAG. All other data are official government figures.

During the 1980s, electronics exports grew more than sixfold, rising from around U.S. $3.2 billion in 1981 to U.S. $7.1 billion in 1986 to U.S. $22.1 billion in 1990 (Kassim and Saleh, 1993, p. 16). In 1987, electronics became Malaysia's largest export sector. The share of chip testing and assembly, which accounted for 82 percent of electronics exports in 1986, began to decline as the range of exported products increased. Exports of chips fell to around 58 percent in 1990 and to 46 percent in 1993. Conversely, consumer goods increased to U.S. $4.2 billion (26 percent) and industrial electronics rose to U.S. $3.9 billion (28.3 percent) by 1993. The diversification trend continued in 1994 and 1995 with new investments in disk drives, computers, and a large influx of Japanese color TV manufacturing.

As in Korea and Taiwan, progress has not been without its setbacks. For example, as a result of international recession, total investment in electronics fell from the peak of U.S. $1.7 billion in 1990 to just U.S. $0.5 billion in 1993. The FDI position began to recover in 1993 with firms from Taiwan, Singapore and Hong Kong making up for the fall-off in Japanese and U.S. foreign investment.

Innovation within the TNCs

Research conducted to assess innovation patterns within twelve major TNCs (Table 5.5), shows that there was little or no long-term R&D into new materials, novel product designs, production technologies, or advanced software. By contrast, most firms carried out substantial innovative activity related to near-term production process improvements. Some firms employed large numbers of engineers and technicians (in the case of Sony, 1,300 or 16.2 percent of the workforce and at MEMC, 120 or 18.8 percent of the workforce).

Not surprisingly, most innovation was incremental rather than radical in character. The TNCs had learned to improve chip handlers, tapers, markers, burn-in ovens, solder plating processes, die bonding materials, jigs, automation machinery, stamping dies for lead frames, and molds for injecting epoxy resin for integrated circuit packages. In a few cases, TNCs carried out product design work (mostly for new models within a standard range) including prototyping. In larger companies, substantial design-for-manufacture was conducted to ensure that new models could be mass produced efficiently.

Extensive process engineering was undertaken by most TNCs, as well as creative modifications to older capital equipment. In the case of SEH this had resulted in patents. SEH, a Japanese TNC, had developed a new wafer polishing system in Malaysia as well as automated etching and slicing machines, leading to significant productivity, quality gains, and several patent applications. Firms such as Intel, Motorola, and Siemens regularly carried out reliability analysis, used statistical process control techniques, and designed low-cost, simple products (e.g., cordless telephones and opto-electronic devices). Many firms had introduced organizational innovations resulting in continuous improvements to processes and productivity, including modular manufacturing, delayering, personnel empowerment, and total quality management.

Compared with South Korea and Taiwan, Malaysian technological innovation was at an earlier stage of development, but it appeared to be catching up quickly. Managers of the TNCs argued that parent companies were commercially motivated to transfer technology, but that success depended on local plant capabilities. Without the capabilities to receive knowledge, specifications, and machinery, the transfer process would be hindered and new investments risked. Local successes in minor innovations had improved performance, leading to further investments. Engineering advances had improved the efficiency of the subsidiaries and enabled them to respond quickly to changes in product demand.

Global Strategies for TNC Innovation

As with Singapore and Thailand, innovation in Malaysian electronics has to be understood within the context of the global strategies of the TNCs. Despite advances, most R&D and core product design was, naturally enough, carried out in the TNC host country. As an example, most of Intel Penang's innovations were concerned with the short-term needs of local assembly and testing. The core of Intel's worldwide technological activity was carried out in the United States, where it invested around U.S. $1.1 billion in R&D in 1994. Intel Penang depended, to a large extent, on the parent headquarters for strategic decisions, including major investments, choice of capital goods, design work, and so on.

However, the technological activities of the subsidiaries in Malaysia should not be dismissed as unimportant. Research and developments, although often stressed, is only a small proportion of total corporate technological activity. Strictly speaking, R&D amounts to the tip of the iceberg, usually well under 15 percent of corporate turnover and often less than 10 percent. Most TNC technological activity involves design, engineering, and operating tasks. These activities are essential for productivity, quality, and competitiveness, and their requirements often shape corporate R&D strategy and provide much of the demand for R&D.

The technology activities of the TNC subsidiaries in Malaysia therefore constitute one essential element of overall operations. Through time, the subsidiaries progressed from basic assembly into higher stages of technological activity, such as process engineering. This process required substantial technological learning and company investment in skills, training, and education. At the present time, most Malaysian subsidiaries are situated between higher technology operations in countries such as the United States, the United Kingdom, and Singapore and lower cost operations in countries such as China. This reflects the general level of development and the relative factor costs of each economy. To progress further in the future, the TNC subsidiaries in Malaysia (and their suppliers) will need to build up further capabilities in precision engineering, prototype building, and product design, as well as R&D.

OEM VERSUS TNC-LED INNOVATION STRATEGIES

A Note on Export Performance

Among the three NIEs examined in this chapter, there was considerable variety among government policies, industrial structures, and patterns of ownership in electronics. These models reflect the distinctive histories and development styles of each economy, including the entrepreneurial overseas Chinese character of Taiwan, the large vertically integrated South Korean *chaebol*, and the TNC-led path of Malaysia.[19] Although it is not possible here to assess the relative performance of OEM and FDI, country data on exports indicate interesting contrasts.[20] Table 5.6 (see p. 152) presents information on GDP and electronics exports for the three cases examined earlier, plus Singapore. Note that the data are not strictly comparable, as figures for electronics are calculated from a variety of sources. Nevertheless, the data suggest that rather than South Korea, which is normally assumed to be the leading NIE, the TNC-led industry of Singapore (with a tiny population and much smaller GDP) leads in terms of total electronics exports.[21] Although it would be revealing to compare contributions to value added, such data are not available. However, in Singapore, electronics was the largest electronics sector in the early 1990s, accounting for around 34 percent of gross manufacturing value added (around U.S. \$4.5 billion in 1992; Economic Development Board, 1992a, p. 2, p. 21) and 40 percent of manufacturing production, a very respectable contribution to overall value added. This suggests that TNCs are not merely "screwdriver" plants and play an important part in industrial development.

Also surprising is the Malaysian performance, almost at the

---

[19] Note that these contrasts are a matter of degree and apply mainly to developments since the 1970s. For instance, foreign TNCs were important during the early stages of South Korean and Taiwanese growth as shown earlier.

[20] Such an assessment would need to account for many factors. Each of the NIEs began with different starting positions, capabilities, and income levels. Different options were open to each country and these partly determined the different routes taken. Factors other than the institutional system for innovation also had a bearing on performance, including government policy, international market trends, and, no doubt, a degree of luck as well as entrepreneurial skill and company strategy. Still, it is very interesting to compare the broad data on electronics exports.

[21] Hobday (1995) shows that progressive technological learning in Singapore occurred within the TNCs.

same export level of South Korea, despite a much smaller GDP, a late start in electronics, and a relatively backward stage of development. Taiwan is not far behind South Korea, in spite of a dependence on SMEs and smaller GDP. The data raise the interesting (but unanswerable) question of how South Korea and Taiwan would have fared had they remained as open to FDI and TNC-led growth as Singapore and Malaysia. However, what would or could have occurred cannot be assessed here or indeed ever known for sure.

Common Success Factors

Given the striking differences in policies, ownership, and industrial structure, one must turn to similarities to try and explain success. These can be divided into (1) the environment for innovation, especially policy and infrastructural similarities, and (2) firm-level innovation process similarities. At least four important similarities at the environment level help explain each country's development success in electronics:

- First, firms benefited from relatively stable macro-economies (say, compared with Latin America), with low rates of interest, low inflation, and high savings. Relative stability provided industry with an environment for long-term planning and investment (World Bank, 1993).
- Second, firms benefited from the outward-looking, export-led industrial policies of each country. These encouraged local firms to overcome their initial dislocation from international markets (Rhee et al., 1984). Exports, whether within TNCs or from local firms, acted as a focusing device for technological learning and investment.
- Third, each NIE government worked to remove illiteracy, deliver sound general education, and provide vocational training for industry. Each country ensured a sufficient supply of skilled workers, technicians, and engineers for industrial development (Wade, 1990; Amsden, 1989).
- Fourth, as and when necessary, governments intervened to ensure that entrepreneurial resources were strong enough to lead industrialization. Policies to overcome what might be called entrepreneurial failure took various forms.[22] In Malaysia

[22] Entrepreneurial failure can be seen as a particular form of market failure that occurs when firms are insufficient in numbers or capability (or both) to lead industrialization.

(as in Singapore and Thailand), government set about attracting TNCs to lead industrialization (Yuan and Low, 1990). In South Korea, the government helped build up the *chaebols* to ensure industrial development. In Taiwan, the government supported scale-intensive chip developments through its technology institute ITRI, which spun off several successful major suppliers.

Basic similarities are also apparent in firm-level innovation paths, across the three cases examined:

- First, both FDI and OEM promoted a gradual learning of technology and enabled enterprise to overcome technological and market barriers to entry. Both TNCs and OEM suppliers engaged in export-led technological learning and acquired successively higher levels of technology.

- Second, to narrow the gap with international leaders, firms in all three countries invested to catch up and assimilate technology, rather than to move the innovation frontier forward. In the case of the TNCs, the subsidiaries often acted as if they were OEM suppliers, making goods to the specification of the headquarters location. In a small number of cases (e.g., Samsung in DRAMs, ACER in PCs), local firms have reached the innovation frontier.[23] At this stage, suppliers require extensive R&D and, often, brand leadership for product acceptance. However, in most cases NIE enterprise still lags well behind the innovation frontier.

- Third, the historical paths of technological progress were similar. Under both FDI and OEM, firms acquired process and product technologies through time, beginning with simple assembly tasks, and graduated toward more complex activities such as process adaptation and R&D. As firms progressed, many relocated some labor-intensive operations to lower-cost Asian locations.

- Fourth, firms in each NIE had to struggle to acquire technology. Success was neither automatic nor painless. The evidence indicates that learning to innovate was a painstaking and difficult process, involving trial-and-error experimentation, investments in training, and, above all, a great deal of human skill and ingenuity.

[23] This can be defined as the point at which R&D becomes central to competitive advantage.

Contrasts with Conventional Wisdom

The innovation paths of the NIEs make an interesting comparison with Western innovation models, which stress new product development, dominant designs, and R&D.[24] The focus of Western literature naturally reflects its concern with leadership strategies, rather than the catch-up strategies of OEM subcontractors or TNC subsidiaries.

In contrast with normal Western models, the NIEs began with mature, standardized manufacturing processes and gradually moved to more advanced stages of technology. Only recently and only selectively have OEM suppliers exploited R&D for future product development. Typically, firms graduated from mature to early stages of the product life cycle, from standard to experimental manufacturing processes, and from incremental production changes to R&D. In this sense, the NIEs progressed "backward" along the normal stages of the product life cycle.

OEM strategies contrast sharply with the Western focus on market creation and advanced product development (Hamel and Prahalad, 1994). Firm strategies had to confront the problem of manufacturing for established export markets and the need to catch up from a technologically weak position. Catch-up learning and innovation enabled NIE firms to expand exports, to improve their production capabilities, and in some cases, to begin new product innovation, as had occurred previously in Japan.[25] This catch-up process appears to be the general sequence of both OEM and TNC subsidiaries in Asia.

The innovation process in electronics also contrasts markedly with popular notions of technological leapfrogging. In contrast with this idea, OEM and TNC firms engaged in an incremental process of learning, beginning with pre-electronic activities (e.g., mechanical and electromechanical engineering). Contrary to leapfrogging, firms tended to enter at the mature, well-established phase of product life cycles, rather than at the early stage.

Finally, the electronics case has implications for theories of production location (Dunning, 1975; Vernon, 1966). With both OEM

[24] See, for example, Utterback and Abernathy (1975), Abernathy and Clark (1985), Clark and Fujimoto (1991), Utterback and Suarez (1993), Hamel and Prahalad (1994), Klepper (1996), and in the marketing literature, (Kotler, 1976).

[25] See Abegglen and Stalk (1985) for Japanese corporate innovation patterns.

and FDI, local enterprise actively stimulated the relocation of production. Indeed, it is doubtful that relocation would have occurred to the same extent without substantial learning and capability building on the part of local plants. In Malaysia, for example, production transfer did not occur as an automatic consequence of an international product life cycle. On the contrary, local subsidiaries needed to generate the skills and competencies to enable foreign technology transfer to occur. Not surprisingly, factory managers were highly motivated to build up local competencies to ensure repeat investments and to prevent TNC migration to other countries. Over the long term, evidence of sustained reinvestment in export capacity is probably a good indicator of local capability building on the part of TNC subsidiaries.

Technological Versus Organizational Innovation

Although this chapter has focused on technology, some of the most important innovations were organizational, including the OEM system itself. This system enabled many local firms to access foreign export channels, overcome barriers to entry, and learn about new markets and technology. As an institutional mechanism, OEM provided a bridge between advanced users in the West and suppliers in the NIEs, forcing continuous improvements on competing suppliers. The OEM (and later ODM and OIM versions) system is new to the marketplace and to the world and therefore constitutes innovation (albeit organizational) in the strictest sense of the term. The regional development that occurred under OEM has no obvious historical parallel and has already proved to be a large-scale feature of economic development in the NIEs.

Problems, Weaknesses and Future Challenges

In spite of their achievements, South Korean and Taiwanese firms continue to suffer from structural weaknesses.[26] A large propor-

---

[26] This section points to remaining weaknesses in OEM and TNC-led systems but does not deal with wider problems of industrial structure or innovation management within firms (e.g., the problem of vertical integration and bureaucratic structures of the *chaebol*) (Chung and Lee, 1989, p. 174). Other problems in Korea include the weakness of the small firm sector and the heavy concentration of the *chaebol* on a few

tion of OEM output remains in relatively low-price, simple goods. Many firms have weaknesses in R&D, capital goods, and new product design. Heavy dependence on Japan for capital goods, core components, and new product designs confront many OEM producers and this has led each country into severe trade deficits with Japan in electronics.[27] Many local firms remain subordinated to Japanese company strategies under OEM arrangements.

Lacking deep technological roots and high-quality brand images abroad, many East Asian firms continue to rely on a repeated cycle of catch-up, imitation-based growth. Even the largest *chaebols* have yet to establish strong capabilities in capital goods, advanced materials, and key components. These weaknesses are even more severe among small firms in Taiwan. Similarly, the TNC subsidiaries in Malaysia (and to a lesser extent Singapore) are weak in new product design and R&D, and depend on low-price, low-end products. As with OEM producers, competencies are concentrated narrowly on manufacturing processes.

Heavy dependence on FDI in Southeast Asia can also bring problems. For example, the fall-off in electronics FDI in Malaysia, discussed earlier, was largely unexpected. Similar reductions have occurred in the past in Singapore. This reliance exposes Southeast Asia to international recession as well as changing global TNC strategies, particularly with the emergence of low-cost competition from southern China and other countries. Indeed, each of the three NIEs confronts low-cost competition from China, Vietnam, Indonesia, and the Philippines. Responding to higher domestic costs, some TNCs (and local OEM suppliers) have relocated production to lower-cost countries, and this poses a possible threat to domestic employment.

Another problem is the lack of integration of the TNCs in the local economies. In Malaysia, as in Singapore, the supply chain of locally owned firms remains weak and lags far behind the back-

product lines (e.g., DRAMs). In Taiwan, firms depend heavily on computer products. As a result both Korean and Taiwanese exporters are highly sensitive to international market trends. Similarly, Malaysia, Singapore, and Thailand are sensitive to FDI flows in electronics.

[27] For details, see for example, Chaponniere (1992, p. 73; Holden and Nakarmi, 1992, pp. 24–25).

ward linkage industries of Hong Kong and Taiwan at similar stages of development. Poor backward linkage restricts the potential for further integration of the TNCs. To some extent, the location of second-tier TNCs into Malaysia from Taiwan and Japan is helping to overcome this problem.

Some of these problems are to be expected due to the path of development. Firms and governments recognize the difficulties and have responded with various strategies. For example, many OEM suppliers have forged strategic partnerships with world leaders to acquire highly advanced technologies. Brand name products continue to increase as a proportion of total sales. R&D spending has grown consistently and firms such as ACER and Samsung have narrowed much of the technology gap.

The TNC subsidiaries in Malaysia (as in Singapore before them) have built up competencies in advanced manufacturing technology and precision engineering. In the future, the TNCs may increase the number of regional headquarters in Malaysia, as they have already done in Singapore. American TNCs (e.g., Texas Instruments, Motorola, and Intel) have grown rapidly in Southeast Asia, revitalizing their operations, learning new skills, and gaining shares of the rapidly growing regional market. Feeling less welcome in Japan and South Korea, many TNCs prefer to invest in Southeast Asia. This has led to wafer fabrication in Singapore and Malaysia and promoted Southeast Asia as an important hub within the global electronics industry.

CONCLUSION

In drawing conclusions it is important to recognize the special characteristics of the electronics industry. It is an example of a fast-growing, internationally traded industry in which the division of tasks across national boundaries is both technologically possible and advantageous to TNCs. It is also a manufacturing-driven, high-throughput industry where labor costs (including skilled workers, technicians, and engineers) are important, both to entry and building competitive advantage. Not all manufacturing industries have these characteristics. Industries such as aerospace, nuclear power, and high-speed trains are subject to different rules and consequently the relevance of electronics is questionable.[28]

However, electronics remains the largest, most dynamic NIE export sector and much can be learned from it. With some qualifications, lessons from electronics apply to other fast-growing export industries including bicycles, clothing, athletic footwear, sewing machines, and so on. Electronics has also had a wide demonstration effect, stimulating new support industries and providing a role model for company strategists and policy makers.

In comparing OEM with FDI, the chapter identified some remarkable similarities in the processes of learning and innovation. Both systems proved to be remarkably successful at enabling enterprises to enter international markets, acquire foreign technology, and utilize exports to force the pace of learning, innovation, and industrial development. As the NIEs climbed the technological ladder, each transferred out labor-intensive activities to lower-cost NIEs and China, deepening Pacific Asian economic integration.

However, both systems endure continuing latecomer disadvantages. Only a small number of OEM suppliers have managed to generate new product innovations. Most are still dependent on their natural competitors for key components, capital goods, distribution channels, and high-quality brand images. Few have managed to succeed in high-price systems, software, and network markets. Many OEM suppliers continue to rely on a repeated cycle of catch-up, imitation, and incremental innovation. Similarly, the TNCs in Southeast Asia lack new product design and R&D capabilities and depend on low-end products for their exports. Despite significant advances in manufacturing technology, all three economies face unrelenting competition from lower-cost countries of the region. Lacking strong R&D capabilities and a thriving capital goods sector in electron-

---

[28] Competitive advantage in these industries is seldom based on volume production costs and incremental process improvements as in electronics (Miller et al., 1995). Entry into systems and capital goods industries is an important competitive challenge for the NIEs. Other types of industries such as petrochemicals, steel, and synthetic fibers also have different characteristics. See Enos and Park (1988) for petrochemicals, synthetic fibers, machinery, and iron and steel. Amsden (1989) looks at automobiles, cement, shipbuilding, textiles, steel, and heavy machinery in Korea. Kim and Lee (1987) compare patterns of technological change in shipbuilding, cement, automobiles, steel, and other sectors in Korea.

ics, the technological roots of the NIEs, by and large, remain shallow.

Despite the macro-economic crisis facing the Asian NIEs at the time of writing, future prospects at the firm level are likely to be strongly influenced by the long-term historical trends and the difficult export-led learning processes described above. TNC-led growth, like OEM, has proved, so far, to be a remarkably successful strategy in electronics, contributing to national economic growth, innovation, and technology absorption. As the chapter showed, Singapore and Malaysia appear to have matched or even surpassed South Korea and Taiwan in their export achievements. Most of the firm-level problems commented on in this chapter are well recognized by firms and governments, which have devised strategies to promote innovation. East Asian OEM suppliers are increasing their R&D expenditures and gradually improving their brand images abroad. Some have gained advantage by transferring basic OEM into neighboring lower-cost countries such as China. Several firms have successfully coupled OEM with new product development strategies, competing internationally with own brand products. Larger Korean companies have forged strategic alliances with TNC leaders to gain access to new technology and distribution channels. In the future, it is likely that more firms will attempt to shed their heavy dependence on hardware production and move toward higher value-added electronics systems, software, network technologies, and information-based services.

To conclude, the NIEs have, so far, defied conventional product life cycle theories of how to compete in electronics, continuously repeating a successful "behind-the-frontier" catch-up innovation cycle. From a remote latecomer starting position, NIE firms have become highly respected international competitors in several key fields of electronics. Despite the regional crises (and the dangers of prediction), given the solid foundation of learning it is likely that the electronics sector in the NIEs will recover from the current difficulties and continue to flourish in the future.

REFERENCES

Abegglen, J. C. 1994. *Sea Change: Pacific Asia as the New World Industrial Center*, New York: Free Press.
Abegglen, J. C., and G. S. Stalk. 1985. *Kaisha, the Japanese Corporation*.

New York: Basic Books.

Abernathy, W. J., and K. B. Clark. 1985. "Innovation: Mapping the Winds of Creative Destruction." *Research Policy*, 14, 3–22.

Amsden, A. 1989. *Asia's Next Giant: South Korea and Late Industrialization*. New York: Oxford University Press.

Bartlett, C., and S. Ghoshal. 1987a. "Managing across Borders: New Organizational Requirements." *Sloan Management Review*, 29(1), 43–53.

Bartlett, C., and S. Ghoshal. 1987b. "Managing across Borders: New Strategic Requirements." *Sloan Management Review*, 28(4), 7–17.

Bell, M., M. Hobday, S. Abdullah, N. Ariffin, and J. Malik. 1995. *Aiming for 2020: A Demand Driven Perspective on Industrial Technology Policy in Malaysia*. Final Report for the World Bank and the Ministry of Science, Technology and the Environment, Malaysia, SPRU, October.

Bloom, M. 1991. *Globalization and the Korean Electronics Industry*. Presentation to the EASMA Conference, "The Global Competitiveness of Asian and European Firms," October 17–19, Fontainbleau, Paris.

Capannelli, G. 1994. "Technology Transfer and Industrial Development in Malaysia: Subcontracting Linkages between Japanese Multinationals and Local Suppliers in the Color Television Industry." Unpublished Master's thesis, Hitotsubashi University, Japan.

Cappelen, A., and J. Fagerberg. 1995. "East Asian Growth: A Critical Assessment." *Forum for Development Studies* (Norwegian Institute of International Affairs), 2, 175–195.

Chaponniere, J. R. 1992. "The Newly Industrialising Economies of Asia: International Investment and Transfer of Technology." *STI Review*, 9, April, OECD, Paris.

Chaponniere, J. R., and M. Fouquin. 1989. "Technological Change and the Electronics Sector – Perspectives and Policy Options for Taiwan." Report prepared for Development Centre Project, May, entitled "Technological Change and the Electronics Sector – Perspectives and Policy Options for Newly-Industrialising Economies." Paris: OECD.

Choi, Y. 1994. "Dynamic Techno-Management Capability: The Case of Samsung Semiconductor Sector in Korea." Ph.D dissertation, Department of Economics and Planning, Roskilde University, Roskilde, Denmark.

Clark, K. B., and T. Fujimoto. 1991. *Product Development Performance: Strategy, Organization, and Management in the World Auto Industry*. Boston, MA: Harvard Business School Press.

Chung, K. H., and H. C. Lee. 1989. "National Differences in Managerial Practices." In K. H. Chung and H. C. Lee (eds.), *Korean Managerial Dynamics*. New York: Praeger, 120–148.

Dahlman, C. J., B. Ross-Larson, and L. E. Westphal. 1985. *Managing*

Technological Development: Lessons from the Newly Industrialising Countries. Washington, DC: World Bank.

Dahlman, C. J., and O. Sananikone. 1990. "Technology Strategy in the Economy of Taiwan: Exploiting Foreign Linkages and Investing in Local Capability." Washington, DC: World Bank, preliminary draft.

Dorfman, N. S. 1987. *Innovation and Market Structure: Lessons from the Computer and Semiconductor Industries*. Cambridge, MA: Ballinger.

Dunning, J. H. 1975. "Explaining Changing Patterns of International Production: In Defence of the Eclectic Theory." *Oxford Bulletin of Economics and Statistics*, 41, 269–295.

Economic Development Board. 1992a. *The Electronics Industry in Singapore*. Singapore: Economic Development Board.

———. 1992b. *The Disk Drive Industry in Singapore*. Special report. Singapore: Economic Development Board.

Egan, M. L., and A. Mody. 1992. "Buyer-Seller Links in Export Development." *World Development*, 20(3), 321–334.

Enos, J. L., and W. H. Park. 1988. *The Adoption and Diffusion of Imported Technology: The Case of Korea*. London: Croom Helm.

Felipe, J. 1998. "Total Factor Productivity Growth in East Asia: A Critical Survey." Manila: Asian Development Bank, working paper.

Felipe, J., and J. S. L. McCombie. 1998. "Methodological Problems with Recent Analyses of the East Asian Miracle." Manila: Asian Development Bank, working paper.

Fok, J. T. Y. 1991, December. "Electronics." *Doing Business in Today's Hong Kong*, 4th ed. Hong Kong: American Chambers of Commerce.

Fransman, M., and K. King. (eds.). 1984. *Technological Capability in the Third World*. London: Macmillan.

Gerstenfeld, A., and L. H. Wortzel. 1977. "Strategies for Innovation in Developing Countries." *Sloan Management Review*, Fall, 57–68.

Garvin, D. A. 1993. "Building a Learning Organization." *Harvard Business Review*, July–August, 78–92.

Guyton, L. E. 1994. "Japanese FDI and the Transfer of Japanese Consumer Electronics Production to Malaysia." Report prepared for UNDP, K. L., Malaysia.

Hamel, G., and C. K. Prahalad. 1994. *Competing for the Future*. Boston, MA: Harvard Business School Press.

Hirschman, A. O. 1958. *The Strategy of Economic Development*. New Haven, CT: Yale University Press.

Hobday, M. 1995. *Innovation in East Asia: the Challenge to Japan*. Aldershot, England: Edward Elgar.

Hobday, M. 1996. "Innovation in South-East Asia: Lessons for Europe?" *Management Decision*, 34(9), 71–81.

Holden, T., and L. Nakarmi. 1992. "How Japan Is Keeping the Tigers in a Cage." *International Business Week*, May 11, 24–25.

Hughes, H. 1988. *Achieving Industrialisation in East Asia.* Cambridge, England: Cambridge University Press.

III. 1988. *Information Industry Yearbook.* Taiwan: Institute for Information Industry.

III. 1991. *Information Industry Yearbook.* Taiwan: Institute for Information Industry.

Johnstone, B. 1989. "Taiwan Holds Its Lead, Local Makers Move into New Systems." *Far Eastern Economic Review*, August 31, 50–51.

Jun, Y. W., and S. G. Kim. 1990. "The Korean Electronics Industry – Current Status, Perspectives and Policy Options." Report prepared for Development Centre Project entitled "Technological Change and the Electronics Sector – Perspectives and Policy Options for Newly-Industrialising Economies (NIEs)." Paris: OECD.

Kam, L. V. 1992. *The Role of Subcontracting in Development of Entrepreneurship in SMIs.* Malaysia: Likom.

Kamien, M. I., and N. L. Schwartz. 1982. *Market Structure and Innovation.* Cambridge, England: Cambridge University Press.

Kassim, H., and I. Salleh. 1993. *Technological Dynamism behind Malaysia's Successful Export Performance.* Malaysia: Ministry of Science, Technology, and Energy.

Kim, L. 1980. "Stages of Development of Industrial Technology in a Less Developed Country: A Model." *Research Policy*, 9(3), 254–277.

Kim, L. 1995. "Crisis Construction and Organisational Learning: Capability Building and Catching-up at Hyundai Motor." Paper presented at the Hitotsubashi Organization Science Conference, October 19–22.

Kim, L. 1997. *Imitation to Innovation: The Dynamics of Korea's Technological Learning.* Boston, MA: Harvard Business School Press.

Kim, L., and C. J. Dahlman. 1992. "Technology Policy for Industrialisation: An Integrative Framework and Korea's Experience." *Research Policy*, 21, 437–452.

Kim, D. K., and L. Kim. (eds.). 1989. *Management Behind Industrialisation: Readings in Korean Business.* Seoul: Korean University Press.

Kim, L., and H. Lee. 1987. "Patterns of Technological Change in a Rapidly Developing Country: A Synthesis." *Technovation*, 6, 261–276.

Kim, S. R. 1996. "The Korean System of Innovation and the Semiconductor Industry: A Governance Perspective." UK Pacific Asia Programme, University of Sussex, England, Working paper SEI/SPRU.

Klepper, S. 1996. "Entry, Exit, Growth, and Innovation over the Product Life Cycle." *American Economic Review*, 86(3), 562–583.

Koh, D. J. 1992. "Beyond Technological Dependency, Towards an Agile Giant: The Strategic Concerns of Korea's Samsung Electronics Co. for the 1990s." Master's thesis, Science Policy Research Unit, University of Sussex, England.

Korea Exchange Bank. 1980. *The Korean Economy.* Seoul, South Korea.

Kotler, S. 1976. *Marketing Management: Analysis, Planning and Control,* 3rd ed. London: Prentice Hall International.

Krugman, P. 1994. "The Myth of Asia's Miracle." *Foreign Affairs,* 73(6), 62–78.

Lall, S. 1982. *Developing Countries as Exporters of Technology.* London: Macmillan.

Lall, S. 1992. "Techological Capabilities and Industrialisation." World Development, 20(2), 165–186.

Lall, S. 1994. *Malaysia's Export Performance and Its Sustainability.* Oxford: International Development Centre, Queen Elizabeth House.

Levy, B. 1988. "Korean and Taiwanese Firms as International Competitors: The Challenges Ahead." *Columbia Journal of World Business,* Spring, 43–51.

Lundvall, B. 1988. "Innovation as an Interactive Process: From User-Producer Interaction to the National System of Innovation." In G. Dosi, C. Freeman, R. Nelson, G. Silverberg, and L. Soete (eds.), *Technical Change and Economic Theory.* London: Frances Pinter, 87–103.

Magaziner, I. C., and M. Patinkin, 1989. "Fast Heat: How Korea Won the Microwave War." *Harvard Business Review,* January–February, 83–92.

Mathews, J. A. 1995. *High Technology Industrialisation in East Asia: The Case of the Semiconductor Industry in Taiwan and Korea.* Contemporary Economic Issues Series No. 4. Taiwan: Chung-Hua Institution for Economic Research.

Miller, R., M. Hobday, T. Leroux-Demers, and X. Olleros. 1995. "Innovation in Complex Systems Industries: The Case of Flight Simulation." *Industrial and Corporate Change,* 4(2), 363–400.

MITI. 1994. *Malaysia International Trade and Industry Report 1994.* Malaysia: Ministry of International Trade and Industry.

Myers, S., and D. G. Marquis. 1969. *Successful Industrial Innovations: A Study of Factors Underlying Innovation in Selected Firms.* NSF 69–17. Washington, DC: National Science Foundation.

Nelson, R. R., and H. Pack. 1995. "The Asian Growth Miracle and Modern Growth Theory." Columbia University: School of Public and International Affairs. September (mimeographed).

Nelson, R. R., and N. Rosenberg. 1993. "Technical Innovations and National Systems." In R. R. Nelson (ed.), *National Innovation Systems: A Comparative Analysis.* New York: Oxford University Press, 46–87.

Nelson, R. R., and S. G. Winter. 1982. *An Evolutionary Theory of Economic Change.* Cambridge, MA: Harvard University Press.

O'Connor, D. 1993. "Electronics and Industrialisation: Approaching the 21st Century." In K. S. Jomo (ed.), *Industrialising Malaysia: Policy,*

Performance, Prospects. London: Routledge, 102–146.

O'Connor, D., and C. Wang. 1992. "European and Taiwanese Electronics Industries and Cooperation Opportunities." Paper presented at Sino-European Conference on Economic Development, May.

Porter, M. E. 1990. *The Competitive Advantage of Nations.* London: Macmillan.

Rasiah, R. 1994. "Flexible Production Systems and Local Machine-Tool Sub-contracting: Electronics Components Transnationals in Malaysia." *Cambridge Journal of Economics*, 18, 279–298.

Rhee, Y. W., B. Ross-Larson, and G. Pursell. 1984. *Korea's Competitive Edge: Managing the Entry into World Markets.* Baltimore: Johns Hopkins University Press.

Riedel, J. 1988. "Economic Development in East Asia: Doing What Comes Naturally?" In H. Hughes (ed.), *Achieving Industrialisation in East Asia.* Cambridge, England: Cambridge University Press, 87–92.

Schive, C. 1990. *The Foreign Factor: The Multinational Corporation's Contribution to the Economic Modernisation of the Republic of China.* Stanford, CA: Hoover Institution Press.

Schmookler, J. 1966. *Invention and Economic Growth.* Cambridge, MA: Harvard University Press.

Senge, P. M. 1990. "The Leader's New Work: Building Learning Organizations." *Sloan Management Review*, 9, Fall, 7–23.

Shieh, G. S. 1992. *Boss Island.* New York: Peter Lang.

Singh, A. 1995. "How Did East Asia Grow So Fast: Slow Progress Towards an Analytical Consensus." Discussion Paper No. 97. United Nations Conference on Trade and Development, February.

SPRU. 1972. "Success and Failure in Industrial Innovation." Report on the Project SAPPHO by the Science Policy Research Unit, University of Sussex. London: Centre for the Study of Industrial Innovation.

Stata, R. 1989. "Organisational Learning – the Key to Management Innovation." *Sloan Management Review*, Spring, 63–74.

Suh, S. C. 1974. "The Korean Electronics as Export Industry." Paper presented at the Korea Development Institute-HIID Conference, June 25–28, Seoul, Korea.

UNDP. 1993. "Technology Transfer to Malaysia: Reports Phase 1 and Phase 11 – Electronics and Electrical and the Supporting Industries in Penang." Malaysia: UNDP, K. L.

Utterback, J. M., and W. J. Abernathy. 1975. "A Dynamic Model of Process and Product Innovation." *OMEGA, The International Journal of Management Science*, 3(6), 639–656.

Utterback, J. M., and F. F. Suarez. 1993. "Innovation: Competition, and Industry Structure." *Research Policy*, 15, 285–305.

Vernon, R. 1966. "International Investment and International Trade in the Product Life Cycle." *Quarterly Journal of Economics*, 80(2), 190–207.

Vernon, R. 1975. "The Product Life Cycle Hypothesis in a New International Environment." *Oxford Bulletin of Economics and Statistics*, 41, 255–267.

Von Hippel, E. 1988. *The Sources of Innovation*. Cambridge, MA: MIT Press.

Wade, R. 1990. *Governing the Market: Economic Theory and the Role of Government in East Asian Industrialisation*. Princeton, NJ: Princeton University Press.

Weiss, L., and J. Mathews. 1994. "Innovation Alliances in Taiwan: A Coordinated Approach to Developing and Diffusing Technology." *Journal of Industry Studies*, 1(2), 64–84.

Westphal, L. E., L. Kim, and C. J. Dahlman. 1985. "Reflections on the Republic of Korea's Acquisition of Technological Capability." In N. Rosenberg and C. Frischtak (eds.), *International Transfer of Technology: Concepts, Measures, and Comparisons*. New York: Praeger, 146–171.

Whitley, R. 1992. *Business Systems in East Asia: Firms, Societies and Markets*. London: Sage.

Wood, A. 1994. *North-South Trade, Employment and Inequality: Changing Fortunes in a Skill-Driven World*. Oxford, England: Clarendon Press.

World Bank. 1993. *The East Asian Miracle: Economic Growth and Public Policy*. New York: Oxford University Press.

Young, A. 1994. "Lessons from the East Asian NICs: A Contrarian View." *European Economic Review*, 38(3/4), 964–973.

Young, A. 1995. "The Tyranny of Numbers: Confronting the Statistical Realities of the East Asian Growth Experience." *Quarterly Journal of Economics*, 110, 641–680.

Yuan, L. T., and L. Low. 1990. *Local Entrepreneurship in Singapore: Private and State*. Singapore: Institute of Policy Studies, Times Academy Press.

CHAPTER 6

Technological Learning and Entries of User Firms for Capital Goods in Korea

KongRae Lee

INTRODUCTION

The innovation of capital goods is an important method for providing viability and flexibility to industrial economies because a great portion of the industrial sectors require improved and innovative capital goods for productivity growth. The existence of a well-developed capital goods sector is frequently regarded as one of the critical measures for distinguishing developed countries from developing countries. Developed countries have accumulated the technological capacity to undertake innovation almost routinely through well-developed capital goods sectors.

A group of past innovation studies showed that user firms play a crucial role in the innovation of capital goods (Parkinson, 1982; Foxall, 1986; Rothwell, 1986; von Hippel, 1976, 1979, 1988; Lee, 1996). They argued that user firms generate the ideas for new products and initiate the various stages of product innovation. The user is a primary actor, particularly at the initial stages of the innovation process of capital goods. At the same time, user-producer interaction is a critical dimension of the learning process in the innovation system of capital goods (Lundvall, 1992).

Past innovation studies on the role of user firms have mostly examined developed countries. User firms of capital goods may also play an important role in the capital goods innovation of developing countries, but in different ways. They may first start technological learning by using capital goods, and then evolve through the learning process by repairing, imitating, modifying, and self-designing, and finally, arrive at the initial stage of the innovation process that takes place in the developed countries. The role of user firms in developing countries is still unexplored.

User firms in developing countries have resorted to satisfying much of the demand for capital goods necessary for their productive activities by using imports from developed countries. This phenomenon may cause specialized local suppliers to stay isolated and to lose opportunities to interact with local users and accumulate technological capability. It eventually hinders the development of the capital goods industry in developing countries. Easy access to foreign capital goods has, however, made it possible for developing countries to continue their economic growth without themselves going through the difficult and costly process of developing the capital goods sector.

Korea, a relatively new member of the Organization for Economic Cooperation and Development (OECD), still depends on capital goods of developed countries. User firms have relied heavily on imports for sophisticated capital goods. Due to this high dependency, a great portion of Korea's trade deficit stems from its import of capital goods. There is a growing consensus that building indigenous technological capability to design complex capital goods would not only encourage domestic production of capital goods, but would also improve export performance (Rosenberg, 1976; Fransman, 1982; Fransman and King, 1984; Singh, 1986; Erber, 1986; Kim, 1993; Porter, 1985, 1990).

This chapter examines the evidence concerning technological learning and entries of user firms in the formation and development of the Korean capital goods industry. It addresses the following research questions: (1) Why have user firms attempted technological learning for capital goods technology, if they have done so? (2) To what extent have user firms directly participated in the innovation of capital goods? (3) Have user firms engaged in the commercialization of their technological assets in capital goods?

BRIEF HISTORY OF THE KOREAN CAPITAL GOODS INDUSTRY

Until the early 1970s, the Korean capital goods industry was in its infancy. It was a depressed industrial sector. Domestic machine shops provided repair services and manufactured some basic general-purpose machines such as drilling machines, gear lathes, and engine lathes. However, the manufacture of these machines relied wholly on reverse engineering (Lee and Choi, 1986). The unreliable quality of domestic machines resulted in only small, unsteady domestic orders. A greater portion of the demand for machines was satisfied by imports. The import dependency ratio was at around 80 percent over the 1960s (Kim, 1988). This precluded the possibility of steady and efficient production runs and sales growth. The small demand for domestic producers was further diluted by a supply pool of a fairly large number of small firms. There were 118 machine tool manufacturers in 1966, all small firms with fewer than 100 employees.

The late 1970s represented a major turning point for Korean industry. After the successful completion of the first two Five-Year Economic Plans, government economic policies began to promote the heavy and chemical industries in the Third Five-Year Economic Plan (1972–1976). There was growing recognition that to promote further increases in exports and to develop the defense industry, Korea needed to upgrade the commodity composition of exports in favor of high value-added capital goods (Kim, 1983). The first prominent sign of a change in government priorities was announced in the Heavy and Chemical Industry Development Plan in 1973. The plan called for a rapid buildup of capacity to manufacture capital goods.

Encouraged by government policies, large firms from user sectors made their entrance into the capital goods market. The government supported their entries with preferential loans, tax reduction, construction of special industrial complexes, discounts on public utilities, and other indirect incentives. New entrants were soon able to manufacture machines at industrial complexes with the assistance of foreign technology. The entries of many large firms inevitably created a glut of capacity that disturbed the structure of the industry. Market competition among domestic firms was so severe that many small firms were forced to leave the industry. The number of machine tool producers was 151 in 1974, but it decreased to 91 in 1975. Large new entrants who were both users and producers of capital goods began to gradually dominate the domestic market.

In spite of government protection and support, the self-sufficiency ratio ranged from only 30 percent to 40 percent until the end of the 1970s, illustrating that domestic firms were not yet technologically capable of producing advanced capital goods. This situation led the government to inaugurate a stronger policy toward import substitution called localization (Lee et al., 1990). Domestic production of formerly imported machines has been fostered by the provision of medium- and long-term capital funding for domestic producers.

At the same time, the government imposed quantitative controls on competing imports immediately on the initiation of domestic production (Chudnovsky, 1986). In the early 1980s, strategies for encouraging international competition in domestic markets were adopted and direct controls were gradually removed to increase industrial competitiveness.

With efforts by domestic firms to learn foreign technologies, and through continuous government support for localization, the Korean capital goods industry increased its self-sufficiency ratio from 50 percent to 60 percent in the 1980s. This increase coincided with the rapid growth of the industry in all aspects – output, exports, technological capability, and so on. At the same time, new entries appeared continuously as the domestic capital goods market grew. For instance, the number of domestic machine tool producers rose from 169 in 1980 to 949 in 1994. The output value of machine tools increased remarkably, from $108 million in 1980, to $1,709 million in 1995, in real terms as shown in Table 6.1.

The fast rise of outputs resulting from increases in both domestic demand and export sales has resulted in many technological changes. First, a large number of technical licensing agreements was made to acquire foreign technologies. Industry effectively adopted imported technologies to upgrade its technological capability, which in turn created more demand for advanced foreign technologies. As a result, the industry has successfully developed technological mastery (Westphal et al., 1984) or at least has improved its technological capability.

The growth of machine tool trade during the period is worth noting. Although in small amounts, the industry has been an exporter since 1964. In 1980, its export sales were at best $23 million, but these increased to $334 million in 1995. Although the scale of export value is small relative to other newly industrializing economies (NIEs), its growth rate is considerable. For instance, Taiwan exported about $1.2 billion in machine tools in

Table 6.1. *The growth of the Korean machine tool industry, 1975–1995*

Unit: million U.S. $, %

Year	Number of firms	Output (A)	Imports (B)	Exports (C)	Domestic market size	A/(A + B) (%)	C – B
1975	91	19	85	0.3	104	17.9	−85
1976	132	37	102	0.4	139	26.7	−102
1977	154	83	153	2	234	35.2	−151
1978	187	174	250	4	420	41.0	−246
1979	172	158	311	14	455	33.6	−297
1980	169	108	174	23	259	38.3	−151
1981	171	106	130	31	205	44.8	−99
1982	158	126	87	35	178	59.3	−52
1983	206	169	140	21	288	54.8	−119
1984	239	219	135	22	332	61.9	−113
1985	297	213	229	23	419	48.2	−206
1986	405	364	322	28	658	53.1	−294
1987	512	577	486	37	1,026	54.3	−449
1988	673	955	609	57	1,507	61.0	−552
1989	789	1,144	777	80	1,841	59.6	−697
1990	822	1,581	851	87	1,476	45.5	−764
1991	833	1,461	941	95	2,307	60.8	−846
1992	805	960	967	111	1,816	49.8	−856
1993	915	1,152	709	111	1,750	61.9	−598
1994	949	1,119	972	185	1,906	53.5	−787
1995	1,037	1,709	1,434	334	2,809	54.4	−1,100
AGR 1975–79	17.25	69.81	38.90	161.37	44.63	—	45.85
AGR 1980–89	18.67	29.98	18.09	14.86	24.35	—	18.52
AGR 1990–95	4.76	11.00	11.00	30.87	13.73	—	7.56

Notes: (1) Output statistics are current prices converted to U.S. dollars. (2) Imports, exports and domestic market sizes are at current prices. (3) Domestic market sizes of machine tools are drawn from output plus imports less exports (A + B − C). (4) AGR indicates annual growth rates for the specified periods. *Source:* Korea Machine Tool Manufacturers' Association (KMTMA), *Machine Tool Statistics Handbook*, various years.

1995, which is 3.5 times greater than the Korean exports of $334 million (KMTMA, 1996–97). The annual average growth rate was 14.9 percent during the 1980–89 period and 30.9 percent during the 1990–95 period.

Machine tool imports, however, have expanded at a much faster rate than that of exports, whose growth rate has recently slowed down (11 percent annually during the 1990–95 period). Machine tool imports were $1.4 billion in 1995, a rate that created a large volume of trade deficit. The trade deficits of machine tools totaled $1.1 billion in 1995, which accounted for 10.9 percent of the total

Korean trade deficit of $10 billion that year. As great as the deficit figure is, it represents the market opportunity open to the Korean capital goods industry. With the acquisition of proper technology, the economic burden may be turned into economic fuel.

User firms of capital goods in developing countries may first start technological learning by using. Production activities of user firms entail an inevitable learning process through operating capital goods. As Schmookler (1966) stated, user firms confront many technical problems as they increase production over time. Their problem-solving activities lead to the learning process for capital goods technology through repairing, imitating, modifying, self-designing, and so on. Learning activities of user firms may finally reach the initial stage of the innovation process that takes place in the developed countries. In other words, user firms generate the idea for a new product and initiate subsequent stages of its innovation after a substantial period of user learning takes place.

In Korean user firms, there were increased commissioned purchases of domestic machines as well as the direct manufacture of capital goods to satisfy internal needs. Particularly in the scale-intensive industries, user firms affiliated with conglomerate business groups called *chaebols*, that came into prominence in the mid-1970s, were leading in the learning process of capital goods technology and in entering the capital goods business. Their entries were encouraged by government policies to promote the heavy and chemical industries.

Technological learning by user firms is evidenced by their acquisition of capital goods from foreign firms in Korea. The source of their technological learning is generally formal contracted foreign firms. There are other methods for obtaining foreign technologies – for example, through technical assistance, management agreements, and various forms of technology collaboration. However, this chapter focuses only on learning as a result of formal technology contracts between domestic and foreign firms.

This investigation reveals that technological learning of user firms began at the initial stages of the development of the capital goods industry. Learning was especially active in the late 1970s and the late 1980s, both of which represent periods of high output and investment growth in the Korean economy. On the other hand, there were only a few license agreements by user firms in the sluggish period of the early 1980s.

In the early 1970s, there was only one user firm (Korea Bearing of Korea Explosive Group) that made a technology licensing agreement for capital goods. By the late 1970s, some new entrants from user sectors were found: Samchully (1975), Hyundai Industry (1976), Doosan (1977), Korea Tungsten (1978), and Daehan Heavy (1979). There were no technological license agreements made by user firms in the early 1980s when the Korean economy experienced a severe recession for the first time since embarking on the road to industrialization.

In the late 1980s (1985–89), a surge of technology license agreements emerged from various user sectors. Their imports of capital goods technology seemed to be greatly encouraged by the rapid increase in domestic demand that resulted from the expanded export sales of passenger cars and capacity expansion of the automobile industry. The main new entrants at that time were Kangwon Industry (1985), Hyundai Motors (1986), Hyundai Heavy (1986) and Hyundai Engine (1986) of the Hyundai Group, Goldstar Instruments (1987) and Goldstar Cable (1988) of the LG Group, Samsung Heavy (1988) of the Samsung Group, Ssangyong Precision (1987) of the Ssangyong Group, Mando (1989), and Kukje Kikong (1989).

Technological learning by car assemblers of capital goods shows a distinctive pattern. Hyundai Motors, the largest car assembler, affiliated with the Hyundai Group, accomplished technological learning to implement self-made machines in its plants (Figure 6.1). Hyundai's machine tool division branched into an independent division in 1978. This division supplied approximately 35 percent of the internal demand for special purpose machine tools and 10 percent of the general purpose machine tools in 1996. On the basis of technological accumulation over a few years, it began to manufacture NC (Numerical Control) lathes under a license agreement with Cincinnati Milacron and began selling them to other users in 1986. It also began manufacturing automatic atmosphere furnaces in 1978 and various other special purpose machines thereafter.

Like many other Korean companies whose technology contract typically involves the exchange of personnel for training engineers

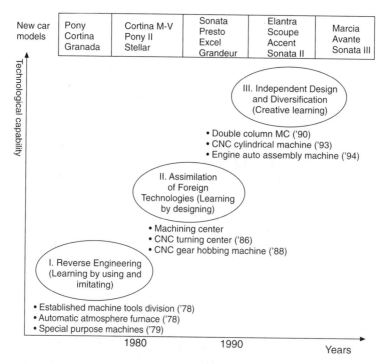

| New car models | Pony Cortina Granada | Cortina M-V Pony II Stellar | Sonata Presto Excel Grandeur | Elantra Scoupe Accent Sonata II | Marcia Avante Sonata III |

Figure 6.1. Technological learning to produce capital goods at Hyundai Motors.

combined with technical assistance (Amsden and Kim, 1986), Hyundai Motors also made large investments in training engineers abroad in order to begin technological learning for capital goods technology, much of it involving on-the-job experience. As a result of this effective means of learning, Hyundai Motors shortened learning time (Westphal, Rhee et al., 1985), rapidly adopting and utilizing foreign technologies to suit its internal requirements better. However, its major activities in technology involved reverse engineering through learning by using and imitating capital goods imported from abroad.

The second phase of Hyundai's learning took place in the 1980s, when it entered a license agreement on machining centers with Shin Nippon Koki, a Japanese supplier, and began selling them to other users in 1984. Hyundai Motors began to produce CNC (Computerized Numerical Control) turning centers under license agreement with Cincinnati Milacron and began selling them to other users in 1986.¹ The late-starting Hyundai made license agreements with a Japanese company, Kasi Fuji, for their technological learning for CNC gear hobbing machines. The condition of the contracts was an initial lump-sum payment of U.S. $80,000 and a running royalty payment of 3 percent over five years.

To learn the licensed technology effectively, Hyundai dispatched qualified engineers to the licensing companies. They quickly understood the principles relevant to their internal requirements. As a result, they significantly shortened development time, for instance, to design foreign capital goods. This learning phase can be termed the assimilation of foreign technologies. Hyundai Motors absorbed technologies of such foreign firms as Shin Nippon Koki, Cincinnati Milacron, Holcroft, Loftus, Kashifuji, ISI, and Norte.

The third learning phase began in the 1990s as Hyundai initiated projects to make independent designs. Using their experience in the manufacturing of foreign machines, Hyundai Motors diversified its production of capital goods. For example, it developed the double column machining center in 1990, the CNC cylindrical machine in 1993, and the engine auto assembly machine in 1994. Their learning mode in the third phase can be described as creative learning, which is more advanced than the first and the second phases. Hyundai Motors is now one of the leading producers of CNC gear hobbing machines. Its machine tool division supplied approximately 35 percent of its internal demand for special purpose machine tools and 10 percent of its general purpose machine tools.

Similar to Hyundai Motors, Kia Motors established a specialized machine tool company, Kia Machine Tools (100 percent share held), to produce machine tools for internal use and for external sales. Kia Machine Tools started producing various machine tools in 1976 based on a technical license from Hitachi Seiki.² Since then, Kia Motors has procured most of its machine tools from Kia Machine Tools.

In addition, Kia Motors has used self-made machine tools produced under its own direct development efforts. About 10 percent to 15 percent of the annual internal demand for production equip-

---

¹ Hyundai Motors Co., company brochures.
² Kia Motors Co. and Kia Machine Tool Co., company brochures.

ment was supplied by its production technology division in 1996. The division has solved various technical problems arising in production lines and has accumulated related technology. The division has been making particular efforts toward increasing the localization of imported machines by cooperating with about forty specialized suppliers.

Unlike Hyundai Motors and Kia Motors, Daewoo Motors did not approach the capital goods market until the beginning of the 1990s. This is partially because it was constrained by its joint company, General Motors (GM). Instead, Daewoo Heavy, one of its sister companies, took up the entry into machines to help solve technical demands. Daewoo Motors did, however, establish a research institute in 1995 to develop production technology and reap technological assets on capital goods. Its active foreign investments generated the establishment of the research institute dedicated to improving overseas plant services. Daewoo Motors had been relatively slow in globalization until it separated from GM in 1992. With the growing need to commercialize its technological assets associated with capital goods, the research institute began commercializing tools, molds, and simple specialized machines.

Patterns of technology acquisition by small and medium-size users are no different from those of large user firms. Shinpoong Paper is an interesting case story on user learning for capital goods technology (see Figure 6.2).[3] Shinpoong, Korea's most profitable paper manufacturer, was founded in 1960. The first phase of Shinpoong's learning was associated with its initial production system in 1962. Shinpoong decided to install a significantly larger capacity system than it could purchase on a turnkey basis. The president of Shinpoong carefully studied paperboard production processes from industry literature, gaining tacit and explicit knowledge about them. He then used secondhand machinery that had been scrapped by a Japanese paper producer.

Shinpoong obtained technical information from literature and from the observation of Japanese papermaking plants. The president designed the basic layout for his plant, used a small Japanese machine shop to produce core parts and fit them to the system.

---

[3] This case story is quoted from Linsu Kim, 1997, *Imitation to Innovation – The Dynamics of Korea's Technological Learning*, Boston: Harvard Business School Press.

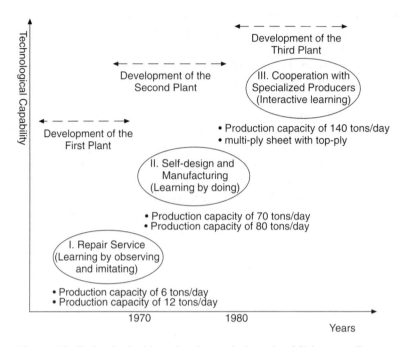

Figure 6.2. Technological learning for capital goods of Shinpoong Paper.
Source: This figure is based on the case study in Linsu Kim, 1977, *Imitation to Innovation: The Dynamics of Korea's Technological Learning*, Boston: Harvard Business School Press.

Debugging was a painful trial-and-error process, but the iterative operation provided the president-engineer with invaluable opportunities to learn the mechanisms of the system. Shinpoong gained a great deal of experience in papermaking machinery and engineering, and excellent opportunities to build the company's tacit knowledge. This tacit knowledge enabled Shinpoong to increase its six-ton-a-day system to eighteen tons a day three years later.

The second phase of Shinpoong's learning took place in 1970, when it decided to install a new production system at its second plant. Instead of purchasing the capital goods from Japan, Shinpoong decided to design its own forty-ton-a-day system. Past technical experience over eight years gave Shinpoong the self-confidence to tackle the challenge. The company subscribed widely to foreign trade magazines and technical journals, which had been a major source of indispensable explicit knowledge. It also arranged with a local capital goods producer to manufacture stock-preparation equipment and dryers, providing an opportunity for that producer to learn about papermaking machinery. With this producer's help, the capacity of the second system was continually improved and expanded to eighty tons a day by 1975.

The third learning phase began in 1978 with a 140-ton-a-day system. Using the experience accumulated during the engineering of the previous two models as a platform, Shinpoong developed designs for Korea's first international-scale papermaking plant. This time, a local capital goods supplier manufactured the system under Shinpoong's supervision. Shinpoong was also encouraged to use a local producer by the government's program to provide preferential financing to purchasers of locally produced capital goods. Had the company contracted to build the plant abroad, the cost would probably have been three to four times more than the $10 million it invested.

In its technological development, Shinpoong had not entered any agreements with foreign firms nor had it received any assistance from local universities, research and development (R&D) institutes, nor engineering firms. It relied completely on the ingenuity, highly effective learning proficiency, and hard work of its president, who developed and used an effective network of local and Japanese capital goods producers. Shinpoong also used the American Pulp and Paper Technical Institute as a major source of new technical ideas.

There are numerous cases of small and medium-size users who have experienced learning activities for capital goods technology. Among them, Sungbo and Taeyang Metal have manufactured automatic loading machines and bolt formers with technical assistance from foreign firms. Taeyang Metal appears to have made substantial use of self-developed technology in manufacturing automatic loading machines, although the basic designs came from foreign firms. Sungbo has cooperated with specialized domestic suppliers to develop bolt formers, its vital process equipment, on the basis of foreign technology.

These three small users (Sungbo, Taeyang Metal, and Myung Sung) have applied self-made machines to account for 10 percent to 30 percent of procured capital goods. Their self-made machines are mostly special purpose machines – for example, an expanded semiautomatic system that became increasingly necessary after the labor disputes of 1987. They are too specialized and idiosyncratic to be produced on a batch basis. Such machines help explain the heterogeneity of capital goods even within the subtypes by which they are described. Specialized domestic producers are reported to have had difficulties obtaining orders for such special purpose machines from customers.

Kongwha Metal is an another interesting small firm that exhibits active learning for capital goods technology. For Kongwha Metal, self-accumulated or self-developed technology was an important enabler for building its technology-learning capability. It has made a variety of machines and tools that are installed in its plants by utilizing internal technical knowledge accumulated through operation, maintenance, and repair. For instance, Kongwha Metal developed assembling machines and testing instruments for producing oil pressure switches. The firm also became involved in the manufacture of electric discharge machines by using its own technological knowledge gained from production experience with various machinery and car parts.

As one can see in these cases, the use of self-developed machines by small and medium-size users is more impressive than those developed by large users. The results of the field survey on four small and medium-size users revealed that all of them actively pursued the direct development of capital goods. To a large degree, they utilized self-made machines. In one firm (Kongwha Metal), which produces thermostats, self-made machines accounted for about 75 percent of the production equipment procured for its internal needs. Self-made machines at this firm vary from assembly machines to testing instruments, some of which have been exported to overseas markets.

To discover the reasons why firms design and make machines for their own internal use, the author conducted interviews with engineers in three large firms employing more than 300 workers, and four small and medium-size firms employing less than 300 workers. Respondents were instructed to weigh the importance of possible reasons on a four-point scale, ranging from 1 (unimportant) to 4 (very important). Table 6.2 depicts the results of the analysis. Mean values of the seven variables weighed by respondents and t-statistics for each variable are presented.

The most important reason for using self-made machines is the "technical incapability of domestic producers" followed by

Table 6.2. *Reasons for developing self-made machines: mean values and t-statistics*

| | Mean values | | |
Reasons	Large users	Small users	t-statistics
Technical incapability of domestic producers	3.333	2.500	1.025
Not available in markets	2.667	3.250	−1.435
Expensive prices of domestic machines	2.667	2.500	0.378
Low performance of domestic machines	2.000	2.000	0.000
Extension of future business	2.666	1.500	1.099
Opportunistic producers	1.000	1.500	−0.845
Fear of leaking information by producers	1.000	0.750	0.845

Source: STEPI field survey conducted in 1996.

"not available in markets" and "expensive prices of domestic machines." The last two variables ("opportunistic producers" and "fear of leaking information by producers") appear to be less significant. There was no significant difference between large users and small and medium-size users in reasons for developing self-made machines.

Meanwhile, the results of a principal component analysis showed that 53.2 percent of the total variance can be explained by the three major variables: "not available in markets," "expensive prices of domestic machines," and "low performance of domestic machines." Another 29.8 percent of the total variance is attributable to the second factor, which is closely correlated with "technical inability of domestic producers" to meet user needs.

These survey results confirm that the technological incapability of domestic producers and unsatisfactory performance-to-investment characteristics of domestic machines have led user firms to become directly involved in learning the technology that will allow them to manufacture their own production equipment. The significance of "expensive prices of domestic machines" implies that domestic production by specialized producers is still inefficient in terms of performance-to-investment.

In general, the sources of technology for user firms pursuing technological learning were mainly foreign technologies. They had acquired this technology initially through the operation process.

Because they could not acquire sufficient technological knowledge this way, user firms made licensing agreements with foreign
producers to complement their lack of internal capability, particularly for advanced technologies.

Another fact worth noting is that most new entrants based on
licenses from foreign firms were mostly large user firms affiliated
with the *chaebols*. This may be because technological learning
based on imported technology requires considerable investment.
Only large firms with substantial capital stock were able to
attempt such technological learning. Their capital formation has
been made through the development of user businesses such as
bicycles, automobiles, shipbuilding, engines, electric cables, metal
products, and so on. It may not be an overstatement to say that
the technological learning and investment of user firms was the
springboard for the development of the Korean capital goods
industry as a whole.

USER INNOVATIONS AND ENTRIES IN CAPITAL GOODS

Having discussed technological learning of user firms, the next
topic of examination is the extent to which user firms directly participated in the innovation of capital goods, if they were involved
in some sort of technological learning linked with capital goods.
User firms pursuing technological learning for and development
of capital goods modified existing technologies to suit their individual requirements. These modifications, targeted at customizing
available technologies, may be regarded as innovation. It is assumed that user firms with patent rights are innovators. Then,
investigating patent activities becomes one method of measuring
innovative activities.

Available statistics on patents granted to domestic organizations allows the comparison of innovative activities between user
firms and specialized producers. Korean firms engaged in capital
goods manufacturing show diversification rather than subsector
specialization. Therefore, the broadly defined concept "the producer of capital goods" is used. Firms engaged in the manufacturing of general machinery are all regarded as producers of
capital goods.[4]

---

[4] General machinery can be defined as machines and equipment included in the code
number 382 (nonelectrical machinery) of the 3-digit International Standard Industrial
Classification (ISIC).

Table 6.3. *Patenting activities by domestic user firms for machine tools in Korea*

	Pre 1974	1975–79	1980–84	1985–89	1990–95	Total
Korean total	0	7	42	123	408	580
Organizations	0	3	17	73	277	370
		(100.0)	(100.0)	(100.0)	(100.0)	(100.0)
Users	0	2	5	28	140	175
		(66.6)	(29.4)	(38.4)	(50.5)	(47.3)
Producers	0	1	12 (70.6)	45	137	195
		(33.4)		(61.6)	(49.5)	(52.7)
Individuals	0	4	25	50	131	210
Foreigners	16	152	275	320	666	1,429
Total	16	159	317	443	1,074	2,009

Notes: (1) Machine tools include the code number B23, B24 and B30 in the International Patent Classification. (2) Figures in parentheses are percentage shares out of subtotal for organization. (3) The user/producer classification of patent holders refers to a particular year 1995.
Source: Korea Institute for Industrial Technology Information (KINITI), KPTN (data base).

Table 6.3 summarizes patenting activities of user firms and specialized producers. The table reveals that on average, 47.3 percent of all patents issued to domestic organizations by 1995 were awarded to user firms. This indicates that user firms had been active suppliers of capital goods innovations in Korea. There also had been considerable proportional increase of user firm innovations over the 1980s. The figures were 29.4 percent for 1980–1984, 38.4 percent for 1985–1989, and 50.5 percent for 1990–1995.

The reason for the proportion of user innovations out of the total innovations seems to be twofold. One reason is that the proportion of capital-goods using firms among the total manufacturers has been rising over the last two decades. It was 18.2 percent in 1975, but increased to 26.1 percent in 1985 and to 37.1 percent in 1994, as shown in Table 6.4. The other reason is the result of intensive technological learning efforts by user firms, which probably led to an increased number of innovations that, in turn, increased the number of their patent registrations.

A considerable proportion of user firms engaging in successful learning have also made commercial entries into capital goods. In particular, user firms attempting technological learning for capital

Table 6.4. *The number of user firms and specialized suppliers for machine tools in Korea*

	1975	1980	1985	1990	1994
Total (A)	22,787	30,823	44,037	68,690	91,372
Users(B)[a]	4,152	6,660	11,478	22,693	33,872
Suppliers(C)[b]	91	172	297	822	949
B/A (%)	18.2	21.6	26.1	33.0	37.1
C/B (%)	2.2	2.6	2.6	3.6	2.8

Notes: [a] Indicates the number of firms in the business of processing and assembling (fabricated metals, general machinery, electric-electronic machinery, transport equipment and precision instrument).
[b] The number of firms producing machine tools surveyed by Korea Machine Tool Manufacturers' Association (KMTMA). The user/producer classification of patent holders refers to a particular year 1995.
Source: Korea Machine Tool Manufacturers' Association (KMTMA), Machine Tool Statistics Handbook, various years.

goods by making license agreements with foreign firms seem to have had commercial objectives from the beginning. One piece of evidence is that a running royalty payment was one of the standard conditions stipulated in their technological license agreements. Firms are obliged to pay royalties for successful sales only. Some firms successfully commercialized licensed technologies immediately following their technological learning for capital goods, competing not only with foreign suppliers but also with other established domestic producers.

Two out of six surveyed user firms having technological learning and innovations on capital goods had sold self-made machines to other user firms. Hyundai Motors is one prominent example of a firm making an entrepreneurial entry into capital goods. Hyundai Motors offers a variety of capital goods ranging from standardized machines, such as machining centers, CNC copy milling machines, CNC turning centers, and CNC gear hobbing machines, to special purpose machines, such as transfer machines, rotary index type machines, flexible transfer machines, and various other kinds of industrial machinery. Total sales amounted to $41 million in 1991 for the 402-employee organization. Hyundai Motors is now a specialized supplier of industrial machinery.

Another firm having successfully sold self-made machines is the small and medium-size user, Kongwha Metal with 250 employees. Kongwha has developed several special purpose machines. Although domestic demand for these machines has been low, Kongwha has successfully sold its machines to foreign customers. The firm has gained many benefits from self-development of capital goods. First, it substantially reduced its capital costs by using in its own operation the machines it had developed. The reduction was almost half the amount it would have had to pay for externally procured machines. Second, it built sound technological capability to design similar machines or to develop more advanced automation systems. Last, the accumulated technology gained from these efforts could be commercialized for profit.

Barriers facing user firms seeking commercial entry were considerable. Both Hyundai Motors and Kongwha Metal had difficulty penetrating the existing market because they either were unable to find customers or lacked the reputation for technical reliability. Interestingly, capital-cost barriers were not as burdening as marketing barriers. Capital accumulation from their original businesses might have been the capital source for entering other businesses.

Hyundai Motors seemed to overcome the marketing barrier by focusing on its fairly large number of subcontracted parts suppliers. In 1990, Hyundai Motors had 433 parts suppliers, most of whom had long-term subcontracting agreements with Hyundai (KAMA, 1991). Such parts suppliers are generally small and medium-size firms whose sales depend entirely on their parent company. They tend to be placed at lower positions in the subcontracting system hierarchy. Hence, they may have readily cooperated with Hyundai Motors' new business efforts for its self-made capital goods. Kongwha Metal shows a similar pattern, with the exception that it has marketed self-developed machines not to its subcontractors but to its customers.

CONCLUDING REMARKS

Summing up, user firms played a significant role in the formation and development of the Korean capital goods industry. They motivated specialized domestic suppliers to embark on the dynamic course of building technological capability. At the same time, they became directly involved in the development and commercialization of capital goods to become innovators and producers of these goods. User learning, coupled with entries into the capital goods market, results in benefits for both user firms and specialized suppliers. Major conclusions can be drawn as follows.

Learning activities of user firms for capital goods existed from the beginning of industrialization. User firms were particularly active in acquiring technological learning at the time when the domestic demand for capital goods was rapidly expanding. Most user firms began with self-developed, special purpose machines. One major reason they initially sought capital goods technology was because domestic suppliers could not meet their technological demand. They mainly relied on foreign technologies to learn capital goods technology.

User firms engaged in self-development of capital goods have modified, improved, and innovated machines to suit their specific requirements. On the average, approximately 47.3 percent of machine tool patents issued to domestic organizations were granted to user firms. The proportion of user innovation has been increasing as a consequence of active technological learning for capital goods. User firms successful in self-development of capital goods have often gone further to make entrepreneurial entries. Some have even experienced commercial success, competing against not only domestic suppliers but foreign firms also.

User firms took an active part in capital goods development by technological learning and commercial entries. They encouraged specialized domestic producers to learn from foreign technologies. They also directly engaged in self-development of capital goods and used self-made machines to a considerable degree. At the same time, some user firms became involved in the commercialization of their self-developed capital goods. As a result of these activities, user firms generated a substantial part of the domestic innovation of capital goods.

What do the learning activities of user firms to gain capital goods technology imply for competitiveness of users themselves and specialized suppliers? Analysis of survey results showed that the impact of user learning and entries on overall competitiveness is greater on the users themselves than on specialized suppliers.

For user firms, cost savings appeared to be the most significant factor, while the quality improvement effect turned out to be the strongest for the specialized suppliers.

These findings imply that active user learning and entries fuel competition not only among the users but also among specialized suppliers. Statistics show that user learning and entries have considerably influenced various technological activities, gradually making competition more severe. The results of the field survey revealed that the impact on users is greatly significant while the impact on producers is moderately significant. This finding implies that user learning for and entries into capital goods stimulate both users and specialized producers to pursue additional technological activities.

For user firms, effect on cost savings, an important measure of competitiveness, appeared to be most significant, followed by quality improvement and new product development.[5] On the other hand, for specialized producers, the effect on quality improvement displayed the highest significance followed by price reduction, increase in product variety, and new product development.

Comparing the responses given by large users and small and medium-size (SM) users, no significant differences were found in the effects of their learning activities and entries on elements of competitiveness except for cost reduction and quality improvement. SM users experienced cost savings from their self-development of capital goods much more than did large users. They also experienced quality improvement much more than did large users in the effects on specialized producers.

The survey findings suggest that SM users are more conscious of cost benefits from the learning and use of their self-developed capital goods than are the large user firms. This also explains why SM users have used more self-made capital goods. One can also see that SM users appreciate quality improvement more than large users do. They are likely to be more sensitive to quality changes made by specialized suppliers because they are more cost conscious than large users.

---

[5] A direct and fundamental determinant of international competitiveness is, with no doubt, technological innovation (Dosi et al., 1990; Soete, 1980, 1981).

REFERENCES

Amsden, A., and Linsu Kim. 1986. "A Technological Perspective on the General Machinery Industry in the Republic of Korea." In M. Fransman (ed.), *Machinery and Economic Development*. London: Macmillan, 93–123.

Chudnovsky, D. 1986. "The Entry into the Design and Production of Complex Capital Goods: The Experiences of Brazil, India and S. Korea." In M. Fransman (ed.), *Machinery and Economic Development*. London: Macmillan, 54–91.

Dosi, G., K. Pavitt, and L. Soete. 1990. *The Economics of Technological Change and International Trade*: London: Croom Helm.

Erber, F. S. 1986. "The Capital Goods Industry and the Dynamics of Economic Development in LDCs: The Case of Brazil." In M. Fransman (ed.), *Machinery and Economic Development*. London: Macmillan, 215–269.

Fransman, M. 1982. "Learning and the Capital Goods Sector under Free Trade: The Case of Hong Kong." *World Development*, 10(11), 991–1014.

Fransman, M., and K. King (eds.). 1984. *Technological Capability in the Third World*. London: Macmillan.

Foxall, C. 1986. *Strategies of User-Initiated Product Innovation*. Bedford, U.K.: Cranfield School of Management.

Kim, Ki-Hwan. 1983. "The Korean Economy: Past Performance, Current Reforms and Future Prospects." Paper presented at the International Forum on Economic Policies and Development Strategies, Seoul, Korea Development Institute (KDI).

Kim, Linsu. 1993. "National System of Industrial Innovation: Dynamics of Capability Building in Korea." In R. Nelson (ed.), *National Innovation Systems – A Comparative Analysis*. Oxford, England: Oxford University Press, 359–383.

Kim, Linsu. 1997. *Imitation to Innovation – The Dynamics of Korea's Technological Learning*. Boston MA: Harvard Business School Press.

Kim, Hwansuk. 1988. Determinants of Technological Change in the Korean Machine Tool Industry: A Comparison of Large and Small Firms, Ph.D. dissertation, The University of London, London.

Korea Automobile Manufacturers Association. *The Korea Automobile Industry*, various years.

Korea Machine Tool Manufacturers' Association (KMTMA). *Machine Tool Statistics Handbook*, various years.

Lee, Jin-Joo, and Dong-Kyu Choi. 1986. *Innovation Process of Korean Industries and Government Policies* (in Korean). Seoul: Korea Economic Research Institute.

Lee, KongRae et al. 1990. *Evaluations and Recommendations for Localization Policy* (in Korean). Seoul: KIET.

Lee, KongRae. 1996. "The Role of User Firms in the Innovation of Machine Tools: The Japanese Case." *Research Policy*, 25, 491–507.

Lundvall, B. A. 1992. *National Systems of Innovation – Towards a Theory of Innovation and Interactive Learning*, London: Pinter Publishers.

Norusis, M. J. 1988. *SPSS/PC Advanced Statistics (V. 2.0)*. Chicago: SPSS Inc.

Parkinson, S. 1982. "Successful New Product Development – Having a Good Customer Helps." *The Business Graduate* (Special Issue), 12(1), 68–69.

Parkinson, S. T. 1982. "The Role of the User in Successful New Product Development." *R&D Management*, 12(3), 123–133.

Porter, M. E. 1985. *Competitive Advantage – Creating and Sustaining Superior Performance*. New York: Free Press.

Porter, M. E. 1990. *The Competitive Advantage of Nations*. London: Macmillan.

Rosenberg, N. 1976. *Perspective on Technology*. Cambridge: Cambridge University Press.

Rothwell, R. 1986. "Innovation and Re-innovation: A Role for the User." *Journal of Marketing Management*, 2(2), 109–123.

Schmookler, J. 1962. "Changes in Industry and in the State of Knowledge as Determinants of Industrial Innovation, in National Bureau of Economic Research (NBER)." *The Rate and Direction of Inventive Activity: Economic and Social Factors*. Princeton, NJ: Princeton University Press, 195–201.

Schmookler, J. 1966. *Invention and Economic Growth*. Boston, MA: Harvard University Press.

Singh, A. 1986. "Crisis and Recovery in the Mexican Economy: The Role of the Capital Goods Sector." In M. Fransman (ed.), *Machinery and Economic Development*. London: Macmillan, pp. 247–268.

Soete, L. 1980. "The Impact of Technological Innovation on International Trade Patterns: The Evidence Reconsidered." Paper presented to the OECD Science and Technology Indicators Conference, Paris.

Soete, L. 1981. "A General Test of Technological Gap Trade Theory." *Review of World Economics*, 117, 638–659.

United Nations. 1979–1988. *International Trade Statistics Year-book*. New York: United Nations.

von Hippel, E. 1976. "The Dominant Role of Users in the Scientific Instruments Innovation Process." *Research Policy*, 5, 212–239.

von Hippel, E. 1979. "A Customer-Active Paradigm for Industrial Product Idea Generation." In M. Baker (ed.), *Industrial Innovation – Technology, Policy, Diffusion*. London: Macmillan, 60–81.

von Hippel, E. 1988. *The Sources of Innovation*. New York: Oxford University Press.

Westphal, L. E., Yung W. Rhee, Linsu Kim, and A. H. Amsden. 1984a. "Exports of Technology by Newly Industrializing Countries – Republic of Korea." *World Development*, 12(5/6), 505–533.

Westphal, L. E., Linsu Kim, and C. J. Dahlman. 1985. *Reflections on Korea's Acquisition of Technological Capability*. In Nathan Rosenberg and Claudio Frischak (eds.), *International Technology Transfer: Concepts, Measures, and Comparisons*. New York: Praeger, 167–221.

Wilder, R. 1990. "The Industrial Property System, Patents, Trademarks, Designs and Know-How." Paper presented to the WIPO Asian Regional Seminar, Geneva, World Intellectual Property Organization (WIPO).

Womack, J. P., D. T. Jones, and D. Roos. 1990. *The Machine That Changed the World*. New York: Rawson Associates.

CHAPTER 7

International Technological Collaboration: Implications for Newly Industrializing Economies

Geert Duysters
John Hagedoorn

INTRODUCTION

Internationalization tendencies in business and economic systems at large receive widespread interest from both theorists and practitioners (see, e.g., Vernon, 1966, 1979; Bartlett et al., 1990; Dunning, 1988, 1993; Reich, 1991; Hu, 1992). Whereas most of the attention in the literature is devoted to the internationalization of production and distribution, much less attention is paid to the internationalization of research and development (R&D) activities (for exceptions see, among others, Lee and Reid, 1991; Pearce, 1989; Graves, 1991; Miller, 1994; Duysters and Hagedoorn, 1996).

In this chapter we aim to identify the major trends in international strategic technology partnering as an important domain within the overall process of internationalization. Given the topic of this volume, we will analyze strategic technology alliances between firms from the developed economies (Triad countries)[1] with companies from newly industrializing economies (NIEs) and in particular South Korea. The alliances that we study are defined as international if at least two firms of the partnership originate from different countries. The term *strategic* is used to denote those partnerships that can reasonably be assumed to affect the long-term positioning of at least one partner. Although production and marketing agreements are also widely reported in the literature, we will limit our analysis to those agreements for which joint tech-

---

[1] Triad countries consist of Japan, the United States, and fifteen European Union member states.

nological activity is at least part of the agreement. Our data set is derived from the MERIT-CATI data bank and covers the period 1980–1994 (see Appendix). Because of the differences between alliances in which two or more companies are involved and alliances between government or academic institutions and companies, we restrict our attention to intercompany partnerships.

In the next section we set the stage for a discussion of international strategic technology alliances. We first present some general rationales for the creation of technology partnerships. This is followed by a broad discussion about the institutional form of the agreement and about the sectors in which technology agreements take place. Examples of different international alliances with companies from NIEs are given throughout these sections. Next we present an empirical analysis of patterns of strategic technology partnering with firms from NIEs. More particularly, we compare international intra-Triad alliances (alliances between European, U.S., and Japanese companies) with strategic technology partnerships between companies from NIEs and companies that are based within the Triad. Within this subset of Triad-NIE alliances we pay specific attention to Triad-South Korean partnerships. Finally, we pay attention to historical patterns of technology transfer to see whether companies from NIEs have gained technological strength through alliances and whether they gradually formed alliances that are somewhat "equal" partnerships of companies with similar technological strength.

INTERNATIONAL STRATEGIC TECHNOLOGY ALLIANCES: STRUCTURAL AND TECHNOLOGICAL DRIVERS

Traditionally, firms have acted as independent self-contained units (Contractor and Lorange, 1988). During the seventies and early eighties a number of companies, however, started to replace their traditional practices, such as mergers and foreign direct investment, with new forms of organization, such as joint ventures, joint development agreements, and other types of technology sharing agreements. The formation of these new forms of cooperation was above all triggered by fundamental changes in the structure of the global economy and by the ongoing process of technological change (Haklisch, 1989). Such structural changes are found in the homogenization of markets, fierce competition, and ongoing globalization tendencies, whereas ever-increasing costs of research and development (R&D) and the increasing complexity of products combined with a strong increase in the speed of technological developments are the main drivers from a technological perspective (Haklisch, 1989).

It appears that even the largest and most diversified firms frequently lack the economic power to successfully enter different geographic markets simultaneously (Ohmae, 1985). Strategic alliances are therefore often seen as an essential part of international corporate strategies (Ohmae, 1990; de Woot, 1990). Strategic alliances make up for the lack of economic power, competence, or foreign experience of at least one of the partners. Strategic alliances are also increasingly used as scanning devices that allow firms to monitor new markets without the need to invest the full amount of resources. If certain market opportunities turn out to be less attractive, then cooperative agreements can be terminated with only a relatively small loss. If, however, new market opportunities materialize further, companies can still decide whether they will pursue these new opportunities through the alliance or on their own (Obleros and MacDonald, 1988).

From a technological perspective other factors also play a role in the formation of strategic alliances.[2] Since the eighties, technology intensive sectors have been characterized by a combination of rapidly rising costs of equipment and R&D, steep learning curves, and ever-shortening product life cycles. The cost of developing a new computer system, car, or microprocessor has gone up to billions of dollars. The development of every new generation of products seems to involve a much higher amount of capital, whereas, due to shrinking life cycles, costs are much more difficult to recoup within such a short time period. With the exception of a few very large multinational firms, no firm seems to be able to finance a wide range of R&D projects all by itself. Even for the largest companies, the risk of failure involved in those capital-intensive R&D projects is likely to be too high. Cost sharing has therefore become a key to a successful innovation strategy (see Mowery, 1988; Link and Bauer, 1989). Cooperation not only lowers the amount of investment but also raises the economies of scale in R&D. By integrating previously separate activities,

---

[2] See Hagedoorn (1993) for a complete overview of motives for strategic R&D alliances.

cooperative agreements raise the total volume of activities, which allows for significant scale advantages.

There are many examples of such cost-reduction and scale-motivated alliances, also in alliances with NIE companies. For instance, in 1993 Texas Instruments and the Korean company Samsung set up a joint venture to jointly manufacture microelectronic components such as 1 and 4 Mbit DRAMs and ASICs. In that same year another Korean company, Daewoo, entered into a joint development agreement with the Russian company Mikoyan Design to jointly develop a military aircraft for the export markets of both companies. In 1992 the Swedish telecom company Ericsson and the Taiwanese company Nanjing Radio Factory formed a joint venture to manufacture radio base stations for analog mobile cellular systems.

Strategic alliances can also be used to reduce lead times for innovative products. A reduction in lead times allows firms to preempt the market and enables them to move faster down the learning curve. Strategic partnerships can therefore play an important role in a joint effort to contract the period between invention and market introduction for a number of projects of each individual company. Examples of alliances that are aimed at the reduction of the time-to-market are:

- The joint development of pen-based palmtop PCs for wireless communication by Motorola and Samsung, which started in 1992
- The development of multifunctional I/O chips by the U.S. company National Semiconductors and the Taiwanese company Acer, which started in 1990.

Strategic partnering is not only used as a scanning device for different product markets but can also be applied as a monitoring device for particular fields of technology. The ongoing complexity of technology and the intersectoral nature of new technologies and the cross-fertilization of scientific disciplines and fields of technology raises the need for flexibility in order to respond quickly to changing market needs and to new technological opportunities. The growing interrelationship between an increasing number of different scientific and technological disciplines in combination with the rising costs of R&D in all high-technology sectors makes it very difficult for a single organization to monitor all the technological developments by itself. Despite successful diversification strategies of many companies, firms often lack competencies in a number of scientific and technological fields. Partnerships with competent partners can create the necessary, complementary technology and scientific inputs enabling these companies to capitalize on economies of scope through joint efforts. Synergy effects arising from technological complementarities among partners often create win-win situations for all the partners involved.

ORGANIZATIONAL MODES OF STRATEGIC ALLIANCES

Traditionally, joint ventures have been the most preferred alliance form. In a joint venture, firms pool their skills and resources in a newly created company that is characterized by joint ownership. Already in the 1980s a larger variety of organizational modes were introduced. Following taxonomies by Auster (1992), Chesnais (1988), Harrigan (1985b), Casson (1987), Contractor and Lorange (1988), and Hagedoorn (1990) we distinguish between equity agreements, such as international joint ventures and research corporations,[3] and a group of so-called contractual arrangements, such as joint development agreements, R&D pacts, and R&D contracts. Many contributions (Auster, 1992; Buckley and Casson, 1988; Contractor and Lorange, 1988; Hagedoorn, 1990; Hagedoorn and Narula, 1996) have shown that these different modes of cooperation have a distinctive impact on the character of technology sharing, the organizational context, and the possible economic consequences for participating companies.

Equity agreements and in particular joint ventures have been extensively used in the international arena. Equity participation creates mutual dependence among the participating companies. If one partner does not behave accordingly then all partners suffer (Buckley and Casson, 1988). The creation of a new firm with usually two parents therefore creates a relatively high degree of organizational interdependence. In terms of Williamson (1985, 1991), this comes close to hierarchical structures with parent companies sharing control over their joint venture. Apart from

---

[3] Research corporations are a subcategory of joint ventures with distinctive research programs.

international joint ventures with companies from NIEs mentioned earlier, there are many other examples. In 1980, Chrysler and Samsung set up what turned out to be a short-lived joint venture to develop automotive parts for Chrysler and other car manufacturers. In 1993, the German company Henkel and the Taiwanese firm SH-Nanji started a joint venture that develops and manufactures PVC plastisols and wax coatings for the car industry. Another example is the joint venture between LG from South Korea and IBM that started developing and producing notebooks, PCs, and servers in 1996.

Whereas these equity agreements are well suited to deal with stable situations that require mutual dependence, an increasing number of companies prefer a more flexible organizational form. Especially in high-technology industries, firms need a certain degree of "strategic flexibility"[4]. Non-equity agreements, more particularly, joint development agreements, are increasingly used by firms that prefer flexibility over stability. Such companies want to be able to switch smoothly from research in one technology to research in another (Obleros and MacDonald, 1988). We understand these contractual, non-equity agreements to cover technology and R&D sharing by two or more companies through undertakings that establish research projects or joint development agreements with shared resources. Although the interdependence in these joint research pacts and joint development agreements is smaller than in the case of joint ventures, the agreements still require a relatively strong commitment of companies and interorganizational interdependence during the joint project. The more flexible non-equity types of agreements are undertaken in particular by large companies that want to explore possible technological opportunities (Duysters and Hagedoorn, 1995; Hagedoorn and Schakenraad, 1994). Because the termination of projects is usually much easier to accomplish in non-equity agreements than in agreements that involve equity, they are often better suited to deal with situations of change or uncertain demand, or when business risk is high (Harrigan, 1988; Kreiken, 1986). We have already presented several examples of such joint research pacts and joint development agreements. In addition to these we can mention

---

[4] Strategic flexibility refers to the ability of organizations "to reposition themselves in a market, change their game plans, or dismantle their current strategies when the customers they serve are no longer as attractive as they once were" (Harrigan, 1985a, p. 1).

some cases of Japanese-Korean collaboration such as the alliance between Toshiba and Samsung to develop 16-Mbit NAND flash memory technologies and the Sumitomo-Samsung joint development agreement to improve semiconductor production efficiency.

Apart from joint development agreements and research pacts there are other non-equity forms. In the case of research contracts, one partner, usually a large company, contracts another company to perform particular research projects. For the initiating party, such a contract can save substantial costs compared to using full-fledged in-house facilities. Disadvantages for those companies are associated with the lack of in-house expertise to assess the value of contract research and the dissociation of R&D expertise from manufacturing expertise (Obleros and MacDonald, 1988; Teece, 1987). For the other contractor, benefits are found in terms of substantial R&D funding and cooperation with experienced partners. For instance, in 1988 the Taiwanese company Acer received an R&D contract from Intel for testing Intel's 80486 processor that enabled it to work within what was at that time a state-of-the-art high-tech environment.

The choice for a particular alliance mode is affected by the tradeoff between minimizing organizational complexity and maximizing control over the alliance by each partner. The more complex interorganizational mode of technology cooperation, such as a joint venture, raises a number of problems of corporate governance. Its quasi-hierarchical nature not only reaches intermediate levels of corporate control, but also introduces dilemmas related to trust, forbearance, and opportunism (Parkhe, 1993). As no separate new administrative element is created in contractual agreements, these appear to involve lesser intraorganizational complexity. However, although contractual agreements in themselves are less complex, companies often engage in several alliances simultaneously with a variety of partners, which introduces an additional level of complexity. This complexity relates to difficulties associated with both the administration of these partnerships and the need to continuously monitor the net benefits accruing from various contractual alliances (Osborn and Baughn, 1990).

These already existing high levels of complexity in alliances are increased once again by their international context. In terms of control, the agreement has to be monitored from corporate headquarters over long distances or from a local or regional subsidiary. However, even in the latter case, there is often no real reduction in the distance of control but it frequently merely results in the introduction of an additional level of corporate governance. Furthermore, companies of different national backgrounds are influenced by their past business experiences as well as by the difficulties of maintaining control over the alliance across borders. Traditional internationalization theory (Buckley and Casson, 1976, 1988; Dunning, 1993; Rugman, 1980) appears to suggest that equity agreements offer a larger degree of control over technology sharing than non-equity partnerships. However, recent contributions (Hagedoorn, 1993; Osborn et al., 1996; Powell et al., 1996) suggest that particularly for technology-related alliances, formal control is probably less relevant than adequate access to new knowledge, flexibility in cooperation, and mutual flows of information for which both complete and incomplete contractual agreements seem adequate.

An interesting question in this context is whether sectors differ with respect to the distribution of equity versus contractual agreements. Studies by Harrigan (1985b, 1988), Link and Bauer (1989), Osborn and Baughn (1990), and Hagedoorn and Narula (1996) suggest that technological stability of industrial sectors is a crucial factor in explaining different patterns for equity and non-equity partnerships. In sectors with low or medium degrees of R&D intensity that we can characterize as low or medium technology-intensive sectors, one will witness a larger share of joint ventures than in R&D intensive sectors, or high-tech sectors, in which we see a general preference for contractual agreements and a higher degree of organizational flexibility in partnerships.

GENERAL PATTERNS IN ALLIANCE FORMATION

The overall number of newly established international alliances in our database has grown from about 100 alliances in 1980 to about 325 alliances in 1989 (see Figure 7.1). In the early nineties we first find a modest slowdown, which is then followed by a strong upheaval in 1993 and a further consolidation of the number of newly established international strategic technology alliances. The same pattern is found in the case of intra-Triad alliances. Although intra-Triad alliances still account for the majority of international

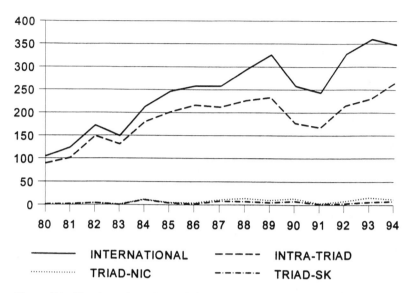

Figure 7.1. Number of newly established international strategic technology
alliances, 1980–94.

strategic technology alliances, the share of non-intra-Triad
alliances appears to be growing.

In the early eighties, only a very small number of firms from
NIEs were involved in strategic technology partnerships. Alliance
activity was very low during the first years of the eighties. In 1984
we witness the first peak in alliance activity with NIEs. In the following years alliances were undertaken on a modest scale, aver-
aging about ten alliances per year. The proportion of alliances
that involve at least one South Korean firm as a percentage of the
total number of Triad-NIE alliances has always been very high.
Until 1985 Korean firms accounted for all the newly established
Triad-NIE strategic technology alliances. In the second half of the
eighties and in the early nineties, their share diminished but
remained eminent. In spite of the much lower magnitude the
growth pattern of Triad-NIE alliances closely resembles the
overall growth pattern of international alliances.

In our preoccupation with international alliances, however, we
should not forget that strategic technology partnering as such has
not necessarily become more internationalized. Although we are

Table 7.1. *Research and development orientation of international strategic technology alliances, 1980–1994*

	80–84	85–89	90–94	Three Periods
Intra-Triad				
R&D	54%	58%	85%	66%
Product/Market	46%	43%	16%	35%
Triad-NIEs				
R&D	24%	27%	72%	41%
Product/Market	76%	73%	29%	59%
Triad-SK				
R&D	17%	27%	85%	43%
Product/Market	83%	73%	15%	57%

witnessing a sharp increase in the number of newly established international alliances, the number of domestic alliances and the number of cross-border strategic technology alliances made within the same international region has also increased quite strongly. In relative terms these domestic and intraregional alliances are still an important phenomenon. Duysters and Hagedoorn (1996) found that, as with the internationalization of company R&D and other aspects of the internationalization of innovative efforts of companies, there is certainly not an explosion of international activities but much more a gradual increase of international alliances in the context of an overall increase of interfirm partnering.

Having discussed both the technological and the competitive drivers that play a role in the formation of alliances, we can view the respective importance of these imperatives in Table 7.1. This table presents the distribution of strategic technology alliances for which we found that joint research and development was the only or by far the most important motive for cooperation set against alliances for which a wider range of incentives such as joint production and joint marketing was also part of the agreement. As we are analyzing international strategic "technology" alliances, it does not come as a surprise that R&D, which plays an important role in technological development, is also a major imperative for companies to cooperate. However, in the case of intra-Triad alliances, the changes over time do suggest that the nineties marks a period in which technological cooperation through joint R&D has become even more important and as such it stresses the relevance of advanced technology pressures that lie behind this phenomenon. The alliances between Triad countries and NIEs show a somewhat different pattern. Although R&D is an important factor in the formation of strategic technology alliances between companies from NIEs and the Triad (including Triad-South Korean alliances), their share is still significantly lower than the share of R&D centerd alliances between Triad countries.

In spite of the relatively low R&D component in the NIE alliances, a sectoral analysis (Table 7.2) also reveals that in the early nineties alliances between Triad countries and NIEs are primarily found in high-tech sectors, especially in the information technology industry. Taken together, computers, microelectronics, software, and telecommunications account for about 56 percent of the total number of alliances in the last period (1990–94). Biotechnology alliances account for 12.3 percent, and alliances in new materials and aerospace account for 7 percent each. Remarkable is the low-tech orientation in terms of sectors in the second period (1985–89). In this specific period only 43 percent of all newly established alliances is found in high-technology sectors. The combined share of newly established strategic technology alliances with NIE companies in high-tech sectors (information technology, biotechnology, new materials and aerospace, aviation and defense) has risen from 76 percent in the first period (1980–84) to more than 82 percent in the last period (1990–94). A striking difference between Triad-NIE alliances and intra-Triad alliances is found in the sectoral distribution within the high technology sectors. The largest number of newly established alliances during the early nineties between Triad firms is found in biotechnology. If we rank sectors according to their number of newly established alliances, we find the biotechnology sector in third place if we restrict our attention to Triad-NIE alliances only. Over a quarter of all newly established alliances with NIEs is established in microelectronics. Computer alliances account for 14 percent compared to 12.3 percent of biotechnology alliances. Also remarkable is the low number of telecommunications alliances

Table 7.2. *Sectoral division of newly established international strategic technology alliances*

	Intra-Triad			Triad-NIE			Triad-SK		
	80–84	85–89	90–94	80–84	85–89	90–94	80–84	85–89	90–94
Biotechnology	15.1%	17.5%	17.9%	4.0%	4.5%	12.3%	4.5%	0.0%	3.4%
Other Information technology	2.4%	3.6%	0.5%	4.0%	0.0%	0.0%	4.5%	0.0%	0.0%
Computers	5.6%	5.3%	6.8%	4.0%	4.5%	14.0%	4.5%	3.8%	24.1%
Microelectronic	16.9%	9.0%	17.6%	40.0%	9.1%	26.3%	40.9%	3.8%	44.8%
Software	8.5%	9.6%	11.2%	4.0%	4.5%	12.3%	4.5%	3.8%	10.3%
Telecommunications	7.6%	11.4%	11.8%	8.0%	9.1%	3.5%	9.1%	3.8%	0.0%
New materials	7.9%	10.0%	8.1%	12.0%	11.4%	7.0%	18.3%	15.4%	0.0%
Aerospace	5.8%	5.2%	9.4%	0.0%	0.0%	7.0%	0.0%	0.0%	3.4%
Automotive	4.6%	7.1%	2.0%	12.0%	18.2%	5.3%	9.1%	23.1%	10.3%
Chemicals	9.6%	7.9%	9.8%	0.0%	18.2%	7.0%	0.0%	23.1%	0.0%
Foods	0.8%	0.5%	1.0%	0.0%	4.5%	0.0%	0.0%	3.8%	0.0%
Industrial automation	5.9%	5.9%	4.0%	8.0%	9.1%	1.8%	4.5%	11.5%	0.0%
Consumer electronics	2.6%	1.4%	1.7%	4.0%	6.8%	1.8%	4.5%	7.7%	3.4%
Electrical machinery	1.0%	1.1%	1.3%	0.0%	0.0%	0.0%	0.0%	0.0%	0.0%
Instrument and medical equipment	3.0%	2.4%	0.9%	0.0%	0.0%	0.0%	0.0%	0.0%	0.0%
Engineering	2.4%	1.6%	1.1%	0.0%	0.0%	1.8%	0.0%	0.0%	0.0%
Exploration services	1.1%	0.4%	0.0%	0.0%	0.0%	0.0%	0.0%	0.0%	0.0%

Table 7.3. *Organizational modes of international strategic alliance partnering,*
1980–1994

	80–84	85–89	90–94	Three periods
Intra Triad				
Equity	35%	39%	24%	33%
Non-equity	65%	61%	26%	67%
Triad-NIEs				
Equity	47%	88%	35%	57%
Non-equity	53%	12%	65%	43%
Triad-SK				
Equity	41%	88%	19%	50%
Non-equity	59%	12%	81%	50%

with NIE companies compared to the relatively high number of such alliances between Triad firms.

It is, however, important to note that for South Korea we find that 86 percent of all their alliances in the most recent period is to be found in high-tech sectors. This marks a considerable shift compared to the second period, in which alliances in automotive and chemicals were dominant. In the most recent period especially, microelectronics and computers stand out as the sectors in which we find the largest number of newly established strategic technology alliances.

Table 7.3 confirms our expectation about the increasing importance of non-equity agreements over time. Overall, the equity/non-equity ratio for intra-Triad alliances decreases from about 65 percent in the early eighties to a mere 24 percent in the period 1990–94. Given the technology focus of the alliances and the fact that most of the alliances are found in high-tech sectors, we expect Triad-NIE alliances to be primarily non-equity agreements. In comparison to intra-Triad alliances, Triad-NIE alliances show a different picture. An initially strong preference for equity agreements is followed by a period in which non-equity agreements can be seen as the most preferred form. This pattern is found in particular in alliances with South Korean companies. These findings are in line with the sectoral data that showed a strong interest in high-technology sectors in the last period compared to a low number of high-technology sector alliances in the second period. This is in line with the assumption that non-equity agreements are better suited to deal with situations of rapid (technological) change, whereas equity alliances are primarily used in more stable environments.

TECHNOLOGY TRANSFER AND LEARNING THROUGH STRATEGIC TECHNOLOGY ALLIANCES

Until the mid-1970s, the technological knowledge base of firms from NIEs was rather underdeveloped, particularly in comparison to their major Japanese, European, and especially U.S. counterparts. The desire to build up a stronger technology base in combination with increased international competitive pressures induced NIE firms to search actively for competent (foreign) partners that were willing to transfer their technological know-how to the domestic NIE firms in the form of one-directional technology flows, such as licenses and second-sourcing agreements. Licensing is generally considered to be a relatively cheap and fast way to acquire a technology. Licensing is also used when capital is scarce or when import restrictions forbid any other means of entry – when a country is sensitive to foreign ownership. In second-sourcing agreements, firms trade the right to make an exact copy of the other firm's product. These unidirectional agreements gave foreign firms fast and cheap access to the newly industrializing economies. Electronics companies based in Europe, Japan, and the United States were leading partners in this respect. Japanese firms such as Toshiba and Sharp were among the first foreign firms to forge ties with companies from the newly industrializing markets by means of licensing and second-sourcing agreements. In Europe, electronic giants such as Philips and Siemens followed the moves of their Japanese competitors. In the United States especially, AT&T, AMD, and Texas Instruments were engaged in a number of licensing and second-sourcing agreements.

Figure 7.2 shows the rapid increase in the number of licenses and second-sourcing agreements until the mid-1980s.[5] These agreements were accompanied by a relatively large number of

---

[5] Data represented in Figure 7.2 and discussed in this section do include second-sourcing and licensing agreements. Both these forms of partnering are not included in the data discussed in the previous sections of this paper.

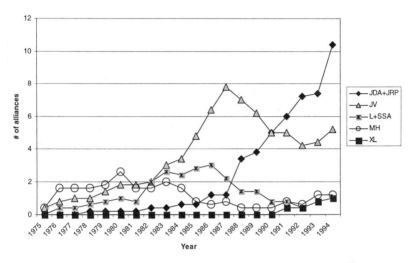

Figure 7.2. Number of newly established strategic technology alliances
(organizational forms), NIEs, five-year moving averages, 1975–94.
Key: JDA + JRP = joint development agreement and joint research pact;
JV = joint venture; L + SSA = licensing and second sourcing agreements;
MH = minority holding; XL = cross = licensing agreements.

minority holdings. Because of the growing importance of the East
Asian region, Japanese companies (e.g., Fuyo, Mazda, and
Mitsubishi) and U.S. firms (e.g., Ford and AT&T) were particularly interested in taking minority stakes in companies from countries such as Korea, Singapore, Taiwan, and Hong Kong. European
firms seem to have been somewhat more hesitant in this respect.

These technology exchange agreements enabled NIE firms,
particularly South Korean companies, to build up a profound
technological knowledge base in a relatively short period of time.
This sophisticated technology base enabled NIE firms to team up
with foreign companies on a more equal level. Instead of mere
one-directional technology flow, firms started to engage in bi-
directional technology agreements such as joint ventures. Many of
these joint ventures were associated with the spreading of risks,
sharing of fixed costs, economies of scale, and, from the perspective of the foreign partner, access to new markets. Joint ventures
had become the most dominant form of partnering until the early
1990s when they were superseded by joint development agreements (see Figure 7.2). Low labor costs in NIEs made it very inter-

esting for companies from high-wage regions such as the United States and Europe to enter into combined technology/production joint ventures with companies from NIEs. A typical example is the 1988 joint venture between Rockwell, KIA, and Daewoo, which was created to produce and design CNCs, servo, and spindle drives in a newly built plant in Seoul.

In the early 1990s, NIE firms already showed their newly acquired sophisticated technological capabilities in production/technology joint ventures. By then, well-developed technological skills of NIE firms were valued more and more at a global scale. South Korea, Singapore, Taiwan, and Hong Kong were no longer considered merely cheap production locations but were increasingly regarded as competent high-technology nations. This view led to the new kinds of alliances that we discussed earlier: joint R&D pacts. The newly created technological capabilities in NIEs attracted a large number of European, Japanese, and U.S. companies that were eager to pursue synergy effects in innovation and technology together with NIE firms. This gave rise to a strong upheaval in the number of joint development agreements and joint research pacts in the 1990s (see Figure 7.2).

Finally, it is important to point to another sign of the maturation of South Korean and other NIE companies through the observation that cross-licenses are increasingly replacing one-directional technology flows from the Triad to the NIEs (see Figure 7.2). Instead of receiving technological know-how, NIE firms increasingly set up cross-licensing agreements with foreign partners on an equal basis. A typical example of such cross-licensing agreement is the agreement between Texas Instruments (U.S.) and Hyundai in which they agreed to cross-license semiconductor and PC patents for the next ten years. Also, the direction of minority holdings has largely been reversed. Instead of U.S., European, and Japanese firms taking minority holdings in NIE firms, nowadays these NIE firms are also taking minority holdings in Triad firms, such as the minority investment of Sun Hill Glycose from South Korea in the U.S. company Phytopharmaceuticals in 1994.

ALLIANCES: THE ROAD TO SUCCESS FOR NIES?

NIEs have increasingly become aware of the importance of building up technological competencies in knowledge-intensive sectors. In a recent report, "Industrial Restructuring for the 21st Century," the Korean Institute for Industrial Economics and Trade (KIET), for example, stresses the need to refocus attention on the knowledge-intensive sectors. Despite the maturation of South Korean and other NIE companies, technological know-how from companies in the developed economies can still be seen as crucial to establishing a prominent (technological) position in high-tech markets. From the perspective of companies from the Triad countries, their ongoing drive to lower costs of technology development and manufacturing often makes them license their technologies to NIE companies.

Recently a number of Japanese (e.g., Fujitsu Ltd., Mitsubishi Electric Corp., and Toshiba Corp.) and American companies (e.g., IBM) have relocated parts of their memory production to NIE foundries. Licensing-in technology from these major players provides an excellent opportunity for NIE companies to learn from their most technologically advanced competitors. The importance of external technological know-how is clearly illustrated by the recent breakup of the alliance between Texas Instruments (TI) and Taipei-based Acer (Taiwan's largest PC maker). TI was the main contributor to the know-how on the submicron process technology that is needed to compete effectively in the high-end memory chip market. For Acer the breakup would make it virtually impossible to develop new state-of-the-art high-end memory chips. Within a week after the announcement of the breakup, Acer signed a deal with IBM about the transfer of IBM's world-class memory and logic technology. Acer's chairman, Stan Shih, acknowledged that this agreement made it possible to replace TI's process technology with IBM's logic processes. By shifting part of its production to Taiwan, IBM benefits from the lower memory manufacturing costs. Currently, Acer and IBM have at least four alliances in the areas of display technology and semiconductors. These alliances have forced other Taiwanese companies to establish their own alliances with foreign companies. For example, Acer's alliance with IBM in display technology was soon followed by a similar alliance between its Taiwanese competitor Walsin Lihwa Company and Toshiba. For almost all companies, teaming up with a competent partner has become a necessity to compete effectively in today's high-tech markets. For these NIE companies, alliances with foreign partners are not only interesting in terms of gaining access to world-class technology but they are also important in terms of gaining credibility, brand recognition, and capital.

CONCLUSIONS

Fundamental changes in the structure of the global economy and the process of technological change are major drivers for the establishment of alliances in high-technology sectors. Structural forces such as the homogenization of markets, fierce competition, and ongoing globalization tendencies in combination with technological forces, such as the ever-increasing costs of R&D and the increasing complexity of products, have heightened the need for new forms of organization.

Today, technological complementarity between partners turns out to be the major driving force behind the growth of international strategic technology alliances. In this chapter we have shown that the number of international strategic technology alliances is rapidly growing. The share of alliances in which at least one partner from a newly industrializing economy is involved, however, remains rather modest. The role of South Korea in these alliances is prominent. South Korean firms are involved in the majority of NIE alliances.

Compared with other international alliances Triad-NIE alliances are increasingly found in high-tech sectors. During the early nineties, high-tech sectors constituted over 82 percent of the strategic technology alliances between the two economic regions, compared to 78 percent for intra-Triad alliances. For instance, a highly research-intensive field such as micro-electronics turns out to generate over 25 percent of the alliances between Triad countries and newly industrializing economies. Together, information technology sectors such as computers, microelectronics, software, and telecommunications account for the majority of all newly established international strategic technology alliances in the first half of the nineties. The focus of the alliances, however, is less oriented toward research than in the case of alliances between Triad firms. Despite the fact that R&D is an important factor in the formation of Triad-NIE strategic technology alliances, other incentives such as joint production and joint marketing are still found to be important drivers in the alliance formation process.

Another important finding is that, in their drive toward flexibility, companies increasingly prefer contractual agreements over joint ventures. The use of contractual agreements, which have dominated intra-Triad alliance formation since the eighties, has become widespread practice for Triad-NIE alliances in the nineties. For South Korean-Triad alliances, we even found that more than 80 percent of all newly established strategic technology alliances have a contractual form. This could indicate that these alliances have reached a general level of confidence and tolerance that is coming close to that of domestic alliances and major trading partners.

This convergence in the pattern of international strategic technology partnering seems to be reflected in the gradual change from just technology transfer from the developed countries to companies from the NIEs to partnerships with more mutual technology exchange and joint development. If one considers the major changes that have taken place from technology transfer through "standard" licensing to cross-licensing and from equity-based alliances to joint R&D pacts, then it is clear that countries such as South Korea and the other NIEs have developed from "junior" partners in the early seventies to important players in the 1990s.

APPENDIX 7.1. THE COOPERATIVE AGREEMENTS
AND TECHNOLOGY INDICATORS (MERIT-CATI)
INFORMATION SYSTEM

The MERIT-CATI data bank is a relational database containing separate data files that can be linked to each other and provide (dis)aggregate and combined information from several files. The MERIT-CATI database contains three major entities. The first entity includes information on over 10,000 cooperative agreements involving some 4,000 different parent companies. The data bank contains information on each agreement and some information on companies participating in these agreements. We define cooperative agreements as common interests between independent (industrial) partners that are not connected through (majority) ownership. In the MERIT-CATI database, only those interfirm agreements are collected that contain some arrangements for transferring technology or joint research. Joint research pacts, second-sourcing, and licensing agreements are clear-cut examples. We also collect information on joint ventures in which new technology is received from at least one of the partners, or joint ventures having some R&D program. Mere production or marketing joint ventures are excluded. In other words, our analysis is primarily related to technology cooperation. We are discussing those forms of cooperation and agreements for which a combined innovative activity or an exchange of technology is at least part of the agreement. Consequently, partnerships are omitted that regulate no more than the sharing of production facilities, the setting of standards, collusive behavior in price setting and raising entry barriers – although all of these may be side effects of interfirm cooperation as we define it.

We regard these as a relevant input of information for each alliance: the number of companies involved; names of companies (or important subsidiaries); year of establishment, time-horizon, duration, and year of dissolution; capital investments and involvement of banks and research institutes or universities; field(s) of technology;[6] modes of cooperation;[7] and some comment or available information about progress. Depending on the form of cooperation, we collect information on the operational context: the name of the agreement or project; equity sharing; the direction of capital or technology flows; the degree of participation in case of minority holdings; some information about motives underlying the alliance; and the character of cooperation, such as basic research, applied research, or product development possibly associated with production and/or marketing arrangements. In some cases we also indicate who has benefited most.

The second major entity is the individual subsidiary or parent company involved in one (registered) alliance at least. In the first place we assess the company's cooperative strategy by adding its alliances and computing its network centrality. Second, we ascertain its nationality, its possible (majority) owner in case this is an industrial firm, too. Changes in (majority) ownership in the eighties were also registered. Next, we determine the main branch in which it is operating and classify its number of employees. In addition, for three separate subsets of firms, time-series for employ-

[6] The most important fields in terms of frequency are information technology (computers, industrial automation, telecommunications, software, microelectronics), biotechnology (with fields such as pharmaceuticals and agro-biotechnology), new materials technology, chemicals, automotive, defense, consumer electronics, heavy electrical equipment, food and beverages, and so on.

[7] As principal modes of cooperation we regard equity joint ventures, joint R&D projects, technology exchange agreements, minority and cross-holdings, particular customer-supplier relations, one-directional technology flows.

ment, turnover, net income, R&D expenditure, and numbers of assigned U.S. patents have been stored. The first subset is based on the Business Week R&D scoreboard, the second on Fortune's International 500, and the third group was retrieved from the U.S. Department of Commerce's patent tapes. From the Business Week R&D Scoreboard we took R&D expenditure, net income, sales, and number of employees. In 1980 some 750 companies were filed; by 1988, this number gradually increased to 900 companies, which were spread among 40 industry groups. The Fortune's International 500 of the largest corporations outside the United States provides information about sales (upon which the rankings are based), net income, and number of employees.

REFERENCES

Auster, E. R. 1992. "The Relationship of Industry Evolution to Patterns of Technological Linkages, Joint Ventures, and Direct Investment between U.S. and Japan." *Management Science*, 38, 778–792.

Bartlett, C. A., Y. Doz, and G. Hedlund. 1990. *Managing the Global Firm*. London: Routledge.

Buckley, P. J., and M. Casson. 1976. *The Future of the Multinational Enterprise*. London: MacMillan.

Buckley, P. J., and M. Casson. 1988. "A Theory of Cooperation in International Business." In F. J. Contractor and P. Lorange (eds.), *Cooperative Strategies in International Business*. Lexington, MA: D.C. Heath, 31–54.

Casson, M. 1987. *The Firm and the Market*. Oxford: Blackwell.

Chesnais, F. 1988. "Multinational Enterprises and the International Diffusion of Technology." In G. Dosi, C. Freeman, R. Nelson, G. Silverberg, and L. Soete (eds.), *Technical Change and Economic Theory*. London: Pinter, 496–527.

Contractor, F. J., and P. Lorange. 1988. *Cooperative Strategies in International Business*. Lexington, MA: D.C. Heath.

Dunning, J. H. 1988. *Multi-Nationals, Technology and Competitiveness*. London: Unwin Hyman.

Dunning, J. H. 1993. *Multinational Enterprises and the Global Economy*. Workingham, England: Addison-Wesley.

Duysters, G., and J. Hagedoorn. 1995. "Strategic Groups and Inter-Firm Networks in International High-Tech Industries." *Journal of Management Studies*, 32, 361–381.

Duysters, G., and J. Hagedoorn. 1996. "Internationalization of Corporate Technology through Strategic Partnering: An Empirical Investigation." *Research Policy*, 25, 1–12.

Graves, A. 1991. "International Competitiveness and Technological Development in the World Automobile Industry." Ph.D. thesis, University of Sussex, Brighton, England.

Gulati, R. 1995. "Does Familiarity Breed Trust? The Implications of Repeated Ties for Contractual Choice in Alliances." *Academy of Management Journal*, 38, 85–112.

Hagedoorn, J. 1990. "Organizational Modes of Inter-Firm Cooperation and Technology Transfer." *Technovation*, 10, 17–30.

Hagedoorn, J. 1993. "Understanding the Rationale of Strategic Technology Partnering: Interorganizational Modes of Cooperation and Sectoral Differences." *Strategic Management Journal*, 14, 371–385.

Hagedoorn, J., and R. Narula. 1996. Choosing Modes of Governance for Strategic Technology Partnering: International and Sectoral Differences. *Journal of International Business Studies*, 27, 265–284.

Hagedoorn, J., and J. Schakenraad. 1994. "The Effect of Strategic Technology Alliances on Company Performance." *Strategic Management Journal*, 15, 291–309.

Haklisch, C. S. 1989. "Technical Alliances in the Semiconductor Industry: Effects on Corporate Strategy and R&D." In Background Papers for Conference on Changing Global Patterns of Industrial Research and Development, Stockholm, June 20–22.

Harrigan, K. R. 1985a. *Strategic Flexibility: A Management Guide for Changing Times*, Lexington, MA: Lexington Books.

Harrigan, K. R. 1985b. *Strategies for Joint Ventures*. Lexington, MA: Lexington Books.

Harrigan, K. R. 1988. "Joint Ventures and Competitive Strategy." *Strategic Management Journal*, 9, 141–158.

Hu, Y. S. 1992. "Global or Transnational Corporations and National Firms with International Operations." *California Management Review*, 34, 107–127.

Kreiken, E. J. 1986. "De coalitiestrategie: creatieve cooperative competitie." In J. Bilderbeek, J. M. L. Jansen, and G. W. A. Vijge (eds.), *Ondernemingsstrategie; theorie en praktijk*. Leiden: H.E. Stenfert Kroese.

Lee, T., and P. Reid. 1991. *National Interests in an Age of Global Technology*. Washington, DC: NAP.

Levinthal, D. A. 1990. "Organizational Adaptation, Environmental Selection, and Random Walks." In J. V. Singh (ed.), *Organizational Evolution: New Directions*. Newbury Park, London: Sage, 61–90.

Link, A. N., and L. L. Bauer. 1989. *Cooperative Research in U.S. Manufacturing: Assessing Policy Initiatives and Corporate Strategies*. Lexington, MA: Lexington Books.

Miller, R. 1994. "Global R&D Networks and Large-Scale Innovations: The Case of the Automobile Industry." *Research Policy*, 23, 27–46.

Mowery, D. C. 1988. *International Collaborative Ventures in U.S. Manufacturing*. Cambridge, MA: Ballinger.

Mytelka, L. 1991. *Strategic Partnerships and the World Economy*. London: Pinter.

Obleros, F. J., and R. J. MacDonald. 1988. "Strategic Alliances: Managing Complementarity to Capitalize on Emerging Technologies." *Technovation*, 7, 155–176.

Ohmae, K. 1985. *Triad Power*. New York: Free Press.

Ohmae, K. 1990. *The Borderless World*. New York: Harper.

Osborn, R. N., and C. C. Baughn. 1990. "Forms of Interorganizational Governance for Multinational Alliances." *Academy of Management Journal*, 33, 503–519.

Osborne, R. N., J. G. Denekamp, C. C. Baughn, J. Hagedoorn, and G. Duysters. 1996. "Embedded Patterns of International Alliance Formation: The Emergence of Hybridization." Working paper, WSU-MERIT.

Parkhe, A. 1993. " 'Messey' Research, Methodological Predisposition and Theory Development in International Joint Ventures." *Academy of Management Review*, 18, 227–268.

Pearce, R. D. 1989. *The Internationalisation of Research and Development by Multinational Enterprises*. London: Macmillan.

Powell, W. W., K. W. Koput, and L. Smith-Doerr. 1996. Interorganizational Collaboration and the Locus of Innovation: Networks of Learning in Biotechnology. *Administrative Science Quarterly*, 41, 116–145.

Reich, R. B. 1991. *The Work of Nations*. New York: Vintage Books.

Rugman, A. M. 1980. "Internationalization as a General Theory of Foreign Direct Investment: A Re-praisal of the Literature." *Weltwirtschaftliches Archiv*, 116, 365–379.

Teece, D. J. 1987. "Profiting from Technological Innovation: Implications for Integration, Collaboration, and Public Policy." In D. J. Teece (ed.), *The Competitive Challenge*. Cambridge, MA: Ballinger, 185–220.

Vernon, R. 1966. "International Investment and International Trade in the Product Cycle." *Quarterly Journal of Economics*, 88, 190–207.

Vernon, R. 1979. "The Product Cycle Hypothesis in a New International Environment." *Oxford Bulletin of Economics and Statistics*, 41, 255–267.

Williamson, O. E. 1985. *The Economic Institutions of Capitalism, Firms, Markets, Relational Contracting*. New York: Free Press.

Williamson, O. E. 1991. "Comparative Economic Organization: The Analysis of Discrete Structural Alternatives." *Administrative Science Quarterly*, 36, 269–296.

Woot, de P. 1990. *High Technology Europe: Strategic Issues for Global Competitiveness*. Oxford: Blackwell.

Commentary

Martin Fransman

The 1997–98 Asian crisis raises important questions about the longer-term efficiency and competitiveness of Asian firms. These questions are particularly important in the case of South Korea where, according to many indicators, some national firms, especially those heavily involved in export markets, appear to have been both relatively efficient and globally competitive. For this reason, this commentary will confine attention largely, though not exclusively, to South Korean firms. (For several reasons that will not be pursued here, Taiwan, the other one of the four original Asian Tigers with the deepest range of domestic firm capabilities, has not experienced the same crisis as South Korea.) Does the current Asian crisis provide grounds for challenging the conventional wisdom regarding the efficiency and competitiveness of South Korean firms? How successful have these firms been in accumulating internationally competitive competencies? And what is meant by "success"? These are the questions that will be examined in this commentary with reference to the four contributions contained in this section of the book.

BACKGROUND: PERSPIRATION OR INSPIRATION?

To examine these questions it is necessary first to go back to pre-crisis times in order to understand how South Korean firms were able to grow as rapidly as they did and, in many cases, perform well in export markets. How is their growth and export performance to be explained?

For some, the development of South Korean and other Asian firms has been unremarkable. For Paul Krugman (1997), the representative of this view with perhaps the highest profile, Asian economic growth, and with it, by implication, the growth of Asian

216

firms, "impressive as it was, could mostly be explained by such bread-and-butter economic forces as high savings rates, good education, and the movement of underemployed peasants into the modern sector" (p. 1). Krugman, therefore, concludes that "Asian growth has so far been mainly a matter of perspiration rather than inspiration – of working harder, not smarter" (p. 1).

How far does this explanation take us in understanding the growth and export performance of South Korean firms? While Krugman's three explanatory variables – high savings rates, good education, and the movement of underemployed peasants – operate at the level of the economy as a whole, it is at the level of the firm that the inadequacy of Krugman's explanation becomes most apparent. For at the level of the firm, it is unclear why and how the availability of investment resources (high savings), together with the availability of labor in general (previously underemployed peasants) and the availability of skilled labor in particular (good education), results in rapid growth in the output of products such as automobiles, steel, ships, semiconductors, and PC monitors, a significant proportion of which are exported in the face of strong international competition. To quote out of context one of the old political economists, Krugman's "perspiration theory of Asian growth" is akin to arguing that the supply of cloth is sufficient for the production of an internationally competitive coat.

At the level of the firm it becomes clear, as Nelson and Pack (1999) have recently demonstrated in great detail, that what is missing in the Krugman story is an explanation of how the inputs that have been made available in South Korea have been transformed into growing outputs and, in many cases, globally competitive output in the form of exports. Krugman implies that the transformation of inputs into globally competitive outputs occurs automatically – a matter merely of "perspiration." However, as some of the studies in this section amply demonstrate, where "perspiration" ends and "inspiration" begins – when the firm's employees begin to work smarter rather than simply harder – is much more difficult to determine than Krugman implies.

But, perspiration or inspiration, what is the significance of the Asian crisis of 1997–98 in general, and the South Korean crisis in particular for the explanation of firm performance in these countries? More specifically, does the crisis provide evidence of weaknesses in firm performance in these countries? To answer these questions it is necessary to understand what caused the crisis, an issue to which we shall return after examining in more detail the process of growth in Asian firms as reflected in the four chapters in this section.

FIRM LEARNING IN GENERAL

In his chapter, David Teece provides a general analysis of the role of firm capabilities in economic development. His overall contention is that "firms are the 'engines' of economic development.... To understand economic development, one must therefore understand the developmental processes inside firms." From this starting point, the "fundamental question" becomes "how does one profitably grow the business?" Teece answers this question in terms of three factors – business processes, market positions, and expansion paths – which, he argues, shape economic development at the level of the firm and determine "a firm's competitive advantage and strategic capability."

In line with earlier work (see, e.g., Teece, Pisano, and Shuen, 1997), Teece emphasizes the importance of "competences and capabilities" as the basic building blocks of competitive advantage. An explanation of the competitiveness of South Korean firms, therefore, requires an explanation of how they have accumulated the necessary competences and capabilities, be it through "perspiration" or "inspiration" or some combination of the two. Particularly important for Teece are those competences and capabilities that are in short supply as a result of being difficult to imitate by competing firms. The reason is that, in the face of sufficient market demand, these competences and capabilities will allow the firms that possess them to earn supernormal profits – in effect, economic rents accruing to resources in scarce supply. In Teece's words, "competences can provide competitive advantage and generate rents only if they are based on a collection of routines, skills and complementary assets that are difficult to imitate."

FORMS OF FIRM LEARNING IN ASIA

Mike Hobday's contribution involves an analysis of two different forms of learning. The first he terms the OEM (original equipment manufacture) system which is to be found in firms in the East

Asian countries of South Korea and Taiwan. If a learning process occurs successfully under the OEM system, it is possible for ODM (own design and manufacture) to emerge. "Under ODM the local firm carries out some or all of the product design (as well as production) tasks needed to make a good, usually according to a general design layout supplied by the [usually foreign] transnational corporation.... As with basic OEM, the goods are then sold under the transnational corporation's (or buyer's) brand name." Even further up the "learning ladder" is *original idea manufacturing* (OIM), a term introduced in the mid-1990s in Taiwan. "Under OIM the product idea is generated by the local firm that designs and manufactures the product, which is then sold under the brand name of the Western or Japanese transnational."

The Mecca, however, for firms in these East Asian countries, is OBM (own brand manufacture), which signifies "a new stage in latecomer product innovation, going beyond the processes learned under original equipment manufacture." It is the Mecca because it allows the East Asian firm to free itself from dependence on the marketing capabilities of its foreign competitors and customers and, as its reward, earn higher profits as a result. However, Hobday concludes that "only a small number of East Asian OEM suppliers have managed to generate new product innovations, build research and development (R&D) capabilities and break free of their dependence on natural competitors for key components, capital goods, and distribution channels."

The second form of learning Hobday calls the "TNC (transnational corporation)-led system," which is dominant in Southeast Asian countries like Singapore and Malaysia. Although this system on the surface appears to be quite different from the OEM system, Hobday concludes from his study that the two systems share "some remarkable similarities in the processes of learning and innovation." Both systems also have their limitations. While in only a few cases has OEM learning resulted in own-brand manufacture (OBM), "the TNC-led system of Southeast Asia has resulted in shallow technological roots and, like the OEM path, weaknesses in new product design capability and R&D." Hobday's ultimate conclusion, however, is that despite these limitations, "both systems have proved to be highly successful strategies for latecomers in electronics, contributing to national economic growth and industrial innovation."

Further evidence of indigenous learning and capability accumulation is provided in KongRae Lee's chapter. This chapter focuses on South Korean firms that have both used and developed their own capital goods, including large car manufacturers as well as a medium-size paper manufacturer. Lee finds that South Korean "user firms played a significant role in the formation and development of the Korean capital goods industry." Although a specialized capital goods sector has emerged in the country, users have to a significant extent vertically integrated the production of capital goods. This is reflected, for example, in Lee's finding that "47.3 percent of machine tool patents issued to domestic organizations were granted to user firms." In pursuing the reasons for this degree of vertical integration, Lee finds that one major reason for a car manufacturer to decide to produce its own capital goods was "because domestic suppliers could not meet their technological demand." This intriguing finding raises a number of questions for further research. For example, why were some South Korean capital goods firms unable to meet the requirements of local users? Furthermore, how did international trade regime-related factors influence the "import-buy local-make yourself" strategic decision?

SUCCESSFUL LEARNING?

The Hobday and Lee chapters provide clear evidence of substantial learning and competence accumulation in South Korea, Taiwan, and Malaysia. While their chapters also point to the limitations of this learning process and the distance that must still be traveled before firms from these countries catch up with competitors in Japan, the United States, and Europe, it is clear that the leading firms in these countries have made significant progress in a number of areas. But how "successful" has this learning been? Clearly, not all learning should be seen as successful learning. For example, it is possible for a firm to make substantial progress through acquiring skills and knowledge that it previously did not possess, but still to remain significantly behind the international frontier in terms of the cost and/or quality of its output. In such cases we may want to conclude that although the firm went through an important learning process, it has not yet been successful, measured in terms of its international competitiveness.

One indicator of successful firm learning is export activity (after allowing for the effects of any subsidies of one form or another). On the assumption that buyers in export markets have other options, their purchase of a firm's products can be taken as an indication of that firm's international competitiveness (in the absence of subsidies). On this basis, for example, it is significant that in 1996 the value of Japanese exports of semiconductors and electronic parts to South Korea amounted to 351 billion yen, whereas South Korea's exports of the same category of products to Japan came to 259 billion yen (*Nikkei Weekly*, p. 1). While it is the case that the South Korean products tended to be technologically less sophisticated than the Japanese ones, and that these figures are subject to exchange rate influences, the fact remains that these statistics do provide an indication of successful learning processes in the South Korean companies that accounted for the bulk of these exports.

Another indication of success is provided in the chapter by Geert Duysters and John Hagedoorn, which deals with international technological collaborations involving firms from the Triad countries (United States, Japan, and Europe) and those from the newly industrialized economies (NIEs), particularly South Korea. According to Duysters and Hagedoorn, interfirm alliances in high-technology sectors have increased significantly in the 1980s and 1990s as a result of fundamental changes in the structure of the global economy. "Structural forces such as the homogenization of markets, fierce competition, and ongoing globalization tendencies in combination with technological forces, such as the ever-increasing costs of R&D and the increasing complexity of products, have increased the need for new forms of organization." More specifically, the authors focus on new forms of organization such as "joint ventures, joint development agreements and other types of technology sharing agreements" in contrast to the "traditional practices, such as mergers and foreign direct investment" that previously dominated.

What conclusions emerge from the study of Triad-NIE (particularly South Korean) alliances and intra-Triad alliances? Duysters and Hagedoorn conclude that although "other incentives such as joint production [and] joint marketing are still found to be important drivers in the alliance formation process," R&D is "an important factor in the formation of Triad-NIE strategic technology alliances." More specifically, the authors find that Triad-NIE alliances are increasingly to be found in the high-tech sectors. "Together, information technology sectors such as computers, microelectronics, software, and telecommunications account for the majority of all newly established international strategic technology alliances in the first half of the nineties." Indeed, Duysters and Hagedoorn conclude that their data provide evidence of a "gradual change from technology transfer from the developed countries to companies from the NIEs to partnerships with mutual technology exchange and joint development." Accordingly, they ultimately conclude, "It is clear that countries such as South Korea and the other NIEs have developed from 'junior' partners in the early seventies to major players in the 1990s."

THE RELEVANCE OF THE ASIAN CRISIS OF 1997/98

The evidence provided in this paper suggests that many Asian firms, particularly in the more advanced countries of South Korea and Taiwan, have accumulated significant competencies through a gradual process of learning but that they still have some way to go. (Linsu Kim's chapter in this book points to some of the changes in South Korea's national innovation system that he feels are necessary if that country's firms are to continue making the progress that is needed.) But what are the implications of the Asian crisis of 1997–98 that hit not only weaker economies, such as those of Thailand, Indonesia, and Malaysia, but also that of South Korea? In South Korea's case, does the crisis point to inherent shortcomings in the capability-accumulation process in the country's firms or is it merely a financial phenomenon that was unrelated to the economic health of these firms, a financial blip that will soon disappear allowing South Korean firms to continue the job of further deepening their capabilities in order to move further into more lucrative and economically beneficial foreign markets?

To answer this question, it is necessary to examine the causes of the Asian crisis, an issue which at the time of writing is controversial and on which there is no consensus. According to one school of thought, the Asian crisis is essentially a currency crisis. However, this view has been challenged by others, notably Paul Krugman (1998), who suggests that "the Asian crisis may have been only incidentally about currencies. Instead, it was mainly about bad banking and its consequences" (p. 7).

In what way is it alleged that the Asian banking system has been "bad"? The answer, according to Krugman, is that Asian governments in effect *de facto* (if not *de jure*) guaranteed the liabilities of Asian financial institutions and, therefore, their creditors. Protected by such guarantees, these financial institutions became "moral-hazard-prone" and engaged in "excessive investment." Since their creditors believed that they were protected from risk, they did not provide the prudent monitoring and controlling functions that would normally be undertaken by risk-bearing creditors. But not only did the Asian financial institutions indulge in excessive investment, they also made "speculative," "over-optimistic" and "unwise" investments. As examples, Krugman cites "office towers and auto plants." Krugman summarizes his story of the Asian crisis:

The excessive risky lending of [Asian financial] institutions created inflation – not of goods but of asset prices. The overpricing of assets was sustained in part by a sort of circular process, in which the proliferation of risky lending drove up the prices of risky assets, making the financial condition of the intermediaries seem sounder than it was. And then the bubble burst. The mechanism of crisis, I suggest, involved the same circular process in reverse: falling asset prices made the insolvency of intermediaries visible, forcing them to cease operations, leading to further asset deflation. This circularity, in turn, can explain both the remarkable severity of the crisis and the apparent vulnerability of the Asian economies to self-fulfilling crisis – which in turn helps us understand the phenomenon of contagion between economies with few visible economic links." (p. 2)

Krugman's suggestion that "over-optimistic" and "unwise" investments were made in automobile plants and, one could add, other investments such as in steel, shipbuilding, and semiconductors, raises a number of further questions. To begin with, why were these investments made (by both Asian as well as Western investors) if they were overoptimistic and unwise? Krugman's explanation is that the "moral-hazard-proneness" of Asian financial institutions led them to be more willing to take *given* risk; that is, the problem lay not with incorrect assessment of the risk itself, but rather with the relatively low degree of aversion to that risk, the result of moral hazard. But if investments in automobile and semiconductor plants were to lead simply to excess capacity, over-supply, and low profits, surely the problem also lay with an incorrect assessment of the risk involved. In turn, this begs explanation.

Closer to the concerns of this commentary, however, is Krugman's suggestion that through the financial intermediation process, financial resources were allocated to economic activities that would not have received funding under a more efficient financial institutional regime. By extension, to the extent that this happened, firms were able to fund their activities and engage in the consequent learning processes, in some cases with the successful results that we have seen, even though these activities were doomed in the longer run to become unprofitable and be eliminated when financial conditions, partly through the effects of financial crisis, were tightened.

To put the issue more concretely, it might be that South Korean semiconductor and consumer electronics firms were able to engage in learning and competence accumulation processes that met the criterion of success defined earlier. But to the extent to which these activities were only possible under an excessively lax financial environment, and would be eliminated once market-determined financial controls were reasserted, the social value of the learning and competence accumulation is obviously diminished. The general implication that follows is that a broader analysis is needed if the benefits of learning and competence accumulation processes are to be evaluated. It is not enough to demonstrate that firms have learned; not even enough to demonstrate that they have achieved internationally competitive outputs. Important too are the longer term rates of return that these learning processes provide since in general it is rates of return rather than rates of learning that drive the capital markets, which are a key component of the selection environment of firms. This much the Asian crisis has made clear. We must conclude, therefore, that the analysis of firm learning and capability development must be complemented by an analysis of long-run financial viability under reasonably open and competitive financial market conditions.

REFERENCES

Krugman, P. 1997. "Whatever Happened to the Asian Miracle?" *http://web.mit.edu/krugman/www/perspire.html*

Krugman, P. 1998. "What Happened to Asia?" *http://web.mit.edu/krugman/www/DISINTER.html*

Nelson, R. R., and H. Pack. 1999. "The Asian Miracle and Modern Growth Theory." *Economic Journal*, 109, 416–436.

The Nikkei Weekly, February 9, 1998, p. 1.

Teece, D. J., G. Pisano, and A. Shuen. 1997. "Dynamic Capabilities and Strategic Management." *Strategic Management Journal*, 18(7), 509–533.

PART III

Innovation Policies

Policies for Science, Technology, and Innovation in Asian Newly Industrializing Economies

Mark Dodgson

INTRODUCTION

Despite remarkable technological achievements in the newly industrialized economies of East Asia,[1] enormous challenges remain for government policies for science and technology development. This chapter examines the relative strengths and weaknesses of science and technology in East Asian newly industrializing economies (NIEs) and analyzes the policies being pursued to assist the development of science, technology, and innovation. Among the most technologically advanced East Asian NIEs – Korea, Taiwan, Singapore, and to a lesser extent China and Malaysia – a major challenge lies in developing and improving the scientific research base, and where this already has some substance and scale, improving the linkages between it and industry. For the

The author wishes to thank the following organizations for the information and help they provided in the preparation of this article: National Science and Technology Board and Hitachi Electronics, Singapore; IPTN, Bandung, Indonesia; ITRI and Hsinchu Science Park, Taiwan; Asian Development Bank, Philippines. Appreciation is also due to Hal Hill, Hadi Soesastro, and John Mathews for their helpful comments. All errors are my responsibility.

[1] East Asia is commonly defined as including the ASEAN nations, China, Japan, Korea, and Taiwan. In this chapter, Japan is not included in this definition as its level of technological development and the challenges confronting it are broadly different from those of other East Asian nations.

Reference to matters "East Asian" is at best a simple convenience, as the historical, economic, social, religious, and cultural diversity in the region is so extraordinarily wide. Reference to East Asia includes Singapore with a population of 3 million and China with 1.2 billion and Indonesia with 200 million. It includes broad diversity in income levels as measured in 1996 by GDP per capita with the following range: Singapore ($30,500); Taiwan ($13,130); Korea ($10,730); Malaysia ($4,446); Indonesia ($1,086); Vietnam ($270).

less technologically advanced nations – Indonesia, Thailand, the Philippines, Vietnam – these challenges, although important, are less pressing than the need to improve the capacity to acquire and use science and technology developed elsewhere.

Policies for science, technology, and innovation are developed with a variety of aims in East Asian NIEs, ranging from the need to address pressing health, environmental, transportation, and agricultural productivity problems on the one hand, to more subjective and indulgent considerations of national prestige on the other. Primarily, however, science and technology are seen as tools of industrial development; they are means by which poorer nations can alleviate poverty and diversify away from their reliance on rural and resource sectors, and the wealthier nations can build competitive advantages in global markets for technology-based goods. Science and technology provide mechanisms for meeting the overwhelming demand for improved standards of living throughout the region.

The importance of science and technology for industrial development is shown in Table 8.1, which lists the strategic industries and industrial sectors identified by various East Asian nations and receiving specific and high levels of government support. Although there are differences in the degree of specification of industrial sectors, there are many similarities, and almost all are high-technology based.[2] Government support in the most successful new industry in East Asia, the electronics industry, has been particularly important. "In all countries (in East Asia), governments have played a decisive role in shaping the industry's development, laying down conditions within which companies will operate, and reducing and spreading the risks of investment in advanced technological activities" (Mathews, 1996, p. 4).

Some definitions are required of the terms of analysis used in this chapter. Science, technology, and innovation policy are considered here to be different. Although there are considerable overlaps and blurred boundaries, science policy is here understood to involve government policies for promoting science in universities and research laboratories, while technology policy addresses the development of important generic technologies, such as infor-

---

[2] There is also extensive variation in the extent to which these receive government support, ranging from high levels of intervention in Indonesia, to the more laissez-faire Hong Kong (although this may, of course, change).

Table 8.1. *Strategic industries in some East Asian countries*

Korea	Taiwan	Singapore	Indonesia
Informatics	Information technology	Electronics	Electronics
Advanced Engineering	Aerospace	Aerospace	Aircraft
Precision Engineering	Precision Machinery and Automation	Precision Engineering, Equipment and Components	Turbines/Engines
Fine Chemicals	Specialty Chemicals	Chemicals	Heavy Industry
Biotechnology	Specialty Medical devices	Biotechnology	Shipbuilding
New Materials	Advanced Materials	Disk Media	Explosives
Environmental Technology	Pollution Control		Steel
Oceanography	Communications Consumer Electronics Semiconductors		Rolling Stock Telecommunication Defense

Source: Marsh, 1997, and authorial research.

mation technology (IT) and biotechnology. Crudely, science policy aims at increasing and improving the capacity of nations to create and respond to new scientific opportunities and options, and technology policy aims to develop specific technological resources and infrastructure. By contrast, innovation policy is considered to be those efforts by governments that encourage the accumulation, diffusion, and creation of new products, processes, and services by firms.

These policies are separated for analytical purposes, but not, of course, in reality, from the wide gamut of policies being pursued to encourage industrial development, education, competition and trade. Table 8.2 outlines some of the major features of science, technology, and innovation policy in the East Asian context.

The policy recipe pursued – the combination of science, tech-

Table 8.2. *Science, technology, and innovation policy in East Asia*

Policy	Main features	Recent trends
Science Policy	Scientific education Research in universities and government labs Basic research	Increased numbers of universities Some deregulation of universities and government labs Improved policy advice
Technology policy	Support for the creation of strategic or generic technologies, e.g., information technology, biotechnology Development of technology infrastructure, i.e., integrated services digital network	Highly targeted policies, e.g., semiconductors, aerospace, multimedia Attempts to diversify technologically Concern for environmental technology issues Intellectual property rights protection
Innovation policy	Firm-level focus aimed at building technological capabilities Subsidized research and development	Intermediary development Focus on technology creating capabilities as well as technology diffusion capabilities

nology, and innovation policies and their dynamic adjustment – depends on the level of economic and industrial development within each nation and the features of each nation's systems of innovation, including the range and quality of relevant institutions and the social and economic relationships within them. Although the nexus between science and technology and industrial development is close in every East Asian NIE, the nature of the links vary considerably. The science and technology challenges in highly industrialized Korea are very different from those in less-developed Indonesia or Thailand. Small firms in Taiwan benefit greatly when compared, for example, with their counterparts in the Philippines, through their access to numerous institutions offering technological, financial, and managerial support. In all cases, however, an essential feature of effective policy, derived in major part from the high growth rates enjoyed in East Asia until the late 1990s and the rapid pace of technological development, is the continued need for policy learning and adaptation as the challenges confronting each country change over time.

Science, technology, and innovation policies are ultimately transformed into industrial development by improvements in the technological capabilities of firms. As studies of national systems of innovation show, it is ultimately the technological capabilities of firms that determine nations' technological, and ultimately economic, performance (Nelson, 1993). Given the importance of these technological capabilities, it is worth briefly considering their constitution.

Recent innovation theory and theories of the firm emphasize the importance of concepts such as "dynamic capabilities," "learning," and "knowledge" – those transformative abilities of firms that enable them to reallocate and reconstruct their resources to build competitiveness.[3] This form of analysis has a relatively long history. Edith Penrose's (1959) classic study on *The Theory of the Growth of the Firm* carefully distinguishes "resources" from "services." She conceives of resources as providing the basis for production and of services as the means of activating the potential resources provide. From the perspective of technological capabilities, this distinction is important as it emphasizes the way in which it is insufficient to address deficiencies in resources alone. Although firms may radically improve their resources – through, for example, increased investment in manufacturing technology or IT – it does not necessarily create competitive advantage, which also requires the "services" element in Penrose's terminology.

Technological capabilities are an important element of these services. There are two broad components of technological capabilities. First, there are those that enable firms efficiently to accumulate, assimilate, and adapt appropriate extant technology, here named "technology diffusion capability." This requires a substantial level of capability on the part of the firm in selecting, using, and developing technology. Second is the capacity to create new technologies based on research and development (R&D) and directed at creating first-mover advantages in the market, intellectual property, and licensing income; it is named here "technology creating capability."

The interdependence of science, technology, and innovation

---

[3] Teece and Pisano (1994), Leonard-Barton (1995), Nonaka and Takeuchi (1995).

policy can be seen in the way technology diffusion capacity depends on the government's selection and support of munificent technologies and provision of good technological infrastructure. Technology creating capability depends on good scientific training, opportunities for linking with scientific expertise in universities and research labs, and effective intellectual property rights (IPR) protection.

This chapter considers three major policies pursued in East Asian NIEs to assist the dynamic development of these technological capabilities: the encouragement of direct foreign investment (DFI) by overseas multinational companies; the formation of "national champions"; and the creation and adaptation of intermediary, technology-transfer-type organizations. First, some description is required of the context in which these policies are implemented.

STRENGTHS AND WEAKNESSES IN SCIENCE, TECHNOLOGY, AND INNOVATION IN ASIAN NIES

According to one estimate, by 2005 the East Asian economies will in combination spend more on R&D than the United States (Sheehan et al., 1995). Figure 8.1 shows the commitment to R&D as a percentage of gross domestic product (GDP) in the two most technologically advanced East Asian NIEs: Taiwan and Korea. In comparison to the static or declining commitments in the United States, the United Kingdom, and Germany, Korea, spectacularly, and Taiwan, incrementally, have been investing an increasing proportion of national output in R&D.

There are ambitious development plans among those nations with low national R&D expenditures. Malaysia's seventh five-year plan, 1996–2000, aims to increase gross expenditure on R&D as a proportion of gross national product (GNP) to 1 percent (from 0.4 percent in 1994), and to increase the number of scientists and technicians to 1,000 per million population (compared with 400 in 1992). Its science budget of $1.2 billion targets information and communications technology (ICT), electronics, biotechnology, and manufacturing. Indonesia has similarly announced the intention to reach the level of 1 percent gross expenditure on research and development as a proportion of gross domestic product by 2003

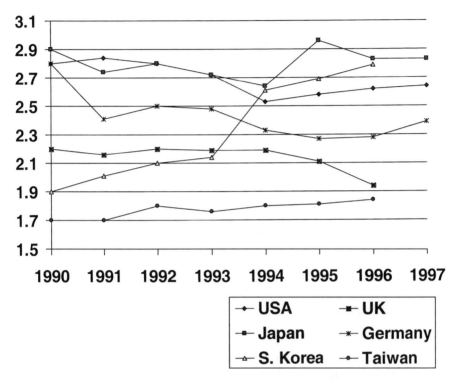

Figure 8.1. Research and development expenditures as a percentage of gross domestic product.

(*Nikkei Weekly*, June 24, 1996), and 2 percent by 2018 (Scott-Kemmis and Rohadian, 1996).

Table 8.3 reveals some of the broad diversity in science and technology capacity in various countries, as measured by R&D expenditure and the numbers of researchers per 10,000 population (the latter statistics suffer notoriously from differences in definitions used). It can be seen that Korea has a relatively large expenditure on R&D, with business expenditure being the major component; Taiwan relies more heavily on government expenditure, but business expenditure still accounts for over 55 percent of total expenditure. Singapore's expenditure is relatively small, and highly reliant on government expenditure; China is a large spender on R&D in real terms, the majority of which, of course,

Table 8.3. *Comparative expenditure on research and development per capita and government expenditure*

	GERD (estimated in 1995 U.S. $million)	GERD/GDP	BERD/GDP	Researchers per 10,000 Population
Korea (1994)	10,120	2.4	1.72	26.3
Taiwan (1994)	4,267	1.8	1.03	29.8
Singapore (1993)	606	1.2	0.75	25.4 (95)[a]
China (1994)	29,939	0.4	0.11	6.8
Malaysia (1992)		0.4	0.17	4.0
Indonesia (1993)	c500	0.2	0.04	
Thailand (1991)		0.2	0.04	
Hong Kong (1995)		0.1	n.a.	
OECD Average		1.94	1.19	
Japan (1994)	77,345	2.64	1.87	45.8
USA (1994)	172,801	2.53	1.80	

Notes: GERD = gross expenditure on research and development.
GDP = gross domestic product.
BERD = business expenditure on research and development.
[a] Data from 1995.
Sources: Various national government and OECD statistical reports.

derives from the government, but its commitment as a proportion of GDP is relatively small. Expenditure on R&D in Indonesia and Thailand is very small, and business commitments there are almost negligible.

Expenditure on R&D provides only one indicator of a nation's technological capacities. Many technological strengths have derived from the purchase of licenses and reverse engineering. Hong Kong's industrial development, in particular, has been based less on R&D and more on imaginative use of technologies developed elsewhere. However, the importance of R&D is recognized by all East Asian governments, and even Hong Kong is considering more active industrial and technology policies (*Far Eastern Economic Review*, October 23, 1997).

Other factors do have to be taken into account, such as the quality of technological infrastructure. Singapore's technological capacity, for example, is considerably enhanced by its superb telecommunications infrastructure. Indicators of technological diffusion are also revealing – for example, at present there are around 4 million Internet users in Asia, compared to around

16 million in the United States, but the figure for Asia is expected to increase by a factor of 10 by 2000 (*Fortune*, August 18, 1997).

Science in Asian NIEs: Features and Challenges

As Lall argues in Chapter 2, the process of technological change in Asian NIEs is generally more a matter of acquiring and improving technological capabilities than innovating at the forefront of knowledge. Science is certainly not a priority among nations such as Thailand and Indonesia, which spend only around $2 per capita per annum on R&D. However, while the science base in East Asian NIEs is relatively weak, there are areas of world-class specific scientific expertise: Malaysia in rubber and palm oil, the Philippines and China in rice, for example. Furthermore, there are also scientific strengths in high-tech industries in Taiwan and Korea, as shown by Figure 8.2, which charts the growth in patenting from these countries in the United States. Singapore leads the world in scientific publications in the fields of engineering and computer science per head of population (Bryant et al., 1996). Nonetheless, the overall picture is of comparative weakness. In 1993, for example, the East Asian NIEs produced only 4.37 percent of international scientific publications, as recorded by the Institute for Scientific Information (ISI) (although this had increased substantially from 0.84 percent in 1981).[4] Combined annual expenditure on basic research in Korea and Taiwan is $2 billion, compared to $31 billion in the United States.[5]

The region still relies heavily on the scientific expertise of the United States. The pattern of international collaborations in research as recorded in the ISI database between 1988 and 1994 shows that Taiwan undertook 73 percent of its collaborative research with the United States, compared, for example, with 9 percent with Japan and less than 0.8 percent with Korea. Korea in turn undertook 64 percent of its international research collaborations with the United States, compared to 20 percent with Japan and 0.7 percent with Taiwan (Bourke and Butler, 1995).

Perhaps the major challenge facing East Asian science is the limited supply of scientists. In response to this shortcoming in

---

[4] Data derived from Bourke and Butler (1995).
[5] Data derived from Indicators of Science and Technology, People's Republic of China, 1996.

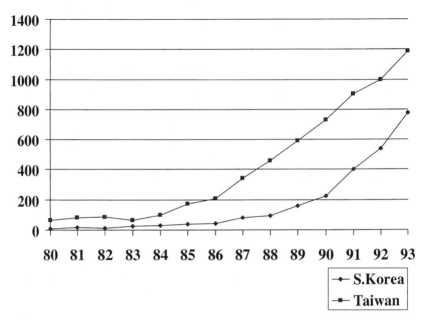

Figure 8.2. U.S. patents granted to inventors from Taiwan and Korea.

science education, East Asian NIEs are increasing the numbers of their universities substantially. Indonesia, for example, plans to open another 100 polytechnics over the next twenty years. In the traditionally highly regulated higher education sector, deregulation is allowing overseas universities to create their own campuses or form joint ventures with local universities; both of these measures are increasing the numbers of science graduates. Recently, some company universities have been created: there are currently three in Malaysia, for example, and one of Korea's best science-oriented universities, POSTECH, was created by a major steel company. However, the extent of the challenge is immense: the demand for university places in Asia is forecast to rise from 17 million in 1990 to 45 million in 2010. It is estimated that to meet this demand a new university will have to be built every three or four days for the next fifteen years (IDP, 1995).

There is also a need for greater deregulation in the controls over university scientists. Only recently have scientists in Indonesia been allowed to undertake research for any ministry other than the Ministry of Education. University scientists in Taiwan are not permitted to engage in industrial consulting, and their incentive system is strongly tied to academic publication rather than broader dissemination of research results.

There has been considerable progress in the development of intellectual property protection in most East Asian countries, and many countries have been signatories to international intellectual property law reforms, such as Trade-Related Aspects of Intellectual Property Rights (TRIPS) under the Uruguay Round of the General Agreement on Tariffs and Trade (GATT). There are still major problems with the implementation of these agreements, however, and few countries have the administrative structures to police the agreements effectively (Turpin and Innes, 1995).

The system of ministerial responsibility for science varies very considerably between East Asian NIEs. In Korea, for example, there is a Ministry of Science and Technology which, as Kim argues in this volume, has had some difficulties in integrating its longterm policies with the more powerful ministries overseeing industry, trade, finance, and education. In Taiwan, in a complex system, there is a National Science Council, whose chairman has equal ministerial status to all other ministries; the Academica Sinica, which has a directly appropriated budget, oversees some basic research institutes, and reports directly to the Office of the President; and the Ministry of Economic Affairs, which oversees research institutes, such as the Industrial Technology Research Institute (ITRI). There appears to be close coordination among these agencies. On the whole, the science and technology administrative systems in Asian NIEs are not only considerably smaller than their equivalents in the major Western economies (as might be expected, given the comparatively limited scale of scientific activities), but they appear not to have undergone many of the changes occurring in their Western counterparts as these organizations search for greater administrative efficiencies, engage in priority-setting mechanisms, and place greater emphasis on accountability.

To address these issues, there is a growing but still relatively small science policy capacity in East Asian NIEs. The major East Asian science policy group is the Science and Technology Policy Institute in Korea. There is also a small policy group within the National Science and Technology Board in Singapore. The Indonesian Institute of Sciences (LIPI), the main science and technology agency in Indonesia, is currently undertaking a World

Bank-funded project that will assist the development of science
and technology (S&T) advice. However, there are still vagaries
and idiosyncracies to be found in policy formulation in East Asia.
In Indonesia, for example, until his elevation to the presidency, the
minister of state for research and technology played the central
role in coordination, prioritizing, planning, implementation,
monitoring, and evaluating all aspects related to research and
S&T policy in Indonesia (Scott-Kemmis and Rohadian, 1996), to
that country's disadvantage.

Technology: Features and challenges (the central role of electronics)

The identification of and support for key technologies has been
one of the major policy initiatives pursued by East Asian NIEs.
Nowhere has this been more evident, or successful, than in electronics, which provides the major technological strengths in East
Asia. Asia has a positive balance of trade in sales of high-tech
products with the United States, largely because of trade in electronics. The number of patents granted in Asia between 1985 and
1990 increased at double the rate of growth in the United States
(although, of course, these grew from a much smaller base). The
greatest proportion of these patents lie in electronics and related
areas (Choung, 1995). As for patenting in the United States, Asian
patents, primarily from Taiwan and Korea, increased fourfold
during the 1970s and tenfold during the 1980s (NSF, 1995).

In a study of high-tech competitiveness of 28 countries, Porter
et al. (1996) developed three indicators: high-tech standing
(current high-tech production and export capability); high-tech
emphasis (the extent to which a nation's exports depend on high
tech); and the rate of change of high-tech standing (Table 8.4).
Their indicators are derived from UN trade data, the Elsevier
Yearbook of electronics production, sales and exports, and expert
panel opinion and are highly dependent on performance in the
electronics industry.

According to these measures, a number of broad characteristics
are discernible among Asian NIEs. First, in respect to technological standing, a group of Asian nations – Singapore, Korea, Taiwan
– are equivalent in performance to Italy, Sweden, and Canada, and
these East Asian nations plus Hong Kong, Malaysia, and Thailand

Table 8.4. *High-tech competitiveness*

Country	High-tech standing	High-tech emphasis	Rate of change
Japan	90.7	67.8	31.1
USA	90.0	53.2	35.7
Germany	60.4	32.3	27.8
UK	49.3	46.7	38.3
France	45.5	35.8	32.4
Italy	31.5	21.0	34.8
Sweden	28.0	31.5	28.5
Canada	24.0	15.1	21.1
Australia	15.6	7.8	30.7
Singapore	35.7	100.0	29.8
South Korea	28.6	59.3	26.6
Taiwan	26.9	58.9	28.5
Hong Kong	22.0	54.7	15.0
Malaysia	24.3	77.4	41.3
China	20.6	24.1	55.5
Thailand	17.1	44.2	47.9
India	13.4	7.4	19.4
Philippines	12.6	33.3	50.5
Indonesia	10.9	6.5	79.9

Source: Porter et al. (1996).

have a greater high-tech emphasis than all the European nations cited here (explained primarily by electronics exports). Although it is occurring from a relatively low base, the rate of change of technological standing in the Southeast Asian nations plus China is larger than the change rate in Asian nations with larger technology bases.[6]

The extent of the ambitions in technology in East Asia is seen in Malaysia's plans to build a 290-square-mile area, named the Multimedia Super Corridor, which aims to attract large numbers of international and domestic IT manufacturing and service companies.[7] Estimates of its cost vary between $15 and $30 billion,

[6] While electronics is the major high-technology industry in East Asia, this indicator leads to some distortions. Malaysia, for example, is shown to have ten times a higher tech emphasis than Australia, but while electronics may be relatively less important in Australia, Australia has huge advantages in the scientific, medical, and resource sectors.

[7] At the time of writing, the currency difficulties facing many Southeast Asian nations has put the future of projects such as this in some doubt. Its planning remains illustrative of the ambitious, technology-led economic development projects in East Asian NIEs.

including the development of two new cities: Putrajaya and Cyber-
jaya, and a $2 billion investment in a fiber-optic communications
system. According to the government, its intention is to assist
Malaysia's transition to the Information Age from its present
labor-intensive, low value-added manufacturing industrial base.
Irrespective of assessments of its likely success, the Multimedia
Super Corridor project is revealing of a number of aspects of
Malaysian technology policy. First is the enormous scale of the
ambition for the project and its clear technological focus. Second
is the way in which it has consolidated and advanced trends in
policy in areas such as the provision of IPR protection, the provision of excellent infrastructure and highly competitive telecommunications rates, and the offering of substantial incentives, such
as tax exemptions for resident companies for up to ten years.
Third, it reveals the pragmatism of the Malaysian government
in overcoming long-established policies that have prevented
foreign ownership and limited the number of overseas workers,
both of which do not apply to firms in the Multimedia Super Corridor. Furthermore – and important in a deeply religious and
strongly governed country – firms will not be subjected to the cen-
sorship of the Internet applied elsewhere in Malaysia (and in
nearby competitor, Singapore). Fourth, the government is using
negative pressure as an incentive: firms that do not move into
the Corridor will be excluded from all government contracts,
which are likely to be in the billions of dollars (*Fortune*, August
18, 1997).

As well as strengths there are also major weaknesses evident in
East Asia's technology base. Royalties and fees paid to U.S. firms
to license use of their proprietary industrial processes nearly
doubled during the 1987–91 period; these were, on average, ten
times the amount paid to Asian firms by U.S. companies (NSF,
1995). Korean semiconductor firms pay up to 30 percent of
revenue in royalties (Mathews, 1996). While this is not always a
weakness if firms are using the licenses as a learning opportunity
to build their own capacity for technology creation capability, few
firms have been capable of using these connections as learning
opportunities.

Another problem confronting technology-based, export-
oriented East Asian firms lies within the electronics industry itself,
major components of which, such as the semiconductor industry,
are notoriously cyclical. Most firms in this sector are relatively

small and compete on the basis of cost advantages rather than technological innovation. Furthermore, although it varies between countries and is declining in aggregate, most East Asian nations depend heavily on Japan for investment (Abegglen, 1994). A major element of Korea's $13 billion annual trade deficit with Japan, for example, is advanced capital equipment. Even the most technologically advanced Asian computer company has difficulty building up its international brand recognition, undertakes incremental rather than world-leading R&D, and is to a significant extent controlled by overseas buyers. For example, Acer, perhaps the Taiwanese electronics firm with the highest market recognition, produces half of its PCs under original equipment manufacturing arrangements for other firms (*Far Eastern Economic Review*, July 25, 1995). Asian firms are also not exempt from the pressures derived from the continuing international increase in the cost of R&D.

Databases on the geographical location of partners in international strategic alliances show that over 90 percent of them occur within the European/Japanese/U.S. Triad (Dodgson, 1993). Hagedoorn, in Chapter 7, shows that the number of Triad-NIE alliances is actually less than 5 percent, with the majority of these alliances involving Korea (these are particularly important with Japanese firms in automotives and with U.S. firms in electronics). Given the usually high technology focus of these alliances, from this evidence it seems that many Asian firms are excluded from major international technology development projects.

Innovation Policy: Features and Challenges

Much of the strength of technologically leading East Asian NIE companies lies in production and project execution (Amsden and Hikino, 1994). These are important skills, but relatively easy to replicate. They do not provide the basis for longer term, sustainable, competitive advantage at a global level. They are transferrable by means of blueprints and explicit information. They exclude the tacit, creative, and intuitive skills necessary to be truly innovative and are argued to be central to the future "knowledge" or "learning" firms and economies (Nonaka and Takeuchi, 1995; Leonard-Barton, 1995; Lundvall, 1992).

Innovation policies in East Asian NIEs have in the past focused on technological diffusion capabilities rather than technological creation capabilities, and they are often associated with nations that have developed infrastructural institutions to assist in the processes of accumulating targeted technology, adjusting it to local conditions, and disseminating it to local firms.[8] Taiwan has been very successful in this aspect of innovation policy. Korean institutions have also been successful in the past at assisting firms in this process, but as Kim (1997b) argues, these institutions may not yet have made the adjustment to the new demands of technological leadership.[9]

The success of East Asian firms in making the transition from technology follower to technology leader is epitomized by Samsung Electronics in Korea (Dodgson and Kim, 1997; Kim, 1997a). Samsung now employs 14,500 researchers, has over 20 research labs, registers over 750 patents a year in the United States, and has attracted collaborative R&D partnerships with many of the world's best high-tech firms. However, there are still weaknesses in the ability of many East Asian firms such as Samsung to manage technological creativity as well as international competitors, particularly in respect to the overbureaucratization (and hence creativity constraints) of the R&D function. While leading Asian companies like Samsung have identified their weaknesses in this area and instigated strategies for overcoming them, shortcomings remain (Dodgson and Kim, 1997).

There are also shortcomings in the systems and methods of training R&D managers. Policies for training technology managers in Asia are generally variable in quality and commonly limited in scale; they often focus on inappropriate European and American models (Minden and Wong, 1996).

For innovation policies to succeed, policy makers must learn to develop and change policies over time (Dodgson and Bessant, 1996). Justman and Teubal (1995) and Teubal (1996) have devised a conceptual framework for the development of technological infrastructure, R&D, and technology policy that distinguishes between basic (infant) and advanced (mature) policies. Basic policies are concerned with market building: providing and stimulat-

---

[8] This diffusion-oriented policy approach has led Mathews (1996) to describe it as a new form of industrialization.

[9] Korea is one of the few East Asian NIEs not to have actively encouraged direct foreign investment. Instead, its policies for technological development, and the encouragement of technological capabilities, has focused on the creation and support of large conglomerate companies.

ing demand for services supporting R&D and innovation (such as consulting and testing). Advanced policies are more selective and focus on creating collaborative networks involved in technology creation. As we shall see in the subsequent examination of technological infrastructure in Singapore and Taiwan, it would be mistaken to assume a formal progression from one set of policies to another as nations become more developed. Singapore is very technologically advanced, but it is in the process of market building for research services among local firms. Taiwan has used network-based policies to encourage technology diffusion. What is important is the ways in which technological institutions adapt and change over time in response to the changing requirements of innovation policies.

THE ROLE OF DIRECT FOREIGN INVESTMENT BY OVERSEAS MULTINATIONALS

East Asian NIEs are major recipients of direct foreign investment (DFI). In 1995, the amount of DFI received in each country was China, $129 billion; Taiwan, $15.6 billion; Hong Kong, $21.8 billion; Indonesia, $50.8 billion; Korea, $14 billion; Malaysia, $38.5 billion; Philippines, $6.9 billion; Singapore, $55.5 billion; and Thailand, $16.8 billion (UNCTAD, *World Investment Report*, 1996).

Such enormous investment substantially improves the resource base of these nations. But investment by overseas multinational corporations (MNCs) may potentially also improve the technological capabilities of local support industries by the transfer of technology, advanced production skills, and management know-how as well as expanded opportunities for self-learning.

The literature tells us that the extent of technology and management know-how transfer between MNCs and local firms depends upon several factors:

- Strategy of the MNC: Japanese firms, for example, are generally believed to desire long-term relationships with suppliers, which may facilitate technology transfer. Technology transfer may occur more readily when the MNC has a controlling interest in the local firm.
- Nature and complexity of the technology: strategic R&D is believed almost always to be located in the MNC home nation;

the more complex the technology, the greater will be the difficulty in transferring it.

- Technological and absorptive capacity of the local firm: without significant technological and managerial capacity, many advanced technologies cannot effectively be integrated into local firms.
- Government policies: the existence of government incentives on the one hand, and fears of sudden localization on the other, affect a corporation's propensity to transfer technologies.
- Concern about the comparative lack of protection for intellectual property.

In practice, despite a huge investment by multinationals, the evidence we have shows that the technological activities of MNCs involve very little development of technological capability in the receiving nation, even as the local level of industrial development increases, governments are very supportive, and investment relationships are long term.

In Indonesia, subcontracting in electronics, food processing, pharmaceuticals, chemicals, and autos has involved little range or depth in the relationship between local companies and MNCs, with little transfer of technology apart from some assistance with quality control techniques and minor product adaptations (Gultom-Siregar, 1995; Hill, 1988; Thee, 1990). However, some firms have developed minor product development capacities. Quality improvements and increased design activities are noted in the textile and garment industry; and within the car industry, up to 0.5 percent of the local firms' expenditure is spent on domestic R&D (Hill, 1995). The minor product developments described by Hill include auto firms developing stronger shock absorbers for local roads, electrical appliances being designed to deal with voltage fluctuations, and bottled drinks and canned food being modified to suit local tastes.

In Thailand, another comparatively weak nation technologically, subcontracting by local firms for MNCs has similarly been in relatively simple components (Supapol et al., 1995), and where there are technological applications involved in joint venture arrangements, these tend to be in low-tech, low value-added manufacturing (Wong, 1995). In the comparatively technologically stronger nations, the situation is slightly different. Malaysia, according to the National Science Foundation, has the greatest potential among the East Asian nations to develop its technological position:

Malaysia is purchasing increasing amounts of advanced technology products and continues to attract large amounts of foreign investment – much of it in the form of new high-tech manufacturing facilities. Even if these facilities are mostly platform (assembly) operations today, Malaysia's strong national orientation (defined by the existence of national strategies and an accepting environment for foreign investment), socioeconomic structure (evidence of functioning capital markets and rising levels of foreign investment and investments in education), and productive capacity (future capacity suggested through assessments of current level of high-tech production combined with evidence of skilled labor and innovative management) suggest that as Malaysia gains technological capabilities, more complex processing will likely follow. . . . Malaysia shows many signs of developing the resources it will need to compete in global technology markets. (NSF, 1995, p. 2)

This development has occurred in circumstances where, until very recently, there has been a relatively weak secondary and tertiary education system, certainly when compared to Korea and Japan at comparable levels of development.

Reliance on MNCs is certainly high: three-quarters of Malaysia's total value of exports are estimated to be provided by MNCs (Lall, 1995). In Malaysia, particularly in the Penang region – which employs over 100,000 workers and where 80 of its 150 electronics factories are foreign-owned (Goh, 1996) – the intense competition between MNCs in the electronics industry has led to some transfers of product and process technologies to local subcontractors that have had to possess high-precision and good quality control techniques. However, this transfer, not surprisingly, has occurred only when the local firm is relatively strong technologically (Rasiah, 1995). And generally, both local and foreign firms perform relatively few high value-added and technologically demanding tasks, such as design and development (Lall, 1995). Indeed, when attempting to replicate the Singaporean survey of the strategic management of technology cited later in the chapter, only fifteen firms were found to be involved in R&D in the Penang region. Even companies like Japan's Matsushita, which have been in Malaysia since the mid-1960s, engage in very little R&D there.

The situation in the People's Republic of China is similar. One of the most comprehensive, case study–based examinations of technology transfer through direct foreign investment was conducted in China. From this study, Lan (1996) found that while valuable technology is tranferred through DFI, the transfer occurs in a limited number of cases and is dominated by transplants of hardware only. Over 70 percent of interviewed foreign investors could not identify technological advantages through their investment. Only a small minority intended to begin any R&D in China.

Singapore has the most aggressive policies in Asia for attracting investment by transnational corporations. Yet even from Japanese MNCs, there has been little transfer of R&D: product and process innovation remains a strategic task back in Japan. Singaporean firms are expected to concentrate on incremental improvement and modification of products (Tang, 1996). Foreign firms investing in R&D in Singapore do so primarily for commercial reasons – such as the desire to develop and adapt products to local markets and be close to lead users and customers – rather than for accessing local technological capabilities and manpower resources (Wong, Loh, and Roberts, 1994).

In summary, subsidiaries of foreign MNCs still contract out a relatively small fraction of the component requirements to unaffiliated local suppliers and hence the possibility for technology transfer is rather limited (Supapol, 1995). As Bell and Pavitt (1993) noted, the depth of accumulated technological capabilities in industrializing countries is limited when technology is incorporated in new production capacity through turnkey projects and direct foreign investment. From this brief review, therefore, it appears that while reliance on policies that encourage investment from overseas corporations may improve the resources of local partner firms and some limited technological diffusion capabilities, the local firms have not built technological creation capabilities.

THE ROLE OF THE "NATIONAL CHAMPION": IPTN IN INDONESIA

As Hill (1995) said, "Technology policy, in all its dimensions, is one of the most debated topics in Indonesia." Yet, Indonesia essentially has no coherent technology policy (Hill, 1995; Kakazu, 1990).[10] Indonesian industry and financial institutions invest little in either R&D or technological innovation. "The national technological effort is small and in the private sector is minuscule" (Hill, 1995, p. 91). In one of the world's most diverse and richest cultures, the culture of technology plays a very small part.

An exception lies in the government-owned "techno-strategic industries" described in Table 8.1. However, there are major problems with these special industrial sectors. Most of them are effectively de-coupled from the bulk of (private sector) manufacturing industry with adverse consequences for the diffusion of technology. And questions abound over their protected status and lack of economic accountability (McKendrick, 1992).

IPTN is the national champion aircraft company. It was formally created in 1976 in Bandung, West Java. It began by manufacturing components for F-16 warplanes and Boeing, and assembling Superpuma and Bell helicopters. With a Spanish partner, CASA, it assembled a thirty-five-seat turboprop, the CN-235. During this partnership IPTN mastered startup and plant operations and acquired the ability to jointly make incremental changes to the aircraft (McKendrick, 1992a). It has itself subsequently entirely designed and manufactured a seventy-seat turboprop, the CN-250 (of which there only a few prototypes in existence). It currently has plans to develop a 130-seat jet plane, the N-2130. The cost of developing the N-2130 is estimated to be around $2 billion (*Financial Review*, February 23, 1996). The total investment in IPTN, prior to the decision to build the PT-2130, is very difficult to assess (IPTN publishes no financial data; it also benefits from considerable "hidden" subsidies in the form of duty-free imports of equipment). Estimates range from $3 billion to $6 billion. This compares with an annual national R&D expenditure of roughly $400 million in 1996–97.

Funding for the N-2130 is planned to come from the private sector rather than from the government. A company, DSTP, has been created to raise the $2 billion, and it has so far raised $100 million. Funds are to be dispersed to IPTN by DSTP only on the basis of approved quarterly reports. So the Indonesian govern-

---

[10] This definition of technology policy is broader than the one identified earlier and includes aspects of what is called innovation policy.

ment has attempted to exert greater financial control over IPTN, but the challenges for DSTP are considerable – not least in raising funds for a product that is not due to be completed until 2004, and is not projected to break even financially until it sells its 326th aircraft in 2013.

There are reasons that Indonesia should consider the development of an aircraft industry. Indonesia comprises a large number of geographical dispersed islands, making communications difficult and air transport crucial. It needs to diversify from its historically resource-based economy, and psychologically the CN-250 gives great optimism to Indonesians concerning their ability to further develop their S&T capabilities beyond aeronautics to support broader industrialization (Scott-Kemmis and Rohadian, 1996).

Nevertheless, critics of the IPTN experiment point to managerial problems such as poor coordination of supplies and work schedules, lack of scale economies, and the pervasive effect of Indonesia's weak educational system (Hill, 1995). While there is a lack of financial information, by any measure, the financial performance of IPTN has been extremely poor (McKendrick, 1992a; Hill and Pang, 1988). There are also critics of the technological performance of the CN-250 (*Business Week*, March 18, 1996). The whole project has suffered from a lack of critical analysis. (One critic of the plane, head of the state-owned airline, Merpati, questioned whether he really had to purchase his aircraft from IPTN and was sacked for his pains.) Others have pointed to a lack of marketing capability. But perhaps the greatest problem considered by the most detailed analysis to date is the lack of management capability, particularly as technology projects become more complex, which reflects the weak educational and R&D base of the country. IPTN is weak in management skills of "coordination, marketing, after-sales service, personnel management, pricing, scheduling and inventory control" (McKendrick, 1992a, p. 65). As Hill (1995) concludes, "It is doubtful whether ambitious 'high-tech' investment projects contribute significantly to efficient, broad-based technology development, particularly when the underlying research and education infrastructure is still rather weak" (p. 119).

The selection of a national champion in the aircraft industry, with little opportunity for munificent technological spin-offs to suppliers and customers, does little to encourage cross-organizational and systemic learning; and while it has improved the quality and level of resources within IPTN itself, it appears to have done little to improve technological capability within IPTN or more generally throughout Indonesia.

DEVELOPING INTERMEDIARY INSTITUTIONS

The National Science Foundation has evaluated the technological infrastructure of various Asian nations using a composite measure including: number of scientists in R&D; purchases of electronic data processing equipment; expert survey data on capability to train scientists and engineers; ability to use technical knowledge effectively; and the linkages of R&D to industry. This indicator is considered to evaluate the institutions and resources that contribute to a nation's capacity to develop, produce, and market new technology. According to this measure, Malaysia and China have relatively strong infrastructure, almost as strong as Korea, Singapore, and Taiwan. Indonesia has relatively weak technological infrastructure (NSF, 1995).

None of the East Asian NIEs, however, has a technological infrastructure of the scale and sophistication as those found in the United States, most European nations, and Japan. This infrastructural deficiency is recognized in East Asian NIEs: Malaysia's seventh five-year plan, for example, allocates 57 percent of its S&T budget to infrastructure development. One of the major future policy challenges facing many East Asian nations as they attempt to develop further their technological capabilities is the need to create an important element of these infrastructures: the so-called intermediary institutions that link suppliers and users of technology, and encourage the accumulation, diffusion, effective use, and eventual creation of technological innovations. These institutions have played a significant but still underdeveloped role in the technological development of Korea, Taiwan, and, latterly, Singapore, but have to date been of little importance in most of the other countries of Southeast Asia.

The role of these institutions elsewhere in the world is extremely diverse. They range from SEMATECH-type organizations focusing on early-stage R&D to relatively simple industrial extension services provided by, for example, the Japanese

Regional Technology Centres (Shapira, 1992) and the U.S. Manu-facturing Extension Partnership (Kelly and Arora, 1996).[11] Inter-mediary institutions are defined as those that proactively operate as a bridge between suppliers and users of technology. Their cre-ation, operation, and nurture is argued to be one of the major ele-ments of effective innovation policy (Dodgson and Bessant, 1996). They are important means of *disseminating* information to firms about new technology and market opportunities. They assist firms to *articulate* their needs and *assimilate* new practices. They can play a central role within networks of firms, particularly among SMEs. Rather than being a purveyor or source of information about finance or science and technology or management capabil-ity, they *coordinate* and *package* support across these areas in a way that is sympathetic to the majority of firms' nonstrategic, time-constrained mode of operating.

They are different from traditional S&T institutions, banks, venture and development capital providers, small firm support agencies, and consultants, although these institutions can fulfill the role of innovation intermediary. These roles are crucially important given the high degree of complexity in the fastest devel-oping technologies that are of such importance to the Asian economies, such as autos, electronics, chemicals, and consumer durables.

The institutional deficiency in intermediary organizations has been recognized by the major development banks. As the World Bank report, "Developing Industrial Technology," argues: "In developing countries, the greatest problem with the science and technology infrastructure (apart from the shortage of human resources to operate it efficiently) has been its lack of effective linkages with the productive sector. Most developing countries have set up networks of technology institutions, but few have been able to harness them to raise productive efficiency in industrial enterprises" (Najmabadi and Lall, 1995, p. 51).

The Asian Development Bank also refers to the institutional failure of what it calls "mentor" organizations (venture capital and development finance institutions, technical standards bodies, and intellectual property law agencies) and "guiding" organizations

---

[11] Numerous case studies of these organizations are presented in Dodgson and Bessant (1996), and Rush, Hobday, Bessant, Arnold, and Murray (1996).

(S&T information and advisory/consultancy services). It describes the risk aversion, low-quality personnel, and ineffective communications of these organizations (ADB, 1995).

There are good examples of government policies for intermediary development and of intermediaries themselves that are adapting and changing over time. Some examples of these infrastructural organizations will now be examined in some depth to explore the ways in which they fit into evolving industrial circumstances and national systems of innovation.

Singapore

Although organizations such as the Singapore Institute of Standards and Industrial Research (SISIR) have been operating since 1973, much of the institutional development in Singapore is of a relatively recent vintage. Between 1985 and 1995 Singapore established nine research centers and institutes focusing on IT, electronics, and biotechnology. According to Tang and Yeo (1995), the mission of these institutes and centers is to (1) provide specialized training, (2) develop pre-competitive technologies, (3) provide services to companies, and (4) transfer technology to industry. The National Science and Technology Board (NSTB) was established in 1991 from the Singapore Science Council, and that same year the National Technology Plan was announced.

Until recently, the overall thrust of Singapore's innovation policy was rather one-dimensional and focused on attracting MNCs and then encouraging them to undertake R&D. For example, NSTB's mission is to develop Singapore into a center of excellence in selected fields of science and technology so as to enhance national competitiveness in the industrial and services sectors. To this end NSTB offers incentives for firms to locate R&D and product design locally. Furthermore, the Singaporean Economic Development Board offers incentives for MNCs to upgrade the technological content of their operations, and subsidies are available for these MNCs wishing to send Singaporeans to headquarters to be trained to implement the transfer of new product lines to Singapore. The EDB has also established the Local Industry Upgrading Program (LIUP) to facilitate technology tranfer. The LIUP involves an experienced engineer from a selected MNC working full-time and wholly paid by the government to provide technical and managerial upgrading assistance to several local supplier firms (Wong, 1995).

The government plans to dedicate $2.85 billion to science and technology between 1996 and 2000. As described by Wong (1996), Singapore's National Technology Plan, while still attempting to encourage R&D by overseas firms, has as its major target the development of indigenous R&D capability among local universities, public research institutes, and firms, including new policies promoting R&D consortia. This approach recognizes the past problems with reliance on MNC research and development, which had some success – for example, according to Singapore's former deputy prime minister, eighty-seven MNCs have significant R&D programs in Singapore (Goh, 1996). But it has also had some deficiencies: as Goh admits, "The R&D activities of these companies must be regarded as peripheral."

The largest deficiency lies in the development of indigenous technology creation capacity. Despite being one of East Asia's most advanced nations technologically, 99 percent of patents in Singapore are registered to nonresidents (NSF, 1995). In their survey of the strategic management of technology in Singaporean firms, Wong, Loh, and Roberts (1994) found marked differences between foreign and local firms. Specifically, foreign-owned firms developed and accepted technology strategy more often; allocated more funds to research; monitored technology more extensively (with Japanese firms being particularly involved with university research); and more often considered themselves technology leaders rather than followers. The survey's authors concluded that technical managers and professionals need to acquire more business skills, and Singaporean companies should make greater use of resources in local universities.

In summary, Singaporean policy has altered in recent times to focus on the active encouragement of R&D and improvement of local technological creation capabilities. Despite rich technological resources, Singapore has not developed the technological capabilities to innovate significantly. Its new policies focus on the development of a research infrastructure, with the aim of embedding technological capabilities in local firms. Its small size will provide advantages over larger economies when attempting to implement the new strategies.

Taiwan

Government-supported technological and scientific research institutes have been indispensable in Taiwan's high-technology industrial development (Castells and Hall, 1994). In contrast with Singapore, Taiwan possesses an older and larger system of R&D institutions. Government has spent more on R&D, and it has had a succession of programs designed to encourage indigenous technological capabilities in strategic technologies. The Industrial Technology Research Institute, for example, which was established in Hsinchu in 1973, has played a major role in developing local technological capabilities in firms. Weiss and Mathews (1994) and Wu (1995), for example, describe how semiconductor wafer fabrication technology developed by ITRI has been spun off into some of Taiwan's most successful semiconductor firms. Numbers of commentators point to the business orientation of ITRI's leaders (Rush et al., 1996), and ITRI is funded on a project basis: while many of its projects are funded by government (for private clients), these projects are won competitively. There is no direct funding or subsidy.

ITRI employs over 6,000 and has an annual operating budget of $500 million. Its technology focus ranges from the high-tech integrated circuits (IC) industry to the textile industry, and its work on factory automation and advanced materials have also been applied in traditional industries. It coordinates multipartner consortia: the Taiwan New Personal Computer (TNPC) alliance formed in 1993, for example, involves thirty-one partners including IBM, Apple, and Motorola. The aims of the alliance are to "bring together firms from all aspects of the IT industry with a clear focus on transferring, uptaking and diffusing the new PowerPC technology in a series of products spanning PCs, software, peripherals and applications such as multimedia" (Poon and Mathews, 1995, p. 2). The initiative behind TNPC lay with the Computer and Communications Laboratory (CCL), one part of ITRI. CCL selected the PowerPC as an important "generic" technology and built the consortium, including negotiating with the U.S. partners. Poon and Mathews (1995) make the observation that this consortium is as much about diffusion of existing technology as it is about technology generation.

ITRI also provides information services, through its Industrial Technology Information Service (which has a staff of 200 and a budget of $10 million), and technical services, such as consulting, training (both technical and managerial), and trouble-shooting.

An ethnographic consideration of the following address by ITRI's executive vice president on its international strategy reveals how comprehensive, considered, and adaptable its approach is to acting as an intermediary.

We aim to: transfer technologies from abroad that would lead to investment in Taiwan and the enhancement of Taiwan's industrial strength; and to participate in international R&D projects and alliances to position ourselves in advanced technologies which are significant to industrial competitiveness in the future.

As an industry-minded R&D institution, we have long been active in transferring foreign technologies to expedite our own R&D and dissemination programs. The challenges ahead are different and broader. To be effective in gaining access to technologies internationally and bringing them to fruition in Taiwan we need to step up our efforts with the following approaches:

First, we regard our international programs as a long-term commitment. This means we will be mindful of both: building long-term capabilities, and producing results on a continuing basis.

The long-term capabilities, we perceive, would reside in an international operations "network" built around regional bases, and the continuous production of results would be attained through "projects" directed at commercialization. The two are mutually reinforcing, with the network supporting and continuously generating project opportunities, and the projects harvesting the benefits of the network.

Secondly, as these international programs are going to be ITRI-wide efforts involving various technical, marketing, planning, and support units, we must organize under a systematic framework to ensure quality and an orderly accumulation of operating experience and assets.

Third, a business opportunities driven attitude and practice should be stressed." (Yang, 1995, p. 2)

As another example of its carefully developed role as an intermediary, in 1996 ITRI opened its Open Laboratory Program based in an extensive new R&D complex in Hsinchu. The OpenLab Program mainly provides space and facilities for joint R&D between ITRI researchers and local businesses, and also has space for business incubation and conference and training facilities. Business incubatees receive "packaged" business and management consulting, financial and legal assistance, and office and administrative support. Entry to the business incubator requires the formal approval of a business plan. Such consultancy activity is, of course, assisted by government policies. Taiwan's technology and management guidance incentives, for example, subsidize 60 percent of the cost of total consulting exercises of firms, up to New Taiwan (NT) $1 million (Smith, 1994).

The intermediary role is additionally important given the small size of most Taiwanese firms. Few have their own research and development departments, and ITRI plays an important role in undertaking R&D and then disseminating the results to these small firms in readily accessible ways.

The collocated Hsinchu Science-based Industrial Park has operated since 1980. It was established to serve Taiwan's high-technology industries and accelerate their development. It offers a wide range of tax incentives, low-interest loans, R&D and man-power training grants, and duty-free importing of equipment and materials. In 1995 it had 170 resident companies, employing 36,000, and in 1994 had sales in excess of $6.5 billion. The Park is expected to reach combined sales of $50 billion by 2003, and has extensive development plans. Its main technology focus is electronics, particularly ICs. It has proven successful at attracting returned expatriates; over 1,000 work at the Park. Initially the government directly invested in the small startups, but increasingly private venture capital companies are assuming this role. Park companies have proved successful technologically, and many have demonstrated sophisticated management strategies when, for example, it comes to managing international strategic alliances (Yuan and Wang, 1995).

The collocation of ITRI and Hsinchu has been very successful. As Castells and Hall (1994) note, a common feature of successful technology institutions is their spatial collocation and integration, and they identify the success of ITRI and Hsinchu Science Park as being dependent upon their coexistence and also being collocated alongside two universities. Local small firms, as well as having the opportunity to link with particular local institutions, are part of an innovative milieu (Cooke and Morgan, 1994).

However, both ITRI and Hsinchu face future challenges in increasing the amount of research being undertaken. There is a concern among senior ITRI managers that more basic research should be conducted. There is also a concern among senior

Ministry of Economic Affairs officials that some companies on
Hsinchu Science Park are more concerned with simple manufacturing (and enjoying the accompanying five-year tax break) than
with conducting research and developing technologies. The challenges of the need to increase research activities are inevitable as
Taiwan reaches the technological forefront in many key areas. The
ability of Taiwan to meet the challenges will require the level of
adaptability and change enjoyed among its institutions in the past.

One of the most astute observers of the Asian technology scene,
Wong Poh-Kam (1995), contrasts the success of state intervention
in hastening technology diffusion among local firms in Taiwan
with the past lack of government concern with public R&D in
Singapore. Public research institutes, he argues,

serve initially to assimilate advanced technology from overseas and
rapidly diffuse them to local enterprises, but increasingly also to serve
as the coordinating nodes to promote indigenous technology creation
via R&D consortia and strategic R&D programs as well. . . . While the
development of the electronics industry in Singapore has been largely
driven by an innovation network model centered on MNCs as the key
nodes, indigenous small and medium entrepreneurial firms – in close
relationship with public research institutes – have been the driving force
in the case of Taiwan. (Wong, 1995, p. 18)

Malaysia

As we have seen, Malaysia has relied heavily on DFI as a means
of encouraging local technological development, and despite the
limited returns to date in building indigenous technological capability it will continue to use such investment as a major element
in its technology development policies (Jegasthesan et al., 1997).
As a complement to this policy it is encouraging the takeover
of foreign firms, the use of original equipment manufacturing
arrangements, and the subcontracting of technology from foreign
firms (Jegasthesan et al., 1997). It has also established a number
of new organizations, such as the Kulim HiTech Industrial
Park and the Malaysian Technology Development Corporation
(MTDC). The MTDC has the aim of commercializing local
research results, introducing strategic technologies, and encouraging the development of venture capital in Malaysia. At the same
time, a number of older Malaysian organizations are adapting and
changing their roles.

An example of this transition is seen in the Standards and Industrial Research Institute of Malaysia (SIRIM), which is a major intermediary institution in Malaysia.[12] SIRIM was established in 1975. It employs 1,200, one-third of whom are scientists and engineers and one-third technicians. Its functions are broad and encompass R&D, prototype testing, standards, calibration, production, export assistance, consultancy, and training. Its mission therefore includes technology diffusion and creation.

Its role has developed along with the Malaysian economy. Previously focused on relatively limited activities related to standards and quality, it is now charged with the development of product development and innovation in Malaysian firms.

To assist this change in strategy, SIRIM was made a corporation in 1996 to remove its activities from some of the constraints of government bureaucracy and to link it closer with industry. Following this move, it separated into two types of activity: statutory or public good services and commercial services (which receive no government funding). The public good services include establishing and operating a number of centers, such as the National CAD/CAM Centre and the National Measurement Centre; acting as contractor for government contracts from specific agencies covering international standardization and SME industry development; and engaging in international science and technology collaborative activities.

Commercial services include contract research and consultancy, commercialization of technology, certification, testing, calibration, providing technical information, and training. SIRIM operates a Joint Research Venture Programme whereby SIRIM funds, facilities, and expertise are used to assist industry partners in turning innovative ideas into marketable products through sharing of costs, equity, and effort. It also has a Tripartite Research Venture Programme, which fosters links through SIRIM-industry-university R&D collaboration. It has run a number of technology business forums (in ceramics, biochemical, CAD/CAM, and industrial automation technologies) where R&D findings are outlined and offered to industry.

SIRIM is highly conscious of the need to balance its long-term

---

[12] This section has relied heavily on an unpublished article by Asmadi M. D. Said, Senior General Manager, SIRIM, "Organisational Change Setting for Greater Effectiveness in the Development and Commercialisation of Technology: The Case of SIRIM."

developmental activities in training and R&D, which will not be funded by the private sector, with commercially attractive projects that will be profitable for it and its clients. The Malaysian government has allocated funds for the continual funding of human resource development in SIRIM and it intends to allocate 50 percent of its R&D expenditure to longer-term, strategic research.

It is obviously too early to assess the outcomes of the corporatization process. SIRIM has been shown to be adaptable in the strategies it has pursued in the past, but the recent changes are radical. They will involve a major transition from a government-owned to a market-oriented organization. Much will depend on the quality of its management in introducing the changes and developing the necessary change in working culture.

It should be noted that Malaysia has had remarkable success in the technology assistance and extension services provided to tropical cash-crop agriculture, such as rubber and palm oil. Government institutes have been very effective in assisting the development of this industry (Barlow, 1978; Barlow et al., 1994).

CONCLUSIONS

Science, technology, and innovation have played a central role in the economic and industrial development of East Asian NIEs. The technological strengths within the region are considerable and rapidly growing. The success of the region could have major consequences for the world technological balance of power, and the policies pursued for technological development hold lessons for other areas of the world (Hobday, 1995).

Yet the challenges for science, technology, and innovation policy in East Asian NIEs are immense. Poverty, disease, transport congestion, and environmental degradation remain endemic in some East Asian nations, and there are pressing societal needs for improved returns from science and technology in these areas. There are also pressing economic needs, ranging from basic industrial development in some nations, to the need to enhance international competitive advantages in others.

The development of science, and scientific and research training, is a particular priority for the more technologically advanced countries. Past heavy reliance on overseas countries, especially the United States, for scientific training and collaborative research may diminish as East Asian NIEs increasingly develop their own scientific infrastructures in universities and research laboratories, and continue to expand the highly successful policy followed by Taiwan and Korea of encouraging expatriate scientists and engineers to return home.

Direct foreign investment and technology policies, particularly those directed at electronics, have been highly effective at building internationally successful industries, based on manufacturing resources and expertise. The challenge for the technologically advanced nations, like Korea, Singapore, and Taiwan, lies in the transition to "knowledge" economies, where competitiveness depends on creativity, speed of learning, and intellectual property. Another challenge is how to diversify into other new technologies, such as biotechnology and new materials. Singapore's National Science Plan, for example, identifies the importance of agricultural biotechnology as a key area of interest. An important policy question for less technologically developed nations, such as Malaysia and Indonesia, is whether the present emphasis on electronics is likely to produce any longer-term sustainable comparative advantages. One might justifiably ask whether emphasis could be better placed on more traditional and historical, but still potentially high-technology, high value-added industries, such as tropical cash crops in Malaysia and textiles in Indonesia.

Many of the challenges confronting all East Asian nations derive from broader international developments: in globalization and the ready transfer of resources across national boundaries in response to cost advantages and available intellectual capital.

To overcome and benefit from these challenges, East Asian nations have to develop the technological capabilities of their firms. These capabilities have to become integrated into the fabric of the industrial structure and the national system of innovation: in the organizational and technological infrastructure on the one hand and in the management practices and routines of firms on the other.

The review of the impact of DFI by overseas multinational companies showed little resulting development of technological capabilities, even among the more industrially and technologically developed nations. The example of IPTN as a national champion showed the dangers of policies driven by national pride and personal egos: it has not and will not develop broad technological capabilities. By contrast, the infrastructure-building policies, shown in the development of "intermediary institutions," have had a distinct impact on the development of technology diffusion and creation capabilities. Part of the strength of these intermediaries derives though their network-oriented focus and emphasis on collaborative activities. In line with recent innovation theory, which analyzes systems of innovation – national, technological, local – their focus is cross-organizational learning (as clearly seen in the ITRI model). The challenge for these intermediaries is to continue to develop, evolve, and adapt as circumstances change.

In the development of effective science, technology, and innovation policies, it is not necessary to reinvent the wheel. There are numerous examples of good practice that can be adopted and adapted from overseas. Learning from overseas experiences is an important element of effective policy of all sorts. There are numerous examples of this having occurred. The development of science parks throughout the region, for example, is based on U.S. experience. The Korea Technology Development Corporation and the Malaysian Technology Development Corporation, for example, were modeled on the British National Research Development Corporation. These institutional replicas are in many ways different from their model and reflect different levels of technological capability in different industries. It is always important to recognize and adapt policies sensitive to national differences. Bureaucratic capacity (and the distortions created by corruption) varies enormously in East Asia, so it is highly unlikely that one single policy model is likely to work.

A question arises of what learning can occur within Asian nations about institutions more appropriate to the specific challenges within the region. East Asia is characterized by very broad differences in industrial structures, government-business relationships, and legal and financial systems as well as by models of management very different from those found elsewhere – for example, in the ubiquity of Chinese family business or in the Korean *chaebol*. The transfer of learning about institutions and the search for complementarities in national technological strengths among various European nations described in Dodgson and Bessant (1996) is, as Stephen Hill points out, also possible and desirable in Asia:

Cultural and organisational dimensions of international S&T are rarely taken into account, yet they could provide the source of potential failure both nationally and in international S&T relations, or, alternatively, the source of potential major advantage through mutually reinforcing solutions to separate national weaknesses in research culture. . . . [A]cross all . . . Asian nations, learning from both the benefits and dis-benefits of each others' research and organisational cultures could be of considerable importance to building resilient and targeted national innovation cultures and policies. (Hill, 1995, p. 5)

The diversity within East Asia provides an opportunity for policy makers to learn and benefit from heterogeneity and, potentially, as trade becomes freer under the auspices of initiatives like APEC, to encourage specialization.

Within the European Union, the European Commission has played a central role in the coordination and transfer of international best policy practice among countries at various levels of development and with different national systems of innovation. Such a role could valuably be replicated by the Asia Pacific Economic Cooperation forum (APEC) within the Asia Pacific region. The transfer and coordination of foresight exercises in science policy, for example, could improve prioritization and encourage diversification. The transfer of best practice in intermediaries could facilitate the greater embeddedness of technology, as has occurred in Taiwan, as opposed to its currently rather shallow roots in many other East Asian NIEs. Furthermore, and probably much further down the track, the confidence to specialize brought about by guaranteed free trade under APEC may encourage diversification away from the currently narrow technology base in East Asia.

Finally, there is speculation about the effects of the Asian financial crisis on science, technology, and innovation policies. The implications of the crisis – which has affected Indonesia particularly severely, but has also adversely affected Korea, Malaysia, and Thailand – on these policies will take some years to assess properly. Some short-term adjustments will undoubtedly occur in national and corporate ambitions, but the long-term technological development trajectories will remain. The crisis arose from shortcomings in financial systems, not government and industry's development and use of technology. Government and business see science, technology, and innovation as fundamental to their efforts to overcome the consequences of the crisis and continue to see it as the basis for future growth. The radical changes occurring in Asian financial systems, with greater transparency and accountability, will lead to more efficient allocation of financial resources for technology projects. Throughout Asian societies, based on past experience, there is a strong belief in the importance of technology and innovation for economic and social progress. This belief is unlikely to be diminished, and if anything is likely to be strengthened as a result of the crisis.

REFERENCES

Abegglen, J. 1994. *Sea Change*. New York: Free Press.
Amsden, A., and T. Hikino. 1994. "Project Execution Capability, Organizational Know-How and Conglomerate Corporate Growth in Late Industrialization." *Industrial and Corporate Change*, 3(1), 111–147.
Asian Development Bank (ADB). 1989. *Regional Cooperation in Technology Ventures in Small and Medium Industry*. Manila: ADB.
Asian Development Bank (ADB). 1995. *Technology Transfer and Development: Implications for Developing Asia*. Manila: ADB.
Barlow, C. 1978. *The Natural Rubber Industry: Its Development, Technology and Economics in Malaysia*. Kuala Lumpur: OUP.
Barlow, C., S. Jayasuriya, and C. Tan. 1994. *The World Rubber Industry*. London: Routledge.
Bell, M., and K. Pavitt. 1993. "Accumulating Technological Capability in Developing Countries." Proceedings of the World Bank Annual Conference on Development Economics, 1992, Washington, DC.
Bourke, P., and L. Butler. 1995. "International Links in Higher Education Research." Report No 37. Canberra: National Board of Emplyment, Education and Training.
Bryant, K., L. Lombardo, M. Healy, L. Bopage, and S. Hartshorn. 1996. *Australian Business Innovation: A Strategic Analysis*, Measures of Science and Innovation 5, Department of Industry, Science and Technology. Canberra: Australian Government Publishing Service.
Business Week, March, 18, 1996.
Castells, M., and P. Hall. 1994. *Technopoles of the World: The Making of 21st Century Industrial Complexes*. London: Routledge.
Choung, J-Y. 1995. "Technological Capabilities of Korea and Taiwan: An Analysis using U.S. Patenting Statistics." Brighton, England: University of Sussex, SPRU, STEEP Discussion Paper 26.
Cooke, P., and K. Morgan. 1994. "The Creative Milieu: A Regional Perspective on Innovation." In M. Dodgson and R. Rothwell (eds.), *The Handbook of Industrial Innovation*. Cheltenham, England: Edward Elgar, 25–32.

Dodgson, M. 1993. *Technological Collaboration in Industry: Strategy, Policy and Internationalisation of Innovation.* London: Routledge.

Dodgson, M., and J. Bessant. 1996. *Effective Innovation Policy: A New Approach.* London: International Thomson Business Press.

Dodgson, M., and Y. Kim. 1997. "Learning to Innovate – Korean Style: The Case of Samsung." *International Journal of Innovation Management,* 1(1), 53–67.

Financial Review, February 23, 1996.

Fortune, August 18, 1997.

Goh, K. 1996. "The Technology Ladder in Development: The Singapore Case." *Asian-Pacific Economic Literature.*

Gultom-Siregar, M. 1995. "Indonesia." In *Transnational Corporation and Backward Linkages in Asian Electronics Industries.* New York: UNCTAD.

Hill, H. 1988. *Foreign Investment and Industrialisation in Indonesia.* New York: Oxford University Press.

Hill, H. 1995. "Indonesia's Great Leap Forward? Technology Development and Policy Issues." *Bulletin of Indonesian Economic Studies,* 31(2), 83–123.

Hill, H., and E. Pang. 1991. "Technology Exports from a Small, Very Open NIC: The Case of Singapore." *World Development,* 19(5), 553–568.

Hill, H., and E. Pang. 1988. "The State and Industrial Restructuring: A Comparison of the Aerospace Industry in Indonesia and Singapore." *ASEAN Economic Bulletin,* 5(2), 152–168.

Hill, S. 1995. "Regional Empowerment in the New Global Science and Technology Order." *Asian Studies Review,* 18(3), 2–17.

Hobday, M. 1995. *Innovation in East Asia.* Cheltenham, England: Edward Elgar.

International Development Program (IDP). 1995. *International Education – Australia's Potential: Demand and Supply.* Canberra: IDP.

Jegathesan, J., A. Gunasekaran, and S. Muthaly. 1997. "Technology Development and Transfer: Experiences from Malaysia." *International Journal of Technology Management,* 13(2), 196–214.

Justman, M., and M. Teubal. 1995. "Technological Infrastructure Policy: Generating Capabilities and Building Markets." *Research Policy,* 24, 259–281.

Kakazu, H. 1990. "Industrial Technology Capabilities and Policies in Selected Asian Developing Countries." Asian Development Bank Economic Staff Paper 46. Manila: ADB.

Kelley, M., and A. Arora. 1996. "The Role of Institution-Building in U.S. Industrial Modernisation Programs." *Research Policy,* 25(2), 265–279.

Kim, L. 1997a. "The Dynamics of Samsung's Technological Learning in Semiconductors." *California Management Review,* 39(3), 86–100.

Kim, L. 1997b. *Imitation to Innovation: The Dynamics of Korea's Technological Learning.* Cambridge, MA: Harvard Business School Press.

Lall, S. 1995. "Malaysia: Industrial Success and the Role of Government." *Journal of International Development,* 7(5), 759–773.

Lan, P. 1996. *Technology Transfer to China through Foreign Direct Investment.* Avebury England: Aldershot.

Leonard-Barton, D. 1995. *Wellsprings of Knowledge.* Cambridge, MA: Harvard Business School Press.

Lundvall, B-A. 1992. *National Systems of Innovation.* London: Pinter.

Marsh, I. 1997. "Economic Governance in Industrialising Asia: Structure, Comparisons and Impact." Sydney: Australian Graduate School of Management Working Paper 97-017.

Mathews, J. 1996. "High Technology Industrialisation in East Asia." *Journal of Industry Studies,* 3(2), 1–67.

McKendrick, D. 1992a. "Obstacles to 'Catch-up': The Case of the Indonesian Aircraft Industry." *Bulletin of Indonesian Economic Studies,* 28(1), 39–66.

McKendrick, D. 1992b. "Use and Impact of Information Technology in Indonesian Commercial Banks." *World Development,* 20(1), 1753–1768.

Minden, K., and P. Wong. 1996. *Developing Technology Managers in the Pacific Rim.* New York: M.E. Sharpe.

"More Like Singapore – Can Industrial Peking Build a High-tech Hong Kong?" (1997, October 23). *Far Eastern Economic Review.*

Najmabadi, F., and S. Lall. 1995. "Developing Industrial Technology." Washington, DC: World Bank.

National Science Foundation (NSF). 1995. *Asia's New High Tech Competitors.* Washington, DC: National Science Foundation 95-309.

Nelson, R. 1993. *National Innovation Systems.* New York: Oxford University Press.

Nonaka, I., and H. Takeuchi. 1995. *The Knowledge-Creating Company.* New York: Oxford University Press.

Penrose, E. 1959. *The Theory of the Growth of the Firm.* Oxford, England: Blackwell.

Poon, T., and J. Mathews. 1995. "Technological Upgrading through Alliance Formation: The Case of Taiwan's New PC Consortium." Paper presented at the "Business Networks, Business Growth" Conference, Sydney, October 19–20.

Porter, A., D. Roessner, N. Newman, and D. Cauffiel. 1996. "Indicators of High Technology Competitiveness of 28 Countries." *International Journal of Technology Management,* 12(1), 1–32.

Rasiah, R. 1995. "Malaysia." In *Transnational Corporation and Backward Linkages in Asian Electronics Industries.* New York: UNCTAD.

Rush, H., M. Hobday, J. Bessant, E. Arnold, and R. Murray. 1996.

Technology Institutes: Strategies for Best Practice. London: International Thomson Business Press.

Science and Engineering Indicators. 1996. Washington, DC: National Science Board.

Scott-Kemmis, D., and R. Rohadian. 1996. "Indonesia: Science and Technology Policy and Development for Industrial Development." Jakarta: Australian Embassy. (Mimeographed)

Shapira, P. 1992. "Lessons from Japan: Helping Small Manufacturers." *Issues in Science and Technology*, 8(3), 66–72.

Sheehan P., N. Pappas, E. Tikhomirova, and P. Sinclair. 1995. "Australia and the Knowledge Economy," Victoria, Australia: Victoria University of Technology, Centre for Strategic Economic Studies.

Smith, H. 1994. "Taiwan's Industry Policy During the 1980s and its Relevance to the Theory of Strategic Trade." Pacific Economic Papers, No 233, July, Australia-Japan Research Centre. Canberra: Australian National University.

Supapol, A. 1995. *Transnational Corporation and Backward Linkages in Asian Electronics Industries.* New York: UNCTAD.

Supapol, A., S. Suebsub-anunt, and P. Arbhabhirama. 1995. "Thailand." In *Transnational Corporation and Backward Linkages in Asian Electronics Industries.* New York: UNCTAD.

Tang, H. 1996. "Hollowing-out or International Division of Labour? Perspectives from the Consumer Electronics Industry and Singapore." *International Journal of Technology Management*, 12(2), 231–241.

Tang, H., and K. Yeo. 1995. "Technology, Entrepreneurship and National Development: Lessons from Singapore." *International Journal of Technology Management*, 10(7/8), 797–814.

Teece, D., and G. Pisano. 1994. "The Dynamic Capabilities of Firms: an Introduction." *Industrial and Corporate Change*, 3(3), 537–556.

Teubal, M. 1996. "R&D and Technology Policy in NICs as Learning Processes." *World Development*, 24(3), 449–460.

Thee, K. 1990. "Indonesia: Technology Transfer in the Manufacturing Industry." In H. Soesastro and M. Pangestu (eds.), *Technological Challenge in the Asia-Pacific Economy.* Sydney: Allen and Unwin.

Turpin, T., and J. Innes. 1995. "Intellectual Property Law in the Asia-Pacific Region." Wollongong, Australia: University of Wollongong, Centre for Research Policy.

UNCTAD. 1996. *World Investment Report 1996.* New York: United Nations.

Weiss, L., and J. Mathews. 1994. "Innovation Alliances in Taiwan: A Coordinating Approach to Developing and Diffusing Technology." *Journal of Industry Studies*, 1(2), 91–101.

Wong, J. 1995. "Technology Transfer in Thailand: Descriptive Validation of a Technology Transfer Model." *International Journal of Technology Management*, 10(7/8), 788–796.

Wong, P. 1995. "Competing in the Global Electronics Industry: A Comparative Study of the Different Innovation Networks of Singapore and Taiwan." Paper presented at the International Symposium, "Innovation Networks: East Meets West," Sydney, August 30–31.

Wong, P. 1996. "From NIE to Developed Economy: Singapore's Industrial Policy to the Year 2000." *Journal of Asian Business*, 12(3), 65–86.

Wong, P., L. Loh, and E. Roberts. 1994. "Global Benchmarking Study on the Strategic Management of Technology: The Case of Singapore." NUS/NSTB/MIT Report. Singapore.

Wu, S-H. 1995. "The Dynamic Cooperating Relationship between the Government and Enterprises – the Development of Taiwan's Integrated Circuit Industry in Retrospect." Taipei: National Chengchi University. (Mimeographed)

Yamashita, S. 1991. *Transfer of Japanese Technology and Management to the ASEAN Countries.* Tokyo: University of Tokyo Press.

Yang, Jin Chang. 1995. "ITRI Stepping Up International Activities." *ITRI Today*, Fall, 20.

Yuan, B., and M-Y. Wang. 1995. "The Influential Factors for the Effectiveness of International Strategic Alliances of High-Tech Industry in Taiwan." *International Journal of Technology Management*, 10(7/8), 777–787.

CHAPTER 9

The Role of Science and Technology Policy in Korea's Industrial Development

Won-Young Lee

INTRODUCTION

This chapter discusses the evolution of science and technology (S&T) policy in Korea's industrial development since the 1960s. Korea has transformed from a low-income, underdeveloped country to a mid-income, industrialized country in about thirty years. Korea joined the Organization for Economic Cooperation and Development (OECD) in 1997 and is striving to become an advanced industrial country in the near future.

The role of S&T policy has not received as much attention as that of industrial policy in the study of Korea's industrial development. Nonetheless, S&T policy played an important role from the initial stage of industrial development and its role continues to expand. Technological capability building in Korean firms owes much to the government's strong commitment.

Science and technology policy formulation at the different stages of industrial development was a challenging task because theoretical foundations for S&T policy suitable to a developing country are fragile. Furthermore, Korea did not have a good benchmark from any other country to follow.

It is true that mistakes were made in carrying out S&T policy at various stages of technological development. However, many policy measures turned out to be quite effective. In this respect, the Korean experience offers lessons for other developing countries facing similar problems. Korea can take advantage of its past experience to design S&T policy for the future.

This chapter postulates that technological development in Korea has undergone three stages: the imitation stage, the internalization stage, and the generation stage. Science and technology policy in each stage is discussed focusing on the following questions: What are the distinctive characteristics of S&T policies at each stage compared to the previous stages? What is the background for the changes in S&T policy? What were the consequences of the policy? The interaction between industrial policy and S&T policy is also discussed. The former is often called the demand side of technology while the latter is regarded as the supply side of technology.

This section classifies technological development stages. First, a conceptual framework for classifying a stage of technological development is discussed. Then, classification of stages during the period from the mid-1960s to the year 1995 are presented.

Conceptual Framework

Jinjoo Lee et al. (1988) identify the three stages of technology development during the course of industrial development: the imitation stage, the internalization stage, and the generation stage. During the imitation stage, foreign technology imitation is the predominant means of acquiring technological capability. The internalization stage starts when local engineers are capable of developing products or constructing new plants through indigenous efforts, or when domestically manufactured products become technically superior to products manufactured in foreign countries. The generation stage begins when a nation is capable of introducing market-leading products and state-of-the-art core technology.

The three stages mentioned are consistent with the stages introduced by Kim and Dahlman (1992), who theorize that the evolutionary path of technology in developing countries follows three stages: the mature stage, the consolidation stage, and the emergence stage. Terminology in Jinjoo Lee et al. (1988) emphasizes technology strategy while that in Kim and Dahlman (1992) focuses on technology characteristics. Criteria for stage classification with both sets of authors are very similar.

Periodic Division of Technology Development Stages

Periodic division of stages is proposed as follows. The transition from the innovation stage to the internalization stage took place in 1980. The transition from the internalization stage to the generation stage occurred in 1990. So, the period from 1962 to 1979 is the imitation stage; the period from 1980 to 1989 is the internationalization stage; and the generation stage starts in 1990 and continues to the present.

The year 1980 is proposed as a transitory period for the following reasons. Technology strategy of Korean firms began to change in the 1980s. Indicators for innovation activities in Table 9.1 show that a drastic jump occurs in the years 1980 to 1985, implying that major structural change occurred during that period. Most significant is the increase in private research and development investment, which increased from 0.21 percent of gross national product (GNP) in 1980 to 1.17 percent of GNP in 1985. Another significant change was the proliferation of the own brand manufacture (OBM) strategy that replaced the original equipment manufacture (OEM) strategy. Leading firms began to introduce their own original models in the late 1970s. The strategy subsequently diffused to other competitors in the early 1980s. LG electronics was able to market own brand-name color TVs in 1976. The firm had been producing TVs as a subcontractor of foreign brands since 1965. Samsung developed its own model of a microwave oven in 1978, followed by LG and Daewoo four years later. Hyundai developed the first automobile with its own brand name, PONY, in 1975.

There also was a significant change in the channel of technology transfer in the early 1980s. The formal mode of technology played an increasing role by the late 1970s. The amount of technology licensing and direct foreign investment increased very rapidly in the 1980s.[1]

The year 1990 is proposed as a turning point in the transition from the internalization stage to the generation stage. Technology strategy of Korean firms began to change from a dependent strategy to a defensive or offensive strategy around 1990. Samsung

---

[1] Note that Kim and Dahlman (1992) also designate the early 1980s as the turning point from the mature stage to the consolidation stage.

Table 9.1. *Major indicators of innovation activities*

	1970	1975	1980	1985	1990	1995
Total R&D (A) (Billion Won)	105	427	282.5	1,237.1	3,349.9	9,440.6
Private R&D (B)	25	141	102.5	930.3	2,698.9	76,597
Governmental R&D (C)	80	286	180.0	306.8	651.0	17,809
A/GNP	0.39	0.44	0.58	1.56	1.88	2.71
B/GNP	0.09	0.15	0.21	1.17	1.52	2.20
C/GNP	0.30	0.29	0.37	0.39	0.36	0.51
C/Total governmental budget	2.2	2.0	2.8	2.8	2.3	2.2
Number of researchers	5,628	10,275	18,434	41,473	70,503	128,315
Governmental/public						
Institutions	2,458	5,308	4,598	7,154	10,434	15,007
Universities	2,011	2,312	8,695	14,935	21,332	44,686
Private sector	1,159	2,655	5,141	18,996	38,737	68,625
R&D expenditure/researcher						
(Thousand Won)	1,874	4,152	15,325	27,853	49,514	73,574
Researcher/10,000 popular	1.8	2.9	4.8	10.1	16.4	28.6
Number of corporate R&D Labs	0	12	54	183	966	2,270
Tech Licensing (import) amount	5.1[a]	26.5	107.2	295.5	1,087.0	1,947.0
(Million $) number	84[a]	99	222	454	738	236
Tech Licensing (export) amount	—	—	—	11.2	21.8	112.4
(Million $) number	—	—	—	7	50	123
Direct Foreign Investment[b]						
amount (Million $)	67,405	203,519	143,136	532,197	802.5	1,941.4
number	115	45	37	127	296	
Overseas Direct Investment[c]						
amount (Million $)	4.8	9.7	15.5	31.5	891	3,059
number	13	11	18	11	344	—
Applied Patents	1,846	2,914	5,070	10,587	25,820	78,499
Utility Models	6,617	7,290	8,558	18,548	22,654	59,866
Industrial Design	4,522	6,707	10,075	18,949	18,769	29,978
Trademark	5,124	9,476	13,558	26,069	46,826	71,852

[a] Statistic for 1972.
[b] Approved Investment (Flow).
[c] Net Investment.

Semi-Conductor was able to introduce the 4 mega dram (MDRAM) chip into the market in 1989, almost in parallel with competitors in the United States and Japan. Korea was capable of producing its own models of large-scale computers in 1991. It was an outcome of the joint R&D efforts by the government and industry. The G-7 project, aimed at developing core industrial technologies, was launched that same year. The total number of corporate research labs exceeded 100 in 1991. The Korean government set up the National Strategies for Information Industries in 1992.

The high-wage period started in 1990. That means Korea could no longer try to catch up in industrial development by taking advantage of low labor costs. Unit labor costs increased by 17.7 percent annually on the average from 1988 to 1990.

INNOVATION POLICY DURING THE IMITATION STAGE

The first five-year economic plan started in 1962. At that time, total R&D investments amounted to 0.2 percent of GNP. There had been virtually no R&D activity in industry and universities. Only public research institutes, whose primary functions were testing and inspection, undertook small-scale R&D projects.

The government recognized the importance of S&T in industrial development. Following the completion of the first five-year plan in 1966, it was determined that more technological manpower and research capability was needed to implement and assimilate foreign technologies. President Park Chung Hee, the architect of Korea's early industrial development, initiated and supervised the establishment of the science and technology infrastructure in the 1960s and 1970s. The Korea Institute of Science and Technology (KIST), the first modern, integrated technical center, was established in 1966. The Ministry of Science and Technology (MOST), was established in 1967. Its primary function was to integrate plans for S&T development, and coordinate governmental R&D, and international S&T coordination and research on nuclear energy. The building of S&T infrastructures continued throughout the 1970s. The Technology Development Law and the Engineering Services Promotion Law were enacted in 1972. The Korea Advanced Institute was set up to office high-caliber master's and doctoral education in 1971. Many specialized research institutions funded by the government were established in the 1970s.

The Korean government invested a larger portion of its budget in S&T than other developing countries at that time. The government budget for S&T promotion increased from 0.18 percent of GNP in 1964 to 0.3 percent of GNP in 1970, and 0.37 percent in 1980. The proportion remained at that level until the 1990s. Korea was also the first developing country to have a ministry-level administration for S&T.

It is well known that S&T policy, the supply side of technology, played only a minimal role during the imitation stage because private demand for R&D was almost nonexistent. Nevertheless, policy makers, including President Park, had strong faith in investing in S&T. The government did not demand immediate return from government-funded research institutes (GRIs), which consumed most of the government's R&D funds. These institutes had full autonomy in the allocation of funds earmarked by the government. The autonomy would not have been possible without the complete trust of the government.

The major contribution of GRIs during this period was to provide the S&T pool to be utilized for the absorption and assimilation of foreign technology and to carry out contract research for the private sector. This alone may not be sufficient to justify the efficacy of resources reserved for the GRIs. Investments in the institutes during the 1960s and the 1970s paid off for other reasons. Government-funded research institutes attracted many Korean scientists and engineers from abroad who otherwise would have not returned. Many of them later played key roles in the development of the heavy and chemical industries and high-tech industries. GRIs also contributed to heightening the social status of scientists and engineers. They received high salaries and enjoyed a high degree of social prestige. As a result, engineering and science-related departments of universities attracted the best students.

Despite a strong commitment by the government on the supply side of technology, its actual role during the imitation stage is believed to have been minimal (Kim et al., 1997). On the other hand, industrial policy, the demand side of technology, greatly influenced the rate and direction of technological advancements in Korean firms. Among the many important aspects of industrial policy, industrial targeting deserves closer attention.

Korean industrial policy is unique in that both export promotion and import substitution are pursued simultaneously. This would not have been possible if Korea had resorted to only trade policy instruments to carry out industrial policy objectives. It was possible because Korea mobilized other policy instruments such as preferential financing, provision of cheap industrial land, and relaxation of antitrust regulations, to name only a few important ones. Labor-intensive export industries were targeted in the 1960s, while the heavy and chemical industries were targeted in the 1970s.

The main objective of industrial targeting is to expand production capacity. But it also stimulates technological capability building. The Korean experience shows that targeted promotion of industries influences technological learning in two ways. First, the interaction with foreign buyers or suppliers provides the opportunity to absorb foreign technology. A survey on the source of technology of exporting Korean firms found that trade-related activities such as employee training abroad, technical assistance from suppliers of parts and raw materials, and technical assistance from buyers are very important modes of technology transfer. For some product innovation, trade-related contacts made up 95 percent of the source of foreign technology transfer (Westphal, Lee, and Pursell, 1981). Second, increase in production enhances technological learning à la Verdoon's law. Experiences in the automobile industry and the electronics industry support this hypothesis.

The Heavy and Chemical Industry Drive in the 1970s was initially much criticized by many economists because it distorted market mechanism. They insisted that the nation's scarce resources would be wasted by over-investment in these industries. These industries indeed suffered from over-capacity and weak technological competency as predicted. In the late 1970s, the average capacity utilization rate dropped to less than 70 percent. These industries, however, overcame most problems by the mid-1980s, the major source of export growth in the following years.

It should be noted that industrial policy and S&T policy were not closely coupled. Industrial policy was mainly administrated by the Ministry of Trade and Industry, while S&T policy was under the control of the Ministry of Science and Technology. The two ministries rarely consulted with each other. Furthermore, the Economic Planning Board, the coordinating ministry of economic-related matters, was preoccupied with other tasks.

Science and technology policy would have been better served for assisting technological development in industries if industrial policy and S&T policy had been closely coupled. S&T policy could have addressed the technological needs of industries more effectively if it had been closely coupled with industrial policy. The GRIs are often criticized by industry because they tended to choose projects that were of little commercial value.

However, this arrangement also produced some benefits. Most

important, S&T policy was consistent. It would never have gained stability if it had been too closely coupled with industrial policy, which was very unstable. Korea's industrial policy was very much influenced by the business cycle and the political situation.

Direct foreign investment and contractual licensing have been recognized as important channels of international technology transfer from the beginning of industrial development. Korea, however, adopted the selective approach in approving the entry of foreign firms to its domestic market. Experiences under the Japanese colonial period bred apprehension toward foreign ownership of domestic firms.

Legal provisions for regulating foreign investment were installed by enactment of the Foreign Capital Investment Act. At that time, entry regulation and quality control of foreign investment were not of primary concern. After normalizing diplomatic relations with Japan, Korea introduced measures to regulate entry of foreign investment, which lasted until 1984. Joint ventures were preferred to wholly owned enterprises. Government authorities had the discretionary power to reject "undesired investment." Performance requirements such as local content requirement and mandatory export quotas were imposed.

Policies toward technology licensing were more lenient. Technology licensing required approval from the government authorities. But the criteria for approval were minimal. The approval process was not intended to discourage technology licensing per se but to help the domestic licensee in reducing royalty payments or shortening contract duration. The government could also impose performance requirements through this approval process.

Korea's policy at that time was characterized by a restrictive policy toward direct foreign investment (DFI) and a lenient policy toward technology licensing. This policy as a whole is often called an unpackaging strategy because foreign capital and technology are acquired through separate channels (Lee, 1989).

The restrictive policy toward DFI, fortunately, did not discourage the flow of capital and technology in significant proportions. Foreign investors were plentiful, while potential recipients of these investments were scarce during the 1960s and 1970s. Unpackaging also turned out to be a less costly means of financing because world interest rates at that time were low. Unpackaging also contributed to internalizing transferred technology.

Studies show that the technological absorption level is negatively correlated with the degree of foreign control (Yong, 1983).

Technology policy during the imitation stage can be summarized as follows. First, Korea committed a relatively large amount of the government budget to building the S&T infrastructure. Government-funded research institutes, which spent the bulk of the government's S&T investment, were an important institutional innovation. Second, industrial policy, the demand side of technology, played a more crucial role in building the technological capability of strategic industries. The S&T policy, however, was not closely coupled with industrial policy. Third, the policy toward DFI was selective. In other words, only the investments that met the various governmental restrictions were allowed to enter.

INNOVATION POLICY IN THE INTERNALIZATION STAGE

The Korean economy experienced a negative growth rate in 1979 for the first time since Korea had begun active industrialization. Many industries suffered from over-capacity. The newly installed government in 1980 realized that the extensive intervention during the heavy and chemical industry (HCI) drive had created too much distortion in the market mechanism. Stabilizing measures were introduced, which included financial market liberalization, trade liberalization, and devaluation of the won, the Korean currency. Industrial targeting was gradually phased out. Functional incentives were emphasized instead of sectoral incentives.

Tax incentives for R&D were extended. Tax credits for R&D were excluded in calculating the upper ceiling of the total tax exemption a firm could receive under corporate taxation. Custom duties on R&D equipment were either abated or exempted. Tax credits for corporate expenditures on human resources development were also introduced. Policy loans to support technological development were expanded even though policy loans in general were shrinking at that time. To assist commercialization of technology, venture capital companies were promoted. The government relegated administration of policy finance to public venture capital companies. Legal foundations for private venture capital companies were introduced. This policy had significant impact since the entry of financial institutions had been very tightly controlled. From 1987 to 1992, over fifty new venture capital companies were created.

These policies may have contributed to the fast increase in the private sector's R&D investment later. However, they also resulted in disguising non-R&D investment as R&D investments, as firms exploited the incentive scheme. A popular scheme was to shift testing and quality control functions to the R&D units. In Korea, R&D expenditures for tax purposes are defined as expenditures by R&D units.

The administration of the government's R&D was also changed. The most significant change in the scope and direction of governmental R&D investments was the establishment of the National R&D Programs (NRDP) in 1982, by MOST. The NRDP under MOST included six research categories. Among these, the Highly Advanced National (HAN) project was the most unique. The main objective of the HAN project was to develop industrial technologies of strategic importance. Private sector participation was encouraged in the project. Private companies provide some proportion of the research funds and they are able to claim ownership of the research results in return. It was also the first large-scale inter-ministerial R&D program.

The introduction of the national R&D programs brought two important changes. First, universities and private firms could participate in governmental R&D programs. They could compete against GRIs to acquire R&D projects. Direct subsidy to the GRIs, on the other hand, shrank. Second, the government was able to pursue technology targeting that was of strategic importance. In the past, the GRIs had had autonomy with little control by the government. Now, the government was able to take the initiative in planning and implementing R&D projects.

The introduction of the NRDP opened a whole new issue regarding the orientation of S&T policy. With the initiation of the HAN project, the government signaled that Korea's S&T policy was shifting to being mission-oriented.[2] The shift was favored by bureaucrats because it increased their discretionary power.

In principle, the change was an improvement, but it also created many undesirable consequences. Consistency in policy became

---

[2] Ergas (1986) classified S&T policy into two categories: diffusion-oriented and mission-oriented.

a major problem in planning government projects. It became common for newly appointed ministers or high-ranking government officials in charge of the NRDP to change concepts and alter priorities, which in turn created instability. It should be noted that positions in the government change very often. Second, introducing NRDP schemes raised administrative costs of R&D projects. Researchers became too much occupied in getting projects, leaving little time for research. To remedy this problem, monitoring and evaluation were emphasized. But this turned out to be very difficult. Last, the introduction of NRDP resulted in the increased allocation of funds to help *chaebols* who had greater lobbying power than small and medium-size companies.

One of the most expensive S&T projects during this stage was the construction of the Daeduk Science Town located near the city of Taejon. One intention of this project was to relocate the GRIs to Daeduk. Many GRIs were located either in metropolitan Seoul or the Changwon industrial complex. The primary purpose of the project was to encourage mutual cooperation among the GRIs. However, a more important reason for this project was to disperse people from the over-populated Seoul metropolitan area. The project officially started in 1974, but actual construction and relocation mostly took place in the 1980s.

The Daeduk Science Town project was a failure for the following reasons. It did not generate as much cooperation among the GRIs as the government had intended. Joint projects involving multiple GRIs were still very rare. Nor did it contribute to downsizing of the GRIs. The number of administrative and support personnel at the relocated GRIs did not decrease. GRIs found difficulty in attracting qualified scientists and engineers, who usually prefer to live in the Seoul metropolitan area. The relocation also made industry-GRI cooperation more difficult. Daeduk is not close to any of Korea's large industrial complexes. The government did try to incubate new technology-based firms around Daeduk, but it did not generate significant results.

The building of the Daeduk Science Town surely contributed to dispersing the population from Seoul. However, it is doubtful that this benefit sufficiently compensates for the costs. In recent years, construction of local innovation systems has become an important issue. The role of the GRIs is very limited because they are concentrated in one location.

Polices regarding DFI and technology licensing were revised considerably during this period. Since 1980, the Korean government has gradually liberalized its foreign investment policy. The Foreign Capital Inducement Act, for example, was revised in December 1984, to encourage direct foreign investment. One of the most important changes was the introduction of a negative loss of industrial activities, which, in effect, made it easier to lower the number of activities that were prohibited or temporarily restricted to foreign investors.

Another significant change concerns the new time-saving approval system. Projects that are not on the negative list, that have a foreign equity share of less than 50 percent, that involve foreign investment amounting to no more than one million U.S. dollars, and that do not require tax exemption will be immediately and automatically approved by the Ministry of Finance without having to go through a committee review or reference to the relevant ministries. Furthermore, restrictions concerning the proportion of externally owned equity have been greatly relaxed except in a few limited cases.

Although provisions for exemption and reduction of customs duties on imported capital goods for foreign investment projects are still retained, various tax advantages given exclusively to all foreign investments have been abolished to provide a fair environment for competition among foreign and domestic firms. Special tax concessions, however, may still be granted.

Policies regarding technological licensing also have been much less restrictive since the revisions of 1978 and 1979. Automatic approval is given for licensing arrangements that meet the following criteria: first, the life span of the project must be less then ten years; second, the running royalty payments must be less than 10 percent of the total sales value; and third, front-end payment must be less than one million U.S. dollars.

Further liberalization was introduced in 1984. The approval system has been replaced by a reporting system. Companies that want to import foreign technology only have to report their intention to the relevant ministry. If the ministry makes no objections and requests no additional information or changes within twenty days after the report is submitted, arrangements for technological import are automatically accepted.

The main theme of S&T policy in the internalization stage can be summarized as enhancement of the private firm's capacity for innovation. Tax and financial incentives for R&D expenditure and manpower development were reinforced to help the private firm's efforts to accumulate in-house R&D capabilities. Technology acquisition through DFI and licensing contracts were encouraged. The government significantly reduced the entry barrier to DFI. Regulation measures to control the quality of DFI and technology licensing were also reduced.

The role of the government as a supplier of technology was less emphasized. The ratio of government R&D investment to GNP and to the total governmental budget outlay had not increased during the 1980s, as shown in Table 9.1. To be precise, the ratio had declined in the first half of the 1980s and recovered in the latter half of the 1980s. Government R&D investment did not increase, primarily because of the small government policy of the 1980s. However, that also reflects the significant change in the attitude of policy makers toward government R&D. They began to pay more attention to efficacy of investment.

INNOVATION POLICY IN THE GENERATING STAGE

The primary goal of S&T policy in this stage was to build national innovation systems similar to those of the highly advanced countries. Balanced development of research capability among industry, academia, and public research institutions was an important policy goal. Furthermore, networking among the main actors of R&D was emphasized.

This intention was clearly reflected in the seventh Economic and Social Development Plan, which covers the period from 1992 to 1997. The most important policy objective is to enhance research capability in universities. Universities had been primarily educational institutions with few research activities even though they have the largest proportion of the nation's qualified scientists and engineers. With about 80 percent of all the nation's Ph.D. holders in science and engineering, universities only received 7 percent of government R&D funds.

To promote cooperative research, the government introduced the Cooperative R&D Promotion Law in 1993 to provide the legal basis for priority funding of cooperative research. The Ministry of Science and Technology introduced a new R&D program to support research in the universities. Science Research Centers and Engineering Research Centers were created in 1990 to help finance basic research in the universities. The Ministry of Education also introduced a new program to support research-oriented universities in 1995. Under this program, six research units in five universities receive five billion won for five years. These funds will be used to upgrade the infrastructure for R&D and to hire more researchers.

The policy for enhancing research capability in universities did not progress as intended for the following reasons. First, the ministries in charge of government R&D were more interested in funding GRIs associated with the respective ministries than in funding universities' R&D. Second, built-in rigidity in allocating the government budget hindered any significant increase in investment for the enhancement of research capabilities at universities. As a consequence, the allocative pattern of governmental R&D has not changed significantly. Government-supported research institutes still received 79 percent of the total governmental R&D expenditures in 1994. The proportion was 90 percent in 1990. Third, the universities were very slow in adapting to the new environment. Universities had neither the capability nor the will to adjust to the changing environment. Korean universities are notorious for inept management. The concepts of efficiency and competition are absent in many aspects of university administration. Professorship is a guaranteed lifetime job. Universities do not have to compete to attract students since there is a very excessive demand for a university education in Korea. Too many regulations on the management of universities by the government also contribute to the passive management style.

Another significant change that took place at this stage was the diversification of government R&D programs. Many ministries began hosting R&D programs of their own: the Ministry of Information, Ministry of Agriculture and Forestry, Ministry of Environment, Ministry of Health and Welfare, and the Ministry of Ocean and Fisheries. This activity shows that R&D policy has come to be considered by the ministries as a viable instrument in carrying out their policy objectives.

Among these, the R&D program hosted by the Ministry of Information is by far the largest and most important. The Telecommunication Technology Program, started in 1992, has brought about many successful results. R&D projects such as BISDN and CDMA are good examples. The Ministry of Information program has two advantages over other programs. It is possible to put a relatively large amount of money in a narrowly defined area because funding originates not from the government budget but from the proceeds of the Korea Telecommunications Corporation. Second, marketing the R&D results is supported by the procurement policy. The ministry and the public sector are the largest buyers of telecommunications equipment.

Coordination and cooperation among ministries have become important issues as the number of participating ministries has been rising. The Interministerial Council on Science and Technology chaired by the prime minister is responsible for this cooperation. However, the council has not been able to function adequately because the budget office, under the Ministry of Finance and Economy, does not respect the recommendations of the council. To cope with this problem, Korea established the Ministerial Meeting of Science and Technology in 1996, chaired by the deputy prime minister. The budget office is under the control of the deputy prime minister who is also the minister of Economy and Finance. It is still too early to tell whether this new arrangement will produce better results. The key issue is whether MOST will be effective. Legally, it is responsible for coordinating government R&D programs and hosting ministerial meetings. But MOST lost credibility as a neutral coordinator because it has its own R&D programs that compete for funds with other ministries.

A notable change at this stage regarding technology transfer was the globalization of Korean firms. *Chaebols* have been quite active in pursuing global networking and technology outsourcing. Ernst and O'Conner (1992) concluded that the major source of rapid development of the electronics industries in East Asian countries has been the active acquisition of technological sources as well as successful utilization of international networking. A study on the technological development of Samsung in the production of semiconductors also confirms the importance of international sourcing and networking (Choi, 1994).

Government policy responded to accommodate this new trend. *Segewha*, a Korean term for globalization, has become an important slogan since 1995. The policy package for Segewha includes a diverse spectrum that covers almost all aspects of government policy.

Segewha in science and technology includes the following: The Korean government's R&D is open to foreign nationals. This position was a significant departure, although the areas open to foreigner researchers are somewhat restricted. The role of government-supported technical information centers has been expanded. Many regional technical centers were established to help small and medium-size companies. Programs to invite foreign scientists and engineers have been expanded. Cooperation with former communist countries such as Russia and China has received special attention. The policy package of Segewha also includes the reform of laws regarding intellectual property rights protection and a strategic approach to standardization.

Protection of intellectual property rights (IPR) has received increased attention as the Korean technological strategy shifts from imitation to innovation. During the imitation stage, protection of these rights was not regarded as important because Korea generated few patents or other forms of intellectual property. The government tried instead to minimize IPR protection to help domestic firms use foreign intellectual property. Laws and regulations were formulated in such a way as to meet minimal international standards. Furthermore, enforcement of the law was less than strict.

However, over recent years, the environment has changed: First, foreign pressure to strengthen intellectual property protection increased. The pressure from the United States was especially acute. Second, Korean innovators increasingly demanded more protection. Significant reforms have been made since the late 1980s to strengthen intellectual property protection. The Material Patent Law category was introduced in 1986, the Computer Program Protection Law took effect in 1987, and the new Patent Act was promulgated in 1995.

CURRENT POLICY ISSUES AND FUTURE DIRECTION

Korea's innovation policy is now at a turning point. Many believe Korea needs to completely overhaul its innovation policy; its foundation was built in the early stages of industrial development and is now outdated. Despite numerous adjustments and reforms at various stages of technological development, Korea's innovation policy is believed to be grossly inadequate for fostering the innovation-led economic growth and industrial development of the future.

Responding to these criticisms, the Korean government legislated the Special Law on Science and Technology Innovation in 1997. The main objective of the law is to improve and modernize Korea's S&T capability to the level of advanced countries in five years. The law is valid for five years starting in July 1997 and ending in June 2002. In addition, the Five Year Plan for Science and Technology Innovation, mandated by the special law, went into effect in 1998. The key elements of the law are as follows.

First, the government will increase budget outlays for research and development. Over the past two decades, the ratio between governmental R&D investment and gross national product did not increase significantly, although the ratio between private R&D investment and gross national product increased very rapidly. The share of governmental R&D investment of the total national R&D investment dropped from 38 percent to 19 percent in 1995.

Specific targets for governmental R&D investment are not specified in the law. Instead, the targets are announced in the Five Year Plan for Science and Technology Innovation. The target for governmental R&D investment is projected at 5 percent of the total governmental budget outlay by the year 2002. This means a significant increase in governmental R&D, which was only 2.8 percent in 1997.

Second, the planning and coordination efforts of S&T policy will be revamped. Institutes specializing in monitoring and evaluating the government R&D programs of the various ministries will be designated to support planning. The law stipulates that all ministries should provide information on R&D programs if requested by the Ministry of Science and Technology.

Third, the government will increase investment in basic research. The law also endorses more assistance to vitalize universities and provides legal grounds to fund management of large-scale, common-use, research facilities for basic research.

In addition, the law addresses the following issues: enlargement of the S&T promotion fund, expansion of technology extension services for small- and medium-size enterprises, creation of the Fund for Science and Technology Culture, introduction of new financing options allowing the use of technology and intellectual property as collateral, and strengthening tax incentives for R&D and manpower development.

The law will bring more consistency to the process of formulating S&T policy and better coordination among the related ministries. Science and technology policy has been very unstable over the recent years. The main direction of the policy was greatly influenced by the cycle of the economy and the personal preferences of high-ranking government officials.

The main motive for the legislation, led by the Presidential Commission on Science and Technology, has been to encourage drastic increases in governmental R&D investment. A heated issue during legislation was whether to specify specific targets for this investment. These targets were opposed by the budget office of the Ministry of Finance and Economy. In compromise, a target will be included in the Five Year Plan for Science and Technology Innovation, without binding power.

The special law on S&T innovation and the five year plan on S&T innovation will become steppingstones for shaping innovation policy in the future. They specify several important policy goals and identify policy instruments for achieving those goals. These goals include an increase in public R&D investment, proliferation of university research and basic research, strengthening of small and median-size firm innovative capability, better coordination among ministries hosting R&D programs, and other important objectives.

Unfortunately, these efforts fail to properly address the issues related to reengineering Korea's national system of innovation. More specifically, they do not properly cite policy reforms for fostering diffusion and interactive learning among the major actors of innovation.

It is well known that networking is the primary weakness of Korea's national innovation system. About 80 percent of total government R&D funds are allocated for government-supported public R&D institutes, with the remaining 20 percent being distributed to industry and university R&D establishments. The majority of national R&D projects are carried out within GRIs. In comparison to other countries, Korean governmental R&D is too skewed toward the GRIs. In addition, private R&D activities are mainly oriented toward in-house R&D, accounting for 83 percent of the total private R&D funding. It should also be noted that large companies are proportionally more inclined to favor in-house R&D in comparison with smaller firms.

Labor movement among different R&D organizations is also hindered by rigid practices built into the private and public sectors. Most organizations, including private firms, universities, and research institutions, have adopted lifetime employment principles and seniority-based promotion schemes. Thus, the job market in mid-career is not at all competitive. The career path of an average university professor will likely consist of a single assignment. The same is true for researchers at GRIs or firms, although their mobility is slightly less constrained.

Encouraging networking and interactive learning among the major actors of innovation requires a much broader spectrum of policy instruments than public R&D investment. To improve university-industry relations, incentives for outsourcing R&D are needed: corporate tax laws need to be altered. To strengthen the relationship between industry and GRIs, the management style of the GRIs needs to be changed. To improve researcher mobility, the labor management style and the compensation scheme of firms, universities, and GRIs need to be changed. To facilitate information flow, intellectual property rights need be strictly protected.

Reengineering Korea's national innovation system is an immediate need. However, it involves not only S&T policy reforms but also economic and social system changes. Many elements are deeply rooted as cultural traits and are very resistant to change.

The special law and the five year plan will play catalytic roles in increasing public R&D investment and introducing more efficient management of governmental R&D programs. But these alone cannot raise Korea's innovation capability to the level of the advanced countries. Social institutions and economic systems need to be reformed in parallel to adjust to the new technological paradigm. These will prove to be challenging tasks for policy makers in the future.

CONCLUDING REFLECTIONS

The main theme of this chapter is the evolution of science and technology policy in the three stages of technological development in Korea. Dividing the evolution into stages is helpful to explain S&T policy changes in the course of Korea's industrial development. The following discusses lessons to be learned from the Korean experience.

First, industrial targeting played an important role in building the technological capability of Korean industries. Export promotion in the earlier stages of industrial development facilitated exposure to foreign source of technology. Interaction with foreign buyers or capital goods suppliers was conducive to technology transfer. The heavy and chemical industry drive in the 1970s created over-investment. But it paid off in the 1980s because these industries accumulated technological capability and obtained competitive advantage through learning by doing. Industrial assistance also contributed to the rise of high-tech industries in the generation stage. For example, Samsung Semiconductor Corporation was allowed to set up production facilities in Yongin near Seoul in exception to the zoning regulation. The personal computer industries received import protection throughout the 1980s. Telephone Exchange System (TDX) and Code Division Multiple Access (CDMA) technology received market support through governmental procurement policies.

Second, technology targeting did not generate good results. Technology targeting officially began by the introduction of national research and development projects. The HAN project is a notable example of technology targeting. But the success rate so far has been very small. In the HAN project, the development of MDRAM is the most frequently cited success. The success, however, is very much attributed to the strong commitment by *chaebols*. The contribution of the government R&D program is estimated to be very small.

Acute disagreements remain about the role of the government in the area of industrial technology. Frequently cited theoretical reasons for direct involvement of the government in industrial technology are as follows. First, R&D rivalry among countries is a worldwide trend. Virtually all governments of industrial countries are involved in industrial technology targeting. Second, markets may fail even in the area of industrial technology. However, these arguments ignore the fact that the government too can fail. The government did not have adequate information or the flexibility of the private firms. This problem is most critical in the area of emerging technology, usually the major objective of technology targeting.

Third, Korean policy toward DFI and technology licensing cannot be emulated by other countries. Korea applied a restrictive policy toward DFI. Entries of foreign firms were selectively allowed. Consequently, capital and technology were imported separately, the former by foreign loans and the latter by technology licensing. This policy did not hamper the transfer of technology, mainly because Korea had the managerial capacity to carry out this unpackaging. In addition, Korea was lucky in that there were not many competitors in the world getting foreign investment or technology. A low world interest rate in the 1970s also provided favorable condition for this strategy.

Fourth, government investment in S&T infrastructure in the imitation stage paid off in the long run. Korea's strong S&T policy in the imitation stage was an exceptional accomplishment considering the fact that R&D was not relevant at that time. Korea put high priority in building up the science and technological infrastructure during the imitation stage. The share of government R&D investment in the total budget increased rapidly until 1980. The government also established many GRIs. These institutes set standards for research and development activities in the private companies, and also contributed to graduate education in science and engineering.

Fifth, under-investment and under-commitment by the government since the 1980s have strained Korea's national innovation system. The ratio of governmental R&D expenditures to GNP has not increased in any significant proportion, even though the ratio of private investment to GNP showed a tenfold increase from 1980 to 1995. The proportion of governmental R&D investment in the total governmental budget outlay also has not increased. In addition, institutional reforms to move the national innovation system from imitation to innovation have not been successfully carried out. The most significant reform during the 1990s was the reform in the tax incentive scheme for private R&D activities. But these are minor changes in what was already established in the 1970s. Korea would have been in a better position if the government had committed more resources in building S&T infrastructure during the 1980s and the 1990s.

Sixth, the introduction of the Special Law on Science and

Technology Innovation in 1997 is an important turning point in shaping S&T policy. It is expected to contribute significantly to expanding the government's role in building scientific and technological infrastructures and upgrading the technological capabilities of the private sector. However, many unresolved policy issues remain related to the transition of social and economic environments to more innovation-friendly ones.

REFERENCES

Choi, Youngrak. 1996. *Dynamic Techno-management Capability: The Case of Samsung Semiconductor Sector in Korea.* Aldershot: Avebury.

Ergas, Henry. 1987. "Does Technology Policy Matter?" In Brooks, Harvey, and Bruce Guile, *Technology and Global Industry.* Washington, DC: National Academy Press, 191–245.

Ernst, D., and D. O'Connor. 1992. *Competing in the Electronics Industry: The Experience of Newly Industrializing Economies.* Paris: OECD.

Kim, Linsu, and Carl J. Dahlman. 1992. "Technology Policy and Industrialization: An Integrative Framework and Korea's Experience." *Research Policy* 21, 437–452.

Kim, Young Woo, Youngrak Choi, Dalwhan Lee, Young Hee Lee, Hyun Pyo Ha, and Dong Hoon Oh. 1997. *History of Korea's S&T Policy during the Last 50 Years.* (in Korean). Seoul: STEPI, Jung-Chak-Yeon-Gu, 97-01.

Lee, Jinjoo, Zong-Tae Bae, and Dong-Kyu Choi. 1988. "Technology Development Processes: A Model for a Developing Country with a Global Perspective." *R&D Management* 18, 235–250.

Lee, Won-Young. 1989. "Direct Foreign Investment and Technology Transfer." *Industrial Policies of Korea and the Republic of China.* Seoul: Korea Development Institute, Conference Series 89-01.

Westphal. L. E., Y. W. Lee, and G. Pursell. 1981. "Korean Industrial Competence: Where It Comes From." Washington DC: World Bank, World Bank Staff Working Paper No. 469.

Yong, Se-Jung. 1983. "A Study on the Difference of Technological Absorption Level in the Foreign Direct Investment Companies." *Kyoung-Young-Kwa-Hak-Hoe-Gee*, 8(1), 85–93.

Commentary

Morris Teubal

SUBJECT MATTER AND GENERAL ISSUES

The authors of Part III analyze the policies implemented by Asian newly industrializing economies (NIEs) for the promotion of science, technology, and innovation. A wide variety of specific policies are covered: targeted and selected support of key technologies and industries such as electronics and heavy and chemical industries; the promotion of "national champions" (Indonesia's IPTN); support of technological infrastructure and intermediary organizations such as Korea's government-funded research institutes (GRIs); the provision of telecommunications infrastructure (e.g., in Singapore and Malaysia); technology licensing; and the provision of incentives to innovation both to national firms and to multinational corporations. While the chapter by Dodgson frequently emphasizes the actual state of affairs in a wide range of Asian NIEs – both the more technologically advanced countries such as Taiwan and Korea and others such as Malaysia, Hong Kong, and Thailand – Lee's exclusive focus is a systematic analysis of the evolution of Korea's science and technology policies since 1962. Both authors consider the institutional underpinnings and the impact and effectiveness of policies. Throughout, attention is given when relevant to issues and problems associated with the transition of Asian NIEs from an early phase of technology imitation to a subsequent phase of technology generation. Despite some clear successes, both authors note that the task of policy restructuring and adaptation to the new technology *generation* needs of some of the most advanced Asian NIEs has been only partially accomplished.

291

DODGSON

Objectives and Conceptual Framework

Dodgson provides an excellent overview of science, technology and innovation policies in Asian NIEs. His chapter covers a wide variety of countries, policies, and quantitative indicators of strengths and weaknesses in science, technology, and innovation. The approach followed is based on a distinction between science policy (roughly associated with support of science and university graduates), technology policy (e.g., support of intermediary institutions involved in absorbing and diffusing technologies from abroad), and innovation policy (see Table 8.2). In his analyses the author makes a distinction between technology diffusion capability – which enable firms to efficiently accumulate, assimilate, and adapt appropriate extant technology – and technology creating capability, which is aimed at creating new technologies based on research and development (R&D) and directed at creating first-mover advantages in the market, intellectual property, and licensing income. Diffusion capabilities require a good technological infrastructure and government selection and choice of generic technologies, while technology creating capabilities depend on good scientific training, opportunities for linking with scientific expertise in universities and research labs, and effective intellectual property rights (IPR) protection. Thus the actual combination of science, technology and innovation policies and their dynamic adjustment depends on the level of economic and industrial development of the country. This points to a third major distinction proposed by the author – that between the more advanced Asian NIEs (e.g., Taiwan, Korea, Singapore, Hong Kong, and possibly Malaysia) and the less advanced Asian countries (China, Thailand, and Indonesia).

A final point in the author's approach is recognition that an effective feature of successful policies "is the continued need for learning and adaptation as the challenges confronting each country change over time." Insufficient learning probably underlies the difficulties in the shift in focus from policies promoting technological diffusion capabilities to those promoting technological creation capabilities. Success in the former – as exemplified, for example, by Taiwan and Korea – does not assure success in the latter. It is arguable whether Korea's policy institutions have already made the required adjustments to the new demands of technological leadership.

General Analyses of Strengths and Weaknesses in Science, Technology, and Innovation

The conceptual framework described is subsequently used by Dodgson in two main directions: first, to describe and analyze in *general terms* the strengths and weaknesses in science, technology, and innovation, and how these vary among Asian NIEs; second, to apply them to *in-depth analyses* of specific policies.

Concerning the first point, there are considerable differences in R&D\GDP ratios and on researchers per 10,000 population among countries, in the quality of their infrastructure, and on the high tech\electronics export orientation among the two groups of Asian NIEs. On the other hand, a measure of strength of some East Asian countries is the *technology* standing of high-tech industries (following a measure suggested by Porter) of Singapore, Taiwan, and Korea. It is as high as that of Western countries such as Italy, Sweden, and Canada.

A final general point concerns the weaknesses of Asian NIEs, even the more advanced ones, which emphasized electronics production. These include (1) the existence of many small producers of electronic components whose markets are notoriously cyclical and who compete on the basis of cost advantages rather than on the basis of technological innovation; (2) the difficulty in building international brand recognition, even in the case of ACER, the most technologically advanced computer company among the Asian NIEs; and (3) the management of technological creativity within large conglomerates. The following quote from the author transmits the gist of the argument. "Most of the strengths of the technologically leading East Asian NIE companies lies in production and project execution. These are important skills but relatively easy to replicate. They do not provide the basis for a longer-term, sustainable, competitive advantage at a global level. They are transferable by means of blueprints and explicit information. They exclude the tacit, creative, and intuitive skills necessary to be truly innovative."

In-Depth Analysis of Specific Policies

Three cases are considered:

- Encouragement of direct foreign investment (DFI)
- Formation of national champions
- Creation of intermediate, transfer-type organizations.

My comments will focus on the first two.

Comments on the Impact of DFI and on DFI Policies

Dodgson concludes that the huge flow of DFI to the NIEs of Asia had, according to existing evidence, little impact on the development of technological capabilities "even as the level of industrial development increases, when governments are very supportive and DFI relationships are long term." That is, the problem of weak spillovers from foreign investment is not only the case of Thailand and Indonesia but also of Malaysia and Singapore. Concerning Singapore, "even for Japanese multinationals there has been little transfer of R&D; product and process innovation remains a strategic task back in Japan"; and "foreign firms investing in R&D in Singapore do so primarily for commercial reasons ... rather than accessing local technological capabilities and manpower resources."

The link between the weak impact of DFI and DFI policies is not fully developed in the paper. The first issue to my mind is to ascertain whether the promotion of R&D and technological "spillovers" figured as an objective of such policies, since one may presume that in many contexts not many automatic spillovers would occur without explicit promotion. DFI policies may have been very successful in terms of other objectives (employment, exports, etc.). Where spillover promotion did not figure among the objectives of policy it is important to ask why this was the case. Moreover, it may be important to ask why follow-up programs favoring DFI did not incorporate the promotion of technological spillovers as a major objective, once the nature and importance of such effects had become fully recognized. This in turn would probably point to possible flaws in the process of government learning[1] and in the process of setting science, technology, and innovation priorities and programs for the economy.

---

[1] One possibility could be absence of a routine of systematically undertaking program impact valuations with the help of impartial experts.

Another possibility (assuming that the spillover objective was there in the actual DFI promotion schemes, as it seemed to be at least at some stage in the case of Singapore) could be flawed program design and\or problems in program implementation. A program explicitly aimed at promoting technological spillovers definitely cannot be circumscribed to the setting of incentives and to financial controls. Explicit targeting of investments with large potential spillovers may have to be undertaken. Moreover, an identification of the desirable types of spillovers and some quantitative indicators of their scope should be established, and this may have to be done for specific enterprises or enterprise types rather than "in general." All this implies that effective promotion of spillovers within a DFI promotion scheme requires *strong policy capabilities* within government, or at least fast learning by relevant agencies on how to achieve such a goal in subsequent or follow-up programs.

The Role of the National Champion IPTN (Indonesia): Some Comments

The author provides an interesting and rich discussion of the context in which the national champion aircraft company, IPTN, was created in 1976: its initial activities, capability development, and international partnering; its product line; and the special status accorded it by the Indonesian government (particularly by Dr. Habibie, minister of state for Research and Technology during part or all the period analyzed). An important point is that Indonesia does not seem to have had an explicit technology policy at all – except support of government-owned "techno-strategic industries." From manufacturing components for F-16 warplanes and Boeing, and assembling Superpuma and Bell Helicopters in the early years, the company (with the help of CASAS, a Spanish partner) gradually acquired a capability for jointly making incremental changes in aircraft. It then began designing and manufacturing turboprop and jet planes. Up to one year ago it had plans to develop a 130-seat jet plane, the N2130, at enormous cost and without clear market prospects. The accumulated investment in IPTN is estimated to lie between 3 and 6 billion dollars, which compares with the national R&D expenditure budget of approximately 400 million dollars in 1996–97.

There are two interrelated issues that are considered in the analysis of IPTN: one is why such a targeted promotion of the industry seems not to have been successful; two is why a science, technology, and industry policy focused disproportionately on the promotion of such a company is inadequate in the sense of covering the wide range of areas required for effective promotion of growth. The former is covered very well and convincingly by the author. Despite the potential advantages of having an aircraft industry in Indonesia, "critics of the IPTN experiment point to managerial problems . . . lack of scale economies, and the pervasive effect of Indonesia's weak educational system." Among the various possible reasons, the author puts emphasis on "lack of management capability, especially as technology projects become more complex, which reflects the weak educational and R&D base of the country."

The author comments also on the broader implications for Indonesia of such policies. He suggests that selection of a national champion in the aircraft industry implies, through weak spillovers to suppliers and customers, weak opportunities for "cross-organizational and systemic learning." This certainly is part of the overall story. A fuller analysis of the social cost of a national champion-based technology policy, however, would require additional information on non-IPTN policies and a broader conceptual framework. I will focus my comments on the latter, broader issue, under the assumption that the non-IPTN set of technology and innovation policies has been weak and partially empty.

First, let us note the increasing importance of diffusion and diffusion policies, which have focused so much attention on the antidiffusion bias of the technology and innovation policies of many advanced, industrialized countries (see Ergas, 1987; Soete and Arundel, 1993; and the Green Paper, European Commission, 1995). This is a result of worldwide trends such as globalization and the ongoing technological revolution – both enhance the possibility and desirability of acquiring technology and technological knowledge from sources outside the firm. It means that the economic cost of devoting relatively few resources explicitly to technology adsorption and diffusion may indeed be quite high. This is implied by the author's emphasis on the important role played by intermediary organizations in fostering technical change and growth in East Asian countries.

The antidiffusion bias can be set within a broader perspective of policies for successful transitions of national systems of innovation, a process involving first and foremost the restructuring of the business sector (Teubal, 1997b). In periods of rapid change and in contexts similar to those of many of the countries of Asia considered in the analysis, the successful promotion of enterprise restructuring requires a *combination of horizontal and targeted policies* (Indonesia's policies would seem to have been disproportionately biased toward "targeting"). Horizontal policies would aim at the widespread penetration and adoption of new activities such as technology transfer and diffusion, R&D, and so on, and support firms *directly* through incentives and other means (Teubal 1996, 1997a). Targeted technological and innovation policies, on the other hand, are aimed at specific technologies or other components of the structure supporting enterprise innovation such as technology centers, venture capital companies, or universities. They would further support innovation and the restructuring process of business enterprises by providing *indirect, system support.* Targeted policies would also be aimed – as mentioned by Dodgson – to generate new technological capabilities of potential value in the future. In most cases both types of policies – horizontal and targeted – are important.

The upshot is that Indonesia's implied technology and innovation strategy with an almost exclusive focus on supporting IPTN had two significant implications. The first is a strong presumption of absence of important programs directly supporting the technology adsorption, innovation, and restructuring of firms broadly throughout the business enterprise sector. (Horizontal programs could be very useful in this connection.) The second is the limited spillovers from the national champion aircraft company. Both would have implied weak overall stimulation of innovation and restructuring in the business enterprise sector.

LEE

The chapter by Lee presents a very interesting analysis of the evolution of science and technology (S&T) policy in Korea since 1962, during which period the country was transformed from a low-income, less-developed country to a mid-income semi-industrialized country striving to join the ranks of the world's advanced industrial nations. The analysis is organized around the three major phases of technological development of the country: the *imitation* phase (1962–80); the *internalization* phase (1980–90); and the *emergence* phase (after 1990). Imitation of foreign technology is the predominant means of acquiring domestic technological capabilities during the first phase. In contrast, during the third and most sophisticated emergence phase, "a nation is capable of introducing market-leading products and state-of-the-art core technology." The intermediate second phase is therefore one of maturation of indigenous technological capabilities – an "internalized" capacity "of developing new products or constructing new plants . . . or when domestically manufactured products become technically superior to products manufactured initially." While the capabilities of the internalization phase are more sophisticated than those originally acquired from foreign technology transfer, they are not yet situated in the world technological frontier and they did not enable Korean firms to create "first-mover advantages" in world markets.

The period around 1980 represents the transition from the imitation to the internalization phase: there is a drastic increase in the share of total R&D expenditures to GNP (from 0.58 percent to 1.56 percent) and in the share of R&D performed in the private sector over total R&D (from 36 percent to 75 percent). Leading firms such as Samsung, Hyundai, and Daewoo – starting in the second half of the seventies – begin introducing their own brand products into world markets, thus replacing the previously widely held original equipment manufacturing (OEM) strategy. Interestingly, after 1980, technology transfer expenditures and DFI increase very rapidly – a factor that emphasizes the continuing importance of non-R&D sources of acquisition of technology. During the nineties, Korean firms began to change their strategy "from a dependent strategy to an offensive or defensive strategy." The paradigmatic example probably is Samsung Semi-Conductor, which was able to introduce a 4 Megabit DRAM into the market in 1989 almost in parallel with its competitors in the United States and Japan.

In what follows, I will focus on Lee's analysis of science and technology policies during the imitation and internalization phases of Korea's industrial development of the last three and a half decades.

Science and Technology Policies during the Imitation Phase
(1962–1980)

Lee describes science and technology policies during this phase of Korea's economic development in terms of establishment of the basic institutions for science and technology in Korea. These include the Korea Institute for Science and Technology (KIST); the Ministry of Science and Technology (MOST) in the sixties; the Korean Advanced Institute of Science (KAIS); and the network of government–funded, specialized research institutes (GRIs) in the seventies.

The period was characterized by support of the technological infrastructure at GRIs *and* support of targeted industries (what the author terms "industrial policy"). Both promoted the adsorption and assimilation of foreign technology. GRIs also attracted many expatriate Korean scientists and engineers who otherwise would not have returned to Korea. Many of these later played key roles in the new heavy and chemical industries developed in the seventies. Industrial policy, while focused on building productive capacity, promoted technological capabilities as well. Two of the mechanisms mentioned by Lee are (1) interactions with foreign buyers and suppliers – for example, through technical assistance and (2) production experience – related to increases in capacity as the cases of the automobile and electronics industries show. Policies toward licensing and direct foreign investment also have had an impact since licensing and DFI are important mechanisms for transferring foreign technology. The restrictive nature of policy toward DFI did not, according to Lee, restrict the flow of technology to Korea, while the lenient policies toward the licensing of local companies were helpful in more than one way. (Lee asserts that the combination of DFI and licensing policies promoted the unpackaging of foreign technology, which also helped in "internalizing" the transferred technology.)

Supply Push and the Bias against Innovation in
Firms: Comments

Lee's analysis of the imitation phase focuses on the creation of the institutions that form the technological infrastructure of the country. The policies are characterized as being undertaken in the absence of a clear "demand" for the services of these institutes and for R&D, more generally speaking. Thus it would not be inconsistent with Lee's analysis to characterize them as being largely *supply push* policies. In his paper there is no discussion of policies *directly* supporting technological activities within business enterprises, such as support of R&D or technological adsorption and learning activities. Nor is there mention of programs supporting business enterprises interested in undertaking projects at (and possibly jointly with) the infrastructural organizations created during this phase.

Absence of demand for innovation on the part of business enterprises during this early phase may have reflected lack of implementation of broad programs that *directly* supported enterprises in this activity (Teubal, 1997a). Moreover, both the awareness of the need to restructure or to undertake innovation and a capacity to proceed and implement such a change in "firm strategy" may require a combination of programs – direct support of innovation and support of new technological infrastructures (Teubal, 1997b).

It would therefore seem that Korean technology and innovation policies of the sixties and seventies might have been unbalanced, having a clear bias against direct support of innovation within business enterprises. Although a certain bias could be justified due to the need to set up a network of basic technological infrastructure institutions, a greater emphasis on direct support to firms – through a learning, demand-creating process – might have generated more rapid and more effective technical change. In a world where the linear model of the innovation process doesn't hold, support of the technological infrastructure would not automatically lead to significant enterprise innovation. A measure of direct support of technology transfer and of modernization and innovation in enterprises would also be required.

Technology and Innovation Policy in the Internalization Phase

Radical changes in policy occurred within the internalization phase with a clear shift from policies supporting technological infrastructure (the GRIs) to (1) policies directly supporting innovation and technological capabilities of individual enterprises and (2) policies supporting financial aspects of the technology support system (Lipsey and Carlaw, 1997). The latter includes support of venture capital companies. Lee also mentions that there was a phasing out of industrial targeting in favor of targeting technologies and extension of "functional incentives."

Policies directly supporting innovation in firms during this period seem to have been of two major types:

- horizontal technology policy programs
- targeted policies supporting industrial technologies of strategic importance

Horizontal technology policy programs included tax incentives to R&D, tax credits for human capital development, reductions in custom duties on imported R&D equipment, and loans for technological development. Sometimes incentives seemed to be extended to enterprise "aggregates" (e.g., tax incentives to R&D); in other cases they might have been given to individual projects. Although horizontality seems to have been present, some of the incentives might not have been extended within strictly horizontal programs in the sense of being available in principle to all firms in all industrial sectors.

Targeted policies supporting strategic technologies were supported in the HAN project, the most unique of six research categories supported within the National R&D Programs (NRDP) implemented in 1982. Lee mentions that private sector participation was encouraged in the projects. Private companies provided some proportion of the research funds and they were able to claim ownership of the research results in return. This seems to imply that at least some of these projects were executed cooperatively. Because of this reason and because of the activity supported (industrial technologies of strategic importance), I would not be surprised that the Highly Advanced National (HAN) research project is a technology promotion program supporting technological infrastructure – that is, cooperatively developed technological capabilities aimed at several users/uses (Justman and Teubal, 1995).

If the above presumption is true, the restructuring of technology and innovation policy during the internalization phase has simultaneously promoted two, *new* components of the supporting infrastructure: new, non-GRI technological infrastructures and venture capital companies. In addition, a new set of programs and tools was introduced *directly* favoring innovation at individual enterprises. (The liberalization of DFI and the further liberalization of licensing of foreign technology must also have strengthened innovation and technical change within enterprises.) The outcome would be a more balanced technology and innovation policy portfolio in a period that also witnessed an enormous growth both of total R&D and of the share undertaken by the private sector. Overall, the changes seem to have been extremely favorable, although several new problems have arisen.

Other Changes in the Nature and Effectiveness of Policies

Lee mentions that the introduction of the National Research and Development Projects (NRDP) enabled universities and private firms for the first time to compete for projects with the GRIs. This, together with the other tax and loan incentives to enterprise R&D, could have been a momentous development in policy since it must have set the base for the growth of R&D executed by the business sector and for the eventual shift in dominance in R&D execution from GRIs to private firms.

A second point relates to the shift from targeting of industries to targeting of critical technologies of strategic importance – what Lee refers to as an increase in the mission orientation of technology and innovation policy. A critical issue is how the targeting process is being done, since the actual impact of this policy may be disappointing due to deficiencies in implementation. Lee mentions a number of problems, such as lack of coherence and continuity in policies, undue influence of *chaebols*, and weakness of coordination and coordination capabilities in the execution of NRDP (e.g., in the establishment of Daeduk Science Town.)

REFERENCES

Ergas, H. 1987. "The Importance of Technology Policy." In P. Dasgupta and P. Stoneman (eds.), *Economic Policy and Technological Performance*. Cambridge, UK: Cambridge University Press, 51–96.
European Commision. 1995. *Green Paper on Innovation*. Brussels-Luxembourg: EGKS-EG-EAG.
Justman, M., and M. Teubal. 1995. "Technological Infrastructure Policy:

Generating Capabilities and Building Markets." *Research Policy* 24(2), 259–282.

Lipsey, R., and K. Carlaw. 1997. "Technology Policies in Neoclassical and Structuralist-Evolutionary Models." Paper presented at the OECD meeting, "Best Practices in Technology and Innovation Policies," Vienna, May.

Soete, L., and A. Arundel. 1993. *An Integrated Approach to European Innovation and Technology Diffusion Policy*. Brussels: Commission of European Communities.

Teubal, M. 1996. "R&D and Technology Policy at NICs as Learning Processes." *World Development*, 24(3), 449–460.

Teubal, M. 1997a. "A Catalytic and Evolutionary Approach to Horizontal Technology Policy." *Research Policy*, 25, 1161–1188.

Teubal, M. 1997b. 2000. "Enterprise Restructruring and Embeddedness: A Policy and Systems Perspective." *Industrial and Corporate Change*. Forthcoming.

PART IV

The End of the Road?

CHAPTER 10

The Dynamics of Technological Learning during the Import-Substitution Period and Recent Structural Changes in the Industrial Sector of Argentina, Brazil, and Mexico

Jorge Katz

INTRODUCTION

Trade liberalization, the deregulation of economic activities, the privatization of public assets, and much more careful management of macroeconomic policy are bringing about far-reaching changes in Latin America. A more competitive atmosphere is gradually gaining ground in the various countries of the region as firms, markets and institutions[1] adapt themselves to a new macro and micro scenario.

Neoclassical economists have presented a rather derogatory view of what import-substitution industrialization (ISI) policies managed to attain in Latin America during the postwar period. In their opinion, active industrial policies benefited only corrupt government officials and rent-seeking entrepreneurs.

In our view, such a conclusion derives from the highly particular lens through which mainstream economists have chosen to look at the world economy. This lens fails to capture the complex learning dynamics that underlie the ISI process, particularly in the larger countries of the region (Brazil, Mexico, and Argentina). At

---

[1] The term *institutions* is used by economists with at least three different meanings. First, it is sometimes used to denote rules or norms that discipline economic behavior. In this sense, the patent law constitutes an "institution" that regulates property rights over new technological knowledge, thus inducing expenditure in research and development. Second, the word is sometimes used to refer to habits. It is in this context that David (1994) speaks of the custom of greeting a stranger with an open, unarmed hand, indicating a friendly approach. This habit has evolved through time into a universal greeting convention. Finally, we also speak about institutions when we refer to organizations, such as the university or the central bank. In relation to this topic the reader should see David (1994), Granovetter (1985), and Nelson and Sampat (1998).

307

the same pace with the expansion of industry, a sophisticated manufacturing culture developed in these countries as they successfully managed to absorb a vast array of technological skills, working habits, and norms of behavior. A massive volume of "social capital" – frequently overlooked in the neoclassical account of the facts – was built up, together with this expansion of industry, and such capital appears now to be of crucial importance for future capitalist development.

During the course of this process, many individual firms managed to accumulate a proprietary stock of technological skills and engineering capabilities that permitted them to increase their productivity and competitiveness significantly, gradually closing the gap with the international technological frontier.

The learning microdynamics involved in such a process will be examined in the second section of this chapter in relation to Brazil, Mexico, and Argentina. We will show that a rapid expansion of labor productivity and of manufacturing exports displaying an increasing degree of technological sophistication occurred in all three of these countries as a result of the development of domestic technological capabilities arising concurrently with the industrialization process.

Exports of capital goods, of engineering services, and of complete manufacturing plants sold on a turnkey basis to other less-developed countries (mostly inside Latin America), provide strong evidence of the accumulation of technological capabilities in parallel with the expansion of industry.

In spite of its richness, however, the process of manufacturing expansion and of a gradual accumulation of technological skills came to an abrupt halt during the 1980s in all three of the countries under consideration. Why was this so? External as well as internal forces must be examined to explain what happened.

The debt crisis, which unfolded in the early 1980s, was a major determinant of the macroeconomic turbulence and disequilibrium that threw all three of these countries into social and economic disarray. External factors – such as the dramatic increase in the international interest rate after the second oil shock of 1979, a sharp fall in terms of trade during the early 1980s, and the reduction in external financing after the Mexican moratorium of 1982 – played a major role in engineering the debt crisis to which Latin American countries simply had to adapt. In addition, poorly designed and implemented macroeconomic stabilization policies made things even worse. The industrial sector was particularly hard hit by a major contraction in aggregate demand as well as by the massive arrival of imported goods, which were substituted for local production. Domestic firms found it almost impossible to cope with the simultaneous impact of a major downturn in demand and the arrival of cheaper – and, sometimes, better – foreign substitutes.

We shall argue here that the contraction and structural transformation experienced by the industrial sectors of Argentina, Brazil, and Mexico during the 1980s resulted more from these macroeconomic circumstances – and from their impact upon aggregate demand, savings, investment, uncertainty, and entrepreneurial spirit – than from an obvious failure or misconception of the industrialization strategy. In a different macroeconomic and institutional setting, industrial policies of the same sort brought about a successful expansion of industry in some of the Southeast Asian economies – Korea and Taiwan among them. Certainly, the rate of investment, the efforts made by firms to build up their human capital and technological capabilities, their need to adapt their operations to more competitive local markets and, above all, the pressure they received from public authorities to expand export ratios all play a significant role in explaining why Southeast Asian firms have attained a better long-term growth performance than their Latin American counterparts.

In view of these conditions, we cannot really argue that, had domestic macroeconomic management been better than it actually was, many "inward-oriented" Argentine, Brazilian, or Mexican firms would have become world-class success stories comparable to Samsung, Lucky Goldstar, or Hyundai, but we do feel confident in arguing that many of the features of the learning microdynamics found in the case of Korean or Taiwanese firms can also be found in many Argentine, Brazilian, or Mexican companies. On the other hand, the institutional and macroeconomic environment was clearly different, as was the role of government, in monitoring the quid pro quo basis on which subsidies were extended in exchange for performance in the Southeast Asian economies. In our view, it is these latter differences that explain a great deal of the observed long-term differences in growth performance between Southeast Asian and Latin American companies.

In addition, we will argue that the contraction of the 1980s could have been much less dramatic – 7,000 firms closed in Chile during that decade and 15,000 did so in Argentina – had macroeconomic stabilization policies been better designed and implemented in these countries. The fact that macroeconomic mismanagement is not normally taken into consideration when judging the results of the import-substitution period in Latin America has induced many economists to believe that it was the industrialization strategy per se that was wrong. True enough, the industrial sector that developed during the import-substitution period had important weaknesses of its own, but many of the difficulties that Argentine, Brazilian, or Mexican firms experienced during the 1980s (and continue to experience today) derive from circumstances that were and are well outside their immediate sphere of responsibility. In our view, ill-advised macroeconomic policies and the fragility of the institutions underlying the relationship between government and industry explain a significant part of the long-term underperformance of manufacturing production in Latin America.

The opening up of the economy to external competition and the deregulation and privatization of economic activities were undertaken throughout the 1980s and in the early 1990s in the expectation that market forces would bring about a better long-term manufacturing growth performance than these countries had attained in the 1960s and 1970s under the guidance of the state. Have these expectations been fulfilled?

Under the new macroeconomic policy regime, the industrial sectors of Argentina, Brazil, and Mexico have been changing quite dramatically in structure and performance. Labor-intensive sectors – such as textiles, leather goods, and garments – and engineering-intensive industries – such as machine tools and metalworking industries (excluding the automobile industry) – have felt strongly the impact of the transition to the new incentive regime. On the other hand, natural resource-processing industries and assembly-type industries (*maquiladoras*) have expanded quite rapidly in terms of output, labor productivity, and exports. In the third section of this chapter we will look at some of the micro and meso features of this restructuring process, paying particular attention to the way that different industries have adapted to the new macro-economic signals and incentives.

Differences in adaptation capabilities have prevailed not only between industries but also between firms within given industrial sectors. Most firms have reacted defensively. They have introduced labor-saving changes in production organization while not committing themselves to major new investments or the strengthening of their local technological efforts. Firms following this strategy have basically been reducing their demand for labor while keeping their level of production roughly constant. A major employment absorption problem has emerged in all three of the countries under consideration as a result of this behavior. On the other hand, a much smaller number of companies have reacted proactively, erecting new plants much closer to international technological standards and simultaneously expanding both their demand for labor and their exports to world markets. As a result of defensive and proactive strategies, the structural heterogeneity within industries has increased and so has the observed rate of business concentration.

At the same time, the sources and nature of technical progress have undergone a significant change with the opening and deregulation of the economy. The relative cost of capital has gone down, inducing many forms of capital-labor substitution on the part of manufacturing enterprises. For the first time in many decades the industrial sector of these countries has not been creating new jobs at a pace compatible with the expansion of the labor force.

Are the Argentine, Brazilian, or Mexican industrial sectors attaining a better overall performance in terms of long-run productivity growth than the one obtained during the ISI period? To answer this question, the fourth section of this chapter looks at labor productivity growth and at the gap between labor productivity in these three countries and the United States over the period 1970–96. As far as aggregate manufacturing production is concerned, the available evidence shows that the three countries have managed to narrow the existing labor productivity gap with the United States, particularly during the 1990s. When we disaggregate at the three-digit level, however, a picture of great heterogeneity emerges. It is only in certain industries, and even then, in particular firms within such industries, that such a successful outcome can be identified. It is mainly large domestic conglomerates and local subsidiaries of multinational corporations in raw material-processing industries and in the automotive sector that have managed to perform well under the new incentive regime, thereby reducing the gap with international productivity standards. Many large local companies, as well as most domestic subsidiaries of multinational corporations (MNCs), have managed to incorporate modern, computer-based, flexible organizational arrangements into their manufacturing production processes. As a result, they have significantly expanded their productivity and exports in recent years. In contrast to their experience, however, a large number of domestically owned small firms have failed to adapt themselves to the new rules of the game. Hundreds of firms producing such items as garments, leather goods, furniture, and machine tools closed down in Argentina, Brazil, and Mexico during the 1990s and many more are struggling for survival in today's much more competitive environment. Imperfect access to factor markets, a lack of institutional support, and limited entrepreneurial capabilities to confront the needs of a more competitive environment appear to be the main reasons that small and medium-size enterprises (SMEs) have suffered so much in recent years. As a result, the benefits of the transition toward a more competitive and deregulated policy regime are still far from evenly distributed among different firms in the economy. New forms of government intervention in the face of such an outcome are probably needed if we are to attain a better pattern of distribution of the benefits of recent changes in the global incentive regime.

THE ISI PERIOD: ITS LEARNING DYNAMICS, PRODUCTIVITY GROWTH AND EXPORTS

Learning Dynamics

When Argentina, Brazil, and Mexico emerged from World War II, they were isolated from the world's major economic powers and strongly influenced by the Cold War atmosphere and by central planning ideas fashionable at that time. This explains why the policy agenda of the immediate postwar years was particularly biased in favor of public production in areas such as telecommunications, energy, and transportation as well as in the so-called heavy industries – steel, petroleum and petrochemicals, and coal.

Because of the disruption of world trade that resulted from the breakdown of multilateralism and of the gold standard, capital goods and consumer durables could not be imported for a rather long period of time, which began even before the war. Long waiting lists for household durables and production equipment were the norm throughout Latin America. Prodigious repair and maintenance efforts were undertaken by both firms and households just to keep old pieces of machinery and vehicles running, since there was no chance of replacing them. Thus, excess demand and a new policy that granted high tariff protection and cheap finance for new firms entering the market rapidly attracted new ventures. These were mainly small industrial firms interested in producing copied versions of old designs of household goods, machines, parts and components for motor vehicles, textiles, pharmaceutical products, leather goods, and so forth. Obviously, such products were exclusively for the domestic market.

The new industrial policies were initially thought to be transitory, in that most public officials expected a quick return to multilateralism and free trade after the war, as had happened in the 1920s. This time, however, there was no such return to a prewar free-market scenario. On the contrary, a new public policy agenda originating with Keynes, Beveridge, and other prominent politicians and social thinkers of the time enhanced the role of the state as an "engine" of growth and provider of "public goods," such as health, education, and social security. A completely new institutional atmosphere – featuring a strong degree of protectionism – developed at the worldwide level during those years.

In Argentina, Brazil, and Mexico, this international climate strongly supported the highly nationalistic local outlook that attributed a central role to public enterprises in the defense sector as well as in energy, telecommunications, and transport. Through different subsidies, it encouraged the creation of thousands of new small and medium-size family enterprises for the production of simple capital goods, consumer durables, fine chemicals, shoes, and apparel for the local market. Two major actors of the import-substituting industrialization (ISI) model – public firms and SMEs – expanded quite rapidly in the late 1940s and early 1950s in these three countries.

A third major actor, the MNC, entered the stage during the late 1950s. Multinationals had been in Latin America prior to that time, but within less than a decade, hundreds of large, multinational enterprises erected new, vertically integrated production facilities under the incentives of tariff protection, import permits, and subsidized credits. Some 200 local subsidiaries of MNCs came on stream in Argentina between 1958 and 1964, and a somewhat larger number did so in Brazil and Mexico. These firms were basically interested in catering to domestic consumers. They arrived in these countries with product designs and organization technologies clearly superior to the ones being employed by local companies. Thus, their entry brought about major changes in the prevailing industrial culture. The impact of their arrival was more strongly felt in industries such as motor vehicles and pharmaceuticals (fields in which MNCs were more actively involved). However, the externalities of foreign investment diffused rapidly throughout the production structure through the mobility of labor and the widespread utilization of new quality control practices, production organization principles, and other techniques.

Having so far identified the three major actors of the ISI model, let us now examine the micro-learning dynamics of the period.

Local industrial plants were normally very small, only about 10 percent the size of comparable production facilities in developed countries (DCs). The factory layout and the organization of production were considerably less sophisticated than those to be found in comparable firms in more industrialized nations. Firms normally started by copying versions of foreign products that were one or even two decades behind the world's technological frontier. Many of these firms used secondhand or self-produced machinery. The degree of vertical integration was much higher than it was in comparable plants in more mature countries. Their output mix was much broader and their degree of production specialization much lower than those of industrial firms in more developed countries. A very fragile and immature domestic production fabric forced many firms to supply themselves with parts and components that would normally have been purchased from specialized subcontractors in more developed countries.

Static as well as dynamic efficiency suffered severely due to these initial organizational features of production. The small size of the plants, a high degree of vertical integration, poor factory layout, and imperfect knowledge and understanding of organizational principles of production accounted for a great deal of down time and inefficiency, resulting in high unit production costs and low product quality. Even though domestic wages were just a fraction of what they were in DCs, the products being made could not readily have been exported to more sophisticated markets.

These circumstances convinced many companies to set up their own engineering departments whose main purpose was to produce incremental units of technical knowledge as a basis for upgrading product designs, production processes, and organizational technologies. Such activities gave rise to a highly idiosyncratic and "firm-specific" flow of incremental know-how. The learning process was geared to solving localized production problems and bottlenecks as well as to expanding utilization of locally produced parts and components and adapting to the local environment production processes originally brought from more mature industrial countries.

The learning dynamics underlying these circumstances and the subsequent impact of that learning process on efficiency and competitiveness need further examination. Many aspects of these dynamics have simply been ignored by neoclassical economics because of the extreme assumptions on which conventional theory has been constructed in relation to access and utilization of technical knowledge by firms in newly industrializing economies.

Consider a company that has an imperfect understanding of the technology with which it is operating, and knows it could do much better in terms of unit costs, down time, product quality, and lead time to the market. Therefore, it decides to expand its engineering and organizational knowledge as a basis for upgrading its current routines.

Neoclassical economics has never attributed much importance to an evolutionary strategy of this sort, even though this is the customary approach among engineers who normally think in terms of improving production routines (Box, 1960; Clark et al., 1971). Conventional theory regards technology as a given, perfectly understood, and completely specified factor of production that is freely available from a public shelf, a view that has led economists to adopt a rather naive way of looking at these matters. Such a view hinders the understanding that an adequate use of "generic" technical and organizational knowledge – available from blueprints, patents, and engineering books – normally requires a significant amount of firm-specific and localized knowledge-generation efforts on the part of the user. Search, trial and error, and frequent changes in routine are common at the shop floor level.

A number of studies carried out by the author throughout the 1970s and 1980s (Katz, 1976, 1986, 1987) show that engineering efforts of this kind were undertaken by many Latin American firms during the ISI years. Furthermore, as much as two-thirds of the observed rate of productivity growth of many of the firms examined in these studies could be explained by in-house, incremental knowledge-generation efforts of this sort.[2] In many of the studies we also found that the rate of productivity growth attained by the firm was significantly higher than the outward expansion of the world's technological frontier, thus permitting it to gradually catch up with international productivity standards.

Learning dynamics of this sort can be expected to lead to a stronger export commitment on the part of the firm. The incremental units of knowledge generated by the firm during its learning process clearly had market value as they could be fruitfully used by entrepreneurs in other developing countries with market and production-organization limitations similar to those the learning firm had set out to solve. It is not surprising to find that many Argentinean, Brazilian, and Mexican firms expanded into exports and into licensing activities during the late 1970s, thanks to their rapid rate of productivity growth and increasing competitive capabilities, particularly within Latin American markets where they enjoyed preferential status. A growing degree of technological sophistication allowed many metalworking firms producing vehicles, machine tools, agricultural equipment, and capital goods for the food industry to gradually enter third markets: Initially these firms exported just a small fraction of their output, but eventually their foreign sales moved into the 10 percent to 20 percent range. Moreover, not only did many firms expand their exports of increasingly sophisticated industrial products, but some of them also managed to export pure technology. This was in the form of licenses, engineering services, and complete manufacturing plants delivered on a turnkey basis to enterprises of other less-developed countries, mostly inside Latin America (*World Development*, 1984).

---

[2] Our research at the individual firm level shows that the lion's share of productivity growth came from process optimization efforts, production planning and organization activities, and other such disembodied forms of technical progress. Significant in-house engineering efforts were also devoted to the adaptation and upgrading of existing machines before replacing them with new equipment. See Katz (1987).

The preceding account of the learning dynamics underlying the industrialization process of Argentina, Brazil, and Mexico and its implications in terms of a steady expansion into foreign markets fits in well with the evidence we found in studying the long-term performance of many small firms as well as different local subsidiaries of large multinationals in all three of the countries under consideration.

We also found a similar process of moving along the learning curve when studying public sector enterprises and their subcontractors during the immediate postwar years. Firms such as PEMEX in Mexico, YPF in Argentina, and Petrobras in Brazil – or their equivalents in telecommunications services, energy generation, and so on – had their own R&D and engineering departments and trained thousands of subcontractors and suppliers, gradually teaching them to improve production routines and quality control practices. As a result of these activities, a massive process of knowledge generation and diffusion – that is, learning – was taking place in the public spheres of the economy, as well.

In spite of the successes, there were major shortcomings and fragilities characterizing the industrialization process. Although exports were gradually expanding, the whole effort remained basically inward oriented. Although firms carried out in-plant technology generation efforts and many had their own R&D facilities, most were limited to minor technological improvements and did little in terms of basic research. The interaction of firms with technical colleges, public research and development institutes, and universities was almost negligible. Our point, however, is that many of the microlearning dynamics that different authors have found in the industrialization process in Korea or Taiwan were also present in Argentine, Brazilian, or Mexican firms during the 1950s and 1960s. In our view, many aspects of the technological catching-up process experienced by many Southeast Asian firms are not at all different from those of Latin American firms. This being so, an explanation for the less-successful long-term performance of Latin American firms must lie elsewhere and not in the industrialization process per se.

Before turning to an examination of the 1980s and the major changes in industrial structure and performance that have derived from the debt crisis, let us briefly look into the impact of the learning dynamics described earlier.

Productivity Growth and Manufacturing Exports during the ISI Process

The 1960s and a large part of the 1970s were particularly successful years for the industrial sectors of Argentina, Brazil, and Mexico. Manufacturing output, labor productivity, and industrial exports expanded at a fast pace, as Figures 10.1 and 10.2 show for Argentina. Comparable evidence is available for Mexico (Casar, 1990) and for Brazil (Suzigan and Villela, 1997).

Manufacturing exports of an increasing degree of technological sophistication resulted from an evolutionary process of the sort we have discussed. Exports of capital goods and engineering services provide evidence of an increasing degree of technological maturity.

Figure 10.2 shows that total exports grew in Argentina from U.S. $1.5 billion to nearly U.S. $4.0 billion between 1964 and 1974. Close to 25 percent of the last figure corresponds to exports of manufacturing products of an industrial origin. Some 130 Argentine manufacturing and engineering firms managed to export U.S. $350 million worth of capital goods, engineering services, licenses, and turnkey production facilities during 1970–74. Cuba, Bolivia, and Paraguay were the main recipients of such exports within Latin America (Ablin and Katz, 1982).

Studies by Sercovich for Brazil and by Dahlman and Cortes for Mexico show that similar developments took place in these two countries. Lall presents a similar picture for India (*World Development*, 12 [5/6] 1984). Molero does so for Spain (Molero, 1992).

Some 145 Brazilian firms – 112 manufacturing enterprises and 33 consulting and engineering companies – exported U.S. $1.382 billion worth of turnkey plants, engineering and licensing services, and made-to-order capital goods during 1976–81. Such exports were primarily absorbed by Paraguay, Bolivia, and Uruguay, but also by Nigeria, Algeria, and Iraq (Sercovich, 1984).

Dahlman and Cortes have shown that between 1975 and 1979 Mexican engineering and consulting firms exported engineering services in connection with the construction of hydroelectrical plants, pipelines, sanitation facilities, oil exploration platforms, glass production plants, and similar services. Domestic capital goods were frequently part of this outward expansion, resulting in

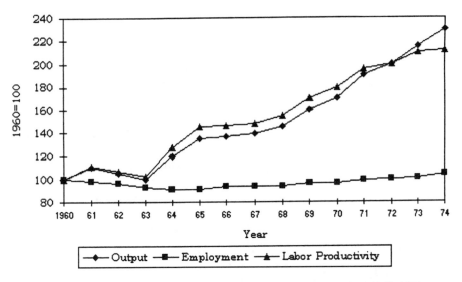

Figure 10.1. Output, employment, and productivity in Argentina: 1960–1974.

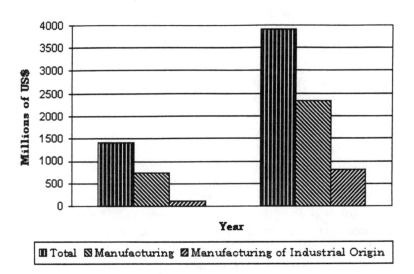

Figure 10.2. Exports for Argentina: 1964 and 1974.

exports of electrical machinery, precision instruments, trucks, and other goods (Dahlman and Cortes, 1984).

A study by Teitel and Sercovich for the Inter-American Development Bank in 1983 presents comparative evidence for these three countries in relation to the increasing technological sophistication of their industrial exports (Teitel & Sercovich, 1984). In the same issue of *World Development*, similar results are reported for India, Korea, Taiwan, and other developing countries.

Yet, in spite of these signs of success and increasing outward orientation, manufacturing industry ceased to grow in the mid-1970s in Argentina, and in the 1980s in Brazil and Mexico. It contracted severely thereafter. Why did this happen?

We shall argue here that the decaying industrial performance of Argentina, Brazil, and Mexico during the 1980s can be explained largely by the external disequilibrium that followed the debt crisis of the late 1970s, compounded by falling terms of trade, lack of foreign financing, and an abrupt rise in the international interest rate. Another important contributor was poorly designed macroeconomic stabilization policies that helped to propagate the external sector's difficulties and transmit them to the fiscal and monetary spheres of the economy, inducing a major episode of macroeconomic turbulence. In other words, rather than being the consequence of a misconceived industrialization strategy, the decaying industrial performance of the 1980s appears to be the consequence of macro-economic mismanagement in the aftermath of the debt crisis of the late 1970s.

The deteriorating external balance of the economy pushed Argentina, Brazil, and Mexico into conventional macro-economic stabilization efforts in the late 1970s and early 1980s. As foreign funds were no longer available for these countries, the public sector was forced to borrow domestically, crowding out other borrowers from local capital markets. This strongly reinforced the speculative climate already prevailing in the economy in the wake of major monetary devaluations and increases in the real domestic interest rates. The economy entered a period of economic turbulence and social disarray, which badly damaged domestic savings, manufacturing investment, and the entrepreneurial spirit, as we see in Table 10.1. A much higher degree of uncertainty and recurrent episodes of hyper-

Table 10.1. *Gross fixed investment as a percentage of gross domestic product: Argentina, Brazil, and Mexico*

	1970/79	80/81	82/84	85/88	1989
Argentina	21.7	20.9	13.8	12.0	9.9
Brazil	24.5	22.0	17.5	17.6	17.6
Mexico	23.0	25.7	18.6	16.8	17.9

inflation induced significant capital flight during the early 1980s in all three countries.[3]

It is somewhat unrealistic to blame the industrialization process for these macro events. Gross domestic product contracted sharply as a result of seriously mismanaged macro-economic stabilization efforts, as did domestic savings and manufacturing investment as a consequence of economic uncertainty. A dramatic contraction of aggregate demand and an increasingly speculative atmosphere explain why firms found it more attractive to engage in financial operations than in long-term engineering or technological activities. Many of them decided to reduce or completely cut off R&D and engineering efforts, limiting themselves to short-term speculative ventures. Their planning horizon fell dramatically as the degree of turbulence augmented and the economy moved into high inflation.

Successive macroeconomic stabilization programs failed in each of these countries, greatly increasing the degree of uncertainty and private agents' mistrust of government policies. Stabilization efforts invariably involved large currency devaluations, increases in the real domestic interest rate, and major reductions in real wages, actions that had a serious impact across the production and social structure. They acted as a strong selection mechanism, discriminating against industries catering to the domestic market and favoring export-oriented raw material processing industries. The latter rapidly gained ground within the manufacturing sector. In addition, economic stabilization programs also had a differential impact on SMEs, on the one hand, and on large domestic con-

---

[3] Close to U.S. $20 billion fled from Argentina between 1979 and 1982 while nearly U.S. $30 billion did so from Mexico between 1979 and 1983. In the case of Brazil, capital flight took place somewhat later, amounting to some U.S. $24 billion between 1984 and 1987.

glomerates or local subsidiaries of MNCs, on the other. They afforded greater freedom to the MNC subsidiaries, which had greater access to capital markets than small and medium-size family enterprises. We will now turn to an examination of these topics.

The Restructuring of Manufacturing Production toward Maquiladoras and Raw Material-Processing Industries

The pattern of specialization that occurred in Argentina, Brazil, and Mexico during the 1950s and 1960s was significantly biased toward the metalworking sector – that is, toward industries producing capital goods, automobiles, consumer durables, agricultural equipment, and similar products. Many of these sectors managed to accumulate a significant stock of technological capabilities during the import-substitution period, with some successfully expanding into export activities. However, a large number of these industries had great difficulty sustaining their rate of expansion in the 1980s. The contraction of domestic demand first, and later the massive arrival of foreign substitutes, explain why many metalworking firms as well as many producers of garments, shoes, and furniture could not continue growing in the 1980s as they had during the 1960s and 1970s.

In sharp contrast to the experience of these industries, raw-material processing sectors in Argentina and Brazil and *maquiladoras* in Mexico expanded quite rapidly throughout those years, in both output and exports. In the late 1970s and throughout the 1980s a large number of modern and highly capital-intensive plants emerged in Argentina and Brazil for the production of pulp and paper, petrochemicals, steel, aluminum, vegetable oil, fishmeal, minerals, and similar products. Also, a large number of *maquiladoras* came on stream in Mexico, producing garments and electronic products.

Consider the Argentine vegetable oil industry, which currently accounts for nearly one-fourth of the country's total exports. Table 10.2 shows the dramatic change this industry has undergone over the last two decades in structure and performance. Fewer firms, a

Table 10.2. *Number of plants, employment and productivity in the Argentine vegetable oil industry: 1973–74 and 1993–94*

Years	Plants in operation	Workforce	Total Tons	Tons per plant	Tons per worker
	(number)	(number)			
1973–74	67	6.895	1.740	26	252
1993–94	59	4.934	12.196	207	2.472

Source: Obtchatko, 1996, p. 17.

much higher output per plant and per man/year, and a lower overall level of employment in the sector as a whole characterize the industry today, compared to its structure and behavior two decades ago. A similar picture can be found in the Brazilian pulp and paper industry (Katz and Bercovich, 1993), in the Mexican and Brazilian petrochemical sector (Chudnovsky, 1997), and in many other resource-based processing industries of these three countries.

The share of natural resource-processing industries increased in Argentina from 36.5 percent to 46.7 percent between 1974 and 1990. In Brazil, this share went from 36.9 percent to 39.7 percent between the same years. On the other hand, the share of *maquila*-type production increased quite significantly in Mexico during the 1990s, presently representing close to 45 percent of total Mexican exports. Thus, the shift toward raw-material processing industries in the Southern Cone of Latin America and toward labor-intensive assembly industries in Mexico, appears as the central feature of the recent industrial restructuring process taking place in the region.

A clear exception to the generalized decay of the metalworking sector can be found in the automotive industry, which also expanded quite significantly in Argentina, Brazil, and Mexico in recent years. In none of these three cases was the expansion of the automotive industry between 1989 and 1995 attributable to trade liberalization efforts. On the contrary, its expansion was triggered by conventional, import-substitution-type industrial policies in Argentina and Brazil, and in Mexico, by changes in corporate strategy involving the use of that country as an export platform for the U.S. market. State-of-the-art automotive plants began to be set up in Mexico in 1986 by Ford, General Motors, and Nissan in order to export world-class automobiles to the U.S. market. The plants were moved to Mexico to take advantage of Mexican wages – which are just a fraction of U.S. hourly wages – and thus to compete with Japanese producers located within the United States. In Argentina and Brazil, the automotive sector began to expand in 1991. This expansion was triggered by an upswing in domestic demand, following the reduction in real interest rates in the wake of the economic stabilization efforts of the early 1990s, and by conventional industrial policies implemented by both governments in 1991 and 1992. Such policies, which involved concerted action by trade unions, enterprises, and government, permitted car prices to fall by nearly 30 percent after taxes were lowered significantly by the government and corporate profits were substantially reduced. In the former inward-oriented strategy, firms operated with a high degree of vertical integration, producing old models in old plants, mostly for the local market. This model has been discarded, and firms have now restructured their operations in an outward-oriented direction, producing world-class vehicles in state-of-the-art plants, with a much higher import content than before.

It is not just the structure of industry that has been affected by the new macro-economic policy regime now prevailing in Argentina, Brazil, and Mexico. The new more competitive and deregulated economic atmosphere has also acted as a powerful nonneutral selection mechanism, winnowing certain types of enterprises from others and inducing a strong process of economic concentration throughout the production structure. Domestically owned SMEs have found it difficult to adapt to the new rules of the game. Thousands of them closed during the 1980s, and many still face that possibility as a result of serious imperfections in factor markets – that is in their access to capital and technology. Let us briefly examine the nonneutral impact of recent trade liberalization and market deregulation efforts.

MNCs, Conglomerates, and Locally Owned SMEs

Four different groups of firms can normally be identified in the production fabric of any given society: (1) SMEs, many of them family owned; (2) large domestic firms belonging to vertically or horizontally integrated conglomerates; (3) local subsidiaries of transnational corporations; and (4) public enterprises. Significant differences frequently prevail among these four groups of firms in their access to factor markets, technological information, management practices, and other aspects.

Consider first the case of SMEs. These firms normally produce goods such as shoes, garments, furniture or machine tools. As a result of their imperfect access to capital and technology markets as well as their difficulties in adapting to a more competitive environment, thousands of SMEs were forced to abandon the market in Argentina, Brazil, and Mexico during the 1980s. Most of them were saddled with small and outmoded facilities that could not be easily upgraded to compete with foreign substitutes once tariff protection was brought down. The ones that have managed to survive have done so by significantly changing their business strategy, concentrating more on end-line assembly operations based on imported parts and components, and abandoning the local manufacture of intermediate parts. Many others have survived by becoming subcontractors of large domestic or international firms (Posthuma, 1995) or by specializing in small market niches. Only a small number of SMEs are presently doing well after having significantly upgraded their production and organizational technologies through importing capital goods, licensing new product designs, and retraining their human resources.

Then there is the group of large domestic conglomerates that are primarily involved in raw material-processing industries. Contrary to the experience of the smaller firms, local conglomerates expanded quite rapidly during the 1980s (Bisang, 1996). A considerable number of highly capital-intensive raw material-processing plants started up during these years, most of them owned by large local conglomerates. The majority of these plants were built to cater to the domestic market but later turned to exports when domestic demand contracted as a result of economic stabilization efforts (Stumpo and Bielchowsky, 1996). More recently, large domestic conglomerates have entered strategic alliances with foreign banks and world-class public utilities operators (such as Telefónica de España or Gas de France) taking part in the privatization of public utilities in telecommunications, energy production and distribution, and postal and transport services. Such alliances have strongly reinforced the market and political power of large local conglomerates.

A third group of firms is made up of the local subsidiaries of large MNCs, which are heavily involved in producing automobiles, petrochemicals, and pharmaceuticals. The flow of direct foreign manufacturing investment contracted in the 1980s in Argentina, Brazil, and Mexico as a result of market turbulence and uncertainty. This flow has regained its momentum since the beginning of the 1990s, but the more recent investments involve quite different and more globally oriented production and marketing strategies. The privatization of public assets and the purchase of debt paper on secondary markets (Fuch, 1990) opened up a vast array of new investment opportunities for transnational corporations in Latin America in the early 1990s. Since trade liberalization, many MNCs have reduced their output mix, abandoned domestic engineering activities, and concentrated on the assembly of imported parts and components and on marketing imported versions of products they used to produce locally.

A fourth and final group of enterprises is composed of large public firms, many of which were formerly involved in the production of steel, petroleum, telecommunication services, and energy. All three of the countries under examination have privatized many of these companies in recent years. In some cases the privatization has been carried out for fiscal reasons, when the government was in urgent need of funds. Often there was not an acceptable regulatory framework to ensure efficient microeconomic functioning and the protection of consumers after the assets were transferred to the private sector.

After having been a major economic actor during previous decades, public enterprises have now seen a decrease in their share of gross domestic product and have also relinquished their leading role in the generation of technology and in the training of human capital.

Trade liberalization and the deregulation and privatization of economic activities have acted as a powerful nonneutral selection mechanism or screening device whose effects extend across the entire universe of manufacturing firms. The share of SMEs and public enterprises in manufacturing output has significantly contracted while domestic conglomerates and local subsidiaries of MNCs have expanded quite rapidly. Imperfect access to capital and technology markets provide the most likely explanation of the decaying performance of SMEs over the last decade.

Another area in which trade liberalization and market deregulation efforts appear to be having a strong nonneutral effect is employment, discussed next.

The Factor-Saving Bias of Recent Structural Changes

We have previously argued that many firms have reacted defensively to the opening up and deregulation of economic activities. This reaction has frequently involved major changes in the organization of production that have allowed firms to produce the same physical volume of output with a much smaller labor force. In many sectors – typically in the textile and metalworking industries – overall employment has fallen dramatically, to one-half or even more of the total payroll of the 1970s. Argentina is clearly the most extreme case of the three under examination here. Taking the industrial sector as a whole, total employment in the Argentine manufacturing sector today is only about 60 percent of what it was two decades ago. Figure 10.3 shows evidence to this effect. Notice the sharp difference between the 1970s, when the expansion of output involved a rapid rate of labor absorption, and the 1990s, when these two variables are moving in opposite directions. The labor-saving bias of recent structural changes is related to a massive transition to more capital-intensive and computer-based production techniques. Thousands of firms currently appear to be engaged in transitions of this sort.

Although so far the problem of labor absorption is less serious in Mexico than in Argentina or Brazil, Mexican policy makers are now convinced that manufacturing can no longer be expected to act as a major source of job creation in the years to come. Also Mexican firms are thought to be very actively engaged in capital labor substitution efforts as well as in the transition toward flexible manufacturing production and organization principles.

Our previous discussion summarizes some of the recent structural changes resulting from the transition to a new macroeconomic incentive regime. Trade liberalization and the deregulation and privatization of economic activities were undertaken in the expectation that they would result in better long-term growth than was attained by the manufacturing sector during the import-

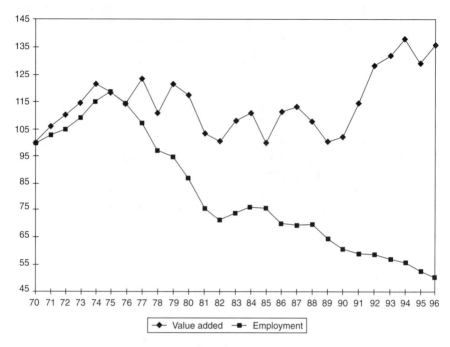

Figure 10.3. Manufacturing output and employment in Argentina, 1970–1994.

substitution period. Have these expectations been fulfilled? In the final pages of this chapter we examine this question.

LABOR PRODUCTIVITY DIFFERENCES IN MANUFACTURING PRODUCTION

This section examines the relative gap in labor productivity between manufacturing activities in Argentina, Brazil, and Mexico, on the one hand, and the U.S. industrial sector, on the other. Is this gap expanding or narrowing over time? Has Latin America's relative performance improved following trade liberalization and market deregulation efforts? Do we find significant interindustry differences in this respect? We have tried to shed light on these questions by examining time series for labor productivity growth for the three countries from 1970 to 1996 both at the aggregate level and for twenty-seven branches of industry at the three-digit level of the International Standard Industrial Classification (ISIC).

Catching Up or Lagging Behind?

Available information indicates that circa 1970 Argentine, Brazilian, and Mexican industries had attained only about one-quarter of the observed labor productivity of U.S. manufacturing industries. Between 1970 and 1996, labor productivity grew at 3.72 percent per annum for Argentine industries, at 2.87 percent in Mexico, and at 2.80 percent in Brazil, while it grew at 2.27 percent per annum in the U.S. industrial sector. For industry as a whole, therefore, the large labor productivity gap prevailing in 1970 seems to have been reduced somewhat during 1970–96. In spite of the above our figures indicate that in the 1990s labor productivity in Argentina, Brazil, and Mexico is still in the range of 50 percent to 60 percent of U.S. labor productivity.

Note that the pace at which these countries are catching up has accelerated in recent years – in 1990–96 in Argentina and Brazil, and in 1985–94 in Mexico. A partial explanation for this acceleration is that there was a large amount of unused production capacity in Argentina and Brazil in 1989–90 prior to their economic stabilization efforts. For these countries, the annual rate of labor productivity growth reached an all-time record of 8.4 percent and 9.7 percent in 1990–96. The figures are lower for Mexico, though productivity growth increased after trade liberalization and market deregulation actions in the mid-1980s.

In all three cases the evidence suggests that a more competitive and deregulated environment has forced many firms into defensive, labor-saving efforts that have indeed increased the rate of expansion of labor productivity. In other words, much of the observed reduction in the relative labor productivity gap between Argentine, Brazilian, and Mexican industries and their U.S. counterparts was attained during the more recent years in which industry has been forced to operate in a more competitive and deregulated climate. So far our discussion has been concerned with labor productivity growth at an aggregate level. What can we say about interindustry differences?

An Interindustry Perspective

If we examine labor productivity growth at the three-digit level of aggregation, we find a significant interindustry variance both within each of the three countries and in comparison with U.S. industries. Some industries have managed to do quite well domestically and have, simultaneously, been able to make a significant reduction in their labor productivity gap vis-à-vis their U.S. counterparts. Conversely, other industries have done badly domestically and have been systematically losing ground relative to the international productivity frontier (see Table 10.3).

On the basis of these figures, we can make the following comments:

• First, there are substantial interindustry differences in labor productivity growth in the three countries. Successful sectors have managed to grow two, or even three, times faster than manufacturing as a whole.

• Second, successful sectors in these three countries include iron and steel, motor vehicles, glass and glass products, and scientific instruments. In these sectors labor productivity growth attained above-average performance. They also made significant progress in closing their relative labor productivity gap with U.S. industries. Together with the pottery and the garment industries in Mexico; the chemical, electrical machinery, and furniture industries in Argentina; and the petroleum, nonferrous metals, and textile industries in Brazil, these are the industries exhibiting above-average labor productivity growth.

• Third, in sharp contrast with the previous group of industries, the leather goods and the shoe industries, together with plastics and the pottery sector in Argentina and Brazil, as well as the nonelectrical machinery and textiles industries in Mexico, show a below-average rate of labor productivity growth and have systematically been losing ground vis-à-vis the international productivity frontier.

What is the most likely explanation for these interindustry differences in labor productivity growth? Most of the successful sectors – iron and steel, glass, pottery, nonferrous metals, textiles – are ones in which large domestic conglomerates are actively

Table 10.3. *Labor productivity growth in Argentina, Brazil, Mexico and the United States: 28 branches of the manufacturing sector, 1970–1996*

ISIC		Argentina	Brazil	Mexico	USA
311	Food processing	2.351	0.967	3.300	2.046
313	Beverages	3.214	−0.655	1.655	3.931
314	Tobacco	3.098	−0.160	2.230	8.461
321	Textiles	3.093	2.849	0.784	1.541
322	Wearing apparel	−0.927	0.557	4.614	1.270
323	Leather	0.636	0.446	3.175	1.952
324	Footwear	−0.263	0.375	−0.210	1.540
331	Wood manufacturing	−0.907	−0.984	2.899	0.837
332	Furniture and fixtures	4.352	−0.499	1.591	0.971
341	Paper and paper products	1.162	2.253	3.785	2.422
342	Printing and publishing	2.170	−1.454	2.616	1.621
351	Industrial chemicals	4.496	1.741	2.226	2.672
352	Other chemical products	5.816	0.618	0.827	3.021
353	Petroleum refineries	2.858	5.075	−2.498	2.023
354	Production of petroleum and coal	3.491	3.541	5.096	1.780
355	Rubber products	1.409	2.457	3.008	1.147
356	Plastic Products	−0.741	0.025	3.176	1.198
361	Pottery	0.695	0.205	7.452	1.730
362	Glass and glass products	3.585	2.937	3.843	1.544
369	Other nonmetallic minerals	2.601	−0.337	3.521	0.996
371	Iron and steel	3.561	2.480	4.301	1.530
372	Non-ferrous basic metals	1.784	3.534	5.069	0.606
381	Manufacture of metal products	3.933	1.103	2.894	0.555
382	Machinery (except electrical)	2.359	0.672	−0.582	1.471
383	Manufacture of electrical machinery	5.794	2.837	4.508	2.475
384	Manufacture of transport equipment	3.263	1.026	4.595	1.942
385	Professional and scientific equipment	3.620	3.572	7.035	1.928
390	Other manufacturing industries	−0.792	−1.188	4.479	1.417

Source: Author's calculations on the basis of Programa de Ánalisis de la Dinámica Industrial. ECLAC.

involved and have been expanding quite rapidly in recent years on the basis of investments in state-of-the-art, highly capital-intensive new production facilities. Subsidiaries of MNCs – also large firms – figure prominently in the motor vehicle industry as well as in the production of scientific instruments, which are also above-average performers. On the other hand, none of the fast-growing industries involve SMEs. These tend to concentrate in industries such as shoes and leather goods, wearing apparel, plastics, and printing and publishing that, unsurprisingly, are among the industries that have performed well below average in labor productivity growth and have lost ground against manufacturing productivity in the United States.

In our view, size of firm is acting here as a proxy variable that picks up the influence of imperfect factor markets, incomplete information, and, more generally, an inadequate perception of what it takes to survive in the new macro-economic incentive regime. It therefore correlates well with the observed interindustry differences in labor productivity growth. Investment in new production facilities and plant upgrading engineering efforts have been considerably lower among SMEs than among large conglomerates or local subsidiaries of MNCs. From this perspective, recent economic stabilization programs have tended to operate as a massive selection mechanism that screens out firms and industries (Nelson, 1995) on the basis of their differential access to technological information and to capital markets. Unfortunately, there is still no suitable macro-to-micro theory of economic growth that can adequately explain why firms of different sizes have very different levels of access to capital and technology markets and therefore different chances of successfully adapting to drastic changes in the global environment. In our view, market failures, imperfect information, and an inadequate perception of the meaning of recent changes in the incentives regime have led to a deterioration in the performance of SMEs and the industries in which such firms figure most prominently.

The evidence presented so far permits us to arrive at an important conclusion: the rate of labor productivity growth has accelerated in recent years, in the wake of trade liberalization and market deregulation measures, and the gap with the international technological frontier is being reduced, even though in absolute terms it is still quite large. The catch-up process, however, has been far from evenly distributed throughout the production structure. Labor-intensive as well as engineering-intensive industries have tended to lag behind, and so have small and medium-size enterprises, many of them family owned and operated. The large domestic conglomerates and subsidiaries of multinational corporations, operating in raw-material processing industries and producing motor vehicles (and in "maquila"-type assembly operations in the electronics and garment industries in the case of Mexico) that have benefited most from the recent transition to a more open and deregulated macroeconomic environment.

REFERENCES

Ablin, E., and J. Katz. 1982. "Tecnología y Exportaciones Industriales." *Desarrollo Económico*, 65, April.

Benavente, J., G. Crespi, J. Katz, and G. Stumpo. 1997. "New Problems and Opportunities for Industrial Development in Latin America." *Oxford Development Studies*, 25(3).

Bisang, R. 1996. "Perfil Tecnoproductivo de los Grupos Económicos en la Industria Argentina." In J. Katz (ed.), *Estabilización Macroeconómica, Reforma Estructural y Comportamiento Industrial.* Buenos Aires: Alianza Editorial.

Box, G. E. "Some General Considerations in Process Optimization." *Journal of Basic Engineering*, 82, March.

Clark, M. E., E. M. DeForest, and L. R. Stechely. "Aches and Pains of Plant Startup." *Chemical and Engineering Progress*, 67, December.

David, Paul. 1994. "Why Are Institutions the 'Carriers of History'? Path Dependence and the Evolution of Conventions, Organizations and Institutions." *Structural Change and Economic Dynamics*, 5(2).

Clavijo, F., and J. I. Casar. 1994. "El Sector Manufacturero y la Cuenta Corriente. Evolución Reciente y Perspectivas." In "*La Industria Mexicana en el Mercado Mundial. Elementos para una Política Industrial.*" Mexico: Fondo de Cultura Económica.

Chudnovsky, D. 1977. *Auge y Ocaso del Capitalismo Asistido*. Buenos Aires: Alianza Editorial.

Dahlman, C., and Mariluz Cortes. 1984. "Mexico." *World Development*, 12(5/6), 601–624.

Fuch, M. 1990. Los Programas de Capitalización de la Deuda Externa Argentina. Buenos Aires: ECLAC. (Mimeographed)

Granovetter, Mark. 1985. "Economic Action and Social Structure: The Problem of Embeddedness." *American Journal of Sociology*, 91(3).

Katz, J. 1976. "*Importación de Tecnología, Aprendizaje e Industrialización Dependiente.*" Mexico: Fondo de Cultura Económica.

Katz, J. 1986. *Desarrollo y Crisis de la Capacidad Tecnológica Latinoamericana. El Caso de la Industria Metalmecánica.* Buenos Aires: ECLAC.

Katz, J. 1987. "Domestic Technology Generation in LDCs. A Review of Research Findings." In J. Katz (ed.), *Technology Generation in Latin American Manufacturing Industries*, London: Macmillan.

Molero, J. 1992. "La Internacionalización de la Industria Española y el Cambio Tecnológico." *Cuaderno de relaciones Laborales N°1.* Universidad Autónoma de Madrid.

Nelson, R. 1995. "Recent Evolutionary Theorizing about Economic Change." *Journal of Economic Literature*, 33, March, 48–90.

Nelson, R. 1996. "The Concept of 'Institutions' as an Attractor, Snare, and Challenge." September, (mimeographed).

Nelson, R., and B. Sampat. 1988. "Making Sense of Institutions as a Factor in Economic Growth." New York: Columbia University. February, (mimeographed).

Nelson, R. 1997. "How New is New Growth Theory? A Different Point of View." *Challenge*, September/October.

Obstchatko, E. 1996. Industrialización Basada en Recursos Naturales. Santiago, Chile: ECLAC. (Mimeographed)

Posthuma, A. C. 1995. "Restructuring and Changing Market Conditions in the Brazilian Autocomponents Industry." ECLAC/IDRC Research Program on Production Restructuring and International Competitiveness in Latin America, Santiago, Chile. (Mimeographed)

Sercovich, F. 1984. "Brazil." *World Development*, 12(5/6), 575–599.

Stumpo, G., and Bielschowsky, R. 1996. "Empresas Transnacionales Manufactureras en Cuatro Estilos de Reestructuración en América Latina: Argentina, Brazil, Chile y Mexico." In J. Katz (ed.), *Estabilización Macroeconómica, Reforma Estructural y Comportamiento Industrial*. Buenos Aires: Editorial Alianza.

Suzigan, W., and A. Villela. 1997. *Industrial Policy in Brazil*. Sao Paulo, Brazil: UNICAMP, Instituto de Economía.

Teitel, S., and F. Sercovich. 1984. "Latin America." *World Development*, 2(5/6).

CHAPTER 11

Korea's National Innovation
System in Transition

Linsu Kim

South Korea (hereinafter Korea) is undergoing a major transition in its economic and technological development. After three decades of phenomenal growth, Korea has recently plunged into an economic crisis with a serious increase in trade deficit and foreign debt. The balance of payment in trade declined from $7.6 billion in surplus in 1987 to $20.6 billion in deficit in 1996. Accordingly, foreign debt increased from $31.7 billion in 1990 to $156 billion in 1997, leading to a bailout by the International Monetary Fund (IMF) in 1997. Unlike past crises, which were evoked largely by external shocks, the current crisis stems mainly from structural weaknesses in the national innovation system (NIS). What has made Korea's NIS, which had functioned relatively effectively in the past, problematic in recent years? This chapter diagnoses the recent problems in the NIS and attempts to provide a prescription for its reengineering.

The national innovation system in a newly industrialized country should be examined in terms of two analytical frameworks: the global technology environment and the institutional environment (Kim, 1997). The global technology environment postulates that industries and firms in advanced countries evolve along a technology trajectory made up of three stages – fluid, transition, and specific (Utterback, 1994). Studies (Kim, 1980, 1993, 1997; Lee, Bae and Choi, 1988) indicate that Korean firms entered the specific stage of the technology trajectory in the 1960s and 1970s, acquiring and assimilating labor-intensive, mature foreign technologies. Imitation was the focus of industrial efforts during this period. Then Korea progressed in the reverse direction toward the transition stage in the 1980s, acquiring and assimilating increasingly knowledge-intensive foreign technologies. Some selected industries even entered the fluid stage in the 1990s to

335

compete neck-and-neck with leading advanced countries. Innovation became the watchword in those industries. That is, the NIS must evolve in response to the changes that occur in technology trajectory.

The institutional environment provides the various economic actors and other elements that influence technological learning in the NIS (Kim, 1997; Lundvall, 1992; Nelson, 1993). They include the government and its policies, the dynamics of the industrial structure, the availability and quality of the educational system, research and development (R&D) infrastructure and its role, the changing nature of sociocultural factors, buyers and suppliers in the international and domestic markets, national R&D investment, corporate management, and the interactions among them. An analysis of the NIS must examine the effectiveness of these actors and elements and their interactions along the evolution of the technology trajectory.

NATIONAL INNOVATION SYSTEM IN DISTRESS

Greek mythology offers an interesting paradox that still has meaning in today's industrial society. The fabled Icarus had powerful wings that enabled him to fly so high, so close to the sun that his artificially waxed wings melted and he plunged to his death (Miller, 1990). The paradox also applies to Korea; the greatest strengths in Korea's NIS in the past became its most serious liabilities in recent years (Kim, 1997). These are discussed in this chapter.

Government: From an Effective Orchestrator to a Rigid Regulator

The strong government in Korea was a major asset in Korea's early industrialization. The government nationalized all banks and monopolized all foreign savings to mobilize financial resources and allocate them for industrial projects according to national priority. Then, the government allocated business licenses to *chaebols*, the Korean version of the Japanese family enterprise *zaibatsu*, to use them as a powerhouse to reach ambitious goals. Such strong leadership pushed Korea's industrial locomotive far faster than in the earlier decades, but it has become a major liability in bringing market mechanisms to the center of the innovation-oriented economy in recent decades. Unlike in the 1960s and 1970s, the state is now in a less advantageous position than is the private sector to understand and respond quickly to the dynamics of the market and technological change.

The government's recent moves have failed to produce desirable results. The government introduced various measures – antitrust and fair trade legislation, trade liberalization, financial liberalization, and investment liberalization. The government also strongly advocates private sector-initiated market mechanisms, but what the government actually does in many aspects mirrors the role of the developmental state, hampering market mechanisms from working properly. While promoting liberalization publicly, government technocrats behind the scene have tried to maintain their orchestrating role even during the 1980s and 1990s. Their self-interest in preserving their bureaucratic power and the inertia to continue the existing practice has inhibited the dynamic growth of private initiatives. As a result, many government developmental programs were inappropriately applied or were many steps behind the private sector.

In addition, two factors also made it difficult for the government to be effective in its developmental role. First, corruption in politics in the late 1970s and thereafter resulted in political collusion between the state and the *chaebols*, leading to irrational allocation of resources and consequently making the government's orchestrating role a major source of inefficiency. For instance, political leaders demanded a kickback from *chaebols* in exchange for a lucrative business license or rescue from financial troubles. It appears that absolute power inevitably leads to absolute corruption. Second, the economic power of *chaebols* grew so strong and their impact on the economy grew so profound that even without kickbacks the government often was forced to rescue poorly managed *chaebols*, too many to name, from financial troubles to protect other firms both upstream and downstream.

The administrative apparatus established in the 1960s became too obsolete to respond to the changing needs of the 1990s. The Ministry of Science and Technology (MOST), the first of this kind in developing countries, was established in 1967 as a central agency to develop the nation's science and technology (S&T) policy and to coordinate S&T activities of various ministries.

MOST made major achievements in establishing a S&T infrastructure during the early decades and in launching national R&D programs. However, its policy coordination activities have largely been ignored by action-oriented ministries that shape industrial, trade, financial, and educational policies. The National Council for Science and Technology, established in 1973, and the President's Science and Technology Advisory Council, created in 1991, never functioned properly to bring about interministerial coordination. Consequently, MOST's long-term science and technology policies were not integrated into national development plans.

Industrial Structure: Chaebols, *both a Burden and an Asset*

One of the most significant ways the Korean government influenced technological learning in the private sector was by fostering its *chaebols*. The Korean government deliberately created and nurtured *chaebols* to use them as engines for rapid economic development. These *chaebols* were the backbone of industrialization in the labor-intensive industries during the early decades. They have generated the lion's share of production and exports from Korea.

The *chaebols* played a major role in expediting technological learning in industry in the past decades. They were in the most advantageous position in attracting the best-qualified entrants to the workforce. They also developed organizational and technical resources to identify, negotiate, and finance foreign technology transfer, taking advantage of their capacity to acquire both explicit and tacit knowledge at a high level from the international community. Their demonstrated economic viability and political collusion enabled them to obtain new business licenses and preferential financing from the government and to invest again to accelerate learning in new projects through organized in-house training and development efforts. The highly diversified but centrally controlled *chaebols* applied experiences gained in one field of business to another, resulting in a rapid diffusion of technological capability across subsidiaries. These firms could enter risky and expensive new businesses, as they were cushioned by their size and diversified portfolio. The *chaebols* also spearheaded the dramatically expanding and deepening industrial R&D activities in

Korea. And they have technical and financial resources to globalize their R&D activities and to monitor and tap the state-of-the-art technologies at the frontier.

Behind the successful story of rapid technological learning by *chaebols*, there are, however, serious tolls in the market. Collusion with powerful government forces resulted in the misallocation of resources and the economic inefficiency at the macro level. Unless financial institutions are completely liberalized, this problem will linger. The concentration of economic power in the hands of a small number of *chaebols* also resulted in monopolistic exploitations at the micro level, such as creating scarcities, price gouging, and predatory behavior in the protected domestic market. The concentration of economic power is, however, likely to be mitigated in the near future. The continuing import liberalization will limit opportunities for *chaebols* to make monopolistic exploitations in the domestic market.

The most serious consequence of the promotion of *chaebols* was the impediment to the healthy growth of small and medium-size enterprises (SMEs). Only during the early 1980s did the government belatedly begin promoting SMEs by establishing sanctuaries for them and helping them get loans by requiring banks to comply with its compulsory lending ratio program. Such programs made a significant dent in the industrial structure, increasing the SME share in manufacturing value-added from 23.7 percent in 1976 to 34.9 percent in 1988. Nevertheless, an imbalance between the large and small sectors still remains. As a result, *chaebols* assembling end-products have to rely heavily on Japan for technology-intensive parts and components, thus critically constraining innovation at both large and small firms. Without fluid support from capable small parts and component suppliers, Korean firms will remain behind in product and process innovation and highly vulnerable in price and quality competition relative to Japanese competitors (Porter, 1990).

Chaebols created many problems, but they are still more assets than liabilities in Korea's technological learning. They play a major role in strengthening Korea's technological capability and spearheading the globalization of Korean businesses because they have the necessary organizational, technical, and financial resources.

Export Market: From North America to the Third World

The government's export drive has decisively affected the NIS on the demand side of technology by creating a highly competitive market environment in which firms had to survive. This policy created business opportunities and concurrently imposed crises forcing firms to undergo a life or death struggle in the competitive international market. To survive the crises, Korean firms had to accelerate learning by importing and rapidly assimilating production and design technology from abroad. In addition, Korean exporters made lump-sum investment for capacity in excess of local market size to achieve economies of scale. This resulted in crises, forcing local firms to accelerate their technological learning to improve productivity and in turn improve international competitiveness so as to maximize capacity utilization. As a result, firms in export-oriented industries learned significantly more rapidly and grew faster than firms in import-substituting industries.

Korean firms relied heavily on foreign, especially American, original equipment manufacturer (OEM) buyers for the international marketing of their products through the 1980s. Such heavy dependence on OEM arrangements gave advantages to Korean firms in the early decades. OEM buyers provided invaluable technical help through interactive tutorial processes to ensure that Korean products met their technical specifications. Their strong marketing capability allowed Korean firms to direct their resources primarily to the development of production capabilities. Problems, however, have emerged over the more recent decades. Korean producers with huge production capacity lost their market share in the United States rapidly when Korea lost its comparative advantage as a production locale and OEM buyers shifted their buying source from Korea to second-tier countries like China. The OEM dependency also retarded the accumulation of international marketing capability and the globalization of Korean firms.

Facing eroding competitiveness in the U.S. market, Korean firms diverted their exports to Third World markets. Nevertheless, the export market is still an important source of stimulus for technological learning. Competitive stimulus, however, is not as strong from these markets as from the U.S. market.

Foreign Technology Suppliers: Increasingly Reluctant to Transfer

As Korean firms approach the technological frontier more closely, they face increasing difficulty in acquiring necessary technologies from foreign suppliers. When technology was simple and mature and patents had already expired, Korean firms with sufficient capability reverse-engineered foreign products, producing knock-offs or clones. This was particularly true for small firms. When the technology involved was complex yet mature enough (Specific Stage) for foreign firms to transfer willingly to Korean firms, and if the Koreans had insufficient capability to reverse-engineer the complex technology, they largely resorted to licensing. This strategy enabled Korean firms to acquire both tacit (e.g., through training and supervision) and explicit knowledge (e.g., blueprints, product specifications, production manuals), which they assimilated in the shortest possible time.

When the technology involved was in the growing stage of its life cycle (Transition Stage) with unexpired patents, foreign firms were usually protective and unwilling to transfer technology to Korean firms. Korean firms with insufficient capability could not progress further. But with the assistance of local, public R&D institutes or smaller foreign firms, some Korean firms built sufficient capability to crack technology through advanced reverse-engineering (in contrast to simple reverse-engineering of low technology). Foreign firms often filed suits against Korean firms for infringement on intellectual property rights. Legal settlements led eventually to formal licensing.

When emerging technologies were involved (Fluid Stage), foreign firms were naturally protective and unwilling to transfer technology to Korean firms. Technology was so near the frontier that it could not be learned from alternative sources such as local, public R&D institutes. Korean firms have to develop sufficient capability to crack the emerging technology on their own.

Education: From Driving Force to Bottleneck

Deprived of natural resources, Korea heavily invested in education, drastically expanding educational institutions during the early decades. Other catching-up countries also invested heavily in education. But what was unique in Korea was the well-balanced expansion at all levels of education prior to launching the industrialization drive. However, more rapid expansion of education relative to economic development created a short-term unemployment problem; high unemployment among the educated was regarded as a serious social issue in the 1960s. The formation of educated human resources, albeit relatively poor in quality, laid an important foundation for the subsequent reverse-engineering of mature foreign technologies.

The rapid expansion of formal education in Korea produced a vast quantity of human resources with enough initial tacit knowledge to make sense of explicit knowledge embodied in foreign technology, or to absorb the tacit knowledge transferred to them in the early decades. Formal education also imbued important social norms and beliefs, which were essential for organized activities in technological learning. Furthermore, such an abundance of human resources with entrepreneurship, competitive capability, and hardworking determination enabled Korea to prosper in the hostile environment of the past.

The government's myopic development strategy, however, retarded the development of educational institutions. Underinvestment in education over the recent decades has resulted in a major bottleneck in Korea's technological learning. The problem of underinvestment is most acute at the university level. Given deterioration in the quality of education and research at universities over the past three decades, all but a few universities have remained oriented primarily toward undergraduate teaching rather than toward research. Relatively low tacit knowledge caused by underinvestment in education compared to increasingly complex technological tasks facing Korean firms is expected to retard R&D productivity in Korean firms. The scarcity of research-intensive universities also preempted the emergence of technology-based small firms. The government is belatedly contemplating the idea of making a major educational reform. Its implementation and effects remain to be seen.

Although there are a few encouraging signs on the quality of university education, there is yet a long way to go. First, the number of scientific publications (by Koreans) quoted by the Science Citation Index (SCI) increased very slowly from 27 in 1973 to 171 in 1980, but very rapidly to 1,227 in 1988 and to 9,124 in 1997, climbing from thirty-seventh in the world in 1988 to seventeenth in 1997. The annual growth rate (28.97 percent) in

1973–94 was the highest in the world, but the ranking is still significantly low compared to Korea's rank of eleventh in terms of GNP. Second, a few universities, such as KAIST, POSTECH, and Seoul National University, have intensified their efforts to upgrade their quality of research to the international level, but it has not been enough to support Korean industries. Third, the government promoted the development of science research centers (SRCs) and engineering research centers (ERCs) to intensify university research, but it will take time and resources before they can become centers of excellence. In short, universities have a long way to go to become first-rate research institutions, and education is a major bottleneck in the national innovation system (OECD, 1995).

Science and Technology Infrastructure

Given the inadequacy of university research activities in Korea, the government developed a network of government-funded research institutes (GRIs) that would play a major role in advanced industrial R&D in Korea. The Korea Institute of Science and Technology (KIST) and its spin-off GRIs spent the lion's share of the nation's total R&D expenditure in the early decades. They, however, suffered from poor linkages with industry during the 1960s and 1970s. Most Korean scientists and engineers recruited by the government came from either academic institutions or R&D organizations that undertook advanced research. However, there was no demand from industry for the kind of expertise available at the GRIs.

Nevertheless, the GRIs played an important role in helping firms acquire foreign technology in the early years of industrialization. GRIs, for instance, helped firms strengthen their bargaining power in acquiring foreign technology. Joint research with GRIs provided opportunities for the firms to acquire prior knowledge about technology, enabling the firm to identify prospective technology suppliers. Once imported, experience gained in the joint research enabled the firm to assimilate and to adapt technology rapidly. GRIs have also been the backbone of the national R&D projects since 1982. These projects cover a wide range of mission-oriented, applied research projects ranging from aerospace to application-specific integrated circuits (ASICs), paving the way in advance for the private sector's entry later.

The GRIs, however, have had major problems in their role in the NIS in recent years. First, the role of GRIs has been weakened vis-à-vis the university laboratories and *chaebols'* corporate R&D centers over time. The GRIs face difficulties in retaining competent researchers, as they move to either academic institutions for prestige and freedom or to corporate R&D laboratories for the dynamic environment and better economic incentives. Second, GRIs have been far less dynamic than corporate R&D centers. The former is under the bureaucratic control of the government, which often stifles the vibrant life of creative individuals by imposing rigid regulations that create serious motivational problems. In contrast, corporate R&D centers are under market control, responding dynamically to market and technological changes for survival. Third, although the GRIs receive the major portion of public R&D funding (81 percent in Korea compared to 24 percent in the United States, 41 percent in Germany, and 47 percent in Japan), they lack diffusion mechanisms to transfer research results to industry. Fourth, a defiant labor union organized by researchers and support staff aggravates the GRIs' inflexibility in management.

Beside the GRIs, there are also technical supporting institutions for SMEs. The government has been so preoccupied with mission-oriented projects that it has failed to develop an effective infrastructure for small firm promotion. The technical extension networks developed in the 1980s have not been sufficiently adequate to help SMEs grow technologically. In the 1990s, Korea belatedly established a few industry-specific R&D institutes for SMEs, such as those in the areas of auto and electronics parts, but their effectiveness remains to be seen.

Seeing that *chaebols* developed an extensive network of their own R&D centers, the government institutes should have adjusted their roles to find their own niche in the areas of agriculture, public health, environment, nuclear energy, and other noncommerce-oriented projects.

In-House Research and Development Efforts: Rapid Growth but with Diminishing Returns

Facing the need to shift to higher value technology-intensive products to overcome high wages and increasing difficulty in acquiring technologies from foreign technology suppliers, Korean industries have drastically raised their R&D investment in recent decades. Though the Korean economy recorded one of the world's fastest growth rates, R&D expenditure rose even faster than GNP. Research and development increased its share of GNP from 0.32 percent to 2.81 in 1971–96, surpassing that of the United Kingdom. The share of industry increased from 29 percent in 1975 to 78 percent in 1996.

The growth rate is the highest in the world. For instance, the average annual growth rate of a nation's R&D investment per gross domestic product (GDP) in 1981–91 was the highest in Korea (24.2 percent) compared to 22.3 percent in Singapore, 15.8 percent in Taiwan, 11.4 percent in Spain, and 7.4 percent in Japan. The average annual growth rate of business R&D per GDP was also the highest in Korea (31.6 percent) compared to 23.8 percent in Singapore, 16.5 percent in Taiwan, 14.0 percent in Spain, and 8.8 percent in Japan (DIST, 1994).

The total R&D in Korea is, however, only about the same as that of a leading company in advanced countries. General Motors and Siemens spend as much as Korea does for R&D. As a result, Korea is squeezed between the advanced countries that have a far stronger technological base and the second-tier developing countries that are rapidly catching up. Korea is, indeed, at a turning point in its modern history.

Other important indicators of Korea's rapid growth in industrial R&D are patent registrations in Korea and abroad. Patent activities in Korea have jumped significantly in the last two decades compared to the first two, increasing a mere 48 percent in the first 14 years (1965–78), but almost tripling in the next 11 years (1979–89). Patent registrations almost tripled in the next four years (1989–93) and more than tripled again in the last four years (1993–97). This reflects the increasing importance of intellectual property rights in the face of declining reverse-engineering. The gap is still great when compared with advanced countries, but Korea is catching up rapidly. Furthermore, the share of Koreans in local patent registration also increased from 11.4 percent in 1980 to 39.7 percent in 1993, indicating the rising R&D activities.

Patent registration in the United States is often used as a surrogate measure of international competitiveness. The number of patent registrations in the United States by Koreans is far below that by Taiwanese, let alone that in the advanced countries. But Korea jumped from being thirty-fifth in the number of patents granted by the United States (among 36 countries listed in an NTIS report) with five patents in 1969 to eleventh with 538 patents in 1992. But despite the fact that Korea spends more than twice the amount for R&D that Taiwan does, the number of patents granted to Koreans by the United States in 1992 was only 538 compared to 1,252 granted to Taiwanese.

University-GRI-Industry Linkage: Weakly Coupled Triad

In the wake of the growing importance of innovation capability in sustaining Korea's international competitiveness over the recent decades, efforts have been made to strengthen university-industry and GRI-industry collaborations.

University-industry collaboration has significantly increased in recent decades. While university R&D expenditure increased drastically from W 2.0 billion ($4.1 million) in 1976 to W 1.02 trillion ($1.28 billion) in 1996, the share of industry-supported university R&D expenditure remained at 50 percent during the same period. Emulating the U.S. experience, the Korean government introduced in 1989 a scheme to establish Science Research Centers (SRCs), Engineering Research Centers (ERCs), and Regional Research Centers (RRCs). The numbers of joint research ventures undertaken by these centers with industry also increased from 24 cases involving 34 firms in 1990 to 415 cases involving 338 firms in 1994 (KITA, 1995). Another important phenomenon that emerged recently is technoparks established or under construction by several leading universities to accommodate joint university-industry laboratories on the campus. Although university-industry collaboration increased significantly, such collaboration is still at the formative stage and the mobility of professional personnel between university and industry is quite limited (Kim, and Yi, 1997).

GRI-industry collaboration also increased over time. The government used several national R&D projects to induce GRI-industry collaborative research. Among the major ones are the Industrial Generic Technology Development Project (IGTDP), Strategic National R&D Project (SNRP), and Highly Advanced National (HAN) R&D Project. These projects are designed for

GRIs to enter into a consortium with the private sector. Universities also have access to these projects. IGTDP concentrates mainly on current problems in existing technology areas with high economic externalities, while SNRP projects focus primarily on future problems in new (to Korea) technology areas with a high risk of failure or with high economic externalities. The most ambitious government vision is the Highly Advanced National (HAN) R&D Project, also known as the G-7 Project, which is aimed at lifting Korea's technological capability to the level of the G-7 countries by the year 2020. For this project, $5.7 billion will be invested jointly by the government, universities, and industries, about half of which will come from the private sector. As a result, while the GRIs' total R&D expenditure increased from W 8.9 billion ($28.2 million) in 1970 to W 1.89 trillion ($2.36 billion) in 1996, the share of industry-funded GRI research increased from 12.8 to 36.2 percent during the same period. Nevertheless, GRIs are squeezed between universities and industry. On one front, universities are expanding their R&D activities rapidly in the basic and applied research areas. On the other front, corporate R&D activities, particularly at large firms, have also expanded rapidly in the development and engineering areas. Consequently, the GRIs' position has been significantly weakened relative to universities and corporate R&D centers. A redefinition of the GRI role is in order.

Financial Institutions: Another Major Bottleneck

The Korean government monopolized the financial sector during the 1960s and 1970s to transform Korea's subsistent agrarian economy into an industrialized economy at the fastest possible speed, in spite of the odds against success. The government nationalized all commercial banks in the 1960s so that it could allocate financial resources. It also borrowed heavily from abroad to channel low-cost foreign finance into industrial projects that were high in national priority, performing its resource allocation function relatively efficiently despite growing corruption.

In the face of increasing complexity in the market and technology, the government denationalized commercial banks and reduced the regulation of nonbanking financial intermediaries during the 1980s, losing much of its power to allocate financial resources. Nevertheless, protecting the local market from foreign financial institutions and political and bureaucratic corruption resulted in gross inefficiencies; Korean banks are still loaded with nonperforming loans – 8.8 percent of total credits in 1992. The government established the country's first venture capital company in 1981, leading to the formation of the venture capital industry in the 1980s. But the venture capital industry is still in its formative stage. In short, the inefficiency of the financial sector is another major bottleneck in Korea's national innovation system.

Preferential finance and tax concessions have been effective in promoting R&D in Korean firms. In Korea, where the private sector takes major initiatives in R&D, accounting for over 78 percent of the nation's total R&D investment in 1996, these financial and tax incentives have enabled the private sector to reduce the cost of R&D activities and human resource development. Nevertheless, preferential finance and tax concessions accounted for only 6.4 percent and 8.73 percent, respectively, of total private R&D investment in 1992 (Lee et al., 1996; Song et al., 1995).

Corporate Management: From Efficiency to Ineffectiveness

In the environment where the state is the major source of constraints and contingencies, corporate managers developed a "conservation-of-power" rationality (Klein, 1977). They sought collusion with powerful politicians and technocrats to be able to enter lucrative businesses and to maximize the predictability of the environment. Few businesses could have grown into a *chaebol* without such political patronage in Korea. The most critical capability was the top manager's political skills at developing and sustaining collusive relationships with the government. It was his entrepreneurship, also, that selected lucrative businesses.

With so much of the firm's success resting on the top manager's personal skills, Korean industry naturally adopted a top-down management style. This management imperative, combined with military rule for three decades, fostered a management style that resembled a military bureaucracy: hierarchical and centrally controlled but relatively less formalized. The notion of Confucian traditions and familism fit comfortably with this hierarchical style of family-centered conglomerates. Unlike highly formalized bureaucratic organizations, Korean firms were adaptable to changes once a decision was made at the top by the "commanding general."

These organizations were quite compatible with and efficient in the imitative reverse-engineering and production-oriented tasks of the 1960s and 1970s.

The developments in the business environment pose new competitive challenges for Korean management. The slowdown of the world economy, protectionist policies in North America and Europe, the rapid growth of real wages in Korea, rising challenges from second-tier catching-up countries, and import liberalization in the home market – all these now require a major reorientation in the organization and management of Korean firms. Furthermore, economic democratization and the consequent disorderly labor movement have increased the workers' dissatisfaction with a military-like, centrally controlled hierarchy.

The efficiency-oriented, militaristic organization style has become a major hindrance to raising the innovation capability of Korean firms. The bureaucratic system that used to maintain order in the large firms of the early decades is now too slow to respond to the dynamically changing technology environment of recent decades. In addition, the development of human resource management techniques has been seriously retarded in Korean firms because they are organized around a task-oriented militaristic bureaucracy.

Many *chaebols* have recognized the problems facing their organizational and managerial style. They have taken various measures to make major changes. However, they found that while the organizational structure and management system could be changed overnight, changing the organizational culture (i.e., the behavior of managers and organizational members to be compatible with the new system) was more difficult. Most Korean managers and workers have never experienced any other type of organization. Some argue that it takes six to fifteen years to change an organizational culture ("The Corporate Culture," 1983), and it may require 5 to 10 percent of the firm's annual budget for that kind of cultural change (Deal and Kennedy, 1982).

Crisis Construction: Can It Be a Tool in the Future?

The government has often created crises to push the *chaebols* to achieve overly ambitious goals. The most dramatic case was the promotion of the heavy and chemical industries (HCIs) at a far greater intensity, much earlier, and in a far shorter time span than originally envisioned as a way to create the defense industry in the wake of the Nixon doctrine in the mid-1970s. The hasty creation of HCIs on a gigantic scale without adequate preparation in terms of technological capability resulted in misallocation of resources, rapid inflation, wage increases, and further concentration of economic power in a few *chaebols*. The most significant effect of the HCI drive, however, was a major crisis in technological learning. The crisis prompted Korean firms to make a quantum jump in technological capability in order to make it creative rather than destructive.

In the militaristic Korean firms, the top management also used crises as a major means of opportunistic learning. Hyundai Motors company, for instance, constructed a series of crises to expedite technological learning by setting overly ambitious goals in acquiring and assimilating foreign technologies (Kim, 1998). A similar learning process is also evident, albeit to a different degree, in other companies and other industries such as electronics, shipbuilding, steel, and machinery.

But as Korea approaches the technological frontier, it will be increasingly difficult to use crisis construction as a means to expedite learning. The pioneering firms must work with a strategic ambiguity that provides only broad direction (Nonaka, 1988).

Deteriorating Sociocultural Factors

Another important element that influenced rapid technological learning in industry in the early decades was the sociocultural environment, which sets the stage for individual behavior and social interaction in Korea. Many Western scholars have attributed the rapid industrial progress of Korea and other East Asian Tigers to Confucianism (Kahn, 1979; Hofstede and Bond, 1988). This argument contradicts previous arguments that the Confucian heritage retarded modernization in East Asia (Levenson, 1958). It also fails to explain rapid industrialization in non-Confucian newly industrializing economies. Confucian culture still permeates Korean society today, but it has undergone significant modification by Christian values and Western civilization, leading to the formation of new Confucian ethics (Tu, 1984). New Confucian ethics – an amalgam of the family or collectively-oriented values of the East with the pragmatic, economic-goal oriented values of the West – is now most visible in Korea. It emphasizes education, clan, harmonious interpersonal relations, action orientation, and discipline. These cultural characteristics must have played a crucial role in inculcating a set of values in the Korean mind.

But neither traditional Confucianism nor new Confucianism alone explains the dynamic energy of Korean society. Many situational factors were also at work (Vogel, 1991). First, the perseverance of the Korean people during the days of turmoil and hardship resulted in a hardworking trait among Korean workers. Frequent foreign invasions, the *han* psyche (the characteristic that drives Koreans to work hard, like codependents in Western society), disciplined work habits formed during the "exam hell" school days, densely populated and severely cold physical conditions, and the memory of deprivation contributed to the formation of the national character. Second, compulsory military service molded young Korean men into disciplined organizational members and gave them invaluable opportunities to learn to manage not only small and large organizations but also complex logistical support systems. Third, the refugee exodus during the Korean War and urbanization afterward resulted in high geographical mobility within Korean society. Rapid expansion of the industrial sectors caused high job mobility, making Korean society far more flexible than before. Furthermore, networking among clan members from school, family, and home town made the society highly interactive, more effectively diffusing imported technology throughout the economy. Fourth, homogeneity (monolanguage and monoculture) and an independent spirit made Koreans highly nationalistic; nationalism grew even stronger during the Japanese colonial oppression. These factors together have played a decisive role in inculcating a strong work ethic in Koreans.

The hardworking spirit and discipline have, however, deteriorated much in the past decade. A drastic shift toward political democratization in the late 1980s triggered the explosion of labor unrest, resulting in work stoppages, missed export delivery deadlines, lowered product quality, and wage hikes exceeding productivity increases. Democratization and the labor movement have also resulted in a significant change in the social and organizational climate; there have been shifts in the power structure and workers have become far less submissive than before. A study shows that the proportion of workers who agreed to comply with seniors' opinions dropped from 77.3 percent in 1979 to 40.6 percent in 1991 and those who agreed to obey superiors' directions dropped from 90.6 percent down to 65.3 percent during the same period. Attitudes have also changed. Those who agreed to view the company as the second family slid from 94.3 percent in 1979 to 59.2 percent in 1991 (Shin and Kim, 1994).

In addition, the new generation brought up in affluence is less willing to work hard compared to the older generation. In an international comparative study of forty-seven advanced and newly industrialized economies, Korea's work attitude, in terms of labor dispute days and absentee ratio, fell from third in 1985 to twenty-fourth in 1994 (BERI, 1992).

Korea also has a negative cultural trait. Korea has a relatively low level of trust compared to such countries as Japan and Germany. Trust is the expectation that arises within a society of regular, honest, and cooperative behavior. A society that does not have trust requires a system of formal rules and regulations, which have to be enforced, many times by coercive means, to bring about interpersonal or interorganizational cooperation. Even those rules are often not properly enforced due to dishonesty and corruption among the enforcing agents. This entails high transaction costs. Such a society finds it difficult to innovate organizationally, since the low degree of trust will inhibit a wide variety of spontaneous social relationships from emerging (Fukuyama, 1995). Widespread low trust in Korean society imposes a kind of tax on all forms of economic activity. For example, familism in big businesses leads to inefficient management. Corruption in government and politics and collusion between the state and big businesses result in misallocation of resources. Predatory behavior in interfirm relations drastically increases transaction costs. And poorly coupled links between R&D actors lead to low productivity in R&D activities. These are all caused by the lack of social capital, which stems from a low level of trust in the society.

In short, Korea's national innovation system (NIS) was relatively effective in the 1960s and 1970s when technology was mature and its acquisition and assimilation were relatively easy. But formal and informal institutions have not been adequately reformed in response to the rapidly changing market and technology environment in the recent decades, and this is leading to structural weaknesses in its NIS.

TOWARD REENGINEERING THE NATIONAL INNOVATION SYSTEM

The remarkable past success has inculcated a "can do" spirit in the minds of the Korean people. Such a "can do" spirit bears fruit when growth depends primarily on hard work, as it did in the labor-intensive era. But when growth relies on collective knowledge and creativity, the "can do" spirit cannot replace an efficient infrastructure, skilled human resources, excellent science, entrepreneurial managers, creative engineers, and a socioculture that facilitates creativity and social interactions across individuals and organizations (OECD, 1995), all of which constitute an NIS in the knowledge-based economy. What then should Korea do to reengineer its NIS in order to sustain its economic development in the future?

First, Korea needs to shift its paradigm from a state-centered to an industry-centered NIS. The former has distorted the role of the state, creating major bottlenecks in industrial innovation. To put industry at the center stage of the NIS, downsizing, decentralization, and democratization in the government and political system are essential. Downsizing will make a smaller government, leaving more room for industry. Decentralization will empower regional governments to take initiatives in strengthening support for SMEs in their regional innovation system. Democratization will foster the mobilization of creativity and initiative in the society as a whole. Such changes are imperative but slow to come under normal circumstances. But they may be expedited under a crisis condition (Kim, 1997).

Second, the government should also restructure its administrative apparatus. A separate Ministry of Science and Technology appears ostensibly to be an ideal structural arrangement to focus its efforts on S&T, but the current ministry has, in fact, no power to function adequately in bringing about effective coordination across different ministries. Its function to formulate and implement S&T policy has been decoupled from the nation's economic and social development programs. To put S&T at the center stage of its developmental effort, responsibility for formulating and implementing S&T policy across different industries should be integrated, as in some advanced OECD countries, with the responsibility for formulating and implementing the nation's economic policy and allocation of resources. The Organization for Economic Cooperation and Development (OECD) (1995) also made a similar recommendation.

Given the country's weaknesses in basic science, another important restructuring task is to integrate responsibility for promoting basic and applied research, as in most advanced OECD countries, with university education. In Korea, the efforts of the Ministry of Science and Technology to promote basic and applied research and to produce high caliber scientists and engineers have not been well coordinated with those of the Ministry of Education (MOE). As a result, most universities under the MOE produce "half-baked" engineers and scientists because the universities lack research personnel and financial support. In contrast, GRIs under MOST have research personnel and financial support, but their research results are not effectively transferred to the rest of the economy due to the lack of links with industry. The integration of the two will enable the government to redefine the role of some GRIs and to expedite its effort to transform some universities into world-class research-oriented institutions.

Third, Korea's advantage over other catching-up countries is the strength of big businesses. *Chaebols* were important assets for Korea's industrialization drive during the early decades. *Chaebols* played a major role in developing mass production systems and exploring the export market in a massive scale in the early decades. They still have an important place in globalizing Korea's businesses. But they have taken their own toll, stifling the growth of small firms. The scarcity of dynamic and innovative SMEs is a major weakness of Korea's industrial structure.

What is desirable is the well-balanced growth of both large and dynamic small firms, as in Japan and Germany. Korea should develop an environment in which more technology-based SMEs can emerge and grow successfully. Although many of these have emerged in the past decade, the number is not sufficient to support the size of industrialization in Korea. A strong surge of technology-based small firms requires two pillars: research-intensive universities and R&D organizations that are able to incubate technical entrepreneurs, and a creative financial service market. The latter includes an effective venture capital industry, a dynamic "over-the-counter" secondary market, and loans on the basis of a new product's potential rather than collateral. The government's recent move to promote venture financing is encouraging, but it will be more costly to the economy if technical entrepreneurs are not technologically competitive in the international market.

In addition, Korea should intensify its network of technical support systems. A network of technical extension services established in the early 1980s has not been effective in helping small firms. Korea needs to emulate the effective network of supporting agencies in Germany or the prefectural laboratories in Japan to develop a systematic network of technical assistance centers throughout the country or at least in industrial areas.

Fourth, facing the increasing reluctance of foreign technology suppliers to transfer sophisticated technologies, Korean firms should seek alternative means to gain access to foreign technologies. These alternatives include R&D outposts, merger and acquisition of foreign firms that have necessary technologies, and strategic alliances. Some leading *chaebols* have established R&D outposts in the United States, Japan, and Europe to monitor the development of emerging technology and have taken equity stakes in foreign firms that possess necessary technologies. Other Korean firms at advanced stages have begun to enter strategic alliances to develop future technology. But the triad – Japan, the United States, and Europe – accounts for 95.6 percent of the total number of strategic alliances. Strategic alliances with newly industrializing economies, including Korea, account for only 2.3 percent of the total (Freeman and Hagedoorn, 1993). Korea must develop its own technologies to expand its global technology network.

Fifth, the most serious bottleneck in Korea's science and technology development, as mentioned earlier, is its inadequate educational system. While Korean children spend far more time studying in both formal and informal educational systems than their counterparts in other countries, an extremely unparticipative educational process with strong rigidities does not favor creativity and initiative. Most, if not all, universities are hampered in becoming first-rate research institutions because of heavy teaching loads, lack of sufficient state-of-the-art equipment, and inadequate research support.

Obviously, unless a major reform effort is made to bring all levels of education, from primary to tertiary, to the level comparable to those of the advanced OECD countries, Korea's future development will be severely retarded. This requires major investment in the years to come. The government can do at least two things. One, it should merge the research function of the Ministry of Science and Technology with the Ministry of Education's university education function to develop a single coordinating body to make state investment more focused. Two, spectacular government projects with great symbolic value are useful for mobilizing energies but they can also be a waste of resources (OECD, 1995). Such projects, if strategically needed, should be launched with universities at the center stage.

If government and industry cannot meet the investment requirements to make major reforms in the quality of the universities, it is imperative that universities be allowed to admit a small portion of its entering students on an endowment basis. Such a scheme would induce parents to shift a huge amount of investment, which has been siphoned to the unproductive informal (tutoring) educational sector, to the formal sector. This strategy could enable at least a dozen universities to develop first-class research capabilities in the short term. In the long run, most universities must acquire world-class, quality education and research capabilities.

Sixth, Korea should further intensify its R&D activities and raise R&D productivity. The government's goal is for the proportion of high-technology industries in manufacturing to increase from 14.8 percent in 1995 to 31.6 percent by 2010. To realize this goal, the government plans for the proportion of R&D investment to GDP to increase from 2.61 percent in 1994 to 4.0 by 2010. But given the downturn in the economic growth rate, it is unlikely that such an ambition can be realized. What is more feasible is for Korea to reform its R&D system in such a way that it can be more productive. Measures to raise the quality of science and engineering personnel, to transform firms into learning organizations, and to promote knowledge diffusion across organizations through increased interorganzational mobility of personnel and cooperation are in order.

Seventh, Korea must remedy another major bottleneck: its inefficient financial sector. The complete opening of the financial sector to foreign institutions to meet OECD membership obligations may be a threat to local financial institutions in the short run, but it will definitely expedite the growth of this sector over the long run.

Eighth, the militaristic style of organization in Korea was an asset in top-down command industrialization. But it became a major liability, impeding bottom-up innovation, in the recent decades. The Korean *chaebols* have to transform themselves into innovation-oriented organizations. Creative imitation and innovation require a highly decentralized, self-contained, strategic business unit structure; an organizational climate that nurtures creative individuals and effective small groups; effective and flexible lateral coordination across R&D, marketing, and production; and bottom-up communications to quickly identify and respond to market opportunities/threats and technological possibilities. This type of organization is almost the opposite of the existing military-style bureaucracy of Korean firms. Korean firms' experience with transforming big militaristic-type organizations into a number of smaller, responsive ones has been extremely difficult. But this is the only way to make firms agile and able to respond to the changing market and technology environment. The sooner firms move in this direction, the sooner they will be in a competitive position.

Ninth, one of the most important reforms Korea should make is to elevate its level of trust, a highly important norm for economic prosperity. Familism in big businesses, corruption in government, collusion between the state and big businesses, predatory behavior in interfirm transactions, and poor links between R&D actors are all caused by the low level of trust in the Korean society. The government and nongovernmental organizations must recognize this as the foremost important issue to resolve. Without elevating Korean society to a high level of trust, the country's national innovation system cannot function effectively. Of three major elements that make up institutions (rules, norms, and their enforcement characteristics), norms are the most difficult and time-consuming to change (North, 1991).

Korean culture also has a problem in its globalization effort. Nationalistic monoculture and monolanguage was an early strength, as the internal cohesiveness of the Korean society brought people together to push for industrialization. But the monoculture/monolanguage characteristic has become a major liability in globalizing the country's economy, posing a major disadvantage and an obstacle for Koreans in learning an international language and understanding different cultures. This disadvantage makes it difficult for Korean managers to manage and work harmoniously with workers from different cultures speaking different languages.

In conclusion, Korea has dynamically achieved phenomenal growth in technological learning over the past three decades. But the country faces many internal problems even as it is being squeezed between advanced countries and the second-tier catching-up countries. Whether Korea will sustain its competitiveness will depend largely on how soon it can reengineer its national innovation system to be compatible with the new market and technology environment. Reform in the educational system is a priority because it can correct many of the major weaknesses in Korea's NIS in the knowledge-based era. Educational reform will strengthen the nation's basic science capability, upgrade human resources that will increase productivity of R&D, and generate new innovations leading to strategic alliances. Educational reform will also allow the emergence of technical entrepreneurs who will create technology-based small firms, and lead to the integration of GRIs with universities, foster individual creativity, and strengthen university-industry links.

After a major economic crisis and the subsequent bailout by IMF, the new government, the first one in Korean history that changed power through a democratic process, launched major reforms in various sectors in 1998. The government is currently undergoing a major restructuring process to be smaller but efficient. The financial sector underwent a major restructuring; many merchant banks closed and large commercials banks were merged to be more efficient. *Chaebols* are also undergoing a major restructuring to focus primarily on a few sectors and prune unprofitable ones. Corruption is being uncovered and prosecuted. State-owned enterprises are being downsized and privatized. It is premature to assess the impact of the reforms, but despite a high unemployment rate, there are several positive signs, such as the foreign exchange reserve, interest rates, and stock prices, indicating that the economy is recovering from the 1997 crisis. If Korea succeeds in its reforms, the current crisis can be a blessing in disguise.

REFERENCES

BERI (Business Environment Risk Intelligence). 1992. *Labor Force Evaluation Measures*. Quoted in Jae-Won Kim. 1995. *Jungyo gyeongjaenggookeo geonro Hyungtae Bigyo (A Comparative Study of Labor Behavior among Major Competitors)*. Seoul: Korea Chamber of Commerce, 162.

"The Corporate Culture." 1983, October 17. *Fortune*, 15–26.

Deal, T. E., and A. A. Kennedy. 1982. *Corporate Cultures – The Rites and Rituals of Corporate Life*. Reading, MA: Addison-Wesley.

DIST (Department of Industry, Science, and Technology). 1994. *Australian Science and Innovation Resources Brief 1994*. Canberra: Australian Government Publishing Service.

Freeman, Chris, and John Hagedoorn. 1993. "Globalization of Technology." Maastricht Economic Research Institute on Innovation and Technology, Working paper 92-013.

Fukuyama, Francis. 1995. *Trust: The Social Virtues and the Creation of Prosperity*. New York: Free Press.

Hofstede, Geert, and Michael Bond. 1988. "The Confucius Connection: From Cultural Roots and Economic Growth." *Organization Dynamics*, Spring, 4–21.

Kahn, Herman. 1979. *World Economic Development: 1979 and Beyond*. London: Croom Helm.

Kim, Linsu. 1980. "Stages of Development of Industrial Technology in a Developing Country: A Model." *Research Policy*, 9(3), 254–277.

Kim, Linsu. 1993. "National System of Industrial Innovation: Dynamics of Capability Building in Korea." In Richard Nelson (ed.), *National Innovation Systems: A Comparative Analysis*. New York: Oxford University Press, 357–383.

Kim, Linsu. 1997. *Imitation to Innovation: The Dynamics of Korea's Technological Learning*. Boston: Harvard Business School Press.

Kim, Linsu. 1998. "Crisis Construction and Organizational Learning: Capability Building in Catching-Up at Hyundai." *Organization Science*, 9(4), 506–521.

Kim, Linsu, and Gihong Yi. 1997. "The Dynamics of R&D in Industrial Development: Lessons from Korean Experience." *Industry and Innovation*, 4(2), 167–182.

KITA (Korea Industrial Technology Association). 1995. *Sanup Gisul Baekseo (Industrial Technology White Paper)*, December. Seoul: KITA Press.

Klein, Burton. 1977. *Dynamic Economics*. Cambridge, MA: Harvard University Press.

Lee, Jinjoo, Zong-Tae Bae, and Dong-Kyu Choi. 1988. "Technology Development Processes: A Model for a Developing Country with a Global Perspective." *R&D Management*, 18(3), 235–250.

Lee, Won-Young, Jong-Kook Song, Jee-Sung Yoo, Woon-Ho Chung, and Dae-Keun Park. 1996. *Gisul Gaebal Keumyung Hwakchoong Bangan (Measures to Expand Technology Development Finance)*. Seoul: Korea Development Institute.

Levenson, Joseph. 1958. *Confucian China and Its Modern Fate*. Berkeley, CA: University of California Press.

Lundvall, Bengt-Ake. 1992. *National Systems of Innovation: Towards a Theory of Innovation and Interactive Learning*. London: Pinter.

Miller, Danny. 1990. *The Icarus Paradox: How Exceptional Companies Bring about Their Own Downfall*. New York: Harper Business.

Nelson, Richard R. 1993. *National Innovation Systems: A Comparative Analysis*. New York: Oxford University Press.

Nonaka, Ikujiro. 1988. "Toward Middle-up-down Management: Accelerating Information Creation." *Sloan Management Review*, 29(3), 9–19.

North, Douglas C. 1991. "Towards a Theory of Institutional Change." *Quarterly Review of Economics and Business*, 31(4), 3–11.

OECD (Organization of Economic Cooperation and Development). 1995. *OECD Review of National Science and Technology Policy: The Republic of Korea*. Paris: OECD.

Porter, Michael. 1990. *Competitive Advantage of Nations*. New York: Free Press.

Shin, Yoo-Keun, and Heung-Gook Kim. 1994. "Individualism and Collectivism in Korean Industry." In Gene Yoon and Sang-Chin Choi, (eds.) *Psychology of the Korean People: Collectivism and Individualism*. Seoul: Dong-A Publishing, 189–208.

Song, Jong-Kook, Sun-Keon Kim, and Hee-Youl Lee. 1995. *Shin Kukje Mooyuk Jilseowa Gisul Gaebal Jiwonjedo (New International Trade Order and Technology Development Assistance Program)*. Seoul: Science and Technology Policy Institute, STEPI Research Report 95–20.

Tu, Wei-Ming. 1984. *Confucian Ethics Today – The Singapore Challenge*. Singapore: Federal Publications.

Utterback, James M. 1994. *Mastering the Dynamics of Innovation*. Cambridge, MA: Harvard Business School Press.

Vogel, Ezra F. 1991. *The Four Little Dragons: The Spread of Industrialization in East Asia*. Cambridge, MA: Harvard University Press.

Commentary

Howard Pack

The chapters by Katz and Kim are part of an ongoing effort by researchers to analyze the differences among economies in which some are encouraged to introduce and master new technologies while others encounter difficulties with this central task of industrialization. Thus the analyses are welcome, providing an interesting contrast. Katz, writing about Argentina, Brazil, and Mexico, argues that their import-substituting industrialization strategies (ISI) through the 1970s were not unsuccessful and that the fruits of the seeds planted in the three decades prior to 1980 did not bear fruit because of changes in macro-economic conditions. He sees few, if any, problems in the industrialization policies followed in the three large Latin American countries. Kim, analyzing the current difficulties of the Korean economy, identifies many flawed policies followed by the Korean government. So the Latin American countries, which had growth rates of per capita income of less than 3 percent per year in the 1960s and 1970s were in Katz's view following few policies that were wrong, while Kim sees the recent dilemmas of the Korean economy as having their genesis during the three decades from 1960 to 1990 when the Korean economy exhibited per capita income growth of 6 percent per year. Thus, the chapters constitute two important views of the contribution of national policies to successful industrialization. How well founded is each of the analyses?

Katz, taking a long-run view, chooses to overlook the extensive documentation of the inefficient short-term performance of the industrial sector in the three countries.[1] He suggests, instead, that the strategies of import-substituting industrialization were successful, largely based on growth in manufacturing *labor* produc-

[1] For a survey and extensive citations, see Pack, 1988.

361

tivity, (presumably value added in constant prices per worker), VA/L, in the three countries.[2] Value added/labor however, increases with growing capital-labor ratios. Since capital intensity was growing in Argentina, Brazil, and Mexico, the question is how much of the growth in labor productivity was attributable to rapid increases in capital per worker. Thus, if he had offered measures of growth of capital intensity, he would have more fully substantiated his views.

Such indicators are important, as the extensive literature analyzing and measuring the effects of import substitution has carefully documented the high rates of effective protection characterizing the Latin American countries in the periods considered. Effective protection measures the rents accruing to factors employed in an industry, which constitute a tax on all sectors other than the protected one. The excessive wages and profits earned by those in the industrial sector represent a tax on those employed in nonprotected sectors, usually those who are much poorer than workers or firm owners in the manufacturing sector. In the three Latin American countries, the protection of the industrial sector may have imposed a 3 percent to 5 percent tax on these poorer segments of society for thirty years. Given that the three countries have income distributions that are among the worst in the world, the imposition of an (implicit) regressive tax of such magnitude must be shown to have had a beneficial long-term outcome to justify the harsh effects.[3] But did it?

The standard measure of static efficiency is the domestic resource cost,[4]

$$\mathrm{DRC}_i = (wz + rk)/(p - mp_m) \qquad (1)$$

where w is the economywide opportunity cost of labor, z the labor

---

[2] Katz's critical Table 10.3 showing labor productivity growth is inconsistent with data reported in the World Bank's *World Development Report, 1994* (WDR) (and other years), which are based on data provided by the national governments. For example, the growth rate of Argentine manufactured value added in the WDR, 1994, for 1970–80 is 1.3 percent and for 1980–90 is 0.4 percent. With even no growth in the labor force, these are inconsistent with Katz's very substantial growth in labor productivity shown in Table 10.3. A similar though smaller discrepancy holds for Brazil and Mexico. The data in the WDR significantly undermine Katz's argument about the success of import substitution even in terms of labor productivity for Argentina in the 1970s.

[3] The share of income of the bottom 60 percent of the population according to the most recent estimates is 24.4 in Mexico and 17.9 in Brazil. (World Bank, 1997, Appendix Table 5).

[4] Bruno, 1972.

per unit of output, r the economywide opportunity cost of capital, k the unit capital requirement, p the c.i.f. price in dollars of an import of the same product or the f.o.b. export price, m the unit import requirement, and p_m the dollar price of imported inputs. The domestic resource cost (DRC) for product i measures the opportunity cost of domestic factors (the numerator) required to earn a net dollar of foreign exchange (the denominator). As shown by Bruno (1972) and others, an economy that systematically enters sectors with low DRCs will maximize its GNP and thus per capita income for a given set of factor endowments.

A decline in DRCs over time is the relevant indicator of improving long-term efficiency in a sector. Katz offers one component of the DRC, namely, z (the inverse of labor productivity), which was declining according to his data. If, however k increased, as other evidence suggests it did, then the DRC may have risen and the tax on the poor may never have had any payoff. Similarly, if p was decreasing due to faster growth of productivity in countries other than the United States, DRCs may have been increasing. In the period considered by Katz, countries such as Japan were experiencing much faster growth in productivity than the United States, and their exports set world prices in many products.

Thus, despite the thoughtful citations of anecdotal evidence of the presence of considerable technological activity during the period of intensive import substitution, Katz does not present a strong case that necessitates a reevaluation of the extensive literature, which has measured the harmful short-term effects of import substitution. He has, however, raised interesting questions for future research.

Turning to the fascinating issues raised by Korean growth, Linsu Kim addresses two questions: (1) Given its spectacular industrialization, how does Korea maintain this pace in the presence of many challenges, particularly from other newly industrializing economies? and (2) Were many of the problems that manifested themselves in late 1997 a result of earlier policies that attempted to stimulate industrialization? Both of these questions can be addressed from a slightly different perspective: Was the extremely close coordination between government and business necessary for Korea's rapid growth and were the *chaebols* an indispensable element in the process?

The flaws in the *chaebol* strategy are now obvious to all knowledgeable analysts of the Korean economy. Kim is concerned that small and medium-size enterprises (SMEs) were neglected during the initial growth spurt, leaving them quite weak. The obvious comparison is development in Taiwan in which government policy was much more neutral among firms of different size. Taiwan now exhibits a robust, flexible, and innovative SME sector and its economy was largely unaffected by the volatility of late 1997 and 1998 that occurred in Korea and other Asian countries. Many observers attribute part of Taiwan's immunity to the financial crisis as reflecting the more conservative balance sheet position of Taiwanese banks and manufacturing firms, a consequence of the more neutral policies. The Korean government in the 1950s and 1960s may not, however, have perceived the SME option as an alternative. Partly, its decisions were influenced by its familiarity with the Japanese *zaibatsu*. But the promotion of the *chaebol* may also have been an understandable response to the much lower education and entrepreneurial levels in Korea in comparison with Taiwan. The flaws in the *chaebol* strategy are now evident though an ex post evaluation of its efficacy, given the initial conditions of the early 1960s, could constitute an interesting exercise in counterfactual analysis.

My own view is that Kim is largely correct and this is not only in hindsight. As early as 1977, the dangers of the *chaebol* strategy were emphasized in a number of World Bank documents and discussions with high Korean officials. The response was dismissive given the spectacular growth rate in the preceding fifteen years (and the ensuing twenty!). Successful strategies, whether in national economic policy or the stock market, are not easy to reverse. Past formulas become the accepted routine and only very astute and politically effective opposition can alter such policies before a major economic crisis. Sometimes even a crisis cannot effect the requisite changes, as post-1990 Japan demonstrates.

Kim is largely concerned with reinvigorating the Korean industrialization effort with still greater research and development (R&D), more emphasis on the SME sector, and improvement in university and post-graduate education. This is indeed part of a sensible and necessary long-run strategy. It risks, however, an error similar to that committed by the government in sticking too long with the emphasis on the *chaebol*. Kim's discussion is focused on the high-tech manufacturing sector. But currently, the weakest private sector is the financial one. To strengthen the private banks and to administer the required regulatory structure will require a large group of officials well trained in financial issues and accounting. More certified accountants and finance specialists familiar with income statements and balance sheets may generate a greater social payoff over the next five years than more electrical engineers and computer scientists. But even in the longer term, the emphasis on high-tech manufacturing is questionable. Hong Kong and Singapore have both entered into services in response to growing competition in manufacturing from lower wage countries. While Korea will continue to have a considerable manufacturing sector, it is necessary to look forward toward the day when its manufacturing sector will inevitably shrink, as has happened in all OECD countries over time. Improved support for the SME sector, greater R&D incentives, and so on may constitute a decreasing part of the desirable long-run portfolio for encouraging rapid economic growth. National innovation systems that Kim knows so well have been much better at preparing for industrial success than at establishing the conditions supportive of nonindustrial growth. Apart from the maintenance of high quality tertiary education, it will be necessary to improve the regulatory environment and the transparency of private and government activities. This may be as difficult as the generation of technological competence in manufacturing, but the transfer of knowledge from the rest of the world should be relatively easy as much of the knowledge is not proprietary and can be shared among governments.

REFERENCES

Bruno, Michael. 1972. "Domestic Resource Costs and Effective Protection: Clarification and Synthesis." *Journal of Political Economy*, 80, 16–33.
Pack, Howard. 1988. "Industrialization and Trade." In H.B. Chenery and T.N. Srinivasan (eds.), *Handbook of Development Economics.* Amsterdam: North Holland.
The World Bank. 1994. *World Development Report*, 1994. Washington, DC: World Bank.
The World Bank. 1997. *World Development Report*, 1997. Washington, DC: World Bank.

Index